Exploiting Images and Image Collections in the New Media

Gold Mine or Legal Minefield?

 International Bar Association Series

Exploiting Images and Image Collections in the New Media

Gold Mine or Legal Minefield?

Edited by

Barbara Hoffman

 KLUWER LAW INTERNATIONAL

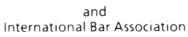 and International Bar Association

Published by
Kluwer Law International Ltd
Sterling House
66 Wilton Road
London SW1V 1DE
United Kingdom

Kluwer Law International incorporates
the publishing programmes of
Graham & Trotman Ltd,
Kluwer Law & Taxation Publishers
and Martinus Nijhoff Publishers

Sold and distributed in the USA and
Canada by
Kluwer Law International
675 Massachusetts Avenue
Cambridge MA 02139
USA

In all other countries, sold and distributed
by Kluwer Law International
P.O. Box 322
3300 AH Dordrecht
The Netherlands

International Bar Association
271 Regent Street
London W1R 7PA
United Kingdom

ISBN 90–411–9721–4

© International Bar Association 1999
First published 1999

British Library Cataloguing in Publication Data
A catalogue record for this book is available from the British Library

Typeset in Bembo 11/12 by Creative Associates, Oxford
Printed and bound in Great Britain by Antony Rowe Ltd, Reading, Berkshire

Table of Contents

Protection and Management of Copyright and Neighbouring Rights in the Digital Era
P.V. Valsala G. Kutty

Use of Images for Commercial Purposes: Copyright Issues under Malaysian Laws
Linda Wang

Legal Protection of Digital Works in Japan
Hirotaka Fujiwara

Museums and Digital Image Archives and the Proposed European Directive on the Harmonization of Copyright: A UK Perspective
Peter Wienand

Interactive Access and Images – Can Copyright Adapt?
John Rubinstein

Copyright and Other Intellectual Property Issues in the Use of Motion Picture Archives, Photo Archives and Museum Collections in the New Media: A Museum Perspective
Christine Steiner

Difficulties of Managing Copyrights, Image and Property Rights to Digitized Works Under French Law
Bruno Grégoire Sainte-Marie and Pierre Gioux

Appendices

Source Material

Forms

About the International Bar Association Intellectual Property and Entertainment and Art and Cultural Property Law Committees

International Bar Association

The IBA is a non-political, not-for-profit membership association, open to members of the legal profession from all nations. Founded in 1947, it is the world's largest international organization of individual lawyers, law societies and bar associations. At the time of writing (April 1999), the Association has more than 18,000 members from 183 countries.

On an operational level, the IBA functions through 60 specialist Committees, which between them cover every aspect of law. The topic of this book had its genesis at a panel which was presented at the 1997 IBA biennial conference in New Delhi. The Committees involved are:

- Art and Cultural Property Law of the Section on Legal Practice; and
- Intellectual Property and Entertainment of the Section on Business Law.

Art and Cultural Property Law Committee

Formed in 1986, this Committee has more than 170 members in 58 countries. Members represent governments, museums, auctioneers and dealers, private owners and collectors, and artists and their estates.

Encouraging and facilitating communications about issues concerning all aspects of the law relating to the art market, international transactions in works of art, cultural property law and museum law, is the mandate of the IBA Art and Cultural Property Law Committee. Recent conferences and panels included subjects as diverse as culture and tourism, museums and the new media, UNIDROIT, international trade in works of art, and gifts of art to museums. Programmes are often sited in historic residences, museums, and other venues of interest to Committee members.

Intellectual Property and Entertainment

Formed in 1970, this Committee has more than 1,500 members in 61 countries. Through 4 sub-Committees, members deal with copyright and entertainment law, patent law, trademark law and the licensing of intellectual property and international treaties. Members of the IBA Intellectual Property and Entertainment Committee seek to achieve an international exchange of dialogue and views about the latest developments and problems that affect their members. Recent conference programmes include:

- building partnerships – production, co-production and distribution structures;
- direct broadcasting satellites (DBS) around the world;
- patenting and ownership of genes and lifeforms; and
- intellectual property audits.

To find out more about the International Bar Association and its activities please contact:

International Bar Association
271 Regent Street
London
W1R 7PA

Telephone: +44 (0)171 629 1206
Fax: +44 (0)171 409 0456
E-mail: member@int-bar.org
Website: www.ibanet.org

Introduction

Barbara Hoffman

The new information technologies have pushed to the forefront the use of images for commercial products as software companies with an expanded appetite for images search to acquire rights to scan photographs of paintings digitally in libraries, photo and film archives and museum collections worldwide.

The London-based *Art Newspaper* writes, 'We are witnessing a wholesale transformation of the market for photographic archives or "stock photography" – the sale and distribution of pictures for newspapers, advertising agencies, graphic and television agencies. The market is worth $1 billion and has an annual growth rate of 10–15%.' Getty Images possesses an archive of more than 30 million pictures, 15 million of which are in the Hulton Getty archive. Other competitors are Kodak, the Image Bank, and Visual Communication in England and Corbis, a wholly owned subsidiary of Microsoft. In 1997, the turnover of Getty Images was $100 million dollars with a gross profit margin of 62 per cent in 1997 figures. Mark Getty states that 'the development of the internet reminds us that in about seven to eight years time 90% of images will be distributed digitally over the net.'

The Corbis Corporation (www.Corbis.com), the publishing subsidiary of Microsoft, has amassed more than 20 million images in its collection, from various sources with the strategy of providing two products: (1) a multimedia stock agency; (2) a series of databases available either via CD-ROM or through an electronic network. Corbis, however, has yet to build up its distribution network and ranks tenth in sales.

'I do have a love of art,' Bill Gates, CEO of Microsoft, has said, 'but this is also very much a business opportunity.' (The name Corbis is derived from 'Core Business'.) Gates initially attempted to purchase exclusive digital rights from museums worldwide and was quickly rebuffed by the museum world. Contrary to the belief of some, the National Gallery, London has not sold its usage rights exclusively to Microsoft or Corbis. Corbis, however, has successfully negotiated limited digital rights deals with Vatican Museum Rome (IBM has digitized manuscripts in the Vatican Library), the Louvre, Paris, the Seattle Art Museum, the Barnes Foundation, the National Gallery and other cultural institutions. In most cases, the agreement entered into with these museums has been a non-exclusive licence agreement for a short period of time which provides the museum with approval and control over the use of images licensed to third parties. While the copyright, if any, in the underlying image is not conveyed, Corbis claims to own a copyright in the digital image. The purchase of the Bettman Picture Library by Corbis is by far its biggest step toward building a huge library of digitally stored images. Many of these images are purportedly in the public domain, which means the image can be used without the permission of the author, because the image was never protected by copyright or the copyright has expired. For those works protected by copyright, purchase of the Bettman archive includes a grant to Corbis of the archive's proprietary rights, including copyright.

The World Wide Web, which transforms sites on the Internet into a graphical interface, has been incorporated by museums like the Smithsonian, the Whitney Museum, Montreal's Museum of Fine Arts, the Warhol Museum, and the Los Angeles County Museum as a medium to make exhibitions, curatorial and archival material available globally. Le Web Museum in Paris, with images pirated from galleries around the world, sends out over 3 million pages of electronic information each week. Originally called Le Web Louvre, it was obliged to change its name by lawyers for the Louvre Museum (based on French intellectual property law) even though most of the works on the web site are public domain images. The Espirit project TISUS, funded by the European Commission in the IV Framework Programme in Information Technology, deals with the creation and the use of a distributed on-line library of historical collections of textiles held by museums and schools. Currently two museums: the Museé de Tissus in Lyon and the Benaki Museum in Athens, two schools: ENSCII/ANAT in Paris and Instituto Tecnico della Seta in Como, and a designer association in Como are joining the project.[1] The website for the Museum of Modern Art in New York ("MOMA") had an estimated 1.2 million users in 1997 with visits approaching actual museum attendance in 1997 (1.65 million). One section of the site is devoted to artist's projects (http://www.moma.org). The Dia Center for the Arts in New York has commissioned artists such as Susan Hiller, Claude Closky, Cheryl Donega, and Tony Oursler, to produce original art for its website since 1995. http://www.diacenter.org.

As museums race to get on line, they are having to rethink concepts basic to their operations. Museum directors throughout the world are using multimedia technology to open up their collections to the public, at the same time such

---

[1]   Discussed at EVA'97 Brussels–Convergence: Creating the Future in Electronic Imaging & the Visual Arts in Brussels, Belgium (26 November 1997).

collections are viewed as financial assets to contribute to the bottom line. On the other hand, museums must respect the legitimate interests of rights holders – artists, donors and the institutions themselves. On the other hand, museums have an obligation to the public to make their collections reasonably available for research, teaching and the education of the public. To avoid the minefields of legal issues surrounding copyright, Elizabeth Brown, Director of the National Museum of American Art in Washington, DC, which offers an array of museum images on the Internet subscription service, America Online, revealed that her museum will focus mainly on online distribution of holdings that are not specifically copyrighted to other owners or artists – 'institutions with alternatives will tend to avoid or diminish involvement with living artists. It will be much more difficult for the arts to find a new basis in society if yesterday's legal structure is allowed to shackle the greatest potentialities of the new media.'[2]

In educational institutions, museums, film and photo archives and libraries, where images have long played a central role, the future use of digital imagery in teaching and research has emerged as one of the central concerns. As American art historian Charles S. Rhyne noted:

'In conducting research, art historians browse photographs, slides, reproductions in books, and other images as avidly as statisticians study numbers... . For the great majority of art historians, who consider the visual experience of the work of art an essential part of its study, no image can fully satisfy... . In contrast, artists most intensively press the demand for free manipulation and innovative use of computer images... . The best education, like the best research, requires flexibility and free exploration... . Images on most CD-ROM's and photo CD's become educationally useful when they are copied onto institutional file servers, where thousands of images can be accessed by many different viewers at the same time... . In large classes where expensive art books cannot be assigned for study, computer images offer for the first time the possibility of assigning high quality color images for student study... . But it may eventually be in the seemingly prosaic provision of an immense number of new, higher quality images, not entirely dependent on but stimulated by the new technology, that digital imagery makes its most significant contribution.'[3]

The electronic revolution is taking educational institutions, museums, archives, and libraries into unchartered legal and technological terrain, causing concerns particularly in the museum and higher education community about the intellectual, aesthetic, and institutional implications of converting visual images to electronic form. It is not only museums which are rethinking concepts basic to their operations such as 'stewardship' and 'exhibition' as well as copyright,

2   Remarks at Panel Discussion, Conference on Intellectual Property Rights and the Arts. The Impact of New Technologies, 43 (13 Dec. 1994) (on file with the author) (sponsored by the New York International Festival of the Arts).

3   Charles S. Rhyne, 'Computer Images for Research, Teaching, and Publication in Art History and Related Disciplines,' *Visual Resources* 12 (1996), pp. 20–25.

connoisseurship, and control; universities, archives, libraries, and study centres are reexamining issues such as the development of international standards for the capture, storage, transmission, and description of images, and the resolution of the complex issues of copyright and fair use.[4] Image archives are both a gold mine and a minefield of intellectual property.

At the same time that digital technologies provide significant opportunity to software companies, publishers, on-line services, cultural institutions, artists, galleries and art educators to explore innovative ways to display, reproduce, study, share, store and create visual images on line and in CD Rom, they pose a challenge to the legal framework for copyright and licensing in cyberspace.

How can images be distributed over networks without compromising their integrity? In the new electronic world, will students be able to freely incorporate into a class report images of works in their local museum? Will museums and archives be able to share with local educational institutions a database of images in their collection made available via a networked environment or on CD-ROM? Will such sharing take place internationally? If so on what terms? Who are the rights holders and what are the appropriate mechanisms for managing rights to use images and compensating rights holders for their use?

In theory, the use of images in the new media raises the same thorny and as yet unresolved issues as in the traditional print media. Yet, the nature of digital images makes more obvious the legal and ethical problems that are still unresolved in the print media.

The new digital technologies permit image, sound, and text to be digitized into zeros and ones; stored and replicated with ease in copies as perfect as the original; permit existing works to be incorporated into new works; and increase the potential for unauthorized alteration and appropriation of copyrighted work. To a far greater extent than photocopying, the digital technologies have eroded traditional roles and boundaries among authors and users, content owners, service providers, producers, publishers and distributors, making it imperative to seek a balance between access to images and protection of authors and publishers' economic and moral rights. Over the past decade, computer technology itself has forced lawmakers and judges worldwide to reconsider, and in some cases redefine copyright doctrine in such areas as originality authorship, fixation, reproduction, infringement and limitations.

Robert A. Baron, a US museum computer consultant, has written that central to all work in the visual arts and the key to our electronic future is the process of finding and using images. We need to know how our online age will affect our range and depth of access, how mundane affairs such as researching images and obtaining permission to sue those images will be affected, and how the *mores* of a digital and electronic present will affect how we use our customary resources in the future.[5]

[4]   Ibid., p. 35.
[5]   Robert A. Baron, 'Digital Fever: A Scholar's Copyright Dilemma,' *Museum Management and Curatorship* 15 (1996), pp. 49–64.

The global information infrastructure and the World Wide Web have facilitated the merging of massive data storage with interactive hypermedia. Information technology is providing the ability to digitize (via high speed international networks) the cultural and academic libraries of the world, to transmit images across the globe, and to provide software producers, consumers, scholars and educators with remote access to the treasures of these libraries. It may be unclear, however, how copyright and other intellectual property rules apply since the simultaneous transmission of digital images to computers worldwide often implicates inconsistent legal regimes. Not only copyright regimes, but trademark, moral rights, rights of publicity, privacy, unfair competition and database protection differ in scope and method of protection.

The objective of this publication is to discuss the special legal concerns and issues in exploiting film, photographic and museum archives and collections by creating electronic or digital image archives and collections and using such archives and collections for commercial exploitation, research, education and artistic production. The digital information environment cannot be contained within the border of any one country. Inevitably, the full exploitation by museums, archives, and educational institutions of the new technologies will require links to an extensive global network. Thus, an understanding of various national laws which provide the legal framework which govern the use and display the images is both instructive and necessary.[6] Software producers and others who seek to exploit museum, film, and photo archives commercially must also be aware of the international context and the laws of countries in which their product will be distributed.

There is a general recognition that there will have to be a better understanding of how the differing systems of countries can be made to cooperate whenever an image, book or database is uploaded from one country and downloaded, distributed and copied in another. Questions include: when does copyright infringement occur; who will have a cause of action to sue;

---

[6]   'The European Economic Community is developing two telecommunications computer networks, one linking libraries, the other linking museums and technical partners. A Visual Arts Network for the Exchange of Cultural Knowledge (VAN-EYCK, http://www.bbk. ac.uk/Departments/HisotryOfArt/van_eyck.html) will provide cross-library access to art history photographic archives and texts. It will link The Witt Library, Courtauld Institute of Art, London: The RKD (Rijksbureau Voor Kunsthisorische Documentatie), The Hague; Cruickshank-Glin Archive, Trinity College, Dublin; Birkbeck College, London; Utrecht University & Vasari Ltd. Telecommunications links to be used include EURO ISDN and academic research telecommunications facilities. A European MuseumsNetwork will provide cross-museum access to images of works in the participating museum collections with accompanying text. It will link museums in Lisbon, Madrid, Paris, The Hague, Bremen, Bremerhaven, Copenhagen, and Hamburg, and provide interactive multimedia access for museum visitors.' See Rhyne, n. 3 above, p. 44, n. 24; Achim Lipp, 'Towards *The Electronic Kunst and Wunderkammer*: Spinning on the European MuseumsNetwork EMN,' *Visual Resources* 10, pp. 101–118.

what national law will apply; what other intellectual property rights are implicated; and what will be the role of national treament?[7]

Given both the importance of copyright to the new media and international efforts at harmonization of national laws by the European Union and through the Berne Convention administered by WIPO (World Intellectual Property Organisation), it is appropriate that this publication had its genesis in a programme co-sponsored by Committee 20 of the General Practice Section and Committee L of the Business Law Section of the International Bar Association at the IBA's New Delhi Conference, India 1997 entitled 'Copyright and Other Intellectual Property Issues in the Use of Motion Picture Archives, Photo Archives and Museum Collections in the New Media'. Papers presented at the programme have been updated and additional essays have been commissioned for this publication, which has as its primary focus the copyright and other intellectual property issues, which grow out of the commercial exploitation and digitization of images in film and photo, archives and museum collections. Because many users of film, photo and museum archives in the new media will involve multimedia applications, additional articles on music licensing and music website use have been commissioned. Topics and issues considered from a policy, legal and practical standpoint include:

- integrity and authorship issues, including multiple authorship issues, in the reproduction of images from motion picture, photo and museum archives and collections;
- protection of motion picture and photo archives, and museum collections as databases or under trademark principles;
- differences in national legal regimes, including the scope of copyright protection, duration and distinction between published and unpublished works;
- copyright protection for digitized versions of public domain works;
- efforts at international harmonization, the EC directive and other initiatives;
- fair use or fair dealing in a global networked environment;
- the role of collecting societies;
- rights of publicity and privacy;
- recent legislative initiatives in Germany, India, Japan, the United Kingdom, the United States, the European Union and WIPO;
- licensing issues with respect to film, photo and museum collections, including both text, image and music;
- practical drafting tips for a digital future, including CD-Rom and on-line licensing agreements for the exploitation of images in picture archives and museum collections by software providers and others and, for the use by museums, of the intellectual property of others.

Thirteen multifaceted articles written by prominent intellectual property lawyers and government officials discuss various issues in the exploitation and

---

[7]   *Columbia Journal of World Business*, 22 March 1996.

protection of motion picture, photographic and museum collections in the
new media. The essays present a national perspective with submissions from
Argentina, France, Germany, India, Japan, Malaysia, the United States and the
United Kingdom · as well as a discussion of efforts at international
harmonization including the World Intellectual Property Organization
("WIPO") Copyright Treaties and the European Commission Data Base
Directive and the European Commission Proposal on the Harmonisation of
Certain Aspects of Copyright and Related Rights in the Information Society.[8]
Collectively the articles draw together and highlight the key differences and
similarities in national regimes with respect to copyright and how such
differences may impact the creation, exploitation and protection of digital
image archives.

In addition to copyright issues, the articles discuss other intellectual property
rights which may effect the exploitation of digital image collections such as the
rights of publicity and privacy and trademark law. Several articles discuss
alternative forms of protection of digital image archives as databases or under
theories of trademark or anti-competition law. As noted above, two articles
focus on the use of music in the new media.

The editor and contributing authors intend that this publication provide
practical and useful information on the current state of the law as it relates to
the creation, profitable exploitation and protection of museum, film and photo
archives. This book is designed to assist the players in the on-line image or
multimedia business and their attorneys to navigate the minefields successfully.

---

[8] A diplomatic conference held in Geneva in 1996 produced two new treaties. The two
WIPO Treaties are known as the WIPO Copyright Treaty (the WIPO Copyright Treaty)
and WIPO Performances and Phonogram Treaty (the Phonogram Treaty). The Copyright
Treaty, which concerns 'literary and artistic' works, is, in the large part, intended to extend
the protection of the Berne Convention into the digital domain. The Phonogram Treaty
addresses the rights of producers and performers in sound recordings.

Under the WIPO Copyright Treaty, computer programs will be protected as literary
works; collective works may be copyrightable based upon the expressive or creative
selection or arrangement of the elements, regardless of the copyrightability of those
individual elements; authors shall be entitled to the exclusive right of public distribution
(subject to the first sale doctrine, as individual nations may elect).

Communication to the Public. Article 8 of the WIPO Copyright Treaty establishes a new
right, which gives authors the right of 'authorizing any communication to the public of
their works, by wire or wireless means, including the making available to the public of their
works in such a way that members of the public may access these works from a place and at
a time individually chosen by them.'

About the Editor and Contributors

BARBARA HOFFMAN
Law Offices of Barbara Hoffman
New York, New York, USA

Barbara Hoffman has practised art, publishing, entertainment and intellectual property law for more than 20 years, engaging in both counselling and litigation. She is an attorney for visual artists, art collectors, museums, directors, writers and producers of independently financed theatrical, TV, motion pictures and multi-media projects, and new media companies. She has acted as legal adviser to various non-profit institutions including the College Art Association which she represented at CONFU, the Catalogue Raisonné Scholars Association, and the International Art Critics Association. She has been a professor of law and taught courses on art and the law, the First Amendment and Intellectual Property. She lectures and writes frequently for such publications as *Artnews, New York Law Journal, National Law Journal* and *Archeology*. Her most recent publications include *Art On-line: From the Virtual Gallery to the Legal Web: Censorship and the Arts* and *A Visual Artists Guide to Estate Planning*.

Ms Hoffman is recent past chair of the Association of the Bar of the City of New York's Committee on Art Law, Chair of Committee 20 and a founder and past president of the Washington Volunteer Lawyers for the Arts. She is an honors graduate from Brown University, with graduate degrees from the Johns Hopkins SATS, the London School of Economics and the Columbia University School of Law. She speaks French, Spanish and Italian.

RACHELLE V. BROWNE
Assistant General Counsel
The Smithsonian Institution
Washington, DC

HIROTAKA FUJIWARA
Hikari Sôgô Hôritsu Jimusho
Tokyo, Japan

Hirotaka Fujiwara is a Japanese attorney-at-law who qualified in 1985. He established the law firm Hikari Sôgô Hôritsu Jimusho in 1995. He works in various areas of laws with an emphasis on intellectual property and general corporate issues. He is involved in litigation involving computer and electronic networking issues and gives lectures on such networking issues and security concerns related to computer and electronic media. His publications include *Introduction to Copyright Law for Programmers* (Gijyutsu-hyôron-sha, 1991), *Security in the Network Society* (Softbank, 1995) and *Cyberspace and Legal Regulations* (Nihon-keizai-shimbun-sha, 1997), among others.

PIERRE GIOUX

Born Bourges, France, 9 March 1963; admitted 1994, Paris. Education: University Paris I (Licence, 1988), University Paris I (Maîtrisc, 1992). Lecturer in Law, Ecole Nationale Supérieure de la Création Industrielle, Institut National des Langues et Civilisations Orientales, Ecole Supérieure de Journalisme de Lille. Author: 'Internet et al Loi Toubon', *Expertises*, August 1997. Member: Association Française du Droit de l'Informatique et de la Télécommunication. Languages: French and English. Areas of Practice: Multimedia Law, Communications and Media Law, Intellectual Property Law, Right to Image.

NORBERT KLINGER

Born in Munich in 1966. Admitted to the Bar: 1996, Munich. 1994 to 1996 assistant to the Institut für Grheber und Nedienrecht (Copyright and Media Law Institute). 1997 to 1998 – legal department of a major media company. Publications: *Rechtstolgen der Beendigong von Filmlizenz Verträgen* (together with Prof. Dr. Mathias Schwarz), 1998 Grur.

BOB KOHN

Bob Kohn is Chairman of the Board of GoodNoise Corporation, The Internet Record Company (www.goodnoise.com), a leading provider of digital music recordings direct to consumers over the Internet. He is also co-author of the 1,500 page book, *Kohn On Music Licensing* (www.kohnmusic.com), a practical guide to the business and legal aspects of the music industry, which he wrote with his father, Al Kohn, retired vice president of licensing for Warner Bros. Music. Prior to GoodNoise, Mr. Kohn served as a chief legal counsel for Pretty Good Privacy, Inc., Borland International, Inc., and Ashton-Tate Corporation. Prior to Ashton-Tate, he was an attorney at the Beverly Hills law offices of Rudin & Richman, an entertainment law firm whose clients included Frank Sinatra, Liza Minelli, Cher, and Warner Bros. Music. He also served as Associate Editor of the *Entertainment Law Reporter*, for which he continues to serve as a member of its Advisory Board.

THE HONORABLE P.V. VALSALA G. KUTTY
Registrar of Copyright, Secretary
Copyright Board & Deputy Secretary to the Government of India
India

ANTONIO MILLÉ
Estudio Millé
Buenos Aires, Argentina

Argentine Lawyer (University of Buenos Aires Law School, 1964) Senior Partner of Estudio Millé legal firm; International Chairman of the Latin American High Technology, Computers and Law Institute (ILATID); Vice-president of the Inter-American Copyright Institute (IIDA); Expert Counsel of WIPO and of UNESCO; Counsel of the Argentinean Computer Industry and Computer Software Commerical Chambers; Publisher of the monthly journal *DAT – Derecho de Alta Technoloía* (Buenos Aires); writer and lecturer in High Tech Law matters; member of the Editorial Board, correspondent or collaborator of different Copyright Law and Computer Law international publications.

JOHN RUBINSTEIN
Manches & Co
London, England

John Rubinstein was educated at Marlborough School and Magdalen College, Oxford University where he gained a BA Hons (Juris). After gaining admission as a solicitor in 1977, he went to New York and worked with Eaton Van Winkle Greenspoon & Grutman, passing the New York Bar and being admitted to practise as a New York attorney in 1979.

He returned that year to England to join the family publishing law firm Rubinstein Callingham and became a partner in 1983. He has remained a partner of the firm through two mergers, the later of which occurred when Rubinstein Callingham Polden & Gale merged into Manches & Co. in 1994. During his career he has increasingly specialized in intellectual property, media and defamation litigation and spearheaded the recognition of Manches Media Group as leading English publishing lawyers. He conducted the first English university course of lectures in Confidentiality at the University of Essex in 1986 and subsequently ran courses at the University of Southampton and the University of Leicester. He has also lectured extensively, written articles and broadcast both on national television and radio on Obscenity, Privacy and Personality issues.

He has been a member of the International Bar Association since 1989 and Co-Chairman (1997-99) of its Section on Legal Practice SGP Committee on Art and Cultural Property Law. He is also a member of the Law Society of England & Wales and the Association of the Bar of the City of New York.

CAROLINA SAEZ
Attorney Advisor Policy and International Affairs
US Copyright Office
Library of Congress
Washington, DC 20559

BRUNO GRÉGOIRE SAINTE-MARIE
FG Associés
Paris, France
Bruno Grégoire Sainte-Marie, a French admitted attorney specializing in intellectual property, has for many years acted as counsel to numerous companies and professionals in the photographic image and multimedia industries. He was co-founder in 1988 with Christiane Féral-Schuhl of FG Associés, a Parisian law firm principally recognized for its strong specialization in information technology, intellectual property and telecommunications law.

PROF. DR MATHIAS SCHWARZ
Schwarz Kurtz Schinewind Kelwing Wicke
Munich, Germany
Admitted to the bar: Munich, 1979; 1984 to 1984 to 1987: head of the legal department of a major media company; in 1990: public accountancy examination; readership at the Munich Hochschule für Fernsehen und Film (Television and Film Academy); chair for media law at Leipzig University since 1995.

Main fields of activity: film and media law; publishing law, broadcasting law, new media, film financing, company law, mergers and acquisitions.

Memberships: 1991 to 1995: Chairman of the Entertainment and Intellectual Property Committee of the International Bar Association, Forum Committee on Entertainment and Sports (ABA); Deutsche Vereinigung für gewerblichen Rechtsschutz und Urheberrecht (GRUR – German Association of Industrial Property and Copyright Law), Institute für Urheber und Medienrecht (Copyright and Media Law Institute), Deutscher AnwaltVerein (German Lawyers Association).

Publications: *Urheberrecht und digitale Medien* (1994, *Copyright Law and Digital Media*); *Der Werbebegriff im rundfunkstaatsvertrag* (1996, *The Concept of Advertising in the German Interstate Broadcasting Convention*), *Urheberracht im Internet* (1996, *Copyright on the Internet*), *Das Recht im Internet* (1997) Publisher, Rechtstolgen der Beendigong von Filmlizenz Verträgen (together with Norbert Klinger), 1998 Grur.

ANTHONY SEEGER
Curator, The Folkways Collection
Director, Smithsonian Folkways Recordings

CHRISTINE STEINER
The J. Paul Getty Trust
Los Angeles, California USA

Christine Steiner is Secretary and General Counsel of the J. Paul Getty Trust, where she provides a wide range of counsel and advice on all legal aspects of the Getty Operating programmes. Prior to her position with the Getty, Ms. Steiner was Assistant General Counsel to the Smithsonian Institution, handling litigation and advice for the Smithsonian's museums and its educational and administrative offices. She earlier served in the Office of the Attorney General of Maryland, representing the state colleges and universities, and subsequently was chief attorney for the Maryland public education system and counsel to the State Board of Education. She has been an adjunct law professor and is a frequent lecturer in the areas of education, museums and the arts.

LINDA WANG
Tay & Partners
Kuala Lumpur, Malaysia

Ms. Linda Wang is a Partner in the law firm of Tay & Partners in Kuala Lumpur, Malaysia. She practises exclusively in the area of intellectual property laws, with an interest in licensing, franchising, sponsorship, media and broadcasting, food and drug, and labelling laws. She is also extensively involved in litigation work relating to infringement of intellectual property rights. She is an active member of both international and Malaysian organizations having an interest in intellectual property rights.

PETER WIENAND
Farrer & Co.
London, England

Peter Wienand specializes in copyright, multimedia and technology law and leads the intellectual property team at Farrer & Co., a firm which has practised at the same London address since 1972. He chairs the firm's Museums and Galleries Group, which services the needs of the firm's museums and gallery clients (among which there are over 20 major institutions), and is a founder member of the Museums and Galleries Copyright Working Group, an independent body set up in the UK in 1996 to represent the interests of museums and galleries in the copyright sphere. Peter Wienand lectures regularly and has recently contributed to such publications as *Art Antiquity and Law*, *The Art Newspaper* and *Museums Journal*. He is also a member of the Intellectual Property Institute and of the Union Internationale des Avocats (UIA).

Intellectual Property Issues in the Creation and Use of Digital Images

Antonio Millé

Estudio Millé, Buenos Aires, Argentina

I. What are Digital Images?

Until the second half of the twentieth century information was destined to be understood, developed and transformed within the human mind. It was externalized by means of different languages and codes (the letters of the alphabet, the combination of colours, musical notes, etc.) and was supported by various material bases (paper, photosensitive film, magnetic tape, etc.). The combination of these techniques produced the 'analogue' information physical media, such as books, magazines, records, audio cassettes, radio and television broadcasting.

Some analogue information reproduction techniques enabled information to be expressed directly on the material base intended for the communication of the content to the end user, for example, drawing or writing on paper, or stone sculpture. Other analogue techniques used different intermediaries between the author's externalization and the material base that reaches the public: this is what happens with photography, whose specimen derives from the developing and printing of a negative, or with the bronze sculpture, that comes from the previous making of model and mould.

The presentation of information has been transformed with the advent of computers. In order to be suitable for being processed in electronic data processing systems, any information must be expressed by employing a binary code, one of whose signs is the presence of current (symbolized by digit '1'), the other being its absence (symbolized by digit '0'). By combining ones and zeros in organized series (seven bits plus one control bit creating eight-bit series called bytes) it is possible to express signs representing basic information units, such as letters, numbers, sound pitches and colours. The sequence of bytes

1

forms files capable of being interpreted directly by the data processing systems and indirectly by the human being.

Thanks to the multiplication of the codes used in the data processing systems and to the existence of a wide range of peripherals which can be connected to the former, it is currently possible to capture almost any phenomenon and enter it into the systems (e.g. recording a video recording directly on the computer memory). It is also possible to translate into digital code an existing representation on analogue base (e.g. scanning the illustration of a book). Representations can also be produced by using systems as an intellectual creation tool (for example, by drawing an illustration 'on the screen').

Digital images are the result of the use of these techniques, all of which provide files in which an image captured, translated or made by computer means is described through a series of bytes. These digital images may be considered from different points of view.

(a) For those who view them on a screen or printed on a solid medium, they are representations perceptible through the sight, and therefore, they are not different as regards their use, purpose and utility from the images whose original support is based on analogue techniques.

(b) For those who consider them from the point of view of their reproduction technique, they are digital computer files. There exist different technical possibilities for the production of files capable of handling 'inputs' and 'outputs' of data corresponding to images.

   (i)   Graphics files contain the description of a design. Bytes indicate to the system the equations or algorithms corresponding to coordinates or vectors that will locate points on an ideal plane, to produce any type of lines, as well as the size and colour of those points. Some graphics files create the feeling of motion to whoever watches them being displayed on screen. This is obtained by changing within certain time intervals the description for the whole or part of the coordinates of the design. Among these files types .3ds, .cad, and .wmf.

   (ii) Image files contain the description of the content of a grid formed by pixels[1] arranged in columns and rows. The description indicates the colour and brightness of each pixel. On being printed or displayed on screen, this group of pixels is perceived by the human being as shapes with colour.[2] Amongst these are types .bmp, .gif, .tga, .jpg, .tif, and .cmx.

   (iii) Files containing the description of images in motion are usually called video files. They are similar to image files, but since they are displayed repeatedly with the frequency necessary to provide the human brain with the illusion of

---

[1] The smaller point directionable in a computer Cathode Ray Tube. To higher pixels density, higher image definition. The word probably comes from the Latin pyxis, which means 'small box'.

[2] Pictorial art has long shown that the feeling of colour can be achieved indistinctly by amalgamating chromatic components in the matter used to paint, or by grouping points of several component colours, so that the mixture is formed 'in the brain' of the public. According to their density, pixels can enable any of these two procedures of chromatic expression.

motion, are used in series of up to 30 frames per second. Generally, they also contain the description of sounds coordinated with images.[3] Some video file families are .avi, .mpg, .vdo, .xdm and .mov.

(c) As regards their legal nature, digital images present the traditional dichotomy between the supporting medium and the content supported, giving rise to the existence of different interests, protected by various legal remedies.

    (i) Contents totally or partially made up of images (illustrated texts, photographs, video recordings of objects, etc.) protected by any of the intellectual property regimes (copyright, trademarks, etc.) or placed by the law in the public domain.

    (ii) *Logical media*, made up of digital files that express the information in such a way that it can be utilized by data processing systems. There exist various systems that can afford legal protection to these files.

    (iii) *Physical media* (magnetic disks, optical disks, etc.) on which a copy of the logical media expressing the contents has been recorded. They have the protection proper to and characteristic of personal property.

II. Processes the Image Files Undergo

Leaving aside the differences between digital images and the original existing in the real world or supported by the analogue medium to which they belong, digital images are rarely commercialized in their 'original' digital state, just as they were captured, translated or made.

A. *Processes to Improve Suitability for Use*

In many cases, digital images undergo processes tending to add practical (and consequently, economic) value to them, being aimed at a certain kind of use.

(a) Modifications, that is to say, additions, suppressions or changes are frequently made in the substance of the content, for example, when the background of the main image in the representation of a monument is 'cleaned'.

(b) By means of restorations an original that suffered damage or degradation in its original analogue medium is either put back into its original state or is enriched by new expression techniques (for example, giving tridimensional effect to an originally 'plane' image).

(c) Compression (through procedures such as unifying redundant information or suppressing the information having ranges beyond the perception capabilities of

---

[3] Sound files contain the numerical description of a sound wave. They enable the reproduction of tones, volumes and timbres, sending the sound reproduction system of the computer an exact copy of the noise or of the music originally recorded. This is achieved by measuring the height of the sound wave at regular intervals of time (i.e. taking 'samples') to describe the curve that the sound wave makes. Musical sound can also be recorded by means of MIDI files that contain the description of the command actions of a musical instrument (e.g. for a piano: pressing force, time during which the key remains pressed, and speed at which pressure on the recording is relaxed). They serve to send musical execution commands to electronic musical instruments or to the sound plate of computers.

human organs) reduces the size of files in order to facilitate their storage, transportation, transfer, communication, etc.

B. *Transformation into Samples 'Without Commercial Value'*

There exist other processes that reduce the commercial value of the digital image transforming it into a mere 'sample' which is useful only for promotional purposes, such as the thumbnail (reduced image) used in catalogues to enable visual identification. These images that the data processing systems show on a small scale, with low resolution, can be easily downloaded and are suitable for meeting on-line distribution and marketing needs. They are not useful for commercial exploitation, so they can be more widely disseminated.

III. The Wrapping of the Digital Image

Files containing digital images processed with a view to their commercialization not only correspond to the different types of files but also can be 'packaged' in logical containers intended to facilitate the storage or distribution by means of certain hardware and software platforms or to protect the rights of those who have produced or distribute the images. These logical containers are usually called digital objects, which Patrice A. Lyons defines as a 'set of sequences of bits, including a single identifier for the object, called *handle*'.[4]

Thus, in the value addition chain we have a content many times coming from the analogue world, but enriched with digital processes, a file serving as a logical support for the content and a digital object as a functional 'wrapper' of the file.

A considerable part of the on-line image commercialization strategies (above all those addressed to the consumer public) are based on the use of digital objects as a security and management too.[5]

The digitization by different operators of the same content originally supported 'analogously' brings about remarkable different results: any format

---

[4]   'Acceso a representaciones digitales de imágenes en color: Una perspectiva desde el derecho de autor y de las communicaciones', DAT, Año VIII, no. 91, p. 1.

[5]   I use as an example the advertising of a service that I found in Http://www.intertrust.com/ products/flow.html: 'The InterTrust Commerce Architecture uses InterTrust's DigiBox secure containers to safely store and transport digital content. These tamperproof electronic packages allow commerce participants to bind business rules such as payment, usage, and metering rules to any kind of digital content – text, graphics, executable software, audio, or video. A creator can specify separate charges for such operations as viewing, printing and excerpting the content in a DigiBox container, and choose from many payment models such as pay-per-view and rent-to-own. The creator can tailor usage and payment rules to past buying patterns, classes of consumers (giving an automatic discount to college students, for example), and other criteria. As permitted by the creator, distributors can specify additional

can be chosen; a higher or lower level of detail can be adopted; different founts, layouts, backgrounds can be used; it can be compressed with more or less effectiveness, and so on. These results will also have different potential for its exploitation, and certainly different market (saleable) value.

IV. The Raw Material of the Digital Image

As state above, digital images can be 'natively' digital (captured by cameras that record images in motion or still images, or designed by means of systems) or come from the digital processing of pre-existing images in the analogue world. Furthermore, digital images can represent objects existing in the real world or purely imaginative creations.

A. *Material Taken from the Analogue World*

The greatest intellectual property problems arise with respect to images representing objects of the real world or which come from the digitization of analogue images. Among these materials we find:

- photographs;
- motion pictures;
- works of art;
- buildings;
- objects not protected by the copyright law that form part of collections.

B. *Processes that Analogue Materials may have Undergone*

Intellectual property problems increase if a considerable part of the material currently handled as digital images comes from the repeated processing of the pre-existing analogue materials. These processes are not necessarily transparent to the user of the digital image, and they may easily go unnoticed. Examples of

---

cont.

rules such as value-added mark-ups. InterTrust thus supports traditional value chain management in the electronic world. A consumer downloads a DigiBox from the distributor's Website content server. After reviewing and accepting the business rules, the consumer accesses the content under the control of the rules. This process automatically creates secure financial and usage records of the transaction and sends them to clearinghouses. Consumers can freely redistribute DigiBox containers to others, who can also use the content subject to the same business rules. The financial clearinghouse processes the transaction records from all users, charges the consumers' accounts, and credits the creator's and distributor's accounts according to the business rules that were packaged with the content. If the business rules in the DigiBox specify the metering of content usage, such usage information is collected when a consumer accesses a piece of content. This usage information is sent to a usage clearinghouse which processes and aggregates metering information, creates usage reports, and passes them on to the creator and distributor.'

these processes include photographs included in printed publications, sometimes with modifications or documentary additions, and printed publications and photographs which have in turn been photographed by third parties so as to obtain slides.

V. The 'Right to Digitize' and the 'New' Authors' Powers

Digital technologies make it possible to carry out operations which were not feasible before, and take advantage of the intellectual creations through new methods. These operations and methods can be seen as new manifestations of the exploitation rights currently recognized by the laws to copyright owners, or as acts not considered by the legislation in force, that claim to be regulated.

A. *The 'Right to Digitize'*

'Digitize' means the action of subjecting any analogue base supporting a content (the paper supporting the text, the cloth that incorporates the plastic work, the phonomagnetic record housing the phonogram, etc.) to the suitable technical process to produce a file supporting the same content.

Although the right to authorize or prohibit the digitization is clearly an act of 'exploitation', it does not appear explicitly in any national or international substantive law text. It does not constitute *estricto sensu* a 'reproduction' in the broad sense of Article 9 of the Berne Convention, though undoubtedly, in the current state of technique, it leads to a 'reproduction', since it is difficult to imagine somebody making such a process not for the purpose of recording the result on a digital storage medium. Since 'digitization' is the first link of the chain of acts (digitize – store – publicize – transmit – communicate) through which a work supported analogously can be exploited in the digital environment, the reservation of this right to the analogue content rights owner should be guaranteed. An explicit provision to that effect, both within national rights and international treaties, would be beneficial.

B. *The 'Storage Right'*

In the on-line distribution process, content is housed in computer memories from which it is taken by users through interactive procedures. As storage is another necessary step in the new chain of acts of exploitation of content (as summarized in the previous point), the points relevant to 'digitization' also apply to the power to authorize or prohibit storage.

C. *The Right of 'Making Works Available to the Public'*

Though the official 'digital agenda' did not explicitly mention 'digitization' or 'storage' rights, the recent WIPO Copyright Treaty made expressly clear in its Article 8 (Right of public communication to the public)[6] that the author's right of 'communicating to the public' comprises 'the making available to the public of their works in such a way that members of the public may access these works from a place and at a time individually chosen by them', clearly referring to the on-line distribution systems. To the effect of the provision cited, 'making works available to the public' is equivalent to storing the copyrighted contents in a site accessible by means of communications. In effect, both powers are exercised in the same way.

VI. 'Rights in a Cascade' in and to Digital Images

The existence of a 'cascade' of rights that arise from the same source and grant to different owners the same powers is typical of copyright law[7] with the peculiarity that many times these rights are labelled as 'exclusive'.[8] Digital images are also subject to the rules of the genre and serve as support for an important plexus of legally protected interests that generally belong to a certain number of different owners.

In some cases, the rights discussed in this chapter receive a practically universal recognition in comparative law; in others, they are treated diversely by different legislations (such as, for instance, the right to authorize or prohibit the reproduction of the image of a work placed within a public place). Certain holders of rights have been authorized by holders of antecedent rights to exploit them, while in other cases no previous relationship or authorization has existed (such as, for example, photographs that show a street including commercial signs or emblems or advertising with registered trademarks). In some cases there exist licence agreement provisions effective and valid between the parties, but that do not bind third parties (for example, in the case of images digitized with authorization from museums); in other cases, the pre-existing rights exploited are in the public domain.

---

[6] The WIPO Treaty on Performances and Phonograms contains Articles 10 and 14 with similar wording as regards the rights of musical performers and of phonogram producers.

[7] It is usual to refer to this branch of law as copyright and neighbouring rights law. *Brevitatis causa*, we will use in this chapter the reduced nomenclature of copyright, including therein the reference to the intellectual property right of performing artists and of the phonogram producers.

[8] Though it seems curious, in practice, this multiple ownership of exclusive powers does not result in conflicts, since the birth of an exclusive power derives from the previous authorization granted by the owner of an antecedent right (for example, the exclusive right of a performing artist to authorize the recording of his performance arises after having been authorized by the composer to perform the work).

A. **Intellectual Property Rights**

The assets protected by different systems affording protection to intangible rights in general, and to intellectual property in particular, that can be contained in a digital image are numerous. The holders of economic and moral rights therein are also numerous if we take into account the heirs, assigns and the never-ending amount of licensees with more or less broad rights in time and space. The protected legal interests of those listed below will be discussed for the purpose of this chapter:

- authors of works of art (painting, drawing, sculpture, architecture, etc.);
- administrators of the public domain, in the countries where the same is under an official trust;
- performing artists;
- photograph or audio-visual works models and 'live dummies';
- celebrities, sports people, and other holders of 'right to the image';
- authors of photographs and audio-visual works;
- editors of printed publications from which images were taken;
- authors of compilations from which images were taken;
- 'manufacturers' of databases;
- those who made the scanning of pre-existing analogue images;
- those who processed the digital image;
- the owners of trademarks represented in digital images.

Any of these holders could have a right of action for the exercise of rights having a bearing on the use of digital images.

B. *Other Rights*

In addition to intellectual property rights, there are other rights protected by ordinary law, such as the personal and real property rights belonging to museums, collectors, governments, and people in general. As some digital images (many, in the case of news miscellany and sports) come from television programmes, the rights of the radio broadcasting entities in their emissions should also be considered.

C. *The Rights of the Creator of Digital Images*

In addition to the rights pertaining to the analogue stage of the image (when the image has that origin), there are such other rights as may belong to the author of the 'digital' version. The creation of the digital image implies a vaster and more complicated operation than the mere capture of the image and its recording on an electronic memory. It requires the making of decisions and choosing among different possibilities on focusing, framing, fixing the 'density' of pixels, establishing the 'palette' of colours, as well as performing a series of other non-compulsory, but very frequent, operations, such as mixing or coordinating the image with others, cutting it out, subjecting it to morphing, changing its background, giving to it different textures, etc.

The addition of value that will enable a wide exploitation of the digital image also requires the exercise of technical and artistic capabilities,[9] above all to describe properly the image with words and codes that facilitate its inclusion in indexes, resulting in its recovery by users interested in that subject or view, and to document certain images so as to connect them with the aspects of reality (geographical, historical, technical, etc.) they express.

The legal nature of the result of the digitization of images is not perfectly defined. Taking into account the nature of the content, it would seem that digital images are works of the fine arts when they show a result of drawing techniques or 'collage' on the screen and that they are 'photographic works' or 'audio-visual works' when they result from the capture and process of a still image or an image in motion taken from the real world or from a pre-existing analogue medium.[10] The distinction may have significance since in many legislations special principles are devoted to 'photographic' and 'audio-visual' works,[11] while the system which is generally more favourable applies to the majority of works, including the fine arts and works of indeterminate genre.[12]

Choosing to stick to the nature of the content is rational, since it would be difficult to sustain that something changes entity (and therefore, legal nature) according to whether its supporting medium is analogue or digital. However, it is common to verify among 'cyber-artists' the conviction about the autonomy of their art, that they identify according to the techniques employed to generate and support the content. If it is shown that these opinions are valid,

---

[9] The complex task of preparing the digital images for the purpose of their on-line exploitation is described by Corbis Archive in its site: 'To carry out its mission, Corbis employs experts in art history, world history, picture editing, scanning, image processing, image management, library science, photography, information processing, intellectual property law, marketing, multimedia production, software development, human interface design and customer service. The Corbis Archive is much more than a collection of images. The company has invested in state-of-the-art hardware, software and processes to provide superior quality and protection for its digital resources and has enhanced their value with full caption and source information. Advanced high-resolution scanning techniques accurately capture the color nuances and composition of each original image, which is then stored in a multimedia database and cataloged with keywords and other text. Sophisticated search-and-retrieval technologies can access images in seconds using text and image-based links, making it possible for content from the Archive to be combined and used in innovative ways.'

[10] In the latter case, there will exist a derivation of the work that will require the authorization of the author of the reproduced work in the event that the same is not in the public domain.

[11] For example, different criteria with respect to their ownership and authorship as in Article L-113-7 of the French Code de la Propriété Intellectuelle, or different protection term as in section 13(1) of the UK Copyright, Designs and Patents Act 1988.

[12] As per Article 2(I) of the Berne Convention, 'every production in the literary, scientific and artistic *domain*' (not *genre*) (author's italics) is eligible for protection, including all original intellectual creation expressed in a reproducible form of indeterminate genre.

the law shall perhaps recognize the existence of a new artistic genre, and study the eventual need of devoting to it certain special principles.

On the other hand, the digitizer of images may aspire to benefit from the protection that the law grants to digital files as such. Some legal protection against the parasitic exploitation by third parties of digital objects has been repeatedly proposed. It is not just a question of granting a proprietary right preventing third parties from digitizing on their own account the content previously digitized by others, but of prohibiting the reproduction of the digital obejct made by others, taking advantage of someone else's effort. This protection can be provided within the existing framework of intellectual property law using such theories as unjust enrichment and unfair competition.[13] Protection can also be afforded by creating a new related *sui generis* right. Objections have been raised to this type of protection by those who consider that digital objects produced by automatic processes do not provide for the addition of the 'substantial investments'.

The fact is that files constitute an economic value (and therefore, a legal interest) in themselves, and the 'makers' of digital objects of any kind (editors or electronic text, digital phonograms, digital or digitized audio-visual works, 'raw material' such as 'samples' or bank images, etc.) are more numerous and make larger more useful investments for the public than those made by the database 'manufacturers'. They undoubtedly deserve a legal protection not less than that which is being organized for them. If such a protection existed, the creators of digital images would benefit from it, adding a legal remedy to those they already have as authors of creations protected in their substance.

VII. Intellectual Property Problems

A. *Problems Relative to Public Domain*

One of the bases of intellectual property is to assure a balance between the interest of creators in enjoying on an exclusive basis the result of their efforts, and the interest of the community in having access to the greatest quantity and best quality of intellectual creations. Since monopoly and free access are antithetical terms, the duration of the copyright protection is an essential resource to assure the balance sought: during their lifetime, and for a term reasonably covering the life of their lineal heirs, authors enjoy exclusive rights; once that term expires, the work comes to be in the public domain and all the members of the community may use and enjoy their works.

'Traditional' copyright had no difficulty in attributing exclusive rights to those who produce works deriving from public domain works. Thus, an asset

---

[13]   For French doctrine and case law, see Phillippe Le Tourneau, *La responsabilité civile* (Dalloz, 1982), p. 641 and Jean-Jacques Burst, *Concurrence déloyale et parasitisme* (Dalloz, 1993). In American Law, see the recent decision in *Tax Analist v. United States Dept. Of Justice* (No. 94-0043, 16 January 1996, US District Court for the District of Columbia).

that was totally in the public domain comes to be private property again partially (in the derived version), but the original version always remains available to the public and to other eventual 'derivers'. The same legal principles can contribute to producing less desirable results if the physical and legal control over certain originals enables *de facto* monopolization for digitization, from which arises *de facto* monopolies for the exploitation in the digital environment of the only or best digital image of that original.

The exercise of the powers emanated from property rights, that allows access to personal and real property to be denied, as well as the limitation to the use of cameras, lighting devices, etc., that the curators of many collections[14] impose, may contribute to the strengthening of those *de facto* monopolies. The same effect may be caused by the *de jure* monopoly created by licence agreements which includes property that does not belong to the licensor's private domain.[15] In this way, the balance of interests that intellectual property law is intended to protect may be altered to the prejudice of the two terms of the commitment, since the fact that property comes to be private again does not enrich the generators of new intellectual creations, and deprives the community of property that the authors assigned to it when the term of exclusiveness expired.

A possible solution to the conflict would be to make free the digitization of any work in the public domain, recognizing that each digitizer has an intellectual property right in and to the derived work produced by him or her, with which the balance of interests would not be different from that obtained in the analogue world.

In the information society global environment, terms of protection should be harmonized, to prevent what is protected in a territory from being freely used in another, and vice versa. Likewise, it would seem fair to tend to a harmonization of the terms of protection for the various categories of contributors to intellectual creation (authors, performers and producers) since, in fact, the disappearance of the right of a rightsholder will not be to the benefit of the community of users but to the benefit of the rest of the

---

14 'Museums and owners claim copyright to the photographs they make of art objects. They also limit use and provide access by licensing their use. In addition, many museums prohibit any gallery photography or insist on conditions guaranteed to produce photographs that are not of publishable quality. For many museums these procedures serve as an important source of revenue.' Robert A. Baron, Museum Computer Consultant, contribution to the CNI Copyright Forum, 31 January 1996, rabaron@nyc.pipeline.com.

15 In the US, the attempt to protect any content under a conventional licence may entail responsibilities: 'While it is well established that rights to intellectual property may be restricted by license, the same is not true of unprotectable data. Indeed, attempts to expand the monopoly power granted a copyright owner to unprotectable material can subject a licensor to a liability for copyright misuse.' Ian C. Ballon, 'Tearing Shrinkwrap in Cyberspace: Enforceable Licenses, Unprotectable Databases and ProCD, Inc. v. Zeidenberg', *Cyberspace Lawyer* 5, p. 2.

rightsholders with a current and valid right, who may thus continue receiving the price that the market assigns to the private domain property but distributing it among less co-owners.

B. *Problems Relative to the Plurality of Rightsholders*

This is also a factual problem. As it arises from the considerations discussed above (see 6.A.), digital images are suitable to support the rights of an increased number of holders. It is not possible for the user to determine how many and which of those holders have rights in and to the image he or she is interested in, and in general, the limited nature of the operation makes it practically impossible to devote the time and resources that would be necessary to make a serious audit of the intellectual properties affected. Many sources of digital images contain a limitation of private use of the material.[16]

In view of the practical impossibility and legal risk posed by the plurality of rightsholders a potential solution may be the use of collective management organizations organized to assure use and distribution of profits among the holders of rights. A solution of this kind has been repeatedly proposed[17] but no attempt has yet been made to put it into practice.

Neither the proposal to create voluntary systems of unified[18] contractual administration nor the one to institute compulsory licence systems have prospered.[19]

For the time being, the solution is to rely on contract whereby the producer or distributor of the digital image acts as guarantor of the legitimacy of the

---

[16]   Thus, the US Library of Congress warns in its site: 'As a publicly supported institution the Library generally does not own rights to material in its collections. therefore, it does not charge permission fees for use of such material and cannot give or deny permission to publish or otherwise distribute material in its collections. It is the patron's obligation to determine and satisfy copyright or other use restrictions when publishing or otherwise distributing materials found in the Library's collections.'

[17]   See for example: 'Just the image of an endless round of letters each asking for the permission to reproduce a particular work has kept many projects on the drawing board....Without a common framework of rights, permissions and restrictions, the development of imaging systems is hampered.' J. Trant, *Imaging Initiative: A Status Report* (The Getty, AHIP, 1997). 'Le principe de la SCAM (Société Civile des Auteurs Multimedia) repose sur le fait que les démarches d'autorization ne font qu'entraver la création. A partir du moment où une œvre existe et qu'elle est inscrite au répertoire de la SCAM, son auteur en autorise implicitement sa diffusion d'autant que les droits afférents seront perçus et lui seront répartis.' Claude Rollin, 'Les modalités de rémuneration des auteurs par les organismes de gestion collective de droits', Séminaire Droits d'Auteur et Multimedia (Paris, November 1993).

[18]   For instance, of the Copymart type, set out by Zentaro Kitagawa in 'Computers, Digital Technology and Copyright', *WIPO Worldwide Symposium on the Future of Copyright and Neighbouring Rights* (WIPO, 1984), p. 115.

[19]   See, for example, Susan M. Jennen, 'Multimedia Licensing Offers Unique Problems', *Les Nouvelles* (December 1993), p. 185.

content offered to the public.[20] However, a contractual solution may appear to be insufficient for certain uses; many licences forbid the electronic distribution of licensed material and thus, would not cover material (articles, advertising, messages, etc.) edited or posted in a web page. Thus material or advertising posted on a web page – one of the most frequent uses of digital images in the on-line environment – would not be protected from risk.

C. *Problems Relative to 'Moral Rights'*

Not all the copyright systems in the world guarantee 'moral rights' to authors, but the respect for the moral right is required under the provision of Article 6*bis* of the Berne Convention.[21] Since the on-line environment, by its transnational nature, is one of the natural ambits for the use of the digital image, the issue of moral rights turns into another problem to be solved – by means of criminal rules by some legislations.

In some countries the moral right is inalienable and cannot be waived. Thus, the right may be exercised by the author or by the author's heirs.

1. Moral Right of 'Integrity'

A digital image (like a photograph or a motion picture) does not constitute a perfect reproduction of the original. The quantity and density of pixels, the quality and range of the palette of colours, the right focusing and framing, the measures of outputs set up by screens and printers, limit the technical possibilities and impose differences with the analogue original more or less perceptible by the public. It is not possible to define with precision and in abstract the boundary between 'innocent' modifications and those implying harm to the honour or reputation of any of the copyright owners that may claim rights in and to the image (for example, the author of the sculpture that disappeared from sight when the framing of the photograph of a building was reduced).

---

[20] This is the policy characterizing the advertising of an important supplier of digital images. 'All Corel Professional Photos are royalty free. Corel has insured that all images are photographer as well as model released. Once you purchase a Corel Professional Photos title you are free to use the images as often as you wish; there are not additional fees.'

[21] '(1) Regardless of the author's proprietary rights, and even after the assignment of these rights, the author shall keep the right to claim the paternity of the work and to object to and oppose any distortion, mutilation or any other alteration thereof or any assault against it causing damage to his honor or reputation.'

2. Moral Right of Paternity

It is hard to define the correct way of attributing the paternity of a work that receives varied contributions, many of which remain anonymous. In addition to the difficulty of supplying information (most commercial digital images do not contain data about their author) there exists the difficulty of displaying that information in a way compatible with usage.

D. *Problems Relative to Fair Use/Quotation Right*

Some of the problems of the users of digital images could be solved by application of the exceptions founded on the fair use of the copyright, or on the 'quotation right' of the civil law countries.[22] Again, globalization introduces the risk of non-homogenous provisions which can be judged according to different criteria by courts distributed throughout the world.

Both exceptions have similar effects, but their justification and extent are different. The quotation right allows critique or essay authors (not mere 'users') to include in their works brief and pertinent citations of the work of other authors. Fair use also protects use (not only mere citation and not only by authors) for educational and journalistic information purposes. But, neither fair use nor the quotation right apply to performances or to rights such as the right to personal image, and the quotation right, in addition to being much more restricted in the amount of usable work owned by someone else, is limited to musical and literary works, not comprising photographs, motion pictures and plastic works (which fair use does comprise), which constitute the main raw material of the digital image.

In brief, except for the very clear case of the brief and pertinent citation of a text or musical phrase, it will be difficult for this type of exception to provide a safe refuge throughout the world for those who may make a non-authorized use for any purpose whatsoever of a digital image with someone else's content. In the on-line uses the solution could perhaps come from the use of hyperlinks that allow the display of digital images that are not reproduced in the page of whoever hyperlinked them or allowed them to be hyperlinked. The hyperlink issue is one of the most intriguing for the current copyright law, and which will be worth watching for future developments.

E. *Technical Protection and Its Legal Defence*

Technical devices for protecting images have been recognized as lawful and in some instances have been incorporated into legislation. These remedies differ from the 'formalities' that some legislation establishes as a requirement for the protection of works of certain genres,[23] such as the intellectual property

---

[22] Berne Convention, Article 10(1).
[23] For example, Article 34 of the Act No. 11.723 (*Ley de Propiedad Intelectual*) of Argentina, that requires photographers to print into the photography the date and place of publication and the author's name as a prerequisite of the work penal protection.

reservation notices of the type that some national legislations or Article III of the Universal Convention still provide for,[24] or the warnings with which authors seek to discourage those who intend to go beyond the limit permitted to legitimate users of a published work. Such technical means are an obstacle to the appropriation of operations on images that the intellectual owner wishes to keep under his or her control.

- Key words (passwords) or personal identification numbers (PIN) constitute the first level of defence. When these safety measures are placed in the points of access to the on-line files, users should identify themselves and/or undertake to respect certain conditions, which may include payments. Although the counter-manoeuvres to 'surround' these filters or to obtain information about valid keys that could be infringed are within the reach of many hackers, these measures are effective with respect to the greater part of the users.

- Another low-level defence (of the 'passive' type) which is specifically used for the protection of digital images is the spreading for advertising and marketing purposes of low-resolution samples which are only replaced by the commercially valuable file when the latter is transmitted to the licensee through a safe channel, after the contract is established and the price paid.

- Another passive technique that enables the low-risk spreading of digital images of medium or high resolution, is their distortion by means of additions or suppressions such as the sectioning, superimposition of signs or words, etc. It enables appreciation of the quality of the original offered and is replaced by the same by equal means and under the same conditions indicated in the previous point.

- 'Watermarks' or 'tattoos' constitute active techniques intended to mark the digital file and/or the screen or printer output that the same produces with distinctive indelible characteristics (perceptible or imperceptible to the eye), repeated throughout the content and that follow the digital object throughout its transfers by communication means and its eventual copies or modifications, that identify the digital image and make it possible, if necessary, to show its origin.[25] Its principal aim is to dissuade professional users from making undue use of the content and to serve as proof in case of conflict.[26]

---

[24] For example, provisions of the US Copyright Act, Chapter 4.

[25] See the examples of the characteristics of two watermarks in the advertising of the Digimarc and FBI systems, accessible respectively at Http://www.digimarc.com/~digimarc/ y http://www.highwaterfbi.com/: 'Digimarc technology allows a digital watermark to be embedded directly into photographs, video, computer images, audio, and other forms of creative property. This watermark is imperceptible to the eye, and imperceptible to the ear, but a computer analysis can read the watermark and discover the message it carries. The watermark is repeated throughout the property. It is robust, and typically survives multiple generations of copying, modification, printing, scanning, and compression. A watermark may carry a copyright notice, a unique serial number, a transaction id, as well as other application specific data.' 'FBI is a new "smart" technology that protects your work by embedding an invisible and highly secure identifier or "fingerprint" within a digital image. FBI fingerprinting is designed to withstand format conversions, compression, resizing, flipping and file transfers between computer systems. FBI fingerprints can even be detected in printed output.'

[26] 'Watermarks' do not limit their usefulness to files with screen and printer output. ARIS Technologies, for example, offer their MUSICODE system to 'tattoo' sound files.

- 'Encryption' of the digital object that supports the digital image is one of the stronger active technical measures. It consists of resorting to a key to 'conceal' the sequences of bytes that make up the file, so that nobody not in possession of the key may 'clear it up'. It is ideal for the distribution of high-cost digital images to usual customers, but – due to the administrative difficulties and the resulting cost of preservation and confidential transmission of keys – is not suitable for small or occasional operations.
- Another strong active technique takes advantage of the virtues of the encryption procedures and the surveillance that the software intelligent agents may keep. Contents are encrypted and housed together with their guardian software in a digital object, circulate enclosed in that digital object during transmission through the network are only decrypted when they get to the final destination.[27]

The WIPO Copyright Treaty has incorporated among the obligations of their member states the granting of a certain level of legal protection to technical protections, establishing in Article 11 (Obligations concerning technological measures)[28] the following:

'Contracting Parties shall provide adequate legal protection and effective legal remedies against the circumvention of effective technological measures that are used by authors in connection with the exercise of their rights under this Treaty or the Berne Convention and that restrict acts, in respect of their works, which are not authorized by the authors concerned or permitted by law.'

This rule – which has not yet been included in national regimes – was the object of strong opposition by those who tried to avoid the disqualification of electric household appliances or computers and computing devices suitable for being used for unprotectedness purposes. Its final wording makes it an obligation to afford protection through civil or criminal law against the conduct of whoever commits 'acts of evasion' of technological measures. It is not required, however, that the member states also provide protection against any person who may provide those infringers with information of technical resources that enable them to behave in such a way. The Treaty imposes two conditions for the right to protection to arise:

(a) that technical measures should be 'effective' (any of the measures we have just mentioned should be regarded as such); and
(b) that the use or exploitation of the work made by who 'surrounded' the technical measures should not have been authorized by the author or person authorized by the law.[29]

---

[27] For example, COPYCAT, a European Esprit program project which can be accessed in the respective site: http://www.mari.co.uk/copicat/page4.htm.

[28] Article 18 of the WIPO Treaty on Performances and Phonograms has a similar wording.

[29] This refers to the fair use and public domain aspects mentioned above and tends to prevent the legal protection of technical protections from ending up granting a legal remedy to annul

F. *Information for the Administration of Intellectual Property*

Files containing digital images (as any other digital medium supporting contents) serve to record, together with the data that encode the image itself, others with different functionality.[30] Among those data there may be information records referring to the identification of the content, its ownership, and the conditions under which its use by third parties is authorized. These records, because they are at the top of the sequence of instructions, have been given the technical name of headers[31] and have been named in the international legal jargon 'Rights Management Information'. Instructions of programs performing information functions about uses and users or protecting the prohibitions imposed by the distributor,[32] may also be included in these records. The processor, on loading the file in the RAM memory of the user computer will read those data and process those instructions.

In the same way that legal protection was organized for technological measures, the information industry has sought to protect the information necessary to manage the intellectual property rights by identification of the digital object, the works, the performances and other intellectual property, and of the holders thereof; the conditions and ways in which use is authorized or forbidden, the rates or fees required, the collecting entities or accounts, etc.

Article 12 of the WIPO Copyright Treaty[33] provides in pertinent part:

'Obligations concerning Rights Management Information
(1) Contracting Parties shall provide adequate and effective legal remedies against any person knowingly performing any of the following acts knowing, or with respect to civil remedies having reasonable grounds to know, that it will induce, enable, facilitate or conceal an infringement of any right covered by this Treaty or the Bern Convention:
  (i) to remove or alter any electronic rights management information without authority;

---

cont.
the public policy exceptions with which the copyright regimes balance in favour of the community the exclusive rights granted to the intellectual property owners.

30 'Computer-based information can also be utilized differently than its paper counterpart. For example, computers can "read" digital information and transform the information or take programmable actions based on the information.' *Digital Signature Guidelines*, Information Security Committee, Science and Technology Section, American Bar Association, p. 6.

31 Their function is 'defining the terms under which the copyright owner makes the work available'. Henry H. Perritt, Jr. 'Permissions Headers and Contract Law', *Proceedings Technological Strategies for Protecting Intellectual Property in the Networked Multimedia Environment* (IMA Interactive Multimedia Association, Annapolis, 1994), p. 27.

32 HTML language instructions may serve these purposes, they are thus utilized by Platform for Internet Content (PICS) an infrastructure for associating labels (metadata) with Internet content using 'Print', 'Save', and 'Quote' commands associated with variables where 0 = disallowed, 1 = conditionally allowed, and 2 = unconditionally allowed.

33 Symmetrical to Article 19 of the OMPI Treaty on Performances and Phonograms.

(ii) to distribute, import for distribution, broadcast or communicate to the public, without authority, works or copies of works knowing that electronic rights management information has been removed or altered without authority.

(2) As used in this Article, "rights management information" means information which identifies the work, the author of the work, the owner of any right in the work, or information about the terms and conditions of use of the work, and any numbers or codes that represent such information, when any of these items of information is attached to a copy of a work or appears in connection with the communication of a work to the public.'

So far, this principle has not be widely implemented in national legislation. It could reasonably be expected that a voluntary agreement among the interested parties (or a new international development) could provide the means to harmonize the location, conformation, configuration and encoding of these records which gives geography and various technical platforms the only practical way to accomplish this principle.

G. *Licences and Implicit Licences*

Licences are valuable to protect digital images that on-line and off-line distributors offer to the public. Large-scale users deal 'face to face' with the owner of the images. However, most of these agreements correspond to a form of adhesion contracts known as shrink-wrap in which the contract offer is expressed in the conditions written in a formula, and the wish to accept through the breaking of a package wrapping or the use of the content after the user has knowledge of such conditions.

The distribution of contents through the Internet has given rise to the development of the variety of licence called point-and-click, which constitutes the on-line equivalent of the shrink-wrap contract. Under these conditions, the user who enters a WWW page is required to click on an icon and accept certain terms and conditions for the use thereof, or he or she is required to type and enter certain information or enter a command or send to the administrator an electronic message with a certain content, as a requirement for being able to download a digital image. To the extent that the user's participation – since physical actions isolated and different from the use of the content are required – is more active and specific than in the case of shrink-wrap licences, the binding value of this type of contract[34] is considered much

---

[34] 'The standard subscriber agreement appears to pass this unconscionability test. First, a subscriber is free to access the electronic bulletin board without the presence of high-pressure tactics. In addition, a subscriber is free to scrutinize all the terms and conditions of the contract. Furthermore, a subscriber enjoys the freedom not to select a particular on-line service and to find a preferred one in the marketplace.' 'Drafting Tips for On-Line Services Agreements', non-signed contribution. *Multimedia Strategist*, 1, p. 1.

safer. The first cases heard by courts as regards the validity of obligations purportedly contracted upon the acceptance of point-and-click agreement proposals seem to confirm this opinion.[35]

Finally, it should be remembered that several opinions[36] have pointed out that whoever fails to resort to any technical or legal means for restricting content in the Internet environment, intends such content to be the object of downloading or of new postings and grants a tacit licence to make said uses. These legal opinions are in keeping with the Nettiquette, and thus, important that those who distribute digital images should stress and highlight any reserved intellectual property rights and that the content is available only on a paying commercial basis.

VIII. Conclusion

The supporting medium and electronic distribution of digital images forms part of the current that gives life to a society abounding in information in suitable languages to make it available to the public. This technique makes it possible to incorporate into that current precious assets that were previously reserved to be used by reduced circles and at the same time stakes the legal interests of a vast variety of rightsholders.

It is important for legal specialists to hone the legal principles that guarantee that all those who contribute immaterial property supported by digital images

---

[35] Hence, for example, the decision made in the US case *CompuServe Incorporated v. Richard S. Patterson and Flashpoint Development* (89 F.3d 1257 (6th Cir. 1996)) in which 'the court noted that Patterson had manifested his assent...by typing "AGREE" at various points in the Shareware Registration Agreement' as reminded by Kent Stuckey in 'Internet and Online Law' *(Internet Law Journal* – http://www.ljx.com/internet/ircomm.html/). Similar doctrine was applied by the court in the case *Hotmail Corporation v. Van Money Pie Inc., et al.,* C98-20064 (N.D. Cal., 20 April 1998).

[36] 'Where a copyright owner deals with the work, or authorizes others to deal with the work, in such a way that it invites others to make use of the work in a certain way, it can be said that the copyright owner has given an implied consent for license to such use, even if there is no specific license given to any individual user...If the copyright owner has permitted the work to be placed on the Web, it can be argued that the owner has implicitly consented to whatever copying or reproduction of the work is necessary to permit the Web page to be accessed and transmitted to the user...Similarly, where a copyright owner places a work on the Internet in such a way that it is freely available, it likely can be implied that any reproduction of the work necessary to permit the work to be perceived by a recipient (such as the loading of the work into the RAM of the recipient computer) has been implicitly consented to.' Michel Racicot *et al. The Cyberspace is not a 'No Law Land'*, (February 1997), p. 286. To the same effect: 'If Web site owners want users to browse – that is, load pages into RAM, and thereby make a copy – they must grant an implied license to make that copy.' Eric Schlachter, 'Caching on the Internet', 1 *Cyberspace Lawyer*, 7, p. 4; and Ellen Poler, 'Frames and License Agreement', ILPN, 20 October 1997, http://www.collegehill.com/ilp-news/poler1.html.

shall obtain the material and moral benefits resulting from their contribution and that at the same time the community enjoys, with respect to the original supported by said digital images, the same freedom of access that the public domain regime traditionally guaranteed. It is equally important that international works assure a sufficient degree of harmonization in the intellectual property law so that these principles may provide legal security to those who create, distribute and use such immaterial assets throughout a global Net.

Copyright Issues in the Use of Visual Images in the New Media

Carolina Saez

Copyright Office, Library of Congress
Washington, DC, USA

This chapter will begin by addressing international harmonization generally, then go on to examine, from a US perspective, aspects of copyright law related to the exploitation of visual works in the digital age. Finally, it concludes with some specific examples of issues raised by such exploitation, drawn from the experience of the Library of Congress.

I. International Harmonization

It is a basic axiom that copyrights are territorial – that they are granted, delineated and enforced in any given country by the operation of that country's laws. Links are forged between those national laws by international relationships, including formal treaties, regional commitments, and the ongoing give and take of trade relations. This foundation of national laws, along with their various international links make up the international legal structure.

Increasingly, there is less divergence among national laws than in the past. A tremendous amount of harmonization has taken place as to the core concepts of copyright. Even with respect to the cutting-edge issues raised by digital technologies, many countries seem to share a common approach. So far, the conclusion internationally has been that existing copyright laws are generally adequate to the task of accommodating the new technologies, and need minor revisions rather than major overhauls. This is reflected in the modest, though important, scope of the recently concluded WIPO treaties.

Differences from country to country will remain, however, no matter how inconvenient this may be in the borderless world of cyberspace. Accordingly, choice of law rules will still be needed. Given the trend toward similarity in national laws, the choice of one country's law over another's is rarely likely to result in widely varying outcomes. In addition, national laws are relatively uniform in their treatment of works of the visual arts. In areas where differences still remain, the choice of law will be crucial. One such area is the term of protection. Many countries, including the US,[1] protect works for 50 years beyond the life of the author, the minimum required by the Berne Convention. In the EU, the member states are required to provide a term of life of the author plus 70 years. This discrepancy makes it complicated to determine when one can freely place older works on the Internet.

The general rule for copyright is to apply the law of the country where the work is exploited. The difficulty lies in determining the place of exploitation for a work made available on the Internet. One possibility is to apply the law of the country where the uploader committed the acts required to place the work on-line. If so, if that country applies the Berne Convention's rule of the shorter term, it may limit protection for the work to the term granted in the work's country of origin. Thus, even if the term in the country of exploitation is life plus 70 years, a US work will never receive protection beyond life plus 50 years. Under this choice of law rule, if someone in the US uploads onto the Internet a European work 60 years after the author's death, the uploader would not infringe the US copyright because the US term has expired. If a person uploaded a US work in Europe, the same result would apply in countries applying the rule of the shorter term. But, if the work is considered to be exploited wherever it is available to the public, the result could be different. The US uploader of a European work could be liable in countries where the term is longer. The uploader of a US work could also be liable in these countries if they do not apply the rule of the shorter term.

II. US Law with Respect to Issues Relating to Visual Works of Art

A. *Copyright Protection for Digitized Versions of Public Domain Works*

1. Scanning of Images

Are digitized versions of public domain works protectable? This issue has not yet been settled by the courts. It has, however, arisen in the US Copyright Office in connection with applications for registration of claims in copyright.

Individuals and companies have tried to register scanned images of visual works, claiming copyright authorship in the scanned image itself, rather then in

---

[1] The 105th Congress (November 1998) enacted Title 1 of section 505, the Sonny Bono Copyright Term Extension Act which extends the term of copyright protection to life plus 70 years.

the underlying work. The Office rejects these applications; it takes the position that such images are not separately copyrightable works. Scanning typically involves mechanical acts, running the work through a machine for example, and does not in and of itself result in new authorship. Even if the work is altered and looks different after being scanned, alterations that result purely from the technology used do not constitute authorship because there is no human judgment involved.

An analogous issue arose with early attempts to register colourized motion pictures as new works. If colourization involves merely using a computer program that assigns colours that are predetermined by objective facts, such as blue sky and skin-coloured faces, then the output is not copyrightable. But the colourization of films can involve more than the automatic work of a computer – creative choices may be made in choosing how to apply colour, and adjusting the final product. The Copyright Office has therefore concluded that some colourized films contain sufficient authorship to justify registration as derivative works.

Whether it is scanning or colourization, the issue is the nature of the acts involved in the creation of the new version – whether and what kinds of choices and judgments were made. Do these acts satisfy the standard of originality required to secure copyright protection in the relevant country?

2. Compilation Copyright for Collections of Digitized Images

Even if there is no copyrightable authorship in a scanned image itself, some protection may be available when it is incorporated into a larger group. Most collections of images can be protected under a compilation copyright. Under US law, a compilation is defined as a work 'formed by the collection and assembling of pre-existing materials or of data that are selected, coordinated, or arranged in such a way that the resulting work as a whole constitutes an original work of authorship'. Some minimal level of creativity must be present in the selection or arrangement of the contents in order for the collection to qualify for copyright protection.

Copyright protection for such a collection of digitized images, however, is quite limited. It extends only to the material contributed by the author of the collection, as distinguished from the pre-existing material. Users would only be barred from copying the collection as a whole, or those elements of protectable selection or arrangement in the collection itself. But the individual images making up the collection are not protected by the compilation copyright, and remain free to be used as long as they are not protected by separate copyrights.

In addition to the protection offered by copyright, the owner of a collection of images has available a variety of means to protect the collection, including contracts, laws of misappropriation or unfair competition, and technical measures such as encryption. The possibility of supplementing these means with a new form of legal protection for databases is under consideration in the US. Such new protection has already been adopted in the EU, known as *sui generis* database protection. Last year, the Copyright Office prepared a comprehensive study on the subject for the Senate Judiciary Committee. A bill is currently pending in the House of Representatives, proposing protection for databases based on a misappropriation model. It would prohibit the taking of all or a substantial part of a database where it would harm the market for the database.

B. *Exemptions in a Global Networked Environment*

1. Fair Use

When visual images are used without authorization, such uses will not infringe if they constitute fair use. The US fair use doctrine excuses certain unauthorized uses of a work that further the public interest, where the present or potential economic value of the work is not substantially impaired. It is a flexible and technology-neutral provision. Its language and concepts apply equally well to all types of uses, including uses in a global networked environment.

With respect to visual works, successful fair use claims may be less common than for literary works. Uses of visual works often involve a taking of the entire work, and are less likely to be 'transformative' in nature. A transformative use, such as parody, is more likely to constitute fair use than a purely consumptive copy.

2. Browsing

Concern has been expressed about potential liability for 'browsing' of images on the Internet. The term 'browsing' however, is an ambiguous term. In the analogue world, to browse usually means to inspect in a leisurely or casual way. Browsing in the digital context also carries this connotation, but raises legal issues because it necessarily results in the making of a copy of the work in the browser's computer.

Under current US law, a browser could in theory be held liable even if he or she did not download a copyrighted work. The courts have held that the reproduction right covers the automatic copying of a work into a computer's RAM memory. Accordingly, if the 'browsing' involves the browser receiving an unauthorized copy of all or a substantial portion of a work in order to view it on his or her computer screen, the conduct could constitute infringement if no defence applies.

Various defences exist, however, which will excuse many acts of digital 'browsing'. Some browsing should qualify as fair use, particularly where the use is non-commercial and purely internal. In addition, many uses may be excused under the doctrine of implied licences, particularly where they are done in the course of an ultimate authorized use or where the copyright owner placed the work on the Internet for unrestricted public consumption. Finally, the market is already resolving some browsing concerns. A number of copyright owners are making excerpts or clips of their works available to consumers at little or no cost.

III. Integrity and Authorship Issues – Examples Drawn from the Experience of the Library of Congress

A. *The National Digital Library*

The National Digital Library (NDL) is a project of the Library of Congress. The goal of NDL is to serve the community not reached by the Library: those who cannot come to Washington DC to use the collections. The project also has preservation implications, because people are able to see works without causing wear and tear of the original. Some libraries are digitizing their historic collections for this reason alone, even without plans to put them up on the Internet.

NDL's American Memory Project draws extensively from the Library's American history collections. The American Memory Project is now made up of about 25 collections, and reflects the multimedia nature of the Library's collections, including such items as sound recordings and films from the turn of the century, photographs, manuscripts, and books.

The Library's institutional enthusiasm about the possibilities of the Internet coexists with the Library's concern about ensuring the proper use of its collections. The NDL project generates new questions every day with respect to the use of works on-line, many relating to copyright law. High priority is given to ensuring that a responsible process is in place to examine these issues. The legal implications of disseminating works in the collection in digital form over the Internet are examined collection by collection, item by item.

1. Example 1: Jackie Robinson Collection

As an example of the steps taken in making a legal assessment, I will describe the facts related to placing on-line the Jackie Robinson collection. The collection concerns a topic often requested by users of the Library: Jackie Robinson, who as the first African-American baseball player in Major League baseball, played a key role in integrating professional baseball. The materials tell his story, and the history of baseball in general. The collection consists primarily of photographs, newspaper clippings, and manuscripts drawn from different divisions in the Library – in total approximately 35 digital images of approximately 20 items.

The initial task is to determine the provenance of the materials – where did the materials come from? How did they enter the collection? At this stage, an important role is played by the people in the collection division of the Library from which the material comes, because they have the highest substantive knowledge of the materials themselves. Furthermore, all correspondence or other documents related to the materials is examined, including any existing permission statements. Even if permission statements exist, however, they are unlikely to include permission to use the work on the Internet. The Library is lucky in some cases. For example, the work and its copyright may have been donated to the Library without restrictions. Or, if the work resulted from a government project, it is in the public domain, since US copyright law does not protect US Government works.

Relying on these basic facts, the Library assesses potential responsibility for the use of the material with respect to copyright (and other rights, including those of privacy and publicity, though these are not discussed here). The first step is usually to determine whether the work is in the public domain, and if it is not, locate the rightsholders. This will usually require a search of Copyright Office registration records. Often such a search is difficult, if not impossible, because many works have no specific formal title or date of copyright identified. It is ironic that as notice and registration of works are no longer mandatory in the world (because of almost universal adherence to the Berne Convention, which prohibits formalities), the importance of centralized records has increased dramatically.

This process is conducted for each item in the collection. For example, with respect to an item of correspondence written by Robinson to a Mr. Rickey, a copyright search was not necessary because the rightsholder was already known. Copyright remains in general with the author from whom the Library will seek to secure rights. In this case, a request for permission was made to Mrs. Robinson, who then granted permission for this use. An on-line notice statement notifies users that these are unpublished works presented with the permission of Mrs. Robinson.

Even when material is clearly in the public domain, the Library is sensitive to ethical issues involving the use of materials, and attempts to contact living persons or heirs to inform them of the Library's intended use.

A restriction statement is developed concerning use of the work by the public. This statement, which appears with the collection, puts the public on notice as to possible limitations on its use of the materials. The statement makes clear that the Library provides access to the materials for educational and research purposes, and that permission of the copyright owners or other rightsholders may be necessary for certain uses. Even where the Library under its own analysis believes the works in a collection are in the public domain, it will not state this definitively in the restriction statement since it cannot take the responsibility of providing legal conclusions to the public.

2. Example 2: The Sanborn Map Collection

This example presents a good model for public–private sector collaboration, to the benefit of the public. An arrangement concerning a collection of maps was reached by the Library and EDR, an environmental research company that provides it clients with maps that show what uses were made of land over time. EDR had recently bought the Sanborn Map Co., which produced fire insurance maps in the 1850s. Included in the purchase were all the copyrights in the Sanborn Collection, but the paper maps actually remaining in the possession of the Sanborn Map Co. were only a small percentage of the total number of maps produced over approximately 100 years. So, while EDR had all the rights, it did not have all the works. The Library on the other hand had copies of all 650,000 of the maps (through copyright deposit) and had stored them on shelves the length of a city block. However, the Library did not own the copyrights, and though many of the maps were public domain, many others were not.

The Library and EDR made a cooperative agreement, therefore, to digitize the whole collection. The Library would provide access to the maps it owned (subject to security and handling requirements), while EDR would undertake the costs of digitizing the entire collection.

The Library sees this collaboration as an opportunity to make the maps easily available to researchers. Otherwise, in the many cases where the maps were still under copyright protection, it would not have had the right to include them in the NDL, and moreover, it lacked the funds to digitize the enormous collection. Furthermore, this arrangement has other benefits, such as reducing wear and tear on the originals and enabling researchers to order from EDR high-quality, hard copy prints of the maps, which the Library's photo-duplication service cannot currently provide with ease. EDR also agreed to give the Library electronic archival copies of the entire collection. On its side, EDR sees an opportunity to have a complete collection available for its clients, with the ability to develop further products that exploit the map images.[2]

---

2   For a full and complete discussion of projects undertaken to promote the application of electronic imaging in the visual arts, particularly in museums, libraries and photo archives, contact VASARI Ltd., Alexander House, 50 Station Road, Aldershot, Hampshire GU11 1BG UK or jamesrhemsley@cix.compulink.co.uk.

A Picture is Worth a Thousand Words: US Intellectual Property Issues in the Exploitation of Visual Images in the New Media

Barbara Hoffman, Esq.,
The Law Offices of Barbara Hoffman, New York, New York, USA

I. Introduction

This chapter discusses the US legal disciplines implicated in content development and distribution of museum collections, film and photo archives in the new media. Digital image collections and archives raise issues which are not addressed by text norms and understanding. Image collections and archives can represent a valuable asset for museums, new media and software professionals. However, such collections and archives present critical technological, ethical and legal issues in their creation, exploitation, protection and distribution in the new media. The specific legal disciplines discussed herein, are copyright, the right of publicity, trademark and unfair competition and licensing. Analysis of the legal issues raised is often complicated because, as with other media, the use of image collections archives may cut across national borders. Digital exploitation and distribution of image collections and archives involve complex issues of choice of law and jurisdiction. Thus this chapter can only highlight the issues.

II. Copyright Basics in US Law

A. Introduction

The source of the US Congress' power to enact copyright laws is article I, clause 8, of the Constitution. According to this provision, 'Congress shall have Power ... To promote the Progress of Science and useful Arts, by securing for limited Times to Authors ... the exclusive Right to their respective

Writings.'[1] For 'Progress in Science and useful Arts' to occur, the courts have stated that others must be permitted to build upon and refer to the creations of prior thinkers. Accordingly, three judicially created doctrines have been fashioned to limit the copyright monopoly and promote its purpose. First, copyright law does not protect ideas but only their creative expression; second, facts are not protected, regardless of the labour expended by the original author in uncovering them; and, third, the public may make 'fair use' of the copyrighted works.

The Supreme Court has acknowledged repeatedly 'the inherent tension in the need simultaneously to protect copyrighted material and to allow others to build upon it.'[2] As Justice Sandra Day O'Connor wrote:

'The primary objective of copyright is not to reward the labor of authors, but "[t]o promote the progress of Science and useful Arts." To this end, copyright assures authors the right to their original expression, but encourages others to build freely upon the ideas and information conveyed by a work ... This result is neither unfair nor unfortunate. It is the means by which copyright advances the progress of science and art.'[3]

The US Congress has implemented its constitution mandate in Title 17 of the United States Code known as the 1976 Copyright Act or Copyright Act of 1976 (Copyright Act).[4] As Mary Levering, Associate Register for National Copyright Programs, US Copyright Office, noted in an address to the College Art Association:

'The genius of United States copyright law is that it balances the intellectual property rights of authors, publishers, and copyright owners with society's need for the free exchange of ideas. Taken together, fair use and other exemptions allowing certain uses of copyrighted works without permission, were incorporated in the Copyright Act of

---

[1]   *Feist Publications, Inc. v. Rural Tel. Serv. Co.*, 499 US 340, 346 (1991). In *Feist,* the Supreme Court sounded the death knell for the sweat of brow doctrine to protect compilations. In finding a white pages telephone directory to be uncopyrightable, the Court held that the sole basis for creativity under US law is creative 'originality'.

[2]   *Campbell v. Acuff-Rose Music, Inc.*, 127 L. Ed. 2d 500, 114 S. Ct. 1164, 1169 (1994).

[3]   *Feist Publications, Inc. v Rural Tel. Serv. Co.*, 499 US 340, 349 (1991).

[4]   17 USC section 106(1) *et seq.* The Copyright Act 1976 became effective on 1 January 1978. All works of art created before that date are governed by the Copyright Act 1909.

   On 1 March 1989, the US joined the Berne Convention, and passed implementing legislation to make it compatible with domestic copyright laws. Copyright in the works of US authors, is protected automatically in all member nations of the Berne Union, and works of foreign authors who are nationals of a Berne country are automatically protected in the US. Due to adherence to Berne, the US changed certain formalities. Copyright notice is no longer required as a condition of copyright protection. Nor is registration required. Registration, however, prior to infringement provides the author with statutory damages and attorney's fees. Registration is a prerequisite to filing suit in a copyright infringement action.

1976, and constitute indispensable legal doctrines for promoting the dissemination of knowledge, while ensuring authors, publishers, and copyright owners protection of their creative works and a return on their economic investments. The preservation and continuation of this balance in the new digital environment is essential to the free flow of information and the development of an information infrastructure that serves the public interest. The loss or diminution of these provisions in the emerging information infrastructure would harm scholarship, teaching, and the operation of a free society.'[5]

In 1993, President Bill Clinton created the Information Infrastructure Task Force (ITF) to implement the administration's vision of the National Information Infrastructure (NII). A Working Group on Intellectual Property Rights, Chaired by Bruce Lehman, Commissioner of Patents and Trademarks, was formed as part of the IITF. The Working Group was charged with evaluating the intellectual property implications of the NII and recommending changes to existing US intellectual property law and policy. The report, titled Intellectual Property and the National Information Infrastructure (the White Paper), was issued in September 1995 by the United States Patent and Trademark Office. Although the White Paper was widely criticized as too restrictive and favourable to the interests of the motion picture, telecommunications, computer software and broadcasting industries, bills based on its recommendations were introduced in 1996 in both the US House and Senate.[6] Both bills died in Committee.

In August 1998, both the House and Senate passed the legislation needed to implement the WIPO Copyright Treaty and Performances and Photograph Treaty negotiated at the 1996 WIPO meeting in Geneva. Following unanimous passage by the Senate, the Digital Millennium Copyright Act (DMCA) was passed by voice vote just days before the House's August 1998 recess. On 1 September 1998 a third version that reconciled differences between the two versions was enacted.[7] The DMCA or WIPO Copyright and Performance and Programs Treaties Implementation Act 1998, was signed by President Clinton on 28 October 1998 after the House and Senate versions were reconciled by a conference committee, which deleted certain

---

[5] Mary Levering, College Art Association Annual Meeting, San Antonio, Texas, January 1995.

[6] See Hon. Marybeth Peters, 'The National Information Infrastructure: A Copyright Office Perspective' (1996) 20 *Colum. - VLA J.L. & Arts* 348. '(1) a group of related amendments intended to make clear that one of the ways in which copies of a work can be distributed to the public is by transmission; and (2) a broadening of the exemptions available to users, specifically, allowing libraries to make digital copies of works in certain circumstances for preservation purposes, and permitting nonprofit reproduction of works in a format accessible to the visually impaired.'

[7] See Statement of the US Register of Copyrights, Marybeth Peters in support of 'World Intellectual Property Organization Copyright Treaties Implementation Act' before the House Subcommittee on Courts and Intellectual Property, Appendix 4, p. 245.

controversial house provisions on database protection[8] and gross market importation.

B. *The Rights of the Copyright Owner in a Copyrighted Work*

To be protected under current US copyright law, a work 'must be an original work of authorship fixed in a tangible medium of expression'. The Copyright Act imposes no requirement of aesthetic merit as a condition of protection. However, a work must have 'at least some minimal degree of creativity'.[9] Works of visual art – a painting, a photograph, a sculpture, a character – are copyrightable subject matter as are film, sound recordings, and databases, although the copyright in the latter is 'thin'.[10] The US Copyright Act was amended in 1980 to extend copyright protection to computer programs as literary works. Architectural plans and drawings were protected under the 1976 Copyright Act. Other forms of architectural works only received protection on passage of the Architectural Works Copyright Protection Act 1990.[11] Ideas, facts, procedures, methods of operation or utilitarian designs are not protectable by copyright. Thus, the simple act of creating an original work in a 'fixed' medium, including electronic, gives the author copyright in the work.

Under section 106 of the Copyright Act 1976, the copyright owner has the exclusive right to:

(a) reproduce the work in copies or phonorecords;
(b) prepare derivative works based on the copyrighted work (which includes the right to recast, transform or modify);
(c) distribute copies by sale or other ownership transfer, or to rent, lease or lend copies;

---

[8] In US copyright law, a database is a 'compilation': 'A work formed by the collection and assembling of preexisting materials or of data.' 17 USC, section 101. Since the decision in *Feist Publications, Inc. v. Rural Tel. Serv. Co.*, notwithstanding a valid copyright, a subsequent compiler remains free to use the facts contained in another's publication to aid in preparing a competing work so long as the competing work does not feature the same selection and arrangement. Databases are copyrightable under both the Berne Convention for the Protection of Literary and Artistic Works and the Agreement on Trade-Related Aspects of Intellectual Property Rights (TRIPs). In 1996, database protection treaty proposals were submitted to the World Intellectual Property Organization. However, the draft proved too controversial and, while database protection remains an issue, formal treaty discussions have been removed from the formal agenda for now. In 1996 the EU adopted a database directive which is currently being implemented by its member nations. The US Congress is likely to consider database protection in the next year. Two basic models have been proposed: (1) an exclusive properly right; (2) some form of unfair competition law.

[9] *Feist Publications, Inc. v. Rural Tel. Serv. Co.*, 499 US 340, 349 (1991).

[10] Ibid. at 349.

[11] An 'architectural work' is defined as 'the design of a building as embodied in any tangible medium of expression, including a building, architectural plans, or drawings'. It includes the overall form as well as the 'arrangement and composition of spaces and elements' in the design of the building, but does not include overall standard features.

(d)   perform the work publicly; and
(e)   display the work publicly.[12]

For certain one-of-a-kind 'works of visual art' and numbered limited signed editions of 200 copies, authors (artists) have the right to claim authorship (attribution) and prevent the use of their names in conjunction with certain modifications of the works and the right to prevent alteration of their work (integrity) under section 106A. Specifically excluded from the definition of 'works of visual art' are 'works made for hire' and 'a motion picture', 'audio-visual work' and 'electronic publication'. The latter two rights – known as *droit moral* or moral rights sourced in the protection of the author's personality – receive limited protection in the US scheme of copyright based on the author's economic rights as compared to France, Germany, Italy and Japan, which are strong moral rights countries.

Ownership of the bundle of intangible rights comprising copyright is separate and distinct from ownership in the work of art. Under current law, absent a writing expressly conveying copyright, the sale, gift, or transfer of the original work of art does not transfer the copyright in the work of art. Under the 1976 Copyright Act, copyright interests can be transferred *inter vivos* or at death and in whole or in part. Any of the exclusive rights comprised in a copyright, including any subdivision of any of the rights specified by section 106, may be transferred and owned separately. The owner of any particular exclusive right is entitled, to the extent of that right, to all of the protection and remedies accorded to the copyright owner. A copyright owner may divide copyright in the work in a number of ways: by the type of use and/or media, by an exclusive licence or non-exclusive licence, by a full interest or a divided interest, by territory or duration (i.e. site licence)[13] to name only a few possibilities. A non-exclusive licence is not a transfer of copyright ownership, but a transfer of a contract right; thus, it need not be in writing. The holder of a non-exclusive licence cannot bring a copyright infringement action.

From a practical stand point, copyright holders are customarily reluctant to agree to broad transfers of rights to future unknown technologies. The grant of rights to a software company to use an image in one medium or for one purpose does not necessarily permit its use in other ways. In particular, ownership of a copy does not necessarily include any of the bundle of intangible rights of copyright and without such grant of rights, licence, or an available defence or exception to those rights, the owner of a copy cannot reproduce, alter, or publicly display the copy. When museums, stock houses, galleries, archives, or publishers purport to license the use of an image, they may be providing access

---

[12]   Under section 101, to 'display a work' is defined as 'to show a copy of it, either directly or by means of a film, slide, television, image or any device or process or, in the case of a motion picture or other audiovisual work, to show individual images non-sequentially'.
[13]   See Saskia Site License, Appendix 11, p. 313.

to a particular copy of the image, on certain terms and conditions. Copyright in the underlying work may be held by the author or his or her heirs.

Authors and copyright holders, in theory, enjoy the same copyright protection in cyberspace as in other media; digital image files are equivalent to paintings, photographs and other works and, if displayed or copied without permission, implicate the right of reproduction and display. However, this simple fundamental concept *ab initio* is not so easily applied in cyberspace. What does and does not constitute the making of a copy? Is reproduction under clause (1) of section 106 to be distinguished from 'display' under clause (5)? For a work to be 'reproduced', its fixation in tangible form must be 'sufficiently permanent or stable to permit it to be perceived, reproduced, or otherwise communicated for a period of more than transitory duration'. Thus, the showing of images on a screen or tube might not be a violation of clause (1), although it might come within the scope of clause (5). Is the mere display of an image on a video monitor a technical violation of the copyright law? Is the transitory storage of an image in a computer memory a copy?[14] What rights of adaptation and reproduction exist for users who download images? Does the right to display accompany transmission of a digital image?[15] Does the first sale doctrine apply to a lawfully acquired digital transmission? How will the law distinguish between an artist's electronic snatches of pieces of art, a software publisher's creating a textbook, and a digitally altered image incorporated in a new work of art?

The WIPO Copyright Treaty incorporates as an international norm the two following rights: Article 6 (the right of distribution) affords authors 'the exclusive right to distribute the original and copies of their works including digital works'; however, no standard is applied with respect to the first sale doctrine; and Article 8 creates a new right of communication to the public

---

[14] The White Paper concludes that temporary storage of a computer file in memory constitutes copying for the purposes of copyright, as does 'scanning', 'uploading' and 'downloading'. In *MAI Sys. v. Peak Computer, Inc.*, 991 F.2nd 599 (9th Cir. 1993), the court ruled that loading of copyrighted software into RAM credited a 'copy' of that software in violation of the US Copyright Act.

[15] *Playboy Enter., Inc. v. Frena*, 839 F. Supp. 1552 (USCD MD Fla. 1993) is one of the first US cases to consider that issue. In finding that an operator of a subscription computer billboard infringed *Playboy* magazine's display right, the Court held that 'the display right precludes unauthorized transmission of the display from one place to another, for example, by a computer system. . . . "Display" covers any showing of a "copy" of the work, "either directly or by means of a film, slide, television image or any other device or process". 17 USC section 101. However, in order for there to be copyright infringement, the display must be public. A "public display" is a display "at a place open to the public or . . . where a substantial number of persons outside of a normal circle of family and its social acquaintances is gathered". Melville B. Nimmer, 2 *Nimmer on Copyright*, section 8.14(c) at 8-169 (1993). A place is "open to the public" in this sense even if access is limited to paying customers.' Ibid. at p. 1557. In *Playboy Enter., Inc. v. Webbworld Inc.*, 991 F. Supp. 543 (ND Tex. 1997), the court held that the two owners of Webbworld were vicariously liable for infringement of copyrights held by *Playboy* by displaying copies of nude images to subscribers on its web site.

which gives authors the right of 'authorizing any communication to the public of their works, by wire or wireless means'. The right blurs the distinction between the right of display, reproduction and performance. This right, similar to the right of transmission in the 1996 legislation, makes clear that the posting of copyrighted material on a web page or on the Internet, which can be accessed by the public, is a copyright infringement. Whether such posting is within the scope of the rights of display, public distribution reproduction, and performance has been the subject of considerable debate in the US. Thus, the copyright owner's exclusive rights to reproduce the work, to display a work publicly and to distribute the work by transmission, are implicated in many NII transactions. While current legal analysis supports the conclusion that digital scanning of images constitutes the making of a copy, and thus infringement, there is no clear legal precedent that establishes whether an intermediate copy may be considered 'fair use' if the end use is fair, or whether an intermediate digital copy is an infringement if the final work is not 'substantially similar'.[16]

The changes that the DMCA makes to current law are significant but few in number. The nature and scope of copyright rights and exceptions are not affected; thus the WIPO rights discussed above are seen as existing in current law. The US had to amend its law only to provide adequate and legal remedies against circumvention of technological measures, and removal of copyright management information.

The DMCA, section 103 adds a new Chapter 12 – Copyright Protection and Management Systems – to the Copyright Act which creates a set of civil and criminal penalties for persons who directly or indirectly circumvent 'a technological measure that effectively controls access to' a copyrighted work. Thus, the DMCA provides copyright holders with an exclusive right to control access where they use technological measures to protect their work. The DMCA goes beyond WIPO in providing teeth to the right by outlawing technology products and services that enable the circumvention of measures used to protect copyrighted works. The DMCA also controls piracy by protecting copyright management information.

The anti–circumvention measures were amongst the most controversial in the battle between the content providers (the film studies, recording and software industries) and the American Library Association, on-line service providers and others.

---

[16] See *Sega Enter., Ltd. v. Accolade, Inc.*, 977 F.2d 1510 (9th Cir. 1993). The Court found that defendant Accolade, a manufacturer of video game cartridges, disassembled the copyrighted computer program of the plaintiff, a video game console manufacturer. Using the 'object code' it obtained, Accolade manufactured video game cartridges compatible with Sega's 'Genesis' video game console. Ibid. at pp. 1514–1515. The Ninth Circuit found the first factor to favour Accolade. Ibid. at p. 1522. In words directly applicable here, it stated that the use at issue 'was an *intermediate* one only and thus any commercial "exploitation' was *indirect* or *derivative*'. Ibid. (emphasis added).

In addition to these protective measures, Title II the 'Online Copyright Infringement Liability Limitation Act' of the DMCA amends Chapter 5 of the Copyright Act to create certain safe havens for on-line service providers who have long been concerned about potential liability resulting from the infringing acts of their users. This Act relieves on-line service providers from copyright infringement liability in most cases. As of the date of enactments, an on-line service provider will not be liable for monetary infringement damages where its users transmit cache, store or provide links to infringing material, provided that certain conditions are satisfied.

C. *Ownership of Copyright*

Two types of property rights must be distinguished: ownership of copyright and ownership of the material object in which the copyright in the work is embodied. The 1976 Copyright Act vests initial ownership of copyright in the 'author' who is the creator unless it is a 'work for hire'. A 'work made for hire' is defined in section 101 of the Copyright Act as:

'(1) A work prepared by an employee within the scope of his or her employment.
(2) A work specially ordered or commissioned for use as a contribution to a collective work, as a part of a motion picture or other audio visual work, as a translation, as a compilation, as a supplementary work, as answer material for a test, or as an atlas, if the parties expressly agree in a written instrument signed by them that the work shall be considered a work for hire.'

III. Special Copyright Concerns and Issues in Creating Digital Image Archives

Images can be original works, reproductions of other works, or, if a reproduction includes original elements, they can be both. Often, a digital image is many generations removed from the original work that it reproduces. For example, a digital image may have been scanned from a slide, which was copied from a published book, which contained a photographic transparency, which reproduced an original work of art.

An original digital image is a work of art or an original work of authorship (or a part of a work), fixed in digital or analogue form and expressed in a visual medium. Examples include graphic, sculptural, and architectural works, as well as stills from motion pictures or other audio-visual works, photographs, and artefacts and objects from museum collections. A reproduction is a copy of an original image in digital or analogue form. The original image in a reproduction is often referred to as the 'underlying work'.[17]

---

[17] See 'Educational Fair Use Guidelines for Digital Images', Conference on Fair Use (CONFU), 15 August 1996.

Images in archives, museums, libraries, and collections may have multiple layers of authorship: the underlying copyrighted work, the photograph of the original work, or its digitized version. A software producer, a museum curator or multimedia producer who obtains rights to use one image does not automatically receive permission to use the other works of authorship.

A. *What Rights does the Museum or Archive Own?*

A software company purchasing a film or a photo archive or a museum collection or a museum seeking to exploit its own collection must use due diligence to establish properly ownership rights. Engaging in or authorizing a reproduction or preparation of a derivative work and the public distribution of the work without the copyright owner's permission is copyright infringement. Determining the copyright status of an underlying image may be difficult for several reasons. Even if a museum, photo or film archive, library, or collection owns an original work of art, it does not necessarily 'own' copyright to the image. Works of art transferred subsequent to the Copyright Act 1976 do not transfer any of the rights of copyright unless accompanied by a written transfer of such rights. Prior to 1978, however, under the *Pushman* doctrine, an artist was presumed to have transferred common law copyright at the time the original work of art was sold unless the artist specifically reserved copyright ownership. Even prior to the Copyright Act 1976, in New York and California statutes were enacted revising the presumption of the *Pushman* doctrine.[18] Determining copyright of ownership in photographs, particularly those taken prior to the Copyright Act 1976 is particularly difficult. In *Lumière v. Robertson-Cole Distributing Corp.*,[19] a photographer was denied any right of copyright in photographs he had taken because a third party had engaged the services of the photographer on behalf of the subject and the photographer was paid for the photographs and his services in taking them. Rights to use images will vary depending not only on the identities of the layers of rightsholders, but also on other factors such as the terms of any bequest or applicable licence.

Any intangible intellectual property rights owned by a museum, film or photo archive must be assignable to a software company or publisher who wishes to acquire rights in the visual images.

The case of *Tasini v. New York Time Co.*[20] addressed the issue of the digital use of a collection of copyrighted works and the scope of licences purportedly granted by the copyright owners. The plaintiffs were six freelance writers who had sold articles for publication in a variety of popular newspapers and

---

[18] *Pushman v. New York Graphic Soc'y*, 287 NY 302, 39 NE 2d 249 (1942).

[19] 280 F. 550 (2d Cir. 1922). See also, *Henri Daumon and Time Inc. v. the Andy Warhol Foundation For the Visual Arts, Inc., The Estate of Andy Warhol and the Andy Warhol Museum*, 96 Civ 9219.

[20] *Tansini v. New Tork Times Co.*, 972 F. Supp. 804 (SDNY 1997), *reh'g denied* 981 F. Supp. 841 (SDNY 1997).

magazines, including the *New York Times* and *Newsday*. The issue determined by the court was whether publishers are entitled to place the contents of their periodicals into electronic databases and onto CD-ROMs without first securing the permission of the freelance writers whose contributions are included in those periodicals. According to the complaint filed by the group of freelance journalists, this practice infringes the copyright that each writer holds in his or her individual articles. The defendant publishers and electronic service providers invoked the 'revision' privilege of the 'collective works' provision of the Copyright Act 1976 under section 201(c). The defendants maintained that they had not improperly exploited plaintiffs' individual contributions, but that they had permissibly reproduced plaintiffs' articles as part of electronic revisions of the newspapers and magazines in which those articles first appeared.

Prior to this action, *Newsday* solicited its freelance contributions in much the same manner as did the *New York Times*. Freelance assignments for *Newsday* were most often undertaken pursuant to discussions between editors and writers and without any written agreements. However, the cheques with which *Newsday* paid freelance writers for their contribution, including those cheques sent to plaintiffs following the publication of their articles, included the following endorsement:

'Signature required. Check void if this endorsement altered. This check accepted as full payment for first-time publication rights (or all rights, if agreement is for all rights) to material described on face of check in all editions published by *Newsday* and for the right to include such material in electronic library archives.'

The court determined that there is no [*sic*] basis for holding that the *Newsday* cheque legends effected an unambiguous and timely transfer of any significant electronic rights in plaintiffs' articles.

In the context of the creation and exploitation of image databases, the following reasoning of the court with respect to collective works and derivative works is instructive:

'Both collective works and derivative works are based upon preexisting works that are in themselves capable of copyright. A derivative work "transforms" one or more such preexisting works into a new creation. ... A collective work, on the other hand, consists of numerous original contributions which are not altered, but which are assembled into an original collective whole. In both instances, the copyright law accounts for the fact that the larger work – although it is entitled to copyright protection – consists of independent original contributions which are themselves protected. ... The copyright in a compilation or derivative work extends only to the material contributed by the author of such work, as distinguished from the preexisting material employed in the work, and does not imply any exclusive right in the preexisting material. The copyright in such work is independent of, and does not affect or enlarge the scope, duration, ownership, or subsistence of, any copyright protection in the preexisting material. ...The aspects of a derivative work added by the derivative author are that author's property, but the element drawn from the pre-existing work remains on grant from the owner of the pre-existing work. So long as the pre-existing work remains out of the public domain, its use is infringing if one who employs the work does not have a valid license or assignment for use of the preexisting work.'[21]

The district court granted summary judgment for defendants. The court held that section 201(c) of the Copyright Act authorizes publishers to reproduce an individual contribution to a collective work (such as a newspaper) as part of the collective work or any revision of that collective work, so long as the publishers make no revisions to the individual contributions. The court rejected the plaintiff's claim that this section does not authorize reproduction in a different media including the electronic media. The court then held that the publication in the electronic media constituted 'revision' of the collective work within the meaning of the statute.[22]

'In sum, both the terms of the 1976 Act, and the pertinent legislative history, reveal a design to extend display rights, in "certain limited circumstances", to the creators of collective works. Thus, so long as defendants are operating within the scope of their privilege to "reproduce" and "distribute" plaintiffs' articles in "revised" versions of defendants' collective works, any incidental display of those individual contributions is permissible'.[23]

Another example of the ownership issue which may arise occurred in a matter settled out of court when the Bettman Archives purchased the INS photographic database. Bettman assumed that it owned the rights to license the images because the negatives were in the library. In fact, the freelance photographers whose work was represented retained valid copyrights in their works and merely permitted the archive to act as an agent for the licensing of their images for which they would be paid a royalty.

If a museum, archive, library, or collection reproduces a work of art, it must obtain the consent of the copyright owner to reproduce the work and, if it is to be a copyright claimant, must add a non-trivial and original contribution not found in the original work of art.

One area of dispute between rightsholders and users is whether photographs of public domain work contain sufficient originality to be entitled to copyright protection. It is a close question, whether a photograph of a painting displays sufficient originality to qualify for copyright protection. According to a leading copyright treatise author, a photograph of a two-dimensional object, for example, a painting or drawing, may lack this quantum of originality.[24] Alternatively, a photograph of a sculpture or other three-dimensional object, which involves the photographer's judgment in selecting camera angles and

21 *Tansini*, 972 F. Supp. at 820.
22 Ibid.
23 Ibid.
24 See 1 *Nimmer on Copyright*, section 2.08(E) at 2-111 (1993).

lighting, is a clearer case of sufficient original authorship.[25] There was sufficient added authorship to a public domain work of art to entitle a small-scale reproduction of Rodin's 'Hand of God' to obtain copyright protection. In the case of *Alva Studios, Inc. v. Winninger*,[26] the court held that the reproduction embodies and results from Alva's skill and originality in producing an accurate scale reproduction of the original. The court emphasized the difference in size, the different treatment of the base and the quality control exercised by the museum's curatorial staff.

Simply because an underlying work may have fallen into the public domain does not necessarily mean that a reproduction is in the public domain or can be copied. In *Woods v. Bourne Co.*,[27] the court commented that a derivative work must be substantially different from the underlying work to be copyrightable. The court stated that the purpose of the term 'original' is not to guide aesthetic judgment but 'to assure a sufficiently gross difference between the underlying and the derivative work to avoid entangling subsequent artists depicting the underlying work in copyright problems'. Is digitization of a public domain image properly considered a process or idea or a mere trivial variation and thus not entitled to copyright protection, or is it of sufficient originality and skill to warrant copyright protection? The United States Copyright Office has accepted digitized versions of public domain works for copyright registration; however, what the Copyright Office requires for registration purposes should not be confused with what the courts have determined or will determine is necessary for copyright protection.

The Bridgeman Art Library, Ltd. v. Corel Corp, et ano 1998 US Dist. LEXIS 17920 recently decided by Judge Kaplan in the Southern District of New York provides some guidance on the issues discussed above. The Bridgeman Art Library, Ltd. (Bridgeman) claimed to represent a number of museums which have 'entrusted plaintiff with the proprietorship of the copyright' to reproductions made from works of art, presumably the originals of which are owned by and/or on display in the museums. Bridgeman claimed to be the sole and exclusive proprietor of all authorized photographic and lithographic reproductions, prints and digital images of works of art of numerous European

---

[25]   For cases involving originality in photographs, see *Gross v. Seligman*, 21 F. 930 (2d Cir. 1914) (the photographer, after sale of the photograph and copyright, took a later picture with the same model and pose but with the addition of a smile on her mouth and a cherry in her teeth, held an infringement) and the related case of *Franklin Mint Corp v. Nat'l Wildlife Art Exch.*, 575 F.2d 62 (3d Cir. 1978) (holding that a later painting by the artist of the same subject was not infringement, as its similarity reflected the common theme). See *also Rogers v. Koons* 960 F.2d 301 (2d Cir. 1991).

[26]   *Alva Studios, Inc. v. Winninger*, 177 F. Supp. 265 (SDNY 1959). See also *L. Batlin & Son, Inc. v. Snyder*, 536 F.2d 486 (2d Cir. 1976); see generally Rhoda L. Berkowitz and Marshall A. Leaffer, 'Copyright and the Art Museum'. 1984 *Columbia Journal of Art and the Law* 8, pp. 249–316.

[27]   60 F.3d 978 (2d Cir. 1995).

master artists, including Michelangelo's Sistine Chapel Ceiling and Leonardo da Vinci's 'Mona Lisa'. Thus, it claimed to have the exclusive rights in photographic transparencies of these works of art and to have transformed those transparancies into digital images in which it also claimed exclusive rights. Corel is a developer, manufacturer and distributor of a variety of consumer software products including CorelDRAW, Corel Professional Photos CD-ROM, Masters I-VII, and a collection of CD-ROM titles containing digitized photographic reproductions of public domain works of a variety of European masters. Bridgeman contended that Corel's CD-ROMs contain digital images of the same works of art and must have been copied from its transparencies. He commenced an action for copyright infringement, Lanham Act violations, common law unfair competition, and tortious misappropriation of goodwill in August 1997, contending that Corel's distribution of its Masters CD-ROM violated Bridgeman's exclusive rights in its alleged reproductions.

Bridgeman's first claim asserted that Corel infringed its copyright in reproductions of public domain works of art by making unauthorized copies of the reproductions and selling and distributing them in Corel Professional Photos CD-ROM, Masters I-VII. Bridgeman's second claim asserts that Corel infringed its copyright or trademark in titling the CD-ROMs 'Masters I-VII', apparently because Bridgeman claims it alone has the exclusive right to title anything 'Master'. Bridgeman further claimed that Corel's use of 'Master' renders a false designation of origin of the reproductions. Finally, Bridgeman asserts state law claims of unfair competition and misappropriation of goodwill.

Corel moved for summary judgment, on the theory that as a matter of law reproductions of any work, let alone works in the public domain for hundreds of years, lack sufficient originality to be copyrightable subject matter. Corel argued that even if Bridgeman owned a valid copyright registration for the individual reproductions, Corel is entitled to judgment on the copyright infringement claim because the 'image transparencies' which were allegedly copied lack the originality required for copyright protection.

Moreover, since Bridgeman has alleged only that Corel copied image *transparencies*, not digitized reproductions, whether Bridgeman's process of digitizing the transparencies made its digitized reproductions sufficiently original is irrelevant. Corel argued that the only issue before the court is whether, as a matter of law, these transparencies are sufficiently original to warrant copyright protection.[28]

---

[28] Under US copyright law an archive could copyright the image as a derivative work. Courts have included that a copyright in such a work is 'thin'. See *Feist Publication* (note 8, above) where the court stated that notwithstanding a valid copyright, a subsequent compiler would remain 'free to use the facts contained in anothers publication to aid in preparing a competing work, so long as the competing work does not feature the same selection and arrangement'. See also discussion in Saez, Chapter 2.

In deciding Corel's motion for summary judgment, Judge Kaplan applied the law of the UK[29] to decide whether copyright subsists in Bridgeman's transparencies since the photographs were published in the UK and the UK has the most significant relationship to the issue of copyrightability. The court held that the transparencies lacked the required originality under the Copyright, Designs and Patents Act 1988. The court them looked to US law to construe English law.

'A work is original if it owes its creation to the author and was not merely copied.... with respect to derivative works, the originality requirement warrants that there be a distinguishable variation between the work in which copyright is sought and the underlying work. Important to this calculus is that the demonstration of some physical, as opposed to artistic skill does not constitute a distinguishable variation.'[30]

Although the decision does not definitively answer the question of whether digitized versions are subject to copyright of public domain works, the rational would seem to support such a conclusion.

With respect to the issue of infringement, the court found no probative similarities between the parties' images. 'When, as here the only similarity between two works is with respect to non-copyrightable elements, summary judgment is appropriate.'[31] The court also dismissed on the merits, Bridgeman's Lanham Act claim.

B. *Is the Image in the Public Domain?*

A source of visual images free of copyright concerns is in the public domain. If an image is in the public domain, one may freely use, copy, adapt, distribute and display it without fear of copyright infringement. This explains the moustache on the 'Mona Lisa' or a Van Gogh self-portrait wearing headphones. Works in the public domain are not protected by copyright, even when incorporated into a copyrighted work. Nevertheless, as discussed above, an artist may make a new or derivative version of a public domain art work which may itself be copyrightable if sufficiently original. The public domain consists of materials that do not enjoy copyright protection as a matter of law. A significant part of the public domain consists of works that once were protected by copyright but have lost that protection by expiration, forfeiture or abandonment. A work enters the public domain when its copyright protection has expired.

Until 1998, the duration of a copyright in the US depended on whether the work was governed by the 1909 Act or the 1976 Act. The duration of copyright in works created as of 1978 was the life of the author plus 50 years. For a work made for hire, the copyright was 75 years from the date of first

---

29   See discussion below on choice of law.
30   1998 US Dist. LEXIS 17920, p. 20.
31   Ibid. at 20.

publication or 100 years from the year of its creation, whichever expires first. Therefore, no copyright in works created under the 1976 Act would expire before the end of 2028. For works published before 1978, the duration depends on whether the work was published or unpublished. Generally speaking, the copyright on works published prior to 1918 has expired. Copyright protection for works of art created prior to 1988 may also have been lost for failure to follow the copyright formalities, primarily the omission of notice on 'published' copyrighted works. However, works like old photographs, for example, that have no affixed copyright notice may not be in the public domain since, if the photographs were never published, neither the 1909 Act nor the 1976 Act required the affixation of any copyright notice. In 1992, Congress amended the Copyright Act to provide that pre-1978 works then in their first term of copyright would be automatically renewed. As a result, copyright in works published between 1964 and 1977 will expire 75 years from initial publication. Recently, by virtue of the Uruguay Round of GATT, President Clinton signed certain implementing legislation which resurrected foreign copyright in works which had entered the public domain in the US for omission of notice or failure to renew. Such works will have the copyright restored for the remainder of the term the foreign work would otherwise have had in the US if the work had not entered the public domain.

The 105th Congress (November 1998) enacted Title 1 of section 505, the Sonny Bono Copyright Term Extension Act, which extends the term of copyright protection to life plus 70 years. In addition works made for hire are now protected for 95 years from publication or 120 years from creation rather than 75 years from publication or 100 years from creation. Libraries, archives and non-profit educational institutions are given greater latitude in using copyrighted works during the extended (20 years) term. If a work is not obtainable at a reasonable price, and not subject to normal commercial exploitation libraries, archives and non-profit educational institutions may reproduce, distribute, display and perform the work for purposes of scholarship, research or presentation.

The Sonny Bono Act accomplishes its principal purpose by adding 20 years to each provision that deals with copyright duration. The Sonny Bono Act does not simply add 20 years to every date in the existing Copyright Act, however. Works which were unpublished and unregistered as of 1 January 1978, and formerly entitled to protection until at least 2002, are not entitled to guaranteed protection until 2022, as might be expected. The copyright in these works will still expire at the end of 2002, unless the works are published before that time. The optional additional protection available for such works, if published before the end of 2002, is extended, however, from 2027 to 2047. Thus, owners of unregistered, unpublished pre-1978 works by artists or authors have an incentive to publish prior to the end of 2002, since publication will provide up to 45 years of additional protection.

The concept of publication was an important concept both under the 1909 Act where publication without copyright notice injected the work into the public domain and under the 1976 Copyright Act, although of somewhat reduces importance, until US adherence to the Berne Convention in 1989. Under the 1909 Act, in general, the law was not entirely clear on whether a non-commercial display of a work of art constitutes publication. Particularly when works have been sold many times, and records are inadequate to establish the publication history of the work, it may be difficult to determine the copyright status of the work. Similarly, limited distribution was held not to constitute publication under the 1909 Act. Many photographs, publicity stills for films, and other images of limited distribution or images provided to archives without limitation may be considered unpublished and therefore not required to have a copyright notice. In general, works which are unpublished not only have a different duration under current copyright law but may be treated differently under Continental legal systems and in 'fair use' analysis.

IV. Exemptions and Limitations on the Copyright Owner's Exclusive Rights

A copyright owner's rights are limited in several respects under existing law. The 'first sale' doctrine permits the owner of a copy of a work to sell or otherwise dispose of the work. Thus, the owner of a CD-ROM of the Barnes collections masterpieces would be free to sell the CD-ROM, but not to copy the copyrighted images on the disk. However, the first-sale doctrine does not translate easily to the on-line environment, where most versions of the work are in an intangible format, whether stored, transmitted, or viewed on-screen. Until the work is printed onto paper (or perhaps saved to a floppy disk), there is no corporeal version of the work under traditional copyright notions. The on-line environment makes it tempting to view copyright law as a relic of the past or the first sale doctrine as a simple inconvenience that can be discarded in favour of copyright protection for every conceivable use of a work.

One limitation on the display right is closely related to the first-sale doctrine: the owner of a work of visual art may display it to the public at the place where it is located. Section 109 of the Copyright Law provides:

'Notwithstanding the provisions of section 106(5) [which grants copyright owners the exclusive right to display publicly copies of a work], the owner of a particular copy lawfully made under this title, or any person authorized by such owner, is entitled, without the authority of the copyright owner, to display that copy publicly, either directly or by the projection of no more than one image at a time, to viewers present at the place where the copy is located.'

Section 110(1) permits the performance or display of a copyrighted work in the course of face-to-face teaching activities in a classroom or similar place of instruction. The privilege to display applies only to those who own the work. Due to its 'face-to-face' requirement, this provision may not protect the telecommunication, transmission and subsequent digitalization of programs embodying copyrighted works. Thus, if an audio-visual work accompanying a museum exhibition is broadcast by closed circuit television from one museum to another location, the exemption would not apply.

Section 110(2) permits the performance of a non-dramatic literary or musical work or display of a work, by or in the course of a transmission, if:

'(A) the performance or display is a regular part of the systematic instructional activities of a governmental body or a nonprofit educational institution; and
(B) the performance or display is directly related and of material assistance to the teaching content of the transmission; and
(C) the transmission is made primarily for –
    (i) reception in classrooms or similar places normally devoted to instruction, or
    (ii) reception by persons to whom the transmission is directed because their disabilities or other special circumstances[32] prevent their attendance in classrooms or similar places normally devoted to instruction, or
    (iii) reception by officers or employees of governmental bodies as a part of their official duties or employment.'

This means that copyrighted drawings, slides, maps, or art prints may be transmitted to a remote site without constituting an infringement; however, movies, videos and other audio-visual works may not. Audio tapes of musical performances would be allowed, but not audio-visual tapes of musical performances. Section 110(2) does not apply to the performance of an audio-visual work.[33]

The situation in which audio-visual works could be transmitted on an electronic network despite section 110(2) is where the use and the portion of the work transmitted is such that it meets the 'fair use' provisions of section 107. Fair use applies concurrently with section 110(2). There appears to be some consensus that section 107 applies to all of the exclusive rights of the copyright holder, but that because of the specific limitations contained in section 110, there may be a higher burden of demonstrating fair use beyond section 110(2).[34] Neither section 110 nor fair use under current interpretations

---

[32] 'Special circumstances' include daytime employment and distance from campus that may interfere with daytime attendance at regular classes. The 94th Congress (2d Session) House of Representatives Report of the Committee on the Judiciary states: 'There has been some question as to whether or not the language in this section of the bill is aimed at undergraduate and graduate students in earnest pursuit of higher educational degrees who are unable to attend daytime classes because of daytime employment, distance from campus, or some other intervening reason. So long as these broadcasts are aimed at regularly enrolled students and conducted by recognized higher educational institutions, the committee believes that they are clear within the language of Section 110(2)(C)(ii).' HR Rep No 94-1476 (1977).

[33] 'Audiovisual works' are works that consist of a series of related images which are intrinsically intended to be shown by the use of machines or devices such as projectors, viewers, or electronic equipment, together with accompanying sounds, if any, regardless of the nature of the material objects, such as films or tapes, in which the works are embodied.' 17 USC, 101.

[34] See CONFU Distance Learning Guidelines, August 1996.

provide complete insulation for universities who wish to digitize completely copyrighted images and produce multimedia works for distribution, subsequent copying and lending to students for later viewing and future use.

The DMCA, section 403 – Limitations on Exclusive Rights: Distance Education – provides that the Register of Copyright no later than six months after the act, after consultation with representatives of copyright, non-profit educational institutions and non-profit libraries and archives shall submit to Congress recommendations on how to promote distance education through digital technologies, including interactive digital networks, while maintaining an appropriate balance between the rights of copyright owners and the needs of users of copyrighted works.

The balancing of the Copyright Act is apparent in the special exemptions for libraries and archives in section 108 and recently enacted amendments permitting digitization of images for archival and preservation purposes.[35] Many have expressed concern that the special exemptions for libraries in section 108 of the Copyright Act are no longer relevant in the digital era. Libraries, of course, may make fair use of copyrighted works pursuant to the provisions of section 107. Section 108, however, provides additional exemptions specifically for libraries and archives. On the one hand, there are those who believe that since licensing of transaction of works in digital form will be a feature of the digital distribution systems of the future, there is no need for library exceptions. Each copying transaction will be cheap and libraries can simply pay for all of the copying in which they engage. On the other hand, there are those who believe that unrestricted copying in libraries should be the rule, without the special conditions and limitations set forth in section 108.

Section 117 of Title 17 of the United States Code establishes an exception to the exclusive rights granted to copyright owners by section 106 for software programs. Section 117 provides that the 'owner' of a copy of a computer program may make or authorize the making of another copy of adaptation of that computer program provided '(1) that such a new copy or adaptation is created as an essential step in the utilization of the computer program in conjunction with a machine and that it is used in no other manner; or (2) that such a new copy or adaptation is for archival purposes....'[36]

A. *Fair Use*

The Berne Convention and various national laws provide exemptions and limitations on the rights of copyright owners, including exemptions for teaching, private copying and the general fair use or fair dealing exceptions of

---

[35] Section 108 has been amended to allow the preparation of three copies of works in digital format, and it authorizes the making of a limited number of digital copies by libraries and archives for purposes of preservation.

[36] 17 USC 117.

common law countries. For example, the Berne Convention includes a general authorization to member countries to permit reproduction for educational purposes. Article 10.2 provides:

'It shall be a matter for legislation in the countries of the Union, and for special agreements existing or to be concluded between them, to permit the utilization, to the extent justified by the purpose, of literary or artistic works by way of illustration in publications, broadcasts or sound or visual recordings for teaching, provided such utilization is compatible with fair practice.'[37]

The US fair use concept is somewhat more liberal and susceptible of broader interpretation than is the concept of fair dealing in UK and Canadian law. It has been described as the most significant and, perhaps, murky of the limitations on a US copyright owner's exclusive rights. Fair use is an affirmative defence to an action for copyright infringement. It is potentially available with respect to all manners of unauthorized use of all types of works in all media. When it exists, the user is not required to seek permission from the copyright owner or to pay a licence fee for the use.[38]

Based originally on judicial decision, Congress codified the doctrine in the Copyright Act 1976. Section 107 of the Copyright Act 1976 does not define

---

[37] Jane C. Ginsburg, 'Reproduction of Protected Works for University Research or Teaching' (1992) *J. Copyright Soc'y US*, pp. 185–86, states:
'This text prompts three pertinent questions: 1. To what kinds of works does it apply; 2. How much of any given work may be reproduced; 3. How many copies may be made? With respect to the first question, the text makes fairly clear that all works protected by the Convention are subject to this exception to the exclusive right of reproduction. Answers to the second and third questions emerge less readily. The phrase "to the extent justified by the purpose" might set some limitation on the amount that may be copied from any given work; it is not always necessary to copy the whole of the work in order to convey the information required for the teaching purpose. On the other hand, the phrase does not preclude the whole of a work in appropriate circumstances. Similarly, the phrase "by way of illustration" may also suggest a limitation on the amount to be copied, but does not clearly prohibit reproducing the entirety of a work....Moreover, Professor Ricketson has stated that Article 10.2 also permits the preparation for teaching purposes of compilations anthologizing all or parts of a variety of works.'

[38] Permissions have generally been sought by publishers for the use of reproductions of art images. Actual practice in the area of illustrating film-related publications has been confused and inconsistent. In October 1988 the International Group of Scientific Technical & Medical Publishers (STM) at its 20th General Assembly in Frankfurt, Germany, adopted a formal policy on electrocopying that said, in part, 'wherever and whenever STM and its members are represented, no electronic storage of information will be permitted without written authorization. The concepts of "fair use" and "private research" that exist in current legislation should not be applied to electronically stored information'. The American Association of University Publishers (AAP) was approached by STM to sign onto this policy statement. The result was a policy issued in February 1989 the final part of which, paralleling the STM statement said: '...it is the position of the AAP that electrocopying of copyrighted works is permissible without authorization only in special limited circumstances where application can legitimately be made of the concept of "fair use" (and similar concepts that exist in other national legislations).' This is further discussed in a position paper for the AAP: Sandy Thatcher, 'Copyright and Optical Scanning in the Distributed Digital Library', 5 May 1995 (on file with the author).

'fair use'. Instead, the preamble to section 107 sets forth certain illustrative examples such as teaching, scholarship and research as examples of a fair use and instructs that this use be considered together with four interrelated factors to determine whether the use made of a work in any particular case constitutes 'fair use'.

The Supreme Court in its most recent discussion on fair use in *Campbell v. Acuff-Rose*[39] stated that all four statutory factors must be considered without favouritism and that fair use must be considered on a case-to-case basis. The doctrine is described as an 'equitable rule of reason' in the legislative history of section 107[40] and the embodiment of the delicate balance of the statutory scheme to promote free dissemination of information, 'thereby benefiting the public by allowing the second author through a good faith productive use of the first author's work...[to create] a new, original work'.

The contours of fair use in the academic environment currently have been shaped by carefully selected test cases brought by book and journal publishers to establish broad principles in areas where substantial licence revenues were at stake. Such decisions as *Basic Books v. Kinko's*[41] and *American Geophysical Union v. Texaco Inc.*[42] placed a limited interpretation on the application of fair use in the context of learning and research. As Association of American Publishers letter to copy-shop owners advises 'that *Kinko's* means that absent permission from the copyright holders, the copying of excerpts from copyrighted works into course anthologies which are distributed to students infringes the copyright in the works excerpted'.

The fair use of materials for academic purposes has rarely been the subject of judicial consideration, primarily because university counsel have a relatively low tolerance for risk and have not sought to push the 'fair use' envelope. There are few cases to date analysing the fair use of images for teaching, scholarship, criticism, or research.[43]

The application of section 107 requires an analysis of both the preamble or paragraph one and the second paragraph. The second paragraph lists four *non-exclusive* factors for determining whether a use is fair. These factors are:

---

[39] 114 S.Ct. 1164 (1994).

[40] A House of Representatives Report of the Committee on the Judiciary noted that any precise definition of fair use was impossible and said that the endless variety of situations and combinations of circumstances that can arise in particular cases precludes the formulation of exact rules in the statute. See HR Rep No 90-83, at 29–30 (1976).

[41] 758 F. Supp. 1522 (SDNY 1991).

[42] 60 F.3d 913 (1994).

[43] See *Ferrato v. Castro*, 888 F. Supp. 33 (SDNY 1995) (plaintiff's motion to dismiss with prejudice granted, holding that the incorporation by the defendant of photographic images of the plaintiff's copyrighted photographs in a mixed media collage under the supervision of the Whitney Museum Independent Studies Program of New York City without the plaintiff's permission for the purposes of exhibition in a show entitled 'The Subject of Rape' and subsequently included in the exhibition catalogue was fair use. The court refused to consider whether or not other uses not before it were fair use).

(1) the purpose and character of the use, including whether commercial or non-profit education;
(2) the nature of the copyrighted work;
(3) the amount and substantiality of the portion used; and
(4) the effect of the use upon the potential market for or value of the copyrighted work.

The four 'fair use' factors 'are to be...weighed together, in light of the objectives of copyright "to promote the progress of science and the useful arts".'[44]

B. *The Purpose and Character of the Use, Including Whether Such Use is of a Commercial Nature or is for Non-Profit Educational Purposes*

As Judge Pierre N. Leval noted at a meeting of the College Art Association on the subject of appropriation art in 1994:

'As to the first and second factors, the statute tells us nothing about what kind of purpose and character of the secondary use, and what kind of nature of the copyrighted work, will favor or disfavor a finding of fair use. In my view (which is not necessarily shared by other judges and copyright scholars), a study of the pattern of decisions reveals that courts have placed great importance on the first factor – the purpose and character of the secondary use. An important question has been: Does this appropriation fulfil the objective of the Copyright Law to stimulate creativity for public instruction? Is the appropriation transformative? Does it use the appropriate matter in a different way or for a different purpose from the original? Appropriation that merely repackages the original will not pass the test. If, on the other hand, the appropriative use adds to the original, if the original is transformed in the creation of new information, new attitudes, new aesthetics, insights and understandings, that is the type of appropriation that the fair use doctrine intends to protect....
   Many other types of critique and commentary also fairly require quotation to communicate their message. An art historian or critic who seeks to make a point about an artist's work cannot effectively do so without showing illustrations.'

Ralph Oman, former Register of Copyrights, noted that:

'in the use of a few frame enlargements to illustrate a classroom lecture versus the reproduction in a book of frame enlargements, the latter would be construed with less latitude from the user's standpoint in a "fair use" analysis than the former. The fact that a university press is "non-profit" will not be dispositive if the work in question would threaten the potential market value for any work that the copyright owner wants to publish – for example a book about the film by the copyright owner – even if the copyright owner has never released such a book in the past.'[45]

---

[44] See *Campbell v. Acuff-Rose Music. Inc.* 114 S. Ct. 1164 (1994).
[45] Letter from Ralph Oman to David Bordwell (7 January 1992) in *Cinema J.* (Winter 1993).

Thus, the courts have placed great importance on the purpose and character of the secondary use and whether the use is 'transformative' and consistent with the goals of the copyright law to stimulate creativity. The US Supreme Court has said that '[t]he enquiry here may be guided by the examples given in the preamble of section 107'.[46]

Educational use promotes the progress of knowledge and the public interest so the use of copyrighted material including images for teaching, research and criticism is more likely to be considered fair use under factor one. Nevertheless, there is no general exemption for education, and factor one must be analysed in conjunction with other factors. For example, many artists, photographers and illustrators may gain substantial revenues from licensing images for textbooks at the secondary and college level. Examples of 'transformative' copying may include the use of an image for purposes of art criticism or artistic parody (but not necessarily appropriation). Courts have rejected fair use where the court perceived only 'piracy' or a quotation to highlight or enliven without any critical comment on the subject.[47] As Justice Storey in 1841 stated in *Folsom v. Marsh*, the leading early American decision on the fair use defence, '[T]he second work must contain real, substantial condensation of the materials and intellectual labor and judgment thereupon, and not merely the facile use of the scissors or extracts of the essential parts constituting the chief value of the work'.

In the *Texaco* case, the court found that factor one tipped against Texaco because citing *Folsom* 'the photocopying "merely supersedes the objects of original creation"....We do not mean to suggest that no instance of archival copying would be fair use, but the first factor tilts against Texaco in this case because the making of copies...is part of a systematic process of encouraging employee researchers to copy articles so as to multiply available copies while avoiding payment.'

C. *The Nature of the Copyrighted Work*

Factor two is a recognition of the fact that there are three types of copyrightable works:

(1) creative or predominantly original works;
(2) compilations; and
(3) derivative works.

---

46 *Campbell*, 114 S. Ct. at 1170.
47 See *Rogers v. Koons*, 960 F.2d 302, 306 (2d Cir. 1991). Court held that artist Jeff Koons' use of photographer Art Rogers 'String of Puppies' was not a fair use to Rogers' claim of copyright infringement in part because it lacked parodic purpose. 'It is the rule in this circuit that though the satire need not be only of the copied work and may, as appellants urge of "String of Puppies", also be a parody of modern society, the copied work must be, at least in part, an object of the parody, otherwise there would be no need to conjure up the original work...this is a necessary rule, as were it otherwise there would be no real limitation on the copier's use of another's copyrighted work to make a statement on some aspect of society at large.'

Thus the Supreme Court has ruled in *Campbell* that factor two 'calls for recognition that some works are closer to the core of copyright protection than others...'. Copyright law gives greater protection to certain classes of works that embody more creativity, such as fiction, photographs, poetry, and art images, compared with more factual materials. The more creative a work is, the greater it is protected. When it comes to original works of art, factor two will almost always go against a finding of fair use because of the innately creative nature of art. Similarly, if a work is unpublished, copying it is less likely to be considered a fair use. Although the fact that it is unpublished does not by itself bar a finding of fair use if such a finding is made upon consideration of all the other factors taken together. On the other hand, the status of a digitally photographed public domain work or 'curatorial photography' is unclear under factor two. For example, a photograph of the 'Mona Lisa' or other examples of 'thin copyright' might provoke a different analysis than a photograph by Dianne Arbus or Richard Avedon or a photograph of a work created by Richard Serra. A US District Court judge in New York has recently held with respect to the analysis of factor two as follows:

'Anyone who has seen any of the great pieces of photojournalism – for example, Alfredo Eisenstadt's classic image of a thrilled sailor exuberantly kissing a woman in Times Square on V-J Day and the stirring photograph of U.S. Marines raising the American flag atop Mount Surabachi on Iwo Jima – or, perhaps in some eyes, more artistic, but nevertheless representational, photography – such as Ansel Adams' work and the portraits of Yousuf Karsh – must acknowledge them as purely fanciful creations. Nevertheless, history has its demands. There is a public interest in receiving information concerning the world in which we live. The more newsworthy the person or event depicted, the greater the concern that too narrow a view of the fair use defense will deprive the public of significant information. Moreover, only a finite number of photographers capture images of a given historical event. Hence, without denying for a moment the creativity inherent in the film clips of actual events relating to the Zaire fight, the degree of protection that properly may be afforded to them must take into account that too narrow a view of the fair use defense could materially undermine the ability of other Ali biographers to tell, in motion picture or perhaps still photographic form, an important part of his story. This of course is not to say that historical film footage loses all copyright protection, only that its character as historical film footage may strengthen somewhat the hand of a fair use defendant as compared with an alleged infringer of a fanciful work or a work presented in a medium that offers a greater variety of forms of expression.'[48]

---

[48] *Monster Communs., Inc. v. Turner Broad. Sys.*, 935 F. Supp. 490 (SDNY 1996).

D. *The Amount and Substantiality of the Portion Used in Relation to the Copyrighted Work as a Whole*

As Judge Leval noted, 'the third and fourth factors direct a court's attention to how much of the work can be taken and how serious a harm has the taking inflicted on the value of the original work. The amount that can be copied as a matter of fair use is a logical function of the first two factors, the purpose of the use and the nature of the work'. For private or personal use there may be occasions when the entire work may be copied.[49]

Normally courts look at both the quantitative and qualitative amount that is taken. The use of a pictorial, graphic and sculptural work will usually involve the whole work. Nevertheless, the Supreme Court in *Campbell* recently held that this factor would not necessarily be determinative and must be considered in light of the purpose and use of the new work. In *Campbell*, the Supreme Court suggested that the extent of copying can provide an insight into the primary purpose of copying, and cautioned that there was a need for more particularized inquiry about the amount taken. Also, the Supreme Court acknowledged in *Campbell* 'the facts bearing on this third factor will also tend to address the fourth factor of market harm'.

E. *The Effect of the Use upon the Potential Market for or Value of the Copyrighted Work*

More important in deciding whether a use is fair is whether the new work that is compiled by using copyrighted material competes with the original work. Prior to the Supreme Court's decision in *Campbell*, lower courts deemed this to be the most important of the four factors. The Supreme Court in *Campbell* made clear, however, that it is only one of four factors to be considered, and it is to receive no greater weight than the others.

The Supreme Court has also stressed the need for evidence about markets for particularized licences – the market for potential derivative uses includes only those that creators of original works would in general develop or license others to develop'.[50] The four factors are not exclusive and other relevant factors may be considered.

A number of cases are pending and several have been decided which consider whether or not a copyright in a work of visual art is infringed by including it within another visual work, and which may serve as precedent for the unauthorized posting of works of copyrighted art on a web site or on a CD-ROM. Perhaps the most important precedent is *Ringgold v. Black Entertainment Television*.[51] *Ringgold* involved an action for copyright

---

[49] *Sony Corp. v. Universal City Studios*, 464 US 417 (1984).
[50] *Campbell*, 114 S. Ct. at 1169.
[51] 126 F.3d 70 (2d Cir. 1997). The author represented the plaintiff Faith Ringgold.

infringement against the producers of a television programme in which a poster of an original artwork was used as set dressing. Defendants contended that the nine instances in their television programme in which portions of the poster were visible, individually and in the aggregate, were *de minimis*, in the sense that the quantity of copying (or at least the quantity of observable copying) was below the threshold of actionable copying. The aggregate duration of all nine segments was 26.75 seconds. The case is important not only for its implication for the virtual gallery, but also for its analysis of the fair use of visual images in film and television. The appellate court reversed the District Court on grounds that the District Court had improperly analysed three of the four fair use factors. The District Court's consideration of the first fair use factor was legally flawed in its failure to assess the decorative purpose for which defendants used the plaintiff's work. Instead, the Court tipped the first factor against the plaintiff because the presence of the poster was 'incidental' to the scene and the defendants did not use the poster to encourage viewers to watch the ROC episode. The first point could be said of virtually all set decorations, thereby expanding fair use to permit wholesale appropriation of copyrighted art for movies and television. The second point uses a test that makes it far too easy for a defendant to invoke the fair use defence. Speaking for a unanimous court, Chief Judge Jon Newman stated with respect to factor one:

'defendants have used Ringgold's work for precisely a central purpose for which it was created – to be decorative. It is not difficult to imagine a television program that uses a copyright visual work for a purpose that heavily favors fair use. If a TV news program produced a feature on Faith Ringgold and included camera shots of her story quilts, the case for a fair use defense would be extremely strong. The same would be true of a news feature on the High Museum that included a shot of "Church Picnic." However, it must be recognized that visual works are created, in significant part, for their decorative value, and, just as members of the public expect to pay to obtain a painting or a poster to decorate their homes, producers of plays, films, and television programs would generally expect to pay a license fee....Considering the first fair use factor with the preamble illustrations as a "guide[]," we observe that the defendants' use of Ringgold's work to decorate the set for their television episode is not remotely similar to any of the listed categories. In no sense is the defendants' use "transformative." '52

With respect to factor three Judge Newman stated:

---

52 Ibid. at p. 79. The Court added: 'We hesitate to say "conclusive" because even existing technological advances, much less those in the future, create extraordinary possibilities. For example, if the news program included a direct shot of an entire story quilt (whether original or poster reproduction), well lit and in clear focus, a viewer so inclined could tape the newscast at home, scan the tape, and with digital photographic technology, produce a full size copy of the original, thereby securing an attractive "poster"-like wall-hanging without paying the $20 poster fee. A news program that recommended this technique would be a weak candidate for fair use.'

'Even if the third factor favors the defendants, courts considering the fair use defense in the context of visual works copied or displayed in other visual works must be careful not to permit this factor too easily to tip the aggregate fair use assessment in favor of those whom the other three factors do not favor. Otherwise, a defendant who uses a creative work in a way that does not serve any of the purposes for which the fair use defense is normally invoked and that impairs the market for licensing the work will escape liability simply by claiming only a small infringement.'

Summary judgment on factor four was inappropriate when Ringgold contended that there was a potential market for licensing her story quilts and stated in an affidavit that in 1995 she earned $31,500 from licensing her various artworks. More specifically, the District Court erroneously assessed the effect of the use on potential markets for the artist's work. Ringgold is not required to show a decline in the number of licensing requests for the 'Church Picnic' poster since the ROC episode was aired. The fourth factor will favour her if she can show a 'traditional, reasonable, or likely to be developed' market for licensing her work as set decoration.

Sandoval v. New Line Cinema[53] further clarifies *Ringgold* and sets forth certain parameters. *Sandoval* was dismissed on a motion for summary judgment prior to the *Ringgold* appellate court decision, holding that the use of ten of the plaintiff's photographs as part of set decoration in the film 'Seven' was fair use. The appellate court affirmed:

'Unlike the artwork at issue in *Ringgold*, where the artwork was "clearly visible" and "recognizable as a painting...with sufficient observable detail for the 'average lay observer'...to discern African-Americans in Ringgold's colorful, virtually two-dimensional style," Sandoval's photographs as used in the movie are not displayed with sufficient detail for the average lay observer to identify even the subject matter of the photographs, much less the style used in creating them....The photographs are displayed in poor lighting and at great distance. Moreover, they are out of focus and displayed only briefly in eleven [9] different shots. Unlike *Ringgold*, in which the court found that brief but repeated shots of the poster at issue reinforced its prominence, the eleven shots here have no cumulative effect because the images contained in the photographs are not distinguishable. In short, this is the type of case the *Ringgold* court anticipated when it observed that "in some circumstances, a visual work, though selected by production staff for thematic relevance, or at least for its decorative value, might ultimately be filmed at such distance"....To establish that the infringement of a copyright is *de minimis*, and therefore not actionable.'

The relationship between licensing and the doctrine of fair use is critical to the digital networked environment. The concern is that technological means of tracking transactions and licensing will lead to reduced application and scope of the fair use doctrine in a network environment. In *American Geophysical Union v. Texaco Inc.*, the Court established liability for unauthorized photocopying

---

[53]   147 F.3d 215 (2d Cir. 1998).

based in part on the Court's perception that obtaining a licence for the right via the CCC was not *unreasonably burdensome*.

Professor Jane Ginsberg notes that the WIPO Berne Protocol proposal identifies that whether or not a use qualifies for a teaching exemption depends on whether or not the use conflicts with a 'normal exploitation of the work'. The proposal recognizes that if the market for excerpts is being exploited by means of collective licensing, the free copying of works for educational purposes poses such a conflict.[54]

Fair use may be considered along a spectrum of uses. Copying and using copyrighted artwork for commercial purposes or broad distribution – such as replicating an image on a T-shirt or incorporating copyrighted images into commercial multimedia products or illustrations in textbooks and distributing many copies or selling them, or simply displaying them on the World Wide Web or reproducing the original artwork as a poster or postcard – is much more likely to be considered a copyright infringement than using the same images or works in a 'classroom' for teaching or in a critical, scholarly article about the artwork in question, or creating digitizing images in research collections, creating thumbnail images and making these searchable by field using copyrighted images in academic course assignments or in fulfilment of degree requirements such as a term paper, thesis or dissertation. The case for 'fair use' in connection with scholarly, analytical, or critical use of images is a strong one.[55]

What is fair use in cyberspace? While the NII and other digital technology present myriad opportunities for fair uses of works:

'[i]t is reasonable to expect that courts would approach claims of fair use in the context of the NII just as they do in "traditional" environments. Commercial uses that involve no "transformation" by users and harm actual or potential markets will likely always be infringing, while non-profit educational transformative uses will likely often be fair. Between these two extremes, courts will have to engage in the same type of fact-intensive analysis that typifies fair use litigation and frustrates those who seek a "bright line" clearly separating the lawful from the unlawful.'[56]

Given the lack of such 'bright lines', interested parties, including the user communities, copyright owners, and those who act in an intermediary role, such as libraries, educators, and publishers, have over the years developed voluntary guidelines to address practical use situations. The genesis of the conference on Fair Use was the Green Paper's call for a 'conference to bring together copyright owner and user interests to develop guidelines for fair uses of copyrighted works by and in public libraries and schools'[57] and 'to

---

54 Ginsburg, 'Ownership of Electronic Rights and the Private International Law of Copyright', 22 *Colum. - VLA J. L & Arts*, p. 191, note 24 above.
55 See *Ferrato v. Castro*, note 43 above.
56 See White Paper discussion above, at p. 4.
57 See Green Paper discussion above.

determine whether educational or library guidelines of a similar nature [to those developed in 1976] might prove attainable in the NII context'. The Working Group added further that 'should the participants in the Conference on Fair Use fail to agree on appropriate guidelines, the Working Group may conclude that the importance of such guidelines may necessitate regulatory or legislative action in that area'.[58]

V. Trademark Publicity and Jurisdictional Issues

Other important issues in the exploitation of digital image archives and collections involve questions of liability for copyright infringement and issues of personal jurisdiction and choice of law. These issues apply to the exploitation of all copyrighted work in the new media.

A. *Copyright Infringement*

To prevail on a claim for direct copyright infringement, a plaintiff must prove ownership of the asserted copyrights and 'copying' by the defendant. Copying is a judicial shorthand for the infringement of any of a copyright owner's exclusive rights. Because direct proof of copying is rarely available to a copyright owner, copying is normally shown by providing that a defendant had access to the copyrighted work, and that there is substantial similarity between the copyrighted work and the accused work. Alternatively, where proof of access is absent, generally copying may be proved by showing a 'striking similarity' between the copyrighted work and the accused work. Direct infringement does not require intent or any particular state of mind. If a museum, photo or film archive owns the copyright in the digital image then displaying, downloading, and using such reproductions in future publications would constitute copyright infringement. Policing piracy, however, may be difficult both legally and technologically. Is an on-line service provider or computer bulletin board operator liable for the infringement of its subscribers? How does one determine where the infringement occurs and what laws apply to the infringement? In what forum should the copyright holder seek redress?

To show vicarious liability, a copyright claimant must prove that a defendant has a direct financial interest in the infringing activity and has the right and ability to supervise the activity which causes the infringement.

---

[58]   See Appendix 5, p. 259 for a discussion and interim report on the Conference on Fair Use (CONFU).

B. *Liability for Copyright Infringement on the Internet*[59]

A full discussion of this issue is beyond the scope of this chapter.[60] As noted above, the DMCA adds a new Chapter 5 to the Copyright Act which exempts from contributory, vicarious and direct infringement liability, Internet service providers who comply with certain conditions. Each safe harbour is accompanied by numerous conditions in order to qualify.

C. *Personal Jurisdiction*

A federal court must have personal jurisdiction over a defendant's person or property to entertain a suit against the defendant.[61] A federal court enjoys personal jurisdiction in a diversity case such as this only if a court of the forum state would have such jurisdiction. The determination of whether a state court would have jurisdiction over a non-consenting, non-resident defendant is normally a two-step process. The first question is whether the defendant is subject to jurisdiction under the applicable state long-arm statute. If defendants are subject to the mechanical provisions of the statute, the second question of due process is reached. Where a long-arm statute is intended to be coextensive with the full reach of the Due Process Clause, the first step is superfluous, and a court need only address the due process requirements. There are two different types of due process analysis in personal jurisdiction: general and specific. General jurisdiction allows a court to entertain a suit against a defendant because of the defendant's general presence in the forum state regardless of whether that presence is related to the litigation at hand. Concerning specific jurisdiction, the Supreme Court has set forth the standard on numerous occasions. In *International Shoe Co. v. Washington*,[62] the Court explained that due process requires that a non-resident defendant 'have certain minimum contacts with [the forum] such that the maintenance of the suit does not offend traditional notions of fair play and substantial justice'. It is essential 'in each case that there be some act by which the defendant purposefully avails itself of the privilege of conducting activities within the State, thus invoking the benefits and protections of its laws'.[63]

It is not clear whether the operation of a web site on the Internet is enough to submit an out-of-state defendant to personal jurisdiction in the forum state. This issue in the US generally involves analysing the forum state's long-arm statute.[64]

---

[59] See Report of the Copyright Office, Appendix 8, p. 287.
[60] Ibid.
[61] Wright and Miller, *Federal Practice and Procedure*, 1063 at 224 (2nd ed., 1987).
[62] 326 US 310, 316, 66 S.Ct. 154, 158, 90 L.Ed. 95 (1945).
[63] *Hanson v. Denckla*, 357 US 235, 253, 78 S.Ct. 1228, 1240, 2 L.Ed. 2d 1283 (1958).
[64] See *Hearst Corp. v. Ari Goldberg*, 1997 US Dist. LEXIS 2065 for an extensive discussion of the issue of personal jurisdiction and web site activity, as well as the literature on the subject.

As the Internet has experienced nearly exponential growth over the past few years, its impact on conventional notions of personal jurisdiction has been hotly debated in courts throughout the country and in countless law review articles and treatises.[65] As one article notes, 'because of its "geographic transparency" and unlimited adaptability to commercial uses, the Internet has begun to test the limits and underlying legitimacy of territorial concepts of personal jurisdiction'.[66] Some courts have differentiated between those cases in which a defendant merely posts information on a passive site on the Internet and those in which the defendant is actually conducting business over the Internet through an interactive site.[67] Generally, despite the Internet's lack of territorial boundaries, the courts have attempted to apply traditional concepts of personal jurisdiction to the Internet, such as whether the defendant intentionally reached beyond its own state to engage in business with residents of the forum state. For example, in *Hearst Corp. v. Goldberger*,[68] the court refused to find personal jurisdiction where the foreign defendant's Internet activity was directed at a national audience and not specifically at the forum state. The court analogized the defendant's web site to an advertisement in a national magazine. Its web site had been accessed by a number of New Yorkers, but no sales had been made in New York.

D. *Conflict of Laws*

The Berne Convention provides that the law of the country where protection is claimed defines what rights are protected, the scope of protection and the available remedies.[69] Choice of law issues in international copyright cases have been largely ignored in reported US cases. For example, several decisions involving a work created by an employee of a foreign corporation have applied the US work-for-hire doctrine without explicit consideration of the conflicts issue. The Nimmer treatise briefly suggests that conflicts issues 'have rarely proved troublesome in the law of copyright'.[70] The 'national treatment' principal of the Berne Convention and the universal copyright convention require that an author who is a national of one of the member states of either Berne or the UCC or one who first publishes their work in any such is entitled to the same copyright protection in each other member state as such other state accords to its own national.

---

[65] See Robert W. Hamilton and Gregory A. Castanias, 'Tangled Web: Personal Jurisdiction and the Internet', 24 *Litigation* 27 (Winter 1998).

[66] Kevin M. Fitzmaurice and Renu N. Mody, 'International Shoe Meets the World Wide Web: Whither Personal Jurisdiction in Florida in the Age of the Internet?' (December 1997) 71 Fla. B.J. 22.

[67] See *Cybersell. Inc. v. Cybersell. Inc.*, 130 F.3d 414 (9th Cir. 1997).

[68] 1997 US Dist. LEXIS 2065, No. 96 Civ. 3620 (PLK)(AJP), 1997 WL 97097 (SDNY 1997).

[69] *ITAR-TASS RUSSIAN NEWS AGENCY, et. al. v. Russian Kurier*, 1998 US App. LEXIS 21016 at 26.

[70] See *Nimmer on Copyright,* § 17.05 (1998).

The Berne Convention provides that the law of the country were protection is claimed defines what rights are protected, the scope of the protection and the available remedies; the treaty does not supply a choice of law rule for determining ownership and the scope of protection afforded, whatever the source, must be applied equally for nationals and foreigners.[71]

In an important decision by the second circuit court of appeals,[72] Circuit Judge Jon O. Newman applied the federal common law on conflicts issues and held that different rules might govern different issues of a case. He held that since copyright is a form of property, the usual rule is that the interests of the parties in property are determined by the law of the state with 'the most significant relationship' to the property and the parties. On the facts before the court, Judge Newman decided that since the works at issue were created by Russian nationals and first published in Russia, Russian law is the appropriate source of law to determine ownership of rights. In so deciding, the court considered only initial ownership and did not consider choice of law issues governing assignment of rights. The court then held that on infringement issues, the governing conflicts principle is usually *lex loci delicti*, the doctrine generally applicable to torts.

The rationale of *Itar-Tass* was further explained and developed by Judge Kaplan in the District Court decision in *Bridgeman Art Library, Ltd.* discussed above. Reiterating the principle that national treatment does not express any choice of law rules, the Court followed *Itar-Tass* and applied the law of the state with the most significant relationship to the property and the parties. In making its determination the Court considered relevant factors such as the nationality of the authors, the place of initial publication and the country of origin as determined under the Berne Convention (country in which the work was first published) and concluded that UK law should apply.

VI. A Brief Overview of Other Intellectual Property Issues

A. *Right of Publicity*

What if a museum or photo archive publishes a poster of a celebrity? What if a museum, film or photo archive reproduces works in its collection which include an image of the celebrity on a calendar or T-shirt? What if the museum or archive either holds the copyright to or is licensed to use the photograph embodying the image?

Unlike Great Britain where there is virtually no protection for the right of publicity, the prospect of a successful claim is much better in the US, where

---

71 See Jane C. Ginsberg, 'Ownership of Electronic Rights and the Private International Law of Copyright' (1998) 22 Colum.-VLA J.L & Arts 165, 167–168.
72 *ITAR-TASS RUSSIAN NEWS AGENCY, et. al. v. Russian Kurier*, 1998 US App. LEXIS 21016 at 26.

the right of publicity is widely recognized and is a matter of the statutory and common law of the individual states. A majority of states recognize some protection against the commercial exploitation of a person's name, likeness and, in some cases, other aspects of persona.[73] However, state law varies widely in terms of whether protection is limited to living persons, the extent and nature of the protection, and the conflict of laws principles used to determine the applicable substantive law.

Indiana, to cite the most extreme example, includes protections against the unauthorized taking of 'distinctive gestures and mannerisms', name, voice signature, photograph, image, and likeness, and provides protection for 100 years after death irrespective of the domicile of the claimant. Queen Victoria's heirs could claim protection in Indiana.

In order to state a cause of action based on the right of publicity, a plaintiff generally must demonstrate that it has a valid and enforceable right in the identity in issue, and that the defendant has infringed upon that right through the unauthorized appropriation of the identity for commercial purposes. To possess a valid right of publicity, the plaintiff must be either the individual whose identity is being infringed, or the heir, assignee, or exclusive licensee of the identity. When the right of publicity of a deceased individual is asserted, the inquiry is whether the right survives death, and for how long. Several states, including New York, Illinois and about seven others, have rejected the concept of the right of publicity after death. A growing number of states, in addition to Indiana, notably California (50 years) and Florida (40 years), however, now recognize this post-mortem right for a set period of years following death.

The easiest cases for the right of publicity are those involving a person's image in advertisements. In nearly every state it is not permissible to use without consent the name or likeness of a living person to advertise a product.

---

[73]   At the time of this writing, courts have expressly recognized the right of publicity as existing under the common law of 16 states (California, Connecticut, Florida, Georgia, Hawaii, Illinois, Kentucky, Michigan, Minnesota, Missouri, New Jersey, Ohio, Pennsylvania, Texas, Utah, and Wisconsin). Of those, five also have statutory provisions broad enough to encompass the right of publicity. In addition, nine states have statutes which, while some are labelled 'privacy' statutes, are worded in such a way that most aspects of the right of publicity are embodied in those statutes. Thus, under either statute or common law, the right of publicity is recognized as the law of 25 states. In only two states has a court expressly rejected the concept and held that a common law right of publicity does not exist in that state. In Nebraska, this rejection was later changed by statute. New York is a special case. The New York courts have rejected the existence of any common law rights of privacy in that state. That rejection was remedied in part by the 1903 New York Statute. While the federal courts and a state court found that a common law right of publicity exists in New York outside of the statute, the latest word from the New York Court of Appeals is that the right of publicity exists but only within the framework of the New York statute, Civil Rights Law, sections 50 and 51. That law prevents the unauthorized use of a person's name or likeness for advertising or trade purposes. For a complete discussion see J. Thomas McCarthy, *The Rights of Publicity and Privacy* (West, 1998).

This protection for the right of publicity exists even if it is clear from the advertisement that the celebrity is not endorsing the product. For example, the use of Spike Lee's image in an advertisement for Sal's pizza restaurant would violate these laws, even though it is unlikely that anyone would think that Spike Lee is endorsing the restaurant.

There are, in any event, many ways that a famous person's name or likeness can be used without running foul of right of publicity protections. As a rule, permission is not needed in order to use a person's name or likeness in a book, newspaper, magazine, TV news show or documentary, or other media purveying news or information. The First Amendment to the United States Constitution[74] provides an unfettered right to write a biography or produce a true TV documentary about a famous person or incident.

Uses of a celebrity's persona in a defined list of media, such as literary works, film, television programmes, radio, and original works of fine art are often exempted from the scope of the right of publicity by statute,[75] as well as anything that has 'political or newsworhty value' or communicates information about an event or topic 'of general public interest'.

B. *Choice of Law/Jurisdiction in Right of Publicity Cases*

Given the wide variety in state law, choice of law becomes a critical determinant of success in a right of publicity case. Some states, including New York, will look to the law of the place of domicile at the time of death of the claimant to determine whether a cause of action exists. A New York court, considering a right of publicity case, would apply its property choice of law rules to select the state whose law determines whether a plaintiff had a protectable right of publicity. The usual rule of US conflict law is to apply the law of the state of domicile of the decedent to determine whether there is a post-mortem right of publicity. Indiana is an exception to this rule and applies its right of publicity law to protect any celebrity whose image is used in connection with any advertising or sale of commercial products in Indiana.

A court has recently held that the first sale doctrine bars right of publicity claims by a baseball player against a company that sells plaques made by framing licensed trading cards of the baseball player.[76]

C. *Section 43(a) of the Lanham Act*

In addition to the state law right of publicity, the use of a person's image may give rise to a claim for false designation of origin or sponsorship under section 43(a) of the Lanham Trademark Act. Such a claim requires a showing that

---

[74] The First Amendment provides in pertinent part that Congress shall make no law abridging the freedom of speech.

[75] See also *Simenov v. Tiegs*, 602 NYS 2d 1014 (Cir. 1993).

[76] *Allison v. Vintage Sports Plaques*, 136 F.3d 1443 (11th Cir. 1998).

consumers are confused into believing that the goods in question are endorsed or approved by the individual.

Section 43(a)(1) of the Lanham Act provides:

'Any person who, on, or in connection with any goods or services or any container for goods, uses in commerce any word, term, name, symbol, or device, or any combination thereof, or any false designation of origin, false or misleading description of a fact, or false or misleading representation of fact, which (A) is likely to cause confusion, or to cause mistake, or to deceive as to affiliation, connection, or association of such person with another person, or as to the origin, sponsorship, or approval of his or her goods, services, or commercial activities, by another person...shall be liable in a civil action by any person who believes that he or she is or is likely to be damaged by such act.'

The Lanham Act may serve to protect a variety of names and likenesses. For example, courts have held that the image and name of an individual is protected under the Act. In *Allen v. National Video. Inc.*[77] and *Allen v. Men's World Outlet. Inc.*,[78] Woody Allen successfully prevented the defendants from using his likeness in their advertisements.

A trademark is a very unique type of property. There is no such thing as property in a trademark except as a right appurtenant to an established business or trade in connection with which the make is employed. The use of a mark to identify goods or services is crucial. It is generally agreed that the Lanham Act cannot provide a federal vehicle for the assertion of infringement of the state law right of publicity since section 43(a) is limited to some form of falsity, while infringement of the right of publicity involves no element of falsity. In many cases, the unpermitted use of one's persona will in addition to infringing upon the right of publicity also infringe trademark or service mark rights in personal identity and/or involve elements of false endorsement. Of course, such a claim might be defeated by the use of a prominent disclaimer to avoid the likelihood of customer confusion.

In the case of *Pirone*,[79] Babe Ruth's heirs, the Babe Ruth League and Curtis Management group, sued Macmillan to prevent the publication of a calendar which used a photograph of Babe Ruth. The US Court of Appeals for the second circuit dismissed on a motion for summary judgment by the defendant, claims of trademark, unfair competition and a right of publicity for failure to state a cause of action. The court stated: 'Here, the calendar uses the name and image of Babe Ruth in the primary sense – to identify a great baseball player enshrined in the history of the game. Such use is not a trademark use and not

---

[77]   610 F. Supp. 612 (SDNY 1985).
[78]   679 F. Supp. 360 (SDNY 1988).
[79]   See *Dorothy Ruth Pirone, Julia Ruth Stevens, Babe Ruth League, Inc. and Curtis Management Group, Inc. v. Macmillan, Inc.*, 894 F.2d 579 (1990) (holding that the Lanham Act was not infringed by the use of Babe Ruth's photo in a calendar).

an infringement....'[80] Furthermore, 'photographs of baseball, its players and assorted memorabilia, are the subject matter of the calendar. The pictures of Ruth no more indicate origin than does the back cover's picture of Jackie Robinson stealing home plate. Both covers are merely descriptive of the calendar's subject matter. In neither case would any consumer reasonably believe that Ruth or Robinson sponsored the calendar.'[81]

The necessity to select specific images of a building, a celebrity, a museum, etc. and use it in connection with a business or trade in order to receive trademark protection was confirmed recently by the sixth circuit court of appeals in the case of *The Rock and Roll Hall of Fame and Museum, Inc. v. Gentile Productions*.[82] The court vacated a preliminary injunction granted to The Rock and Roll Museum and held it unlikely that the Museum would prevail on its trademark infringement claim. Charles Gentile, a photographer, sold posters featuring a photograph of the Museum and the words 'Rock n' Roll Hall of Fame', along with Gentile's signature. The Museum claimed trademark infringement, based on the theory that the images and words were used 'in a manner which reflects a deliberate attempt to confuse, mislead and deceive the public into believing that the posters are affiliated with the Museum'.[83] This theory was rejected by the Court of Appeals which held 'we cannot conclude on this record that it is likely that the Museum has established a valid trademark in every photograph, which, like Gentile's prominently displays the front of the Museum's building...'.[84] The court accepted that a photograph which prominently depicts another person's trademark might use its object as a trademark.[85] In summary, images and databases may under certain circumstances receive protection under trademark law. If the image or database has come to be identified with a particular producer, the unauthorized use of material from the database in a manner that creates a likelihood of confusion as to source may be actionable under the state or federal trademark law;[86] however, the court was not persuaded that the Museum uses its building design as a trademark.

---

[80] Ibid. at 583.
[81] Ibid.
[82] *The Rock and Roll Hall of Fame and Museum, Inc. v. Gentile Productions*, 134 F.3d 749 (6th Cir. 1998).
[83] Ibid. at 750.
[84] Ibid. at 755.
[85] *Coca-Cola Co. v. Gemini Rising, Inc.*, 346 F. Supp. 1183 (EDNY 1972).
[86] See generally J. Thomas McCarthy, *Trademarks and Unfair Competition*, (1996), section 23.

VII. Drafting Intellectual Property Licences for the Exploitation of Film, Photo and Museum Collections[87]

A valuable source of practical considerations is the Koeve/van der heide document provided at the RAMA November 1993 Copyright Workshop on 'Electronic Publishing Licensing of On-Line Databases' which sets out a model licence agreement for the utilization of published works in on-line databases.[88] Key sections include:

(1) Grant of Rights;
(2) Responsibilities of the Database Operator;
(3) Rights and Responsibilities of the Publishing Company;
(4) Type, Amount and Date of Payment of Licence Fees;
(5) Obligation to Provide Information;
(6) Warranty and Liability;
(7) Duration and Termination of the Agreement; and
(8) Consequences of Termination of the Agreement.[89]

The Definitions and the Grant of Licence provisions in a contract between a creator of a collection of digital images and other digital information for licence to third parties for commercial and personal use and an active photographer with approximately 20,500 35mm colour transparencies of travel photography with an emphasis on south-east Asia are provided below. The clauses represent the non-negotiated terms proposed by the Licensee.

'1. Definitions
The following terms as used herein shall have the following meanings whenever capitalized:

(a) "*Element*" means a chemical or analog record of information (e.g., a slide, transparency, print, negative, audiotape, film, printed material or videotape), or a digital file of such record of information sorted in any medium. Each image in the Collection shall be considered an "Element" hereunder. "*Licensed Element*" means an Element which Licensor has licensed to licensee under this Agreement which Element is owned by Licensor or whose owner is represented by Licensor and which has been provided to and selected by Licensee pursuant to this Agreement.

(b) "*Digitize*" and variations thereof means converting an Element into "*Digital*" (i.e., binary) format such that it can be read, utilized and displayed by a device, machine, or any other technology currently in existence or hereafter developed capable of utilizing digital information. As part of the Digitization process, licensee may remove incidental dust, dirt and other particles from the original Elements, and Licensee may use cloning and other image processing techniques to cover incidental dust, dirt and other particles and imperfections that appear in

---

[87] See also the chapter by Christine Steiner and CD-ROM Licensing Agreement at Appendix 12.

[88] Matthew Duncan, *Museums and Galleries New Technology Study: Copyright and Author's Rights – Work Package 4* (December 1996).

[89] Ibid.

the resulting digitized Elements. Licensee also may correct the color and color contrast in the resulting Digitized Elements. However, at all times during the Digitization process, it is Licensee's intent to create Digitized Elements that are substantially true to their respective original Elements. Licensee may crop a Digitized Element under the following circumstances and in the following manner: (i) to create a square or rectangular Digitized Element if the original Element is not square or rectangular in shape, (ii) to remove background objects and materials (such as a wall, an easel or other hanging/holding devices) that are separate from depicted objects in the original Elements, and (iii) to remove picture frames. Licensee is developing and may use copy protection schemes, which may result in encoding or encrypting upon the resulting Digitized Element, in connection with its reproduction, distribution and licensing of the Licensed elements, Licensor acknowledges that licensee may Digitize Licensed Elements in its imaging lab.

(c) "*Element License*" means the license granted by Licensee or its distributor with respect to an individual Licensed Element or group of Licensed Elements for commercial use and personal use by Licensee in any medium, which license does not include any right to use Corbis software (other than the Licensed Element), search and retrieval and/or cataloging tools.

(d) "*Licensee Product*" means products or services created by Licensee which incorporate Licensed elements (and may include other Elements), and which are licensed, sold and/or otherwise distributed by Licensee or its distributors pursuant to a Licensee Product License. Promotional materials, such as a catalog which includes Licensed Elements, distributed on any medium whether now known or hereafter devised, shall not be considered Licensee Products.

(e) "*Licensee Product License*" means the license of Licensee Product granted by Licensee or its distributor to their respective end users for their Personal Use. "*Personal Use*" means an individual's or entity's private, non-commercial use of a Licensed Element, including the display of the Licensed element at various resolutions alone or in combination with other material, the downloading and copying of the Licensed Element, the modification of the licensed Element, the creation of printed versions of the Licensed Element, and the use of the Licensed element and modified versions for reference, research any other private, non-commercial purpose. An electronic display in a public place shall be considered a Personal Use, provided the user or any other entity does not charge a fee or charge for viewing the Licensed Elements. However, the display of Licensed Elements in print form in a public place shall not be considered a Personal Use.

(f) "*Caption Information*" means information that identifies an Element and shall include, as appropriate, the information fields specified on the spreadsheet attached hereto as *Exhibit A* and other formation as may be specified by Licensee. Any license of a Licensed Element shall be deemed to include the related Caption Information, whether prepared and archived with the Element or separately, and no additional sums shall be paid by licensee or the use of Caption Information.

2. License.

Licensor hereby grants Licensee and its representatives, agents and assigns a non-exclusive, worldwide license as follows:

(a) *Grant*. Subject to the Term as defined below, the rights granted herein include the right to digitize use, reproduce, modify, translate into any language and create derivative works based upon the Licensed Elements; to combine Licensed

Elements with Caption Information and other materials; to catalog, index, market, advertise, display, perform, distribute, transmit, license, sell, rent or lease copies of the Licensed Elements in any medium whatsoever, whether now known or hereafter devised; including without limitation in advertising and promotional products. The foregoing rights may be exercised by Licensee and Licensee's through Element Licenses or Licensee Product Licenses. Notwithstanding the foregoing, neither Licensee nor its Licensees or assigns shall have any obligation to incorporate the Licensed Elements into any product or service whatsoever.

(b) Term of Agreement

   (i) *Term.* Subject to the provisions of Paragraph 10 below, the Agreement is for an initial term of twenty (20) years from the Effective Date (the "Term") and shall be automatically renewed for subsequent terms of five (5) years each, unless Licensee or Licensor notifies the other in writing of its intent not to renew at least ninety (90) days before the expiration of the term or any subsequent renewal.

   (ii) *Effect of Termination.* Upon termination of this Agreement Licensee shall no longer be entitled to acquire additional Elements, or to use individual Licensed Elements (other than as part of a pre-existing product) as provided for in this Agreement. For Licensed Elements already acquired by licensee and incorporated into products a services Licensee, its Licensees and/or assigns prior to termination, Licensee and its Licensees and/or assigns shall retain the right to continue using such Licensed Element in the respective product or service after the Term. Such License shall be subject to all restrictions and obligations as provided for herein.

(c) *Updating Licensed Elements.* If Digital technology changes during the Term of this Agreement such that the Licensed Elements are no longer satisfactory for state-of-the-art storage or presentation, the parties will cooperate to provide licensee with, or allow licensee to create, updated Licensed Elements in accordance with the procedures set forth in this Agreement. Licensee will be responsible for all reasonable out-of-pocket expenses associated with supplying and/or creating such updated Licensed Elements.

(d) *Caption Information.* Licensor shall provide licensee with Caption Information related to each Element in accordance with Section 5 below. Licensor shall work closely with Licensee to determine the format that is most compatible with licensee's information processing system. Licensee shall have the right, in its sole discretion, to include some or all of the Caption Information with each Licensed Element, to combine Caption Information provided by Licensor with editorial materials from licensee as well as other sources, and to edit, delete or otherwise change the Caption Information.

(e) *Copyright Information.* These licenses also shall include the right of Licensee to secure copyright protection in Licensee's own name for Licensee products and services containing Licensed Elements and to exploit such copyrights.

(f) *No Clip Photography Products.* Notwithstanding anything in this Agreement to the contrary, neither Licensee nor Licensor will produce a Clip Photography Product that includes the Licensed Elements or grant Element Licenses (or other similar licenses) to third parties for use of the Licensed Elements in a Clip Photography Product. As used herein, "Clip Photography Product" means a product or service that contains multiple uses such as editorial use and commercial use (for example, advertising and promotions), for a one-time fee or purchase price. A product or commercial use (for example, advertising and promotions), for a one-time fee or purchase price. A product or service licensed or sold to customers for Personal Use only shall not be considered a Clip Photography Product.'

Of interest is the attempt by Licensee to address Licensor issues of duration, control, and artistic integrity. Copyright is not synonymous with commercial value and many digital archives and collections may not be able to rely on the copyright monopoly to protect their investment. For the database owner as Licensor of its products, contracts provide a major source of protection complementing the limited protection offered by copyright and trademark and often supplementing it. A study carried out by the US copyright office concludes that 'though terms vary from company to company and from product to product, the core average of database contracts tends to be similar: contracts restrict access, specify permissible conditions of use and set terms for enforcement and remedies'.

Editor's Note

The decision in the *Bridgeman Art Library, Ltd. v. Corel Corp.* 36 F. Supp 2d 191 (S.D.N.Y) was amended on 2 March 1999.

Following the entry of final judgment, the Court was bombarded with submissions. The Court granted a motion for reargument but nevertheless reaffirmed its prior holding that the colour transparencies lacked 'originality' and were therefore not copyrightable. Judge Kaplan rejected new arguments on 'originality' and international copyright issues. On the issue of 'originality' the reader is directed to the fact that the holding is limited to reproductions of colour transparencies of public domain paintings and that the record was devoid of any evidence of Bridgeman's reproduction technique except the plaintiff's statement that it laboured to create 'slavish copies' of the original. The Court decided that the *Graves* case would not change the result and rejected the argument of Professor William Patry, author of a copyright treatise, that the Court erred in applying UK law on the issue of copyright ability.

Protection and Management of Copyright and Neighbouring Rights in the Digital Era[1]

Mrs. P.V. Valsala G. Kutty
Registrar of Copyright, India

I. Introduction

The concept of protection of intellectual property stems from the desire of the human mind to recognize and encourage creativity. Civilized society has always taken pride in rewarding ingenuity, calibre and talent. History is replete with the stories of emperors and kings who patronized writers, artists and musicians. In the early days of civilization, the rights of creators of intellectual property were not much of an issue, as means to reproduce a work were very limited. Copyright protection became a necessity when the printing machine was invented and the massive reproduction of works became the order of the day. However, the need for protection of IPR gained momentum in the wake of its potential for being exploited commercially. With the advent of digital technologies, the concept of copying underwent sea changes. The amazing fidelity with which copies can be made has taken society by surprise and traditional forms of the protection of rights have been rendered obsolete. National governments all over the world debated on the impact of digital technologies on the protection and management of the rights of authors and other owners of copyright and neighbouring rights. Most of the world agreed that the solution lay in adoption of new guidelines for the operation of global digital systems. The leading role in this direction was taken by WIPO, who

---

[1] The Honourable Mrs. P.V. Vasala G. Kutty presented this paper as the keynote address at the November 1997 IBA Conference in New Delhi, India. It has been edited for this publication to include additional information. See generally for this update S. Ramiah, India, in 2 *International Copyright Law and Practice* (October 1997), at IND-9 (Paul E. Geller ed.) (general discussion of India's Copyright Law).

launched a massive exercise to formulate a Protocol to the Berne Convention and a New Instrument of the Protection of the Rights of Performers and Producers of Phonograms. A series of meetings of the Expert Committees set up for this purpose culminated at the Diplomatic Conference in December 1996 where two new treaties were finalized – The WIPO Copyright Treaty and The WIPO Performance and Phonogram Treaty.

The new challenges posed by digital technologies in the protection of copyright and neighbouring rights have impacted all forms of work whether the work is a literary piece, a phonogram or a motion picture. In the case of a motion picture, modern technology allows all kinds of manipulations of any material in digital format. Many such manipulations cannot be wished away as just reproductions. They can be used to bring out changes and modifications where the application of the right adaptation or moral rights may be involved. Undoubtedly, this factor does raise serious concerns for the motion picture industry and for the rightsholders. Although these issues were discussed at length in the Expert Committee meetings, the Diplomatic Conference did not address the rights of performers in audio-visual fixations, due to strong sentiments expressed by delegations having large stakes in the film industry.

The Expert Committees and the Diplomatic Conference deliberated intensively regarding the digital agenda, the rights of reproduction, the right of communication to public, technological measures and rights management information.

II. Right of Reproduction

The basic proposal that was discussed contained a clause under the right of reproduction to include in its ambit all types of reproduction – temporary or permanent, direct or indirect – in any manner or form. Limitations were also proposed to exclude temporary reproduction that has the sole purpose of making the work perceptible or reproduction of a transient or incidental nature provided that such reproduction takes place in the course of legitimate use of the work. These provisions were very vital for the on-line and on-demand transmissions of work. Content-providers in on-line, interactive transmissions systems would confidently be able to provide access to their works using new technologies without jeopardizing their economic interest, under the proposed clause. Those who defended the Article argued that it will not cause any serious set-back to any temporary copying that takes place along a telephone network or in browsing the Internet, as temporary copying is already covered by the Berne Convention and all domestic laws. They further argued that the exceptions and limitations permitted under the proposal will serve the purpose of excluding acts that were not economically relevant. However, many delegations had serious doubts on the intentions of the proposed provisions regarding the right of reproduction. They felt that these provisions ignored the basic reality of how the Internet worked and would automatically impose strict liability on the participants in Internet communications, including Internet-providers and users. They referred to temporary copying known as 'caching' as an essential part of the Internet transmission process, without which messages could not travel through a network and reach the public screen. Creation of an additional liability on the part of Internet participants was seen as a fundamental flaw in the basic proposal. In view of the strong opposition from various groups and the inability to resolve amicably the interests of content-providers and service-providers in the digital system, the issue of the right of reproduction was deferred for future consideration. The general consensus was that the issues relating to reproduction may be appropriately handled by the existing international norms on the right to reproduction and the possible exceptions to it, particularly under Article 9 of the Berne Convention and its well-established and flexible principles.

III. Right of Communication

The rights of communication under the Berne Convention provides for an exclusive right of communication to authors of dramatic or dramatico-musical and musical works when such works including translations are performed in public or communicated through cinematography. With respect to literary work, this is limited to recitations. The proposal considered by the Diplomatic Conference addressed advances in digital transmission technology through the modified right of communication. The text prepared by the Chairman of the Expert Committee provided the authors the exclusive right of authorizing any communication to the public of their works, including making their works available to the public by wire or wireless means in such a way that members of the public may access these works from a place and at a time individually chosen by them. These proposals widened the traditional notion of public to include interactive transmission, not making it mandatory that a group of individuals actually access it. The clause covers all types of works like computer programs and other literary works that were excluded from the traditional right of communication to the public under the Berne Convention.

Although the proposal was meant for protecting copyrighted work in the digital media, many communication industry organizations did not favour it. They felt that Internet-providers do not have proper control over the routes or passages of information traversing across their network. Their contention was that it was not always practically possible to translate each package to determine the contents. The technological companies were not ready to take on the burden of ensuring that only legitimate work got delivered through their systems.

After debating on the proposal on behalf of the content-providers and the service-providers, the Diplomatic Conference arrived at a consensus for a right of communication to the public more or less on the lines of the basic proposal. In addition, there was an understanding that there would be an agreed statement to make it clear that the provisions of physical facility for enabling or making a communication did not in itself amount to communication within the meaning of the new Treaty or the Berne Convention.

IV. Technological Measures

The draft considered by the diplomatic Conference made unlawful the importation, manufacture or distribution of protection-defeating devices. It was contended that this clause will help in eliminating devices such as unauthorized pay-TV decoders, hardware locks used to protect unauthorized copying of computer programs, etc. This clause, intending to safeguard the author's exclusive rights to control the reproduction and distribution of his or her work by providing physical protection, was objected to by many industry groups. Such objections were made on the ground that many innocent manufacturers and distributors would be subjected to liability in cases where their products are used to circumvent copyright protection devices. They felt that such a clause would force many companies to abandon or slow down production of new products fearing liability.

After a considerable amount of argument, the global community agreed that contracting parties may provide adequate legal protection against circumvention of effective technological measures used for exercise of the rights of authors and owners of copyright and neighbouring rights. The finally accepted version in the two Treaties put to rest many of the apprehensions in the minds of industry regarding over-legislation and the restrictions that would have been imposed on fair use provisions by library systems, educational institutions, research organizations, etc., and at the same time making it mandatory for contracting parties to check effectively the use of devices meant for circumvention of technological measures.

V. Rights Management Information

Images, when exploited through digital means, can be easily copied and modified into various forms. With the expansion of markets for works that have been derived in myriad forms from the original works, it becomes necessary to provide for a mechanism for ensuring accessibility to copyright information so that licensing and other authorized forms of exploitation of works become easier. The Copyright Information Management System has been thought to provide easy access to information regarding the copyright holder, term of protection, licence conditions, etc., especially in situations where the collective administration societies are not fully developed or not developed enough to handle the higher demands of digitalized works.

The issues involved were discussed threadbare by various interest groups. At the end of the day, the conference adopted a clause whereby the contracting parties were bound to provide adequate and effective legal remedy against any knowing tampering of electronic rights management information and distribution, import broadcast or communication to the public of works from which electronic rights management information has been removed or altered without authority. The rights management information has been clarified as information which identifies the work, the performer, the author/owner, the terms and conditions of use of the work, etc.

A very significant factor that emerged during the Diplomatic Conference is the realization on the part of the world community about the ever increasing need for striking a balance between the rights of the authors/owners of copyright and neighbouring rights on the one hand and the interests of the society on the other, in the context of framing new legislation whether nationally or internationally. The attempts to offer a foolproof system of protection of copyright and neighbouring rights in the digital era thus culminated in the evolution of two Treaties which address solutions to the threats posed by digital technologies to creative efforts, in a limited way. The hesitation in the minds of large nations all over to legislate on matters which are relatively uncertain, the strong position taken by various interest groups and, to top it all, the unwillingness to compromise on vital issues, did pose a set-back to finding a long-lasting solution to problems. The deletion of the original provisions relating to the right of reproduction is a price which the Conference paid for through its inability to resolve issues in an atmosphere of mutual understanding and trust. At the same time, the solution offered for checking for protection-defeating devices and tampering of copyright management systems have, beyond doubt, proved that it is possible for nations to think alike and come to plausible solutions to the problems that threaten human ingenuity and creative spirits. It is certain that a dialogue has commenced, a dialogue that has stirred up innumerable issues which the nations all over the world will hopefully keep alive and rake up more frequently than ever before.

VI. Indian Scenario

Coming to the Indian scenario regarding copyright and neighbouring rights, it is no exaggeration to say that the Copyright Act 1957, as amended from time to time, the latest amendment being in 1994, is one of the most modern pieces of legislation.[2] The Act confers rights to literary, dramatic, musical and artistic works, sound recordings and cinematograph films. Computer programs and

---

2   The Copyright Act 1957, as passed and amended by the Indian Parliament, is the law currently relating to copyright in India. This Act extends to the whole of India and is a consolidating measure. The Act's 1984 amendment was passed to combat the prevalent piracy in India and to make provisions to the 1957 Act applicable to video films and computer programs. The Act was further amended in 1992 to increase the term of copyright from 50 years to 60 years, running from the year either of death of the author or of first

databases are treated as literary works. In the case of computer programs, sound recordings and cinematograph films, the rights available include rental rights.

Performers and broadcasting organizations are also provided rights under the Copyright Act, although in a limited way. The rights of performers however cease to be available once the performer agrees to incorporate his or her performances in cinematograph films.

Being a large country with diverse and rich cultural heritage, it has become impossible to protect and manage the rights by individual efforts. Realizing the advantages in collective administration of rights, a whole chapter has been devoted in the Copyright Act for setting up such societies. As per these provisions, three societies have already been registered under the Act, for the sound recordings, the performing rights with reference to musical works and for cinematograph films. There is need for setting up more societies to deal with different types of works. Even the existing societies have to be strengthened and modernized to deal with digital exploitation of works.

Some of the definitions given in the Copyright Act are worth sharing. They are broad and encompass all possible elements. Performers, for example, include actors, singers, musicians, dancers, acrobats, jugglers, conjurers, snake charmers, etc. Again the term 'communication to the public' has been defined as making any work available for being seen or heard or otherwise enjoyed by the public, directly or by any means or display or diffusion other than by issuing copies of such work regardless of whether any member of the public actually sees, hears or otherwise enjoys the work so made available. It has been clarified that communication through satellite or cable or any other means of simultaneous communication to more than one household or place of residence, including residential rooms of any hotel or hostel shall be deemed to be communication to the public.

The Indian Copyright Act needs hardly any amendments to make it conform to the provisions of the TRIPS Agreement. The Act requires only minor cosmetic amendments to incorporate the provisions contained in the new treaties.

---

cont.

publication. The Act was again amended in 1994, effective 10 May 1995, changing many provisions: for example, this amendment established copyright-related rights in performances and broadcasts. It was intended to rectify difficulties indicated by copyright owners and users, to give effect to experience with prior law, and to respond to technological developments. See S. Ramiah, India, in 2 *International Copyright Law and Practice* (October 1997), at IND-9 (Paul E. Geller ed.) (general discussion of India's Copyright Law).

Use of Images for Commercial Purposes: Copyright Issues under Malaysian Laws

Linda Wang

Tay & Partners, Kuala Lumpur, Malaysia

I. Introduction

This chapter will seek to consider the commercial and legal implications under Malaysian copyright laws, of dealing with information, in particular information consisting of images in digital form, as something akin to a physical commodity. Copyright issues in Malaysia are governed by the Copyright Act 1987 (the Act). Since its coming into force on 1 December 1987, the Copyright Act 1987 has undergone several amendments. The first, in 1990, provided for the accession of Malaysia on 1 October 1990 to the Berne Convention for the Protection of Literary and Artistic Works 1886 ('the Berne Convention'). In 1996, the Act was further amended, essentially to expand the jurisdiction of the Copyright Tribunal to allow licensing schemes operated by licensing bodies to be referred to it and to allow for the compounding of certain copyright infringements. It also makes reverse engineering non-infringing. (This reverses the decision in *Peko Wallsend Operations Ltd v. Linatex Process Rubber Ltd.* (1993) 1 MLJ, which decided that to reverse engineer is an infringement, as an industrial design is protected by copyright either:

(a) on the basis of its two-dimensional drawings; or
(b) as an original artistic work in the form of a three-dimensional reproduction of the drawings.)

On 4 June 1997, the Act was further amended to cater for the use, exploitation and protection of copyright within the Multimedia Super Corridor (MSC), principally to redefine 'broadcast' to accommodate any future technological development including the transmission of encrypted signals. The 1997 amendments also made provisions to incorporate the WIPO Copyright Treaty

(WCT) and the WIPO Phonogram and Performance Treaty 1996 (WPPT). As at the time of writing, the 1996 and 1997 amendments have yet to come into force.

II. Works Protected by Copyright

Section 7(1) of the Act lists the works eligible for copyright protection in Malaysia and they are to be protected irrespective of their quality and the purpose for which they were created. The works are:

(a) literary works;
(b) musical works;
(c) artistic works;
(d) films;
(e) sound recordings; and
(f) broadcasts.

In respect of a literary, musical or artistic work, it is further provided that the work shall not be eligible for copyright unless sufficient effort has been expended to make the work original in character and written down, recorded or otherwise reduced to material form. 'Material form' is defined as including any form of storage (whether visible or not) from which the work or a substantial part thereof may be reproduced. Thus, the work need not be reduced to any tangible or visible form but may be embedded or stored in a non-sensate form such as electrical impulses on a disk, ROM or EPROM. The concept of 'originality' applied under Malaysian copyright laws is substantially similar to that as applied by English courts. Thus, what is required is that there must be originality in the expression of the idea and this expression of the idea must originate from the author in the sense that the work must not be a copy of another work. In *Lau Foo San v. Government of Malaysia* (1974) 1 MLJ 28, an action brought under the FMS Copyright Enactment (Cap. 73), the Federal Court said that to rebut originality, it must be shown that the appellant's works are nothing more than direct tracings of other original works or drawings.

Where images in films, photographs, paintings, museum archives and other sources are amassed, converted and stored in digital form, though resulting in a single collection, there are, in effect, separate rights in different works, involved with different persons owning those separate rights. For instance, paintings, drawings, etchings, prints, maps, plans, charts, diagrams, illustrations, sketches, works of artistic craftsmanship, photographs not comprised in a film, are all eligible for protection as artistic works under the Act. Where the images contain writings, the writings may be protected separately as literary works. There may also be protection of a work as a film if the definition under the Act is satisfied. A film is defined as a fixation of a sequence of visual images on material of any description, whether translucent or not, so as to be capable, with or without the assistance of any contrivance, of being shown as a moving picture or of being recorded on other material so that it can be so shown. Thus, material of any description upon which images may be fixed and shown as a moving picture, is eligible for protection as a 'film'.

There was doubt initially as to whether the definition, by referring to the fixation of a 'sequence of visual images' would exclude images which are stored or recorded in electrical impulses or digital form. In such instances, the images can hardly be described as fixed in a 'sequence of visual images'. The Supreme Court in *Foo Loke Ying & Anor v. Television Broadcasts Ltd & Ors* (1985) 2 MLJ 35, however, dispelled any doubts of such nature and ruled that there is no requirement that the images be in a state ready for projection, stating that:

'The definition does not require that visual images should be in a state ready for projection in order to qualify as a cinematograph film and it would be enough that they be recorded on any material, translucent or otherwise, and that it should be possible to translate them into a moving picture....'

It was further held by the court that the definition in the Act made no reference to the film-making process, but was primarily concerned with the 'essential characteristics of a sequence of visual images capable of being shown as a moving picture'. The recording of images in the form of electrical impulses on magnetic tapes, such as video cassette tapes, was thus held to be within the definition of 'film' under the Act.

The database or compilation of images created may also be eligible for protection as a 'literary work', defined by the Act to include tables or compilations, expressed in words, figures, or symbols (whether or not in a visible form). The definition seems intended to include computer database for protection as a literary work. In most cases, however, the issue is not so much whether the compilation or database is proper subject matter for protection but whether it has sufficient originality to qualify for protection, considering that a database is essentially a large amount of information, facts and figures which have been amassed from numerous sources. Frequently, also, the information is information which is publicly available. The value of a database, however, lies in the manner or order in which it is compiled, so that it is possible efficiently to access the database, search and retrieve relevant data within a short time. Otherwise, it is nothing more than a jumble of information. Thus, in considering originality, a factor which would be relevant is the amount of skill and effort expended by the designer of the database in the presentation and arrangement of the data, such as would enable quick and efficient access for purposes of searching and retrieving relevant data, by way of an appropriate retrieval program.

The decision of the Federal Court in *Lau Foo Sun v. Government of Malaysia* cited above, seems to require the satisfaction of only a low threshold of originality. This seems in line with decisions of English courts which have tended to fix originality at a low level. This is significant as if a higher threshold of originality is required, works such as computer databases, computer programs or other computer-generated works, which may be immensely useful but not highly creative or original, may fail to qualify and be excluded from protection.

It is worth mentioning that copyright in a literary work consisting of computer database or a 'table or compilation' subsists quite separately from copyright which may subsist in works comprised in the database or compilation, such as copyright in the artistic works or films.

If any of the works are broadcasted, there may also be protection of the works as broadcasts. A broadcast is the transmission, for reception by the general public, by wireless means or wire, of sounds or images or both.

Thus, the package of information or images when offered to the public whether in CD-ROM, through an electronic network, or a stock agency, is a package consisting of a bundle of separate rights, with different copyrights co-existing with one another and various rights split between different people. There can, of course, be agreements between the various copyright owners that copyright should vest in any one or other party. But it would be rare indeed in practice for such an agreement to be reached as the sources of the database would in most cases be varied and many. This separation of rights among different people can therefore make it extremely difficult and complicated in practice, since any dealing in the copyright work will require the consent or licence of everyone who has copyright in any part of the whole work. The duration of copyright protection can also vary, with copyright in different works forming part of the whole work, expiring at different times. It should also be borne in mind that the precise nature of the individual copyright is different in relation to each form of copyright. So, in determining what is, for example, an infringing act, reference must be had to the appropriate part of the copyright legislation dealing with that sort of copyright to determine if the exclusive rights have been infringed. It may also affect questions of subsistence of copyright in Malaysia. The works forming part of the whole are likely also to have different authorship, places of publication or may be unpublished works. Thus, within that compilation or package of works offered to the public, there would be works which are protected elsewhere but do not qualify for protection in Malaysia, works which are protected but for different durations and having different owners with different rights.

As to how such works may be protected and exploited in the context of local laws, it is necessary first to consider briefly the circumstances by which copyright would subsist in a work and the nature of such protection.

III. Subsistence of Copyright

A. *Authors*

The author of a work is the first owner of copyright. Where the work was commissioned or was made in the course of the author's employment then copyright is deemed to be transferred to the person who commissioned the work or the employer, subject to any agreement between the parties excluding or limiting such transfer. There is no requirement that the agreement be in writing. For the purposes of the Act, the following persons are regarded as 'authors'.

(a) in relation to literary works, the writer or the maker of the works;
(b) in relation to musical works, the composer;
(c) in relation to artistic works other than photographs, the artist;
(d) in relation to photographs, the person by whom the arrangements for the taking of the photograph were undertaken;
(e) in relation to films or sound recordings, the person by whom the arrangements for the making of the film or recording were undertaken;
(f) in relation to broadcasts transmitted from within any country, the person by whom the arrangements for the making of the transmissions from within that country were undertaken;
(g) in relation to any other cases, the person by whom the work was made.

For copyright to subsist, the author or any of the authors in the case of a work of joint authorship, must at the time when the work is made, be a qualified person. A 'qualified person' is:

(i) a Malaysian citizen or a permanent resident in Malaysia or, a national or a person who has permanent residence in one of the countries of the Berne Convention;
(ii) a body incorporated in and vested with legal personality under the laws of Malaysia or, a body incorporated in and vested with legal personality under the laws of any one of the member countries of the Berne convention.

'Residence' is not defined. Something more than a visit would be required but the degree of permanence is not clear. Very probably, it will be sufficient to show that the author, at the time the work was made, was living at a place within the country in question as his or her home.

B. *Publication*

Copyright can also subsist in a literary, musical or artistic work or film or sound recording if it was first published in Malaysia, regardless of whether the author was a qualified person at the time when the work was made. A publication shall be deemed to be a first publication in Malaysia if the work was first published:

(a) in Malaysia and not elsewhere; or
(b) elsewhere but published in Malaysia within 30 days of such publication elsewhere.

A work is deemed to have been published only if a copy or copies of the work have been made available with the consent of the owner in a manner sufficient to satisfy the reasonable requirements of the public. This is fairly broad and may cover any form of distribution or of making the work available, whether by way of sale, offer or expose for sale or hire, letting out for hire, rental or lending. The fact that there was no profit or commercial gains derived from making copies of the work available is not relevant.

Literary, musical or artistic works or films first published in one of the countries of the Berne Union, or simultaneously in a country outside the Union and in a country of the Berne Union are also protected in the same way as if the work had been first published in Malaysia. As for sound recordings, under existing Regulations made pursuant to the Act, it is only sound recordings made or first published in the US (including Puerto Rico, Guam and the Virgin Islands) and the UK, that will be granted protection as though they are works made or first published in Malaysia.

Copyright can also subsist in a broadcast if it was transmitted from Malaysia. Only broadcasts transmitted from the UK enjoy protection in the same way as broadcasts transmitted from Malaysia.

C. *Made in Malaysia*

Notwithstanding that the author of a work is not a qualified person at the time the work was made or that the work does not meet requirements of first publication, copyright can subsist if the work was made in Malaysia. Protection extends also to every work eligible for copyright (other than sound recordings, broadcasts and published editions of literary, musical or artistic works) if the work was made in a country of the Berne Convention.

The Act does not define 'made'. Thus, it leaves to be decided (there is as yet no court ruling on this point) whether a work is to be considered made, at the time of creation or at the point when it was reduced to material form. As copyright does not subsist unless the work has been reduced to material form, or affixed as in the case of a sound recording or a film, it makes sense to say that it should not be considered to have been made until this requirement has been fulfilled. But in relation to works which take some time to complete, it is questionable at which point of time this is to be regarded as fulfilled – whether it should be at the time the work was first reduced to material form or at the time of completion. Possibly, there can be copyright as soon as the work is reduced to some material form notwithstanding that it is not completed, so that if the half-finished work is copied there can be action for infringement.

IV. Rights Protected by Copyright

The Act allows the owner of copyright in a literary, a musical or an artistic work, a film, or a sound recording to exclusively control in Malaysia:

(a)   the reproduction in any material form;
(b)   the performance, showing or playing to the public;
(c)   the broadcasting;
(d)   the communication by cable; and

(e) the distribution of copies of the work to the public by sale, rental, lease or lending,

of the whole work or a substantial part thereof, either in its original or derivative form.

A. *Reproduction in Any Material Form*

'Reproduction' is defined by the Act and means the making of one or more copies of the work in any form or version. As to what constitutes reproduction, it has been said that there must be sufficient objective similarity between the two works and also some causal connection between them, the former being an objective issue and the latter, a subjective one (*Francis Day and Hunter Ltd v. Bron* (1963) Ch 587, (1963) 2 AER 16, CA).

In *Longman Malaysia Sdn Bhd v. Pustaka Delta Pelajaran Sdn Bhd* (1987) 1 CLJ 588, in determining whether what had been copied amounted to a substantial part of the plaintiff's book, the Court considered the quality rather than the quantity of the pirated parts reproduced. The Court also held that in that case, the copyists of the relevant diagrams and tables, which were a very vital part of the plaintiff's book, were relieved of the necessity of using their own skill and labour and had therefore taken a free ride on the efforts of the original author and artist. The parts taken were done *animo furandi*, with the intention on the part of the copyists of saving themselves time and labour, such that the defendant's use of the parts taken competed with and affected the sales of the plaintiff's books.

As was ruled in the case of *Peko Wallsend Operations Ltd v. Linatex Process Rubber Bhd*, cited above, the right to control reproduction extends also to the making of an object or thing in three dimensions from a two-dimensional work (e.g. drawings, paintings) or the reproduction in two dimensions of a three-dimensional work.

In general it is an infringement not only to reproduce a work in the same medium or form, but also to reproduce it in another medium. The mode of reproduction of a work is not material.

B. *Performance, Showing or Playing to the Public*

The performance, showing or playing must be in public or to the public. Generally, it can be said that any performance which is not domestic or quasi-domestic will be regarded as being in public, notwithstanding that only a few members of the public are present or that no charge for admission is made. The character of the audience is of relevance and can be decisive in determining if the performance, showing or playing of the work was to the public.

C. *Broadcasting*

'Broadcast' means the transmitting for reception by the general public by wireless means or wire, of sounds or images or both, and 'broadcasting' is to be construed accordingly. Thus, what is covered is the act of initiating the sending by wireless means or wire, waves resulting in a representation of the work, whether visually, aurally, or both. It is to be noted that the transmitting must be for 'reception by the general public'. The Act does not define 'general public'. However, compared with the rights to 'communicate by cable', which specifically refers to reception by the 'public or any section thereof', it would seem that a distinction is intended to be drawn by the use of 'general public' in the definition of 'broadcast'. Probably what is meant by the 'general public' is not to be construed differently from the 'public' in cases of public performances. However, where the broadcast can only be received by paying members of the public or subscribers, and not by the public at large, it would seem that it would not be within the broadcasting rights of the Act.

D. *Communication by Cable*

Communication by cable means the operation by which signals are guided by wire, beam or other conductor device, to the public or any section thereof, for reception. It is thought that the person sending out the signals need not contemplate their reception but that there would be an infringement if the signals were in fact sent out in such a way that are receivable by the public or any section thereof.

E. *Distribution Rights*

It is an infringement to distribute, without the consent or licence of the copyright owner, copies of the work to the public by sale, rental, lease or lending. There were doubts initially as to whether the rights to control distribution extend to original works or whether they were to be read as restricted to infringing copies of works or original unpublished works. The Act refers to 'the distribution of *copies* of the work'. Both 'copy' and 'infringing copy' are defined by the Act; 'copy' being a reproduction of a work in written form, in the form of a recording or film, or in any other material form, and 'infringing copy' meaning any reproduction of any work, the making of which constitutes an infringement of copyright or, in the case of any article imported into Malaysia, the making of which was carried out without the consent of the owner of the copyright.

As the provision defining distribution rights in the Act refers only to 'copies' of the work as opposed to 'infringing copies', it seems that the rights to control distribution extend to both infringing and original works, including works which have already been published or lawfully put in the market by the copyright owner or its licensees. This would have the perhaps unintended effect of allowing copyright owners to control the first and subsequent dealings in the work, whether by way of sale, rental, lease or lending. This would also mean that parallel importation is prohibited in relation to copyright works, notwithstanding that there is clear judicial recognition that it is not Malaysia's policy to prohibit parallel importation. This is certainly the position as regards patent and trademark rights. In *Winthrop Products Inc. & Anor v. Sun Ocean (M) Sdn Bhd* (1988) 2 MLJ 317, it was held that once the owner of a trademark has attached the trademark to goods and put them into the market, he or she cannot prevent further dealings with the genuinely marked goods. In the case of *Smith, Kline & French Laboratories Ltd v. Salim (M) Sdn Bhd* (1989) 2 CLJ 228, the Court similarly held that parallel importation of patented products, which were lawfully put into the market by the patent owner in the first place, was not an act which infringed patent rights.

That the right to control distribution extends to both infringing and original works (notwithstanding that the works had been published or circulated before was judicially affirmed in the case of *Class One Video Distributors Sdn Bhd & Anor v. Chanan Singh Sher Singh & Anor* (1997) 3 CLJ 694. There the Court found infringement as the rental of certain video tapes by the defendant without the consent or licence of the plaintiffs. This was notwithstanding the fact that the tapes were all original tapes, tapes which had been lawfully obtained from the plaintiffs or their licensees. It was held that 'copies' as used in the provision of the Act granting distribution rights must necessarily refer to copies lawfully or unlawfully made. The 1997 amendments do not address this and the wordings granting distribution rights as set out earlier remain unchanged.

V. Infringement

Copyright is infringed (section 36(1) of the Act) where a person does, or causes any other person to do, without the licence of the copyright owner, any of the acts to which the copyright owner has exclusive rights to control (mentioned in paragraph IV of this Article). Although the Act is silent, it is however, generally accepted that a person can be liable for infringement even if there is no actual knowledge nor any reason to believe that he or she is infringing copyright. There is no provision in the Act relieving an innocent infringer from liability to pay damages.

Copyright is also infringed (section 36(2) of the Act) if a person imports an article into Malaysia without the licence or consent of the owner for the purpose of:

(a) selling, letting for hire, or by way of trade, offering or exposing for sale or hire, the article;
(b) distributing the article –
   (i) for the purposes of trade; or
   (ii) for any other purpose to an extent that it will affect prejudicially the owner of the copyright; or
(c) by way of trade, exhibiting the article.

A person can only be liable for importing an article for any of the purposes set out above if he or she knows or reasonably ought to know that the making of the articles in question was carried out without the consent or licence of the copyright owner. Thus, there would be no infringement under this provision of the Act if the articles imported had been lawfully made. However, as seen from the decision in *Class One Video Distributors* cited earlier, the distribution rights granted extend to controlling the sale, rental, lease or lending of both infringing and original works. Thus, even if the importation of original articles or articles which had been lawfully put into the market is not an infringement, it is, nevertheless, an infringement to distribute such articles in Malaysia unless there is consent or licence from the copyright owner. By granting such wide rights to the copyright owner to control distribution, the provision relating to infringement by way of importation, is essentially rendered otiose.

VI. Duration of Protection

A. *Literary, Musical or Artistic Works*

The general rule is that copyright in literary, musical and artistic works subsists for the duration of the life of the author plus 50 years. Where the work had not been published before the death of the author, copyright subsists until 50 years from the beginning of the calendar year next following the year in which the work was first published. If the work is of unknown authorship, the copyright period is 50 years from the end of the year in which the work was first published and if the identity of the author later becomes known, the general rule will apply. In relation to works of joint authorship, copyright expires 50 years from the end of the calendar year in which the last of the authors dies. Copyright in a published edition of a literary, musical or artistic work expires 50 years from the end of the calendar year in which the edition was first published.

B. *Other Works*

Copyright subsisting in a sound recording, photograph, film, works of the government, government organizations and international bodies will all expire 50 years from the end of the calendar year in which the respective works were first published. Copyright in a broadcast shall similarly expire 50 years from the end of the calendar year in which the broadcast was first made.

C. *Duration of Protection for Databases*

Some databases are frequently updated and where that is the case, then a new copyright could conceivably come into existence on each update of the database. On this basis, there would in effect, be perpetual copyright in the database. Whether this will be recognized and given effect remains to be seen, but in principle, provided the requisite amount of skill and labour continue to be expended in the compilation of the database, there is essentially no reason why the database should not enjoy new copyright upon each act of updating.

VII.   Moral Rights

In respect to all works in which copyright subsists, the Act provides that no person may, without the consent of the author or his or her personal representative after the author's death, do or authorize:

(a)   the presentation of the work under a name other than that of the author by any means whatsoever (section 25(2)(a)); or

(b)   the presentation of the work in a modified form by any means if the modification significantly alters the work and is such that it might reasonably be regarded as adversely affecting the honour or reputation of the author (section 25(2)(b)).

For this purpose, 'name' includes initials or monograms. The Act also provides that the right against false attribution of authorship and the right of integrity may be exercised notwithstanding that the copyright in the work is not vested in the author or his or her personal representative. Thus, although such rights exist concurrently with the copyright in a work, they are independent of the ownership of the copyright.

It is to be noted that the moral rights granted by the Act do not include rights for the author to require that he or she be identified or acknowledged as the author. Thus, if the copyright owner reproduces or publishes the work without naming the author, notwithstanding a specific request in writing by the author to be so named, there would be no breach of moral rights. In this regard, the Act may not have fully complied with Article 6*bis* of the Berne Convention which provides, *inter alia*, for the right to be identified as the author.

Moral rights cannot be assigned or transferred, save only in the event of the author's death, in which case such rights may be carried out by the author's personal representative. Any breach of moral rights is actionable at the suit of the author or if the author is dead, by his or her personal representative.

VIII.   Commercial Use of Images in Digital Form

In converting images, whether from films, photographs, pictures and drawings, museum collections or archives, to digital form, there is in effect a reproduction of the original works. To avoid infringement, it would be necessary to obtain permission or licences from the owners of copyright in the original works. As seen earlier, one of the exclusive rights granted to a copyright owner in Malaysia is the right to reproduce in any material form, the whole work or any substantial part of it. 'Material form' includes any form of storage (whether visible or not) from which the work may be reproduced. Thus, the reproduction of the work in any tangible or visible form, or the reproduction of the work to be embedded or stored in non-sensate forms such as electrical impulses on disks, ROM or EPROM, would be within the scope of exclusive rights of the copyright owner.

The right to reproduce in digital form may be secured by way of a licence or an assignment. More commonly, such rights are secured by way of a licence, as opposed to by way of an assignment. The licence or assignment need not be for the entire copyright in the work but may be partial, i.e. specifically for the right to reproduce in digital form. The licence or assignment can be further limited to defined territories, so that the doing of any of the acts licensed or any exercise of the rights assigned outside the specified territories would infringe copyright of the licensor or assignor. It is likely also that the works would have been obtained from numerous sources and as such, would involve many different copyright owners. It makes sense, therefore, to have a standard licence document with all the various copyright owners. Otherwise it may be excessively difficult and cumbersome to monitor all the licences with all the various copyright owners on different terms and conditions. There is also the danger of being inadvertently in breach.

Under the Act any assignment of copyright and any licence for the doing of any act controlled by copyright are required to be in writing. Where the assignment is not in writing, e.g. an oral assignment, it is not void but has effect only as an agreement to assign. Thus, the assignee of an oral assignment is treated as having an equitable right to the copyright assigned. A licence which is not in writing is also not void. Where the licence is not in writing, an exclusive licencee cannot, however, claim the benefits conferred by the Act, that is, of having the same rights of action and be entitled to the same remedies as if the exclusive licence had been an assignment, concurrently with the rights and remedies of the copyright owner.

In negotiating for assignments or licences, an important consideration is the period of copyright remaining in the works. This would be relevant in negotiations for the assignment price or licence fees and in determining the overall costs in developing and producing the database. It is also significant in determining the period of the licence, as the licence should not extend beyond the period of copyright in the work. Where there is uncertainty regarding the period of copyright, because the year of death of the author or the last surviving co-author or, the year of first publication cannot be ascertained, it would be advisable for parties generally to come to an agreement as to the time, after which, copyright in the work will be treated as having expired.

As for Malaysia, it would seem that in addition to negotiating for reproduction rights, it would be necessary also to secure rights to distribute 'copies' of the work. A 'copy' of a work is a reproduction of the work in written form, in the form of a recording or film, or in any other material form (section 3 of the Act). Images reproduced in digital form are 'copies' of the original works. Thus, unless distribution rights as granted by the Act are redefined by Parliament or the case of *Class One Video Distributors Sdn Bhd & Anor v. Chanan Singh Sher Singh & Anor* (1997) 3 CLJ 694, discussed earlier, is judicially redefined, it would seem that the copyright owner has rights to control distribution in Malaysia of any copies of the work which form part of the compilation (in CD-ROM, for example), to the public by sale, rental, lease or lending. This is so notwithstanding that the copies are licensed copies or have been lawfully reproduced.

Additionally, where the digital images are accessible via an electronic network or by telephone dial-up so that the images can be selected, displayed and viewed on screen by the user, it would seem that the licence or the rights obtained from the copyright owner must also provide for rights of 'showing' the work to the public. Under the Act, the 'performance, showing or playing to the public' of the work is also an exclusive right of the copyright owner. 'Showing' is not defined. It is doubtful if such instances of 'showing' was intended by the draftsman of the Act to be covered but having regard to the ordinary meaning of the word, there is no reason why 'showing' would not also include a display of the work on computer screens. On this basis there is presumably a 'showing' of the work if it is exhibited or displayed for viewing by the public or set up in such a way that it is available for viewing by the public.

Depending on whether there is to be any broadcast to the general public of the works in the compilation, a licence to broadcast may also be required. Frequently the database of images would be accessible via an electronic network or telephone dial-up. In such circumstances, permission or rights to communicate by cable would also be required. As discussed earlier, rights to broadcast are probably only infringed where the broadcast is receivable by the public at large. The right to communicate by cable, however, is infringed even where the signals are receivable by only selected members of the public, e.g. those who have paid fees or by reason of membership of an organization or club. Even where the signals are sent and received from a satellite and then distributed by means of wire, beam or other conduct or device, for reception by the public or any section thereof, it is likely that this would be within the exclusive right of the copyright owner to 'communicate by cable'.

The above presumes that copyright subsists in the relevant works in Malaysia. In all probability, the works or images compiled are likely to include foreign works, possibly sourced from different countries. However with Malaysia and a growing number of countries having acceded to the Berne Convention, chances are most works protected in other countries would also be protected by copyright in Malaysia.

A. *Moral Rights*

As mentioned earlier in this chapter, moral rights granted by the Act does not entitle the author to require that he or she be identified as the author. In other words, it does not confer rights of paternity to authors. Thus, assuming moral rights are not waived and the work is reproduced in digital form and published without naming the author (even upon specific request of the author to do so), there would not have been any breach of moral rights. This makes it significantly easier to deal with moral rights in relation to the many works that would be included in the database, at least as far as Malaysia is concerned. In countries where rights of paternity are conferred, it is difficult to envisage how such rights could be exercised without becoming unduly cumbersome for the database owner. Considering that in most cases, authorship and ownership of copyright are vested in different persons, to seek out each and every author or the author's personal representative for a waiver of moral rights or to attribute authorship to each and every work within the compilation, are not viable alternatives.

Under the Act, it is open to authors to object to any derogatory treatment of their works or to a false attribution of authorship. However, as it is unlikely that the use of images in compiling the database would involve any significant or material alteration of the works, there should, in practice, not be much difficulty in dealing with this. Similarly as regards the author's right to protect against false attribution.

The exercise of moral rights may be waived by the author or the personal representative of the author after his or her death. The Act does not require that the waiver be by way of any instrument in writing. In practice, however, this is usually secured in writing, especially, where the work is commissioned work.

Any breach of moral rights under the Act would entitle the author or if the author is dead, a personal representative, to an action for breach of statutory duty to recover damages or to obtain injunctive relief and such other remedy as may be available. The court may also direct the publication of such correction as it may deem fit to restore the author's honour or reputation or to attribute to the author, such authorship as had been falsely or wrongly attributed.

B. *Ownership of Copyright in Database*

Quite separately from copyright in films, drawings, paintings and other underlying works, there can also be copyright in the database of images compiled. Tables or compilations, whether in words, figures or symbols (whether or not in a visible form) is a 'literary work' under the Act and is eligible for protection. The requirement of originality must of course always be met. The arrangement or presentation of the compilation must therefore had been the result of a sufficiently substantial degree of skill and labour.

The first owner of copyright in the database would be its author, that is, the 'writer or the maker' of the work, unless the database was made in the course of employment or the author was commissioned to make the work under a contract *for* services. Under these circumstances, copyright is automatically transferred to the employer or the person who commissioned the work, subject to any agreement excluding or limiting the transfer. There is no requirement that the agreement excluding or limiting such transfer is to be in writing. Thus, it is always prudent in practice to include as a standard term in employment contracts or contracts for services, an express provision to the effect that no circumstances shall in any way be construed as excluding or limiting the transfer of copyright to the employer or person commissioning the work or, as vesting any copyright in the author. This may avoid unnecessary complications arising by reason of the author subsequently asserting ownership to copyright on account of some oral agreement or promises made to him or her. This would be particularly relevant where the development and the making of the work involves several authors, or maybe even a larger number of authors. In addition, for databases, still more people may be involved in the continuous updates that would be carried out on the database.

It is not too careful to bolster further the clause providing for no exclusion or limitation of transfer of copyright, with a clause expressly assigning to the employer or the person commissioning the work, all and any residual copyright that may be vested in the author. Where the work is to be used or exploited in countries around the world, this may be particularly significant, so that any variations that may be found in local laws as regards deemed transfer of copyright, would not turn out to be an unexpected problem. In most jurisdictions, including Malaysia, assignments of copyright are required to be in writing.

C. *Protection and Exploitation of the Database*

Any reproduction in material form of the database is an infringement of copyright. Reproduction means the making of one or more copies of the work in any form or version, including any form of storage (whether visible or not) from which the work can be reproduced. It is not necessary that the whole work be reproduced. It suffices for purposes of finding infringement that a substantial part of the work was reproduced.

As to what constitutes a 'substantial part', it is recognized in relation to more traditional forms of work, that the question is to be decided as a matter of fact and degree and does not depend merely on the physical amount but on the substantial significance of what had been taken. Thus, in *Longman Malaysia Sdn Bhd v. Pustaka Delta Pelajaran Sdn Bhd* (1987) 1 CLJ 588, the court had to consider whether what had been copied amounted to a substantial part of the plaintiff's book and in doing so, it considered the quality rather than the quantity of the parts reproduced. The court also agreed with the English court in the case of *Ladbroke (Football) Ltd v. William Hill (Football) Ltd* (1964) 1 WLR 273 (per Lord Reid) that 'substantiality' depended more on the quality rather than the quantity of what had been taken and that one of the ways of determining this was whether the part taken was novel or striking or was merely a commonplace arrangement of ordinary words of well-known data. In *Longman Malaysia* the diagrams and tables copied were found to be a very vital part of the plaintiff's book and there was infringement. By copying, the defendant was relieved of the necessity of using its own skill and labour and had thereby taken a free ride on the efforts of the original author and artists.

The database compiled is likely to contain many images or many millions of characters in electronic form. However, in use, whether the data is accessed via an electronic network or more directly, from a local storage medium (e.g. compact disc), any copying by the user is likely only to constitute a very small part of the whole work. Thus, in terms of proportion, the parts reproduced in most cases are likely to be immaterial compared to the whole, simply because the total works or information contained in the database is so vast. It would be interesting, therefore, to see how the courts would interpret 'substantial part' in relation to databases, such as would be sufficient to find infringement.

Additionally, copyright in a database is not derived from the underlying works but lies in the manner of arrangement and presentation of the compilation. Thus, where images forming part of the database are reproduced without consent, issue may arise as to whether there is infringement of copyright in the database, as there would not have been any copying of the layout arrangement or presentation of the compilation. However, in the opinion of the present author, it is likely that the courts in determining if there is infringement of such reproduction rights, would construe the right in accordance with the wording of the Act and treat databases like any other works. Thus, the primary consideration would be whether there has been reproduction of the whole or a substantial part of the work. If so, then it would seem that there would be infringement only if a sizeable or substantial portion of the database had been downloaded or copied.

Unauthorized reproduction of any of the underlying works comprised in the database would infringe copyright in that work.

Distribution of copies of the database of images, in compact discs form, for example, by sale rental, lease or lending, without authority or consent, would also infringe distribution rights of the copyright owner. This applies even where the copies are original copies lawfully put in the market by the owner or its licensees.

Where images from the database are projected and shown to the public, there may also be infringement of copyright in those works. There would be infringement of copyright in the database if substantial images from the database as a whole are publicly shown without authority or consent.

Similarly, where the whole of the database of images or a substantial part thereof, is sent or transferred electronically, there would be infringement of the owner's rights to communicate by cable, as well as, infringement of the right to reproduce. Where the database is copied by the user and sent electronically to his friends (via an electronic network), it is questionable if his group of friends would constitute the public or a section thereof, to render the act an infringement. However, considering the ease with which materials may be copied and sent electronically to another, it may be that transmission to even a small group of friends would be sufficient to constitute the 'public' or a section of it. In the case of *Jennings v. Stephens* (1936) Ch 469, which considered what would amount to a performance in 'public', it was said that central to the issue was the importance of the purpose underlining the right of public performance, or for that matter, any of the other restricted rights. That purpose must surely be to preserve the value of copyright in the work by preventing unauthorized use of the copyrighted work. In *Jennings v. Stephen*, the court found that what was of relevance is whether the performance would have the effect of whittling down the value of the monopoly by any substantial extent or injuring the proprietary right of the copyright owner. If the value would be substantially affected, then the performance would be of a public nature. Thus, if this was to be followed, it would seem that the electronic transmission by the user to a small group of his friends can amount to communication to the public and infringing. In these cases, it would be difficult to imagine the rights of the copyrighted owner not being substantially affected as each of those persons in receipt of the copyrighted work, would be able to make further 'communications by cable' to others.

Nevertheless, as mentioned earlier, there is infringement by reason of unauthorized reproduction.

D. *Contractual Protection*

In addition to protection by way of copyright, additional protection may be obtained by having the end user enter into direct contractual relations with the database owner. Where the database is accessed via an electronic network or telephone dial-up, it is common to require the user to enter on-line, into a licence agreement before allowing access. This may or may not involve the payment of a fee by the user. Where the database is distributed in the form of compact discs or other forms of storage, the user may be required to sign a written licence agreement at the time of purchase or the agreement may be supplied with the discs similar to shrink-wrap licences for software.

The contractual terms may provide for a general no copying or reproduction clause or limit the images that may be copied. Thus, in the event of dispute and if the agreement is upheld, the database owner may successfully obtain interim remedies or claim for breach of agreement even though it may not succeed on claims for infringement on account that the images reproduced do not form a substantial part of the whole work.

Effective contractual protection, however, relies to a large extent on the ability to monitor compliance with the terms. In relation to a purchaser of a disc (or other storage device) containing the database of images, the ability to detect non-compliance is, realistically speaking, almost non-existent save where copying is done on a large scale or substantially. Furthermore, contractual obligations are only enforceable against a party to the contract. Thus, where the copying is done by a person other than the party who entered into contract, that third party cannot be liable for any breach of contractual obligations.

E. *Criminal Offences*

It is an offence under the Act to make, distribute or to deal by way of trade in infringing copies of a copyrighted work. It is also an offence to possess otherwise than for private and domestic use any infringing copy or to make or have in possession any contrivance used or intended to be used for the purposes of making infringing copies. Possession of three or more infringing copies is deemed to be otherwise than for private or domestic use.

Offences are investigated and prosecuted by the Enforcement Division of the Ministry of Domestic Trade and Consumer Affairs. Investigations or actions are initiated by lodging a formal complaint with the Division, which has wide powers, including the power to enter any premises or building to search for and seize any materials related to the commission of the offence.

Legal Protection of Digital Works in Japan

Hirotaka Fujiwara

Hikari Sôgo Hôritsu Jimusho, Tokyo, Japan

I. Legal Protection of Digital Works on Networks

A. *Multimedia Era*

Computer technology has developed significantly; computers with the abilities of a huge general-purpose computer of one decade ago are now available for use as personal computers. In particular, due to the rapid progress in calculation speed and storage capacity of personal computers and the introduction of CD media such as CD-ROM, an inexpensive but high-capacity form of memory, personal computers now may handle still images, moving images and sound which basically require a huge amount of data, by using their digitized data. There is also progress in the compression technology of huge amounts of data such as the data of images and the technical progress in software handling images.

As a result so-called multimedia such as texts, numbers, animation, sound, still images and moving images may be handled in combined form. The advantage of multimedia is not only that the scope of data which can be handled by computers is becoming larger and larger, but also that all information may be handled in the form of dialogue with users of computer (*interactive*). Accordingly, the multimedia user may withdraw such information as matches his or her needs. The multimedia may be used not only as a research tool, but can be used for education, presentations related to business activities, games and for other various purposes.

In addition, the Internet of today is fit for very practical use as the infrastructure of our highly information-oriented society, and can provide a wide variety of multimedia information.

B. *Risks of Digitization*

1. Risks Related to Digitization

In the multimedia era, catalogues and the like in PDF format may be sent electronically on the Internet. Compilation works including individual works may be presented on a home page and sent around the Internet. Accordingly, in respect of works circulated on the network, it is necessary to examine closely what legal framework, both domestic and international, is applicable to such works.

In particular, the Internet is rapidly expanding as a global open network, and works are under the serious threat of infringement of rights. Because existing works may be digitized as a whole and circulated on the network, the reproduction and modification of works has become quite easy. The reproduction of digitized works does not harm the quality of such digitized works, and traces of reproduction or modification may not necessarily be left.

In short, due to the digitization of works, the works lose their tangible form and are circulated or distributed as intangibles, thus making it very difficult to discern between the original and its reproduction.

2. Risks Related to Globalization

In addition, if infringement, such as reproduction, of the copyrights of works protected by the Copyright Law of Japan occurs in a foreign country which does not have a copyright act or which is not a signatory to certain intellectual property treaties, the Copyright Law of Japan does not apply to such a case. Accordingly, if a home page is opened in such foreign country and a third-party's work (or, more accurately, its reproduction) is presented on such home page, such work may be circulated or distributed around the world, and it becomes very difficult to take measures against such copyright infringing activities.

3. Risks Related to Anonymity

In addition, with respect to the Internet, anonymity is an underlying feature, and accordingly, it may be very difficult to identify the person infringing the copyright.

4. Responsibilities of the Provider

Accordingly, for the purpose of preventing the infringement of copyrights on the Internet, it is necessary to impose some responsibilities on the provider which permitted the infringing person to open such home page, or to educate the user about copyright law and appropriate ethical behaviour.

C. *What is a Work on the Internet?*

1. Communication Through Personal computers

The main object of communication through personal computers (e.g. Niftyserve) may be literal information, and most of the information circulated there is considered as a 'work' as defined in the Copyright Law of Japan (individually, a 'work', and collectively, 'works'). In contrast, in the case of a very short communication such as chats, individual utterances may hardly be deemed a work.

Article 2, paragraph 2(1) of the Copyright Law defines 'works' as follows: '"Work" means a production in which thoughts or sentiments are expressed in a creative way and which falls within the literary, scientific, artistic or musical domain.' Article 10, paragraph 1 of the Copyright Law illustrates works with examples as follows:

(a) novels, dramas, articles, lectures and other literary works;
(b) musical works;
(c) choreographic works and pantomimes;
(d) paintings, engravings, sculptures and other artistic works;
(e) architectural works;
(f) maps as well as figurative works of a scientific nature such as plans, charts, and models;
(g) cinematographic works;
(h) photographic works;
(i) computer program works.

2. Internet

In contrast, an Internet home page consists of photographs, graphic works and writings (today, sound data or moving images are also included). The respective elements may collectively bear the nature of the works. Since such various kinds of works on a home page are compiled with intellectual creativity, such compilation may often be protected as an independent compilation work under the Copyright Law (individually, a 'compilation work', and collectively, 'compilation works').

Article 12 of the Copyright Law provides as follows:

'(1) Compilations which, by reason of the selection or arrangement of their contents, constitute intellectual creations shall be protected as independent works.
(2) The provision of the preceding paragraph shall not prejudice the rights of authors of works which form a part of the compilations defined in that paragraph.'

3. Multimedia and Moving Images

It is only recently that moving images have come to be handled by personal computers, thanks to the enhanced speed and lowering price of personal computers. Article 10, paragraph 1(7) sets forth cinematographic works as an example of a work. In addition, Article 2, paragraph 3 provides as follows: 'As used in this Law, "cinematographic work" includes a work expressed by a process producing visual or audio-visual effects analogous to those of cinematography and fixed in some material form.' This provision is considered the provision defining the cinematographic work. That is, although cinematography (*eiga* in Japanese) originally refers to cinematography in the form of film for presentation in theatres, videotapes, videodisks and other materials storing continuous images, of which the difference between these and cinematography lies only in their form of storage, such as optical film and magnetic tape or disk, need not be distinguished from cinematography in respect of their functions and therefore also constitute cinematographic works.[1] However, the scope of cinematographic works is not clearly cut. Article 16 of the Copyright Law provides as follows:

'The authorship of a cinematographic work shall be attributed to those who, by taking charge of producing, directing, filming, art direction, etc., have contributed to the creation of that work as a whole, excluding authors of novels, scenarios, music or other works adapted or reproduced in that work; provided, however, that this shall not apply to the case where the provision of the preceding Article is applicable.'

With respect to cinematography, 'those who, by taking charge of producing, directing, filming, art direction, etc., have contributed to the creation of that work as a whole' means the director, producer, cameraman, art director, etc., and cinematography is usually a joint work of such persons. Those persons are generally called modern authors. An assistant director or assistant cameraman who partially contributes to the creation of such work is not included among such persons. However, if those persons are engaged by a movie company and are involved in that work as its business, such movie company shall become the author of that work in accordance with the provision of the legal person's authorship (Article 15 of the Copyright Law). This provision also explains clearly that the authors of a cinematographic work are distinct from the authors of a novel or scenarios adapted into that cinematographic work, music or lyrics reproduced in such work or the author of artistic or other works related to such work.

The relationship between an original work that has been adapted and a cinematographic work based on such original work is the relationship between the pre-existing work and the derivative work. Article 28 of the Copyright Law provides as follows: 'In the exploitation of a derivative work, the author of the pre-existing work shall have the same rights as those the author of the derivative work has under the provisions of this subsection.' Accordingly, in order to exploit a cinematographic work which is a derivative work, the licence from the author of the original work is necessary.

---

[1]   Moriyuki Kato, *Chosakuken-hô Chikujyô Kôghi Shinban* (Lecture on Copyright Law Article by Article, new ed.), p. 47.

Further, Article 29, paragraph 1 of the Copyright Law provides as follows:

'Copyright in a cinematographic work, to which the provision of Article 15, paragraph 1, the next paragraph and paragraph 3 of this Article are not applicable, shall belong to the creator of that work, provided that the authors of the work have undertaken to participate in the creation thereof.'

Accordingly, in respect of a cinematographic work, if an author has entered into a participation agreement with the creator of such work for the making of such work, the copyright as proprietary right belongs to the creator. Article 2, paragraph 1, subparagraph 10 defines the creator of cinematography, as follows: '"creators of cinematography" means those who take the initiative in, and the responsibility for, the creation of a cinematographic work'.

The legislative purpose of this provision is that since the use of a cinematographic work has been traditionally entrusted to the exercise of rights of the creator of the cinematographic work, and cinematography has a special character in that the creator of a cinematographic work invests a substantial amount of money in production expenses, and makes and publicizes cinematographic work as its corporate activities, if all the persons who may be potentially regarded as authors of the cinematographic work are allowed to exercise their respective copyrights, smooth distribution of the cinematographic work will be prevented, and therefore, it is considered most appropriate that the copyrights in ordinary cinematographic works such as cinematographic works presented in theatres are conferred to the creator of such work.[2] In accordance with the above-mentioned provisions, the author and the copyright owner of a cinematographic work may be different persons.

The author of a cinematographic work shall have, as moral rights, the right of making the work public (Article 18 of the Copyright Law), the right of determining the indication of the author's name (Article 19 of the Copyright Law) and the right of preserving the integrity of the work (Article 20 of the Copyright Law). The copyright owner of a cinematographic work shall not have such moral rights but shall have, as proprietary copyrights, the right of reproduction (Article 21 of the Copyright Law), the rights of cinematographic presentation and distribution (Article 26 of the Copyright Law), etc.

However, recently, the Japan Film Director Association (*Nihon Eiga Kantoku Kyôkai*) has submitted to the Agency for Cultural Affairs of Japan a statement demanding that the copyright which confers the right of presentation, broadcasting, etc. of his or her own cinematography should be conferred to directors and that currently the protection of the authors' rights is not sufficient with respect to the secondary use of cinematographic works under the current Copyright Law. In addition, performers such as film actors have shown a similar intention by insisting that it is insufficient that performers do not have the right to secondary use of cinematographic works. As a result, the first subcommittee

---

[2]   Ibid. at 173.

of the Council on Copyrights of the Agency for Cultural Affairs has issued a report to the effect that the Agency will make positive efforts to support the protection of the rights of film directors, performers, etc. in respect of the secondary use of cinematographic works. Therefore, it is possible that the Copyright Law may be amended depending on future discussions on this matter.

D. *Partial Amendment of the Copyright Law*

In using the Internet, if a person accesses a WWW server from his or her personal computer, the information stored in the WWW server will be sent to his or her personal computers and will be shown on the screen. Therefore, such person may have the illusion of watching the various screens on the WWW server through a personal computer although no such screens exist.

A part of the Copyright Law of Japan was amended on 10 June 1997 (having become effective on 1 January 1998), and the former provision of the right of wire transmission has been amended into the provision of the right of public transmission (Article 23 of the Copyright Law), and the performer's and phonogram producer's right of making transmittable has been provided only in respect of live performances and performances visually recorded. This amendment to the Copyright Law reflects the new WIPO Copyright Treaty and the WIPO Performances and Phonograms Treaty (the 'new Treaties') adopted at the diplomatic conference held in Geneva in December 1996.

The new Treaties provide for the author's 'right of communication to the public' and the performer's or the phonogram producer's 'right of making available fixed performances or phonograms', and the protection against the violation of these rights has been provided for in the new Treaties.

The objects of the right of communication to the public are the activities of connecting a server to a network and the activities of transmission, and a violation of copyright shall be deemed to have taken place at the time when a server is connected to a network and made available to the public. Transmission without authorization shall also be a violation, and such transmission includes interactive transmission. In contrast, the right of making available fixed performances or phonograms shall not include the right of transmission, and the performer or the phonogram producer shall have only the right of authorizing the connection of a server to a network.

Article 2, paragraph 1(7-2) of the Copyright Law defines 'Public Transmission' as follows:

'"public transmission" means the transmission of radio communication or wire-telecommunication intended for direct reception by the public, excluding the transmission (other than that of program works) by wire-telecommunication installations one part of which is located on the same premises where the other part is located or, if the premises are occupied by two or more persons, both parts of which are located within the area therein occupied by one person'.

Article 2, paragraph 1(9-4) of the Copyright Law defines 'Interactive Transmission' as follows: ' "interactive transmission" means the public transmission made automatically in response to a request from the public, excluding the public transmission of falling within the term "broadcasting" or "wire diffusion"'. In addition, Article 23 of the Copyright Law provides as follows:

'(1) The author shall have the exclusive right to make the public transmission of his or her work (including the making transmittable of his or her work in the case of the interactive transmission).

(2) The author shall have the exclusive right to communicate publicly, by means of a receiving apparatus, his or her work of which the public transmission has been made.'

Further, Article 2, paragraph 1(9-5) of the Copyright Law defines 'making transmittable' as follows:

'"making transmittable" means the putting in such a state that the interactive transmission can be made by either of the following acts:

(a) to record information on a public transmission memory of an interactive transmission server already connected with telecommunication networks for the use by the public ("interactive transmission server" means a device which, when connected with telecommunication networks for the use by the public, has a function of making the interactive transmission of information which is either recorded on such a part of its memory as used for the interactive transmission (hereinafter in this item referred to as "public transmission memory") or inputted to such device; the same shall apply hereinafter), to add a memory recording information as a public transmission memory of such an interactive transmission server, to convert such a memory recording information into a public transmission memory of such an interactive transmission server, or to input information to such an interactive transmission server;

(b) to connect with telecommunication networks for the use by the public an interactive transmission server which records information on its public transmission memory or which inputs information to itself. In this case, where a connection is made through a series of acts such as wiring, starting of an interactive transmission server or putting into operation of programs for transmission or reception, the last occurring one of these acts shall be considered to constitute the connection.'

Then, Article 92-2 of the Copyright Law provides as follows:

'(1) Performers shall have the exclusive right to make their performances transmittable.

(2) The provision of the preceding paragraph shall not apply to the following:

(i) performances incorporated in visual recordings with the authorization of the owner of the right mentioned in Article 91, paragraph (1);

(ii) performances mention in Article 91, paragraph (2) and incorporated in recordings other than those mentioned in that paragraph.'

Article 96-2 of the Copyright Law provides as follows: 'Producers of phonograms shall have the exclusive right to make their phonograms transmittable.'

According to the above-mentioned amendments to the Copyright Law, it may be considered that the Copyright Law of Japan has responded quickly to the new Treaties in order to prevent the violation of copyrights on the Internet. However, the establishment of provisions itself does not mean that cases of violation of copyrights will disappear, and accordingly, it will be of great importance to provide practically effective means to protect against such violation.

E. *Relationship to Provisions Restricting Rights*

1. Downloading and Reproduction for Private Use under Article 30 of the Copyright Law

Article 30 of the Copyright Law permits reproduction for private use, and under such Article, the activities of reproduction of a work or its reproduction 'for the purpose of the reproducing person's personal use, family use or other similar uses within a limited circle (hereinafter referred to as "private use")' shall not be a violation of copyright. The question is raised as to whether the downloading of a work or its reproduction for the purpose of private use is permitted under Article 30 of the Copyright Law.

Although there is an argument that private use admitted under Article 30 of the Copyright is too broad and such Article should be amended, this argument shall be set aside for the time being, and as interpretation of the current provision of such Article, a reproduction for private use under such Article shall be deemed to have taken place when a member who makes access to a personal computer communication or a WWW server downloads by his or her personal computer a work which is stored in a relevant host-computer or WWW server. In addition, Article 30 of the Copyright Law is considered a mandatory provision, and accordingly, the conditions set forth by a member who uploaded a work may not prohibit such reproduction for private use itself.

Further, since downloading itself is considered a reproduction for private use, a member's downloading shall not be a violation even if the object is an illegally made reproduction. That is because Article 30 does not limit the permission of reproduction for private use only to that of a legally made reproduction but is interpreted as to include also reproductions of illegally made reproductions.

A person's use of such downloaded illegally made reproduction by his or her personal computer for business use does not constitute a violation of copyright unless he or she knew at the time of downloading that such downloaded reproduction had been illegally made.[3]

---

[3] See Article 113, paragraph 2 of the Copyright Law.

2. Uploading and Reproduction for Private Use under Article 30 of the Copyright Law

However, the presentation of a third person's work on an electronic board or a forum in a personal computer communication system is interpreted as not to constitute a reproduction for private use admitted under Article 30 of the Copyright Law.[4] Accordingly, uploading of a third party's program work without authorization on a personal computer communication system (e.g. registering such program work as free software in a data library) shall constitute a violation of copyright.

Provided, however, that in the case where a copyright owner has authorized the reproduction or adaptation of his or her work in advance, as in the case of free software, it will not be necessary to obtain authorization when reproducing or adapting such free software developed by a third party and uploading the same, provided further that consideration to moral rights be duly given.

In addition, attaching a third party's work to a WWW server shall not be considered to constitute a permitted reproduction for private use, and it will be an illegal reproduction unless such party's authorization is obtained.

3. Permission of Reproduction under Article 47-2 of the Copyright Law

Article 47-2 of the Copyright Law permits the reproduction by the owner of a copy of a program work 'if and to the extent deemed necessary for the purpose of exploiting that work on a computer by himself or herself'. Accordingly, a member who downloaded a computer program from a network may make copies of such downloaded computer program for the purpose of making a back-up copy under Article 47-2. Provided, however, that apart from Article 30 of the Copyright Law (since this Article is interpreted by a substantial number of people to be a directory provision) it is possible to conclude that the terms of use set forth by a member who uploaded the concerned program should govern and take precedence over this Article.

F. *Network and Moral Rights*

The Copyright Law provides for certain moral rights of the author. Article 2, paragraph 1(2) of the Copyright Law defines the 'author' as 'a person who creates a Work'. Accordingly, at the time when an author creates a work, the proprietary copyrights and moral rights therein are conferred to the author.

The above-mentioned right of reproduction, right of public transmission and right of adaptation, etc. are proprietary copyrights. Proprietary copyrights are transferable, and accordingly, the owner of a proprietary copyright and the author may be different. On the other hand, moral rights are exclusively

---

[4]   Research Committee on Electronic Information and Use of Network, Report, 16.

personal rights and non-transferable, and accordingly, even when proprietary copyrights are transferred, moral rights remain with the author. The contents of moral rights are as follows:

(a) right of making the work public (Article 18, paragraph 1 of the Copyright Law): 'the right to offer to and to make available to the public his or her work which has not been made public'.

(b) right of determining the indication of the author's name (Article 19, paragraph 1 of the Copyright Law): 'the right to determine whether his or her true name or pseudonym should be indicated or not, as the name of author, on the original of his work or when his work is offered to or made available to the public'.

(c) right of preserving the integrity (Article 21, paragraph 1 of the Copyright Law): 'the right to preserve the integrity of his or her work and its title against any distortion, mutilation or other modification against his or her will'.

Considering the relationship between the structure of a computer network and moral rights, the following issues will be identified.

(i)   When uploading a third party author's unpublished work, it is necessary to obtain the author's authorization regarding its publication and follow the author's will regarding indication of the author's name.[5]

(ii) When uploading a third party author's published work, it is necessary to follow the author's will regarding indication of the author's name, provided, however, that, in the case where the author has indicated a certain name as such author's name in the published work, indication of such name may be considered as following such author's will. Even in the case of free software, the author may often require indication of such author's name when a third party uploads the free software.

(iii) Any distortion, mutilation or other modification made to a third party author's work without such author's authorization when uploading the same on a network shall constitute such author's right of preserving the integrity thereof.

Provided, however, that Article 20, paragraph 2(3) provides for, as an exception to the right of preserving the integrity of a computer program: 'modification which is necessary for enabling use on a particular computer of a computer program work which is otherwise unusable on that computer, or to make more effective use of a computer program work on a computer' and, accordingly, such modifications constituting such an exception shall not violate the right of preserving integrity. In some cases such as free software, the author has permitted modifications to such author's program work, and in such cases, it may be considered that the author has waived in advance the right of preserving integrity.

G. *Responsibilities of the Provider*

Is the provider responsible when an author's work is illegally reproduced on its WWW server and transmitted publicly and such provider takes no measures

---

5   Ibid.

against such situation? The issue of responsibilities of the provider is a difficult one, an issue which is unsolved in many countries.

My opinion is that the provider does not violate copyrights directly, but that the provider's concrete obligation of deletion should be found when certain requirements, such as that the provider knows or ought to know of the activities violating copyrights and that the violation has been furthered by the provider's activities or omission of activities, are satisfied, which follows the idea of contributory infringement discussed in the US. Therefore, if the provider does not delete the related object, such provider shall be liable in tort.

In a case of defamation in an electronic conference on a personal computer communication system (the '*Nifty* case'), where I was an attorney for the plaintiff, the Tokyo District Court rendered a new and very important judgment on 26 May 1996. The judgment states as follows:

'when it is found that a system operator knows concretely that a statement of defamation of a person is presented on the forum under its management and control, it should be admitted that such system operator owes, considering its status and powers, an obligation to act to take necessary measures to prevent the unjust attack of such person's reputation'.

The reasons given for such judgment are:

(a) that taking necessary measures to prevent the unjust attack of a person's reputation should be a part of the management of a forum;
(b) that a system operator may take measures such as deletion of the concerned statement;
(c) that if so deleted, the members may not see such statement thereafter;
(d) that a person the reputation of which is being attacked may not have concrete measures to prevent such statement from being read; and
(e) that there is some description in the membership rules and the operating manual regarding measures against the prevention of defamation.

However, the judgment also states that since:

(i) the system operator may not check the statement appearing in the forum or conference in advance;
(ii) very few system operators concentrate on the business as system operators and many system operators spend only their leisure time on their business as system operators;
(iii) the business scope of system operators is very broad; and
(iv) considering the volume of statements, it is extremely difficult to check, identify and examine the problematic statements, even where a system operator's obligation to take measures is found, the obligation to check statements all the time should not be imposed on such system operators.

The above *Nifty* case is a case of defamation, but the reasoning can also apply to the case of infringement of copyrights.

H. *Jurisdiction and Governing Law*

In principle, in respect of an international civil case, international jurisdiction shall be granted to the court having jurisdiction over the address of the defendant, and further, if, applying the provisions of the Civil Procedure Code of Japan regarding territorial jurisdiction, a Japanese court may have jurisdiction over such case, the Japanese court shall have international jurisdiction over such case, unless there exist special circumstances, such as a circumstance in which allowing such jurisdiction may harm the equality of the parties involved or the idea of due and speedy process.

In the provisions of the Civil Procedure Code of Japan regarding territorial jurisdiction, Article 15 thereof provides that a court having jurisdiction over the place of tort may have jurisdiction over such tort case. Since infringement of copyright is one type of tort, the court having jurisdiction over the place of tort may have jurisdiction over such infringement. However, in respect of the Internet, it is very difficult to determine where the place of tort is.

In addition, according to the Civil Code of Japan, in a case in which the copyright owner demands damages incurred from infringement of copyright, the place to perform the obligation to pay damages shall be the address of the obligee.[6] Since Article 5 of the Civil Procedure Code shall grant to a court having jurisdiction over the place to perform the obligation a jurisdiction over such case, there is no dispute in admitting the jurisdiction granted to the court having jurisdiction over the place to perform the obligation under an agreement between the concerned parties, but there is a strong objection to admitting the jurisdiction granted to the court having jurisdiction over the place to perform the obligation under a tort.

Accordingly, there is no dispute that there is granted international jurisdiction to a country where the injuring party has an address, but further discussion should be necessary to determine whether jurisdiction should be granted to a court having jurisdiction over the address of a related server or to a court of the country in which the injured party is located. In my opinion, considering the situation in which a work on a WWW server is automatically reproduced as a cash file on the personal computer by which a person accessed to WWW server, the tort should be found at the address of the related WWW server and the address of the person who made access.

In addition, I think that jurisdiction based upon a tort on the Internet may be granted to multiple places of tort, and that the injured party may bring a suit in the place where he or she found the fact of infringement of copyright. However, since this is an issue which is not sufficiently discussed, there is no established argument.

---

[6]   Article 484 of the Civil Code of Japan.

II. Amendment of the Copyright Law Related to the Circumvention of Effective Technological Measures

A. *WIPO New Treaties*

Article 11 of the WIPO Copyright Treaty and Article 12 of the WIPO Performances and Phonograms Treaty[7] deals with the circumvention of effective technological measures. Article 11 of the WIPO Copyright Treaty provides as follows:

'Contracting Parties shall provide adequate legal protection and effective legal remedies against the circumvention of effective technological measures that are used by authors in connection with the exercise of their rights under this Treaty or the Berne Convention and that restrict acts, in respect of their works, which are not authorized by the authors concerned or permitted by law.'

This Treaty provides that certain measures should be taken against 'circumvention of effective technological measures that are used by authors', but the scope of its regulation is very vague. The respective stages of circumvention will be the manufacturing and import of equipment for circumvention, sale or other distribution of such equipment and human activities using such equipment, but it is not clear whether all such stages shall be regulated or only human activities shall be regulated. In addition, the scope of technological measures is not made clear either.

There are various technological measures, scrambling technologies, ciphering technologies, etc. which are used not only for the protection of copyrights but also for other purposes, and it is not clear whether all such technologies should be regulated or certain specific technologies should be regulated. In addition, if the activities which are not legally permitted are the object of such provision, the regulations thereunder shall not prevent use which is made in accordance with the restrictive provisions of copyrights, and there arises doubt that the circumventive activities which are made in pursuing the legally permitted activities should be legal. For example, use in accordance with the provisions of Article 30 and so forth of the Copyright Law of Japan or use to which the Fair Use Principle of the US apply should not be considered illegal. Therefore, it is not clear how the problem of interfering with legal use under the Copyright Law is dealt with. As a result, the decision on what kind

---

[7] Article 18 of the WIPO Performances and Phonograms Treaty provides as follows: 'Contracting Parties shall provide adequate legal protection and effective legal remedies against the circumvention of effective technological measures that are used by performers or producers of phonograms in connection with the exercise of their rights under this Treaty and that restrict acts, in respect of their performances or phonograms, which are not authorized by the performers or the producers of phonograms concerned or permitted by law.'

of measures should be taken against circumvention of technological measures was entrusted to the respective countries' discretion under the new Treaties.

B. *Intermediate Report of the Copyright Council, Multimedia Subcouncil, Working Group (February 1998)*

1. Point at Issue

The respective stages of circumvention will be the manufacturing and import of equipment for circumvention, distribution of such circumventive equipment and circumventive activities, and there are circumventive activities in which circumventive equipment is used and those in which such equipment is not used. The circumventive equipment includes such equipment for general use and such equipment solely for copy protection. Therefore, there arises a problem as to what kind of circumventive activities should be regulated in what ways.

2. Circumventive Activities to be Regulated

There is no dispute in regulating the last stage of circumventive activities in the above-mentioned respective stages of circumvention. The contents of such circumventive activities are those which, for the purpose of exploitation, etc. of the works, circumvent the technological measures added by the copyright owners to the works, which are the object of protection of rights under the current Copyright Law.

First, the Intermediate Report states that it is appropriate to regulate the circumventive activities related to technological protective measures added for the purpose of rights provided under the current Copyright Law. Its conclusion is that technological measures to protect the derivative rights such as the right of reproduction shall be the object of such regulation. That seems to mean that the measures which restrict only the use (playing, receiving, etc.) shall not be the object of such regulation. Accordingly, it is anticipated that technologies related to access control such as scrambling technologies or ciphering technologies shall not be treated as the object of such regulation.

As to the electronic watermark technologies, it is stated that such technologies are also related to the regulation regarding the information for control of rights, and the regulation on such technologies shall be considered in the future.

In addition, at this time the regulation against circumventive activities related to technological measures of protection are not limited depending on the kinds of works, etc. However, depending on the difference in form such as between analogue works and digital works, or the difference in ways of communication such as between communication via network or communication by broadcasting, technological measures of protection may be different, and accordingly, technological variety should be taken into consideration when making regulations.

As to circumventive activities, in relation to the current situation where technological measures to be regulated are limited to those for the purpose of protection of derivative rights, such as the right of reproduction, such activities are limited to those the purpose of which is use for reproduction etc. or with notice of illegal reproduction of programs (hereinafter referred to simply as 'use').

Further, there is another problem as to whether technologies should be specified for the purpose of such regulation, and in this respect, although it seems necessary to specify the technologies since they shall become the object of such regulation, there is some apprehension that the development of technologies might be prevented by specifying the technologies, and therefore, the concrete provisions have not yet been introduced.

3. Other Activities to be Regulated

The Intermediate Report states that circumventive equipment which is the object of the regulation consists of, for example, equipment, parts or programs manufactured solely for the use of circumvention of technological measures, and that at minimum, distribution or provision of equipment should be the object activities of the regulation.

However, regulation of circumventive activities itself is an *ex post facto* measure to deal with illegal reproduction which constitutes a violation of copyright, and those activities which come to surface are just the tip of the iceberg, and it is practically impossible to identify and follow up all of the actual circumventive activities. In addition, under the current law, in order to make someone responsible, it must be certain that the concerned use is not in the scope of free use such as private use. Further, it seems that since the distribution etc. of equipment may have a stronger effect on the risk of violation of copyrights of the works, in order to make more effective the regulation against the circumvention of technological measures of protection, it should be insufficient from the point of view of copyright protection unless the manufacturing, import and distribution of equipment which are pre-stages of the circumventive activities are made the object of regulation.

In this regard, the Intermediate Report states that the regulation shall also be applied to the manufacturing, import and distribution of equipment; provided, however, that it is also stated that the equipment to be regulated should be limited to that which are manufactured solely for the use of circumventive activities. The regulation needs to cover distribution or provision of such equipment, but regulation should not apply to equipment for general use. It is pointed out that regulation of such equipment may be avoided by attaching other functions to the concerned equipment.

In addition, since it is stated that at least the finished equipment, parts and software should be the object of regulation, it is unclear to what extent the equipment which is not finished should be regulated.

Further, because the activities to be regulated are concerned with the distribution and provision of equipment to be used solely for circumventive activities, the manufacturing or import of equipment which is a pre-stage to circumventive activities and which should be covered by such regulation may need to be limited to those made with the purpose of distribution.

4. Relationship to the Restrictive Provisions

In the Intermediate Report, as to how the provisions are coordinated with the provisions of Articles 30 and so forth, only the point at issue is stated and the manner in which such problem should be resolved is not stated.

5. Other Matters

In the Intermediate Report, other points at issue, such as the works in respect of which the legal protection has expired, or simple data, may not be used as a result, what kind of legal measures should be taken against the circumventive activities, or the fact that manufacturers may have to bear excessive costs, are also discussed.

Museums and Digital Image Archives and the Proposed European Directive on the Harmonization of Copyright: A UK Perspective

Peter Wienand
Farrer and Co., London, England

I. Museums and Digital Image Archives in the United Kingdom

Many museums and galleries in the UK are currently digitizing or considering the digitization of their image resources. Digitized images are seen as a more permanent form of storage of photographic records than transparencies which fade over time. More importantly, of course, digitizing images of objects in the collection of a museum or gallery is the essential pre-condition for being able to make use of digital communications technologies, principally the Internet or closed networks between schools, libraries or universities.

Clearly, the national institutions with their perhaps greater financial resources are more advanced in this process than many smaller museums and galleries. The National Gallery in London, for example, is in the process of digitizing its images of every painting in its collection, with the avowed aim of putting thumbnail versions of every image onto its web site. However, there are examples of smaller institutions that, with sponsorship or other funding, have digitized significant elements of their image resources. An example here would be the work done by the Norwich Castle Museum for its CD-ROM on the Norwich School of Artists. The Ashmolean Museum in Oxford is participating in a European Commission-funded project called MENHIR, which involves the tagging of digital image files with unique national code identifiers which are perceived as essential for the purposes of rights management.

One of the most potentially interesting initiatives is the Scottish Cultural Resources Access Network (SCRAN) project, funded in part from lottery funds disbursed by the Millennium Fund, one of the distributing bodies of the UK National Lottery.[1] This involves the digitization of images of around 30,000 objects in the collections of museums and galleries across Scotland. The digitized images will form part of a database combined with 1.5 million text records, data, captions and multimedia essays. The images will be available at three levels. Thumbnail images will be available for free via the Internet; educational licences will be made available for a fee, and finally very high-quality digital images will be available for commercial exploitation.

The SCRAN example illustrates one of the principal difficulties facing museums and galleries in digitizing images of objects in their collections – cost. The funding constraints in the museums and galleries sector has perhaps restrained the headlong digitization of museum and gallery image resources around the country. The SCRAN project is, among other things, an attempt to find funding to enable smaller institutions to digitize their visual resources. Apart from the kick-start lottery funding, fees for the educational licences and from commercial exploitation of the images are intended to cover the cost of digitizing museum images.

The latest spending review announced by the UK Government in 1998 announced that an extra £290 million would be made available for the arts and cultural institutions, with £99 million earmarked for museums and galleries. One of the specific objectives of this extra funding is to enable at least national museums and galleries to offer free public access to their collections. The concept of 'public access' has always included intellectual access,[2] but it is not yet clear how much of this extra funding may be used in digitizing images of objects in museum collections to make them more easily available via digital communications networks.

II. The Current Copyright Position in the UK

A. *General Issues Relating to Ownership and Subsistence of Copyright*

A first hurdle is securing the copyright in the underlying image. Museums ought to be in a good position, as the owners of the objects portrayed, to acquire the rights in images of those objects. However, they face the following problems.

(a)   Control over photography and filming in the gallery is crucial if the value of images is not to be diluted by images obtained by visitors, especially those who

---

[1]   More information can be accessed via SCRAN's web site which is http://www.scran. ac.uk/.

[2]   See for example the consultation paper on Public Access for Museums and Galleries published in December 1997 by the Department of Culture, Media and Sport which called for 'the widest possible physical, sensory and intellectual access to [museum and gallery] collections'.

are not members of the general public but are allowed in to take photographs for publishing or other commercial purposes. If the museum's publishing policy were governed solely by commercial considerations, then all visitors should be required to assign their copyright to the museum as a condition of access. This is not always the case.

(b) A 'photograph' is defined for the purposes of UK copyright legislation as meaning 'a recording of light or other radiation on any medium on which an image is produced or from which an image may by any means be produced and which is not part of a film'.[3] This will clearly include digitized images. However, there remains a concern in some quarters that copyright does not necessarily subsist in photographs of, say, paintings or other artistic works, on the basis that the photograph would be an insufficiently original reproduction. But while this may be the case in some other European jurisdictions,[4] this is not the case in the UK, where the legal tradition derives from the treatment of photographs under the Copyright Act 1911.[5] There, copyright belonged to the person who owned the negative at the time when the negative was made. This helps to demonstrate how in the UK all photographs have in principle been deemed to be capable of being original copyright works regardless of their subject matter.

(c) Images have to be digitized for digital exploitation whether in on-line or off-line form. Although no cases under English law specifically confirm this, a new copyright may well arise in the digitization, where sufficient skill and labour went into the manipulation of the technological variables to mark out an area of 'originality'. Such a copyright should be secured by the museum, in the same way as the copyright in photographs, although given the cost of digitizing images, museums often have to consider licensing the digitization to recoup their investment.

(d) If an object is out of copyright, a new right called 'publication right' – introduced following a recent EC Directive – applies to out of copyright works.[6] If such a work has never been published before, then whoever now unearths and publishes it gets a 25-year exclusive publishing monopoly. Under UK law this is a problem mostly for unpublished artistic works and not for other unpublished works since they remain in copyright in the UK until 2039. (Two categories of unpublished artistic works are also unaffected until 2039 – engravings the author of which died before 1989 and post-1957 photographs.) Including a digital image of such an object on a publicly accessible database will amount to publication for these purposes. Obviously museums and galleries – leaving cost aside – should now consider publishing any such unpublished items in their collections. If they

---

[3] Section 4(2) of the Copyright, Designs and Patents Act 1988.
[4] In particular Germany. See also Article 6 of Council Directive harmonizing the term of protection of copyright (93/98/EEC) which provides that 'photographs which are original in the sense that they are the author's own intellectual creation shall be protected....No other criteria shall be applied to determine their eligibility for protection. Member States may provide for the protection of other photographs.'
[5] Copyright Act 1911, section 21.
[6] Regulation 16 of The Copyright and Related Rights Regulations 1996 (SI 1996 No 2967), implementing EC Directive No 93/98/EEC of 29 October 1993.

inadvertently allow someone else to publish such items without negotiating a licence or assignment back of the publication right, they could be stopped from publishing these items themselves.[7]

B. *Databases*

Databanks of digital images may well fall into the definition of databases, which by virtue of a recent change in the law enjoy a specific regime of protection.[8] The definition of 'database' is '...a collection of independent works, data or other materials which (a) are arranged in a systematic or methodical way, and (b) are individually accessible by electronic or other means'. Databases now enjoy a two tier protection.

(a)   Databases which constitute the creator's 'own intellectual creation' should be protected by copyright as literary works.[9]

(b)   Databases which are not 'intellectual creations' but which nevertheless represent 'a substantial investment in obtaining, verifying or presenting the contents' should be protected by a new database right, allowing the owner to prevent the unauthorized extraction (any form of transfer of the contents to another medium) or reutilization (the making available of the database to the public, whether by physical distribution or on-line transmission) of all or a substantial part of the database.[10] The right aims to protect the investment of the person making the database (the person or company responsible for creating the database and who makes the requisite investment). It falls short of full copyright protection, chiefly because it only lasts for 15 years, although any substantial new investment in the interim in updating the database will renew this period.

Museums and galleries that invest in the obtaining, verifying or presenting of digital image databases will therefore in principle be the owners of database rights in those databases.

C. *Clearance*

Identifying and clearing third-party copyrights in material which is being digitized is obviously a problem for museums and galleries concerned with collections of modern art or of other works still in copyright, such as photographs and films. Many have suggested a one-stop-shop approach to reduce the burden of clearing rights for multimedia projects, learning from collective licensing schemes where only one body need be approached to clear

---

7   See Helen Simpson and David Booton 'The new Publication Right: how will it affect museums and galleries?' (September 1997) 2 *Art Antiquity and Law*.

8   By virtue of the Copyright and Rights in Databases Regulations 1997 (SI 1997 No 3032), implementing Council Directive 96/9/EC. The Regulations came into force on 1 January 1998.

9   Copyright, Designs and Patents Act 1988 (as amended), sections 3(1)(d) and 3A(2).

10   Copyright and Rights in Databases Regulations 1997, regulation 16.

all the rights. No such body yet exists in the UK. Individual rightsholders and collecting societies still need to be approached, although consolidation is beginning to occur,[11] and some initiatives are looking at multimedia exploitation, such as IMPRIMATUR.[12] This is a project aiming to devise processes marrying technical and legal strategies to protect and license intellectual property rights. It is currently in year two of a three-year project aimed at developing a consensus and then some server software embodying this consensus. However, apart from SCRAN there is nothing in the museum sector in the UK like the Museum Educational Site Licensing (MESL) project in the US.[13] In the meantime, clearance can only be managed by meticulous identification of rights, negotiating costs to keep within budget and, in many cases, finding commercial partners to share those costs.

D. *Infringement and Enforcement of Copyright and other Rights*

Although UK law has since 1988 recognised the storage of a work in any medium by electronic means as a 'copy' which, if made without the copyright owner's authority would amount to an infringement of copyright,[14] there has been much less certainty as to whether the transmission or retrieval of copyright works via electronic networks are in themselves infringements (although transmitting a work knowing that infringing copies will be made by means of such a transmission is a secondary infringement[15]). Attempts have been made to assimilate such transmissions within the concept of a 'cable programme service',[16] though these have been much criticized and are not helpful in the Internet since the definition of 'cable programme service' excludes interactive services.

It is worth noting that under UK law, authorizing someone to commit an infringement such as copying is as much of an infringement as copying.[17] In the Internet context, this could be helpful in enforcing copyright in relation to certain acts initiated abroad. For example, if someone makes a copyright work available on a web site which is hosted on a server outside the UK, they are implicitly authorizing that work to be copied by each person who visits the site and views (i.e. copies onto his or her own terminal) the work. An action for infringement of copyright could be brought in the UK against the site 'publisher'.

---

[11] Such as the joint venture recently established of the Mechanical Copyright Protection Society (MCPS) and the Performing Rights Society (PRS).

[12] Launched in December 1995 and sponsored by EC DG III. Its coordinating office is at Marlborough Court, 14–18 Holborn, London EC1N 2LE (tel. +44 171 395 0670; e-mail: imprimatur@alcs.co.uk).

[13] Set up in 1994 and supported by the J. Paul Getty Trust Art History Information Program.

[14] Copyright, Designs and Patents Act 1988, section 17(2).

[15] Copyright, Designs and Patents Act 1988, section 24(2).

[16] Notably in *Shetland Times Ltd v. Dr. Jonathan Wills* (24 October 1996), Ct. Sess (Scotland).

[17] Copyright, Designs and Patents Act 1988, section 16(2).

However, there is no doubt that the uncertainties surrounding the copyright implications of Internet transmission and retrieval have influenced the attitude of museums and galleries to the possibility of making images of objects of their collections available on the Internet. While museums and galleries have duties to provide access to their collections to members of the public, they also rely on the income they derive from the sale or loan of images through the picture libraries which many of them operate. The legal uncertainties surrounding digital transmissions and retrieval have helped to retard the use of the Internet as a means of providing remote access to their images of objects in museum collections.

Museums are no different from other publishers in having to enforce copyright from time to time, although not all museums have the resources to mount expensive copyright infringement claims. In common with other Internet publishers, they face the conundrum of enforcing their rights across many jurisdictions.

The 1996 WIPO Treaties[18] – when implemented into national laws – should improve the situation. The draft EC Directive which has just been published[19] (see further below) should achieve this in the EU. But effective enforcement requires not just harmonized laws but effective procedures and remedies. Until content providers, including museums, can be confident about these they may hesitate before putting too much of real value on-line. One solution is to put thumbnail images only – images which should in theory be of little commercial value but satisfy the demands of public access – onto web sites. This is certainly the policy of the National Gallery in London, but other major institutions have not yet followed suit.

E. *Knowledge about Copyright Issues*

Sadly, not all museums and galleries in the UK are as fully aware of copyright issues at they might be. In a survey[20] commissioned by the Museums and Galleries Copyright Working Group[21] a year ago, 105 museums and galleries which might be expected to deal with copyright were questioned. The results were mixed. There was a general interest in copyright, but some responses were less reassuring. Only 49 per cent of respondents considered copyright when acquiring new items; 64 per cent required freelance photographers to assign copyright back to the museum. Only 39 per cent professed to have

---

[18] The WIPO Copyright Treaty and the WIPO Performances and Phonograms Treaty adopted following the WIPO Diplomatic Conference of December 1996.

[19] Proposal for a European Parliament and Council Directive on harmonization of certain aspects of copyright and related rights in the Information Society: COM (97) 628.

[20] Emma Williams, Rights and Reproduction Survey, December 1996. See also the article in (April 1997) *Museums Journal*.

[21] Further information about this organization, founded in 1996, can be obtained from the author.

agreements covering licensed digital exploitation. So it seems clear that there is a need, at least in the UK, to provide more information about the impact of copyright in the museums sector.

F. *Public Access and 'Fair Dealing' and other Exemptions under UK Law*

Many of these issues museums face in common with other publishers of multimedia and digital products. However, in one vital respect museums are not like other publishers. In the UK, they are legally obliged under their founding charters to consider the public benefit of their activities.

For example, the Boards of Trustees of the Victoria and Albert Museum and the Science Museum are expressly enjoined by statute 'generally [to] promote the public's enjoyment and understanding' of, respectively, art, craft and design, and science and technology.[22] The National Gallery, Tate Gallery, National Portrait Gallery and Wallace Collection have similar duties.[23] Most other museums have similar objectives.

Fulfilling these objectives surely involves the reproduction and publication (whether in digital or analogue form) of images of objects in the museum or gallery collections. The creation of reproductions in the form of digital images and their publication, for example via the Internet, will involve an infringement of any copyright in those objects. As we have seen, many such objects may well still be in copyright. However, there is little in current UK copyright law which allows museums and galleries to fulfil these objectives without infringing any such copyright.

UK copyright law recognizes limits to the scope of copyright protection by permitting certain things to be done without infringing copyright, where a less restrictive regime is deemed socially or culturally beneficial. UK law provides for a number of exceptions that may be relevant to the use and exploitation by museums and galleries of digital images.

(a)   'Fair dealing' with a copyright work for the purposes of private study or research does not infringe the copyright in the work.[24] It is likely that the making available of a digital image by a museum to a researcher or for solely private use would come within the exemption. The making available of multiple copies would not, however. Research does include commercial research. It is not clear whether putting thumbnail images on a web site could ever fall within the exemption even if the site contained express statements that viewing or downloading was only permitted for certain purposes because putting a digital file onto a web site might be regarded as tantamount to authorizing multiple copying.

(b)   'Fair dealing' with a copyright work for the purposes of criticism or review of that or another work does not infringe the copyright in the work, provided that

---

[22]   National Heritage Act 1983, sections 2 and 10 respectively.
[23]   Museums and Galleries Act 1992, section 2.
[24]   Copyright, Designs and Patents Act 1988, section 29(1).

the author of the work (not the copyright owner) is identified.[25] In the case of a digital image of a painting in a museum collection, two authors might therefore need to be identified, namely the artist and the photographer (although since the latter is usually never identified when the photograph is published, identifying the photographer would usually not be required). There is little guidance from reported cases on the scope of this exemption. Bona fide criticism rather than merely cursory comment in relation to a work is likely to be required by a court so that, for example, coffee table art books with little real critical content ought not to benefit from the exemption.

(c)   Schools and colleges can copy works 'in the course of instruction or of preparation for instruction' so long as this is done in a classroom context;[26] but museums and galleries will not qualify as they are not 'educational establishments'.[27] However, database right in a database made available to the public is not infringed by fair dealing with a substantial part of its contents if it is extracted for the purpose of illustration for teaching or research and not for any commercial purpose.[28] This is wider in some respects than the equivalent provisions applying to copyright. A museum might be able to rely on this exemption if, for example, it used a portion of a published image database in the course of educational and non-commercial activities within the museum. However, the copyrights in the individual images would still have to be cleared.

(d)   Prescribed libraries, that is, mainly public libraries – including the libraries maintained by museums and galleries – can, for example, supply single copies of articles in periodicals or single copies of extracts from books, so long as the copy is required for research and private study.[29]

(e)   UK law[30] allows the photography or the making of a graphic work representing a building, or a sculpture or work of artistic craftsmanship which is permanently situated in a public place or in premises open to the public. This is of some possible use to museums in that they can currently argue that a sculpture in their collection which is permanently publicly accessible may be photographed by them although of course it also means that members of the public may photograph the sculpture as well.

But (these general provisions aside) there are in the UK no provisions specifically applying to museums. The criticism and review provisions would not extend to reproduction by a museum of images if in-copyright works in its collections for the purposes of conservation or of fulfilling its duty of educating the public. A museum wishing to exploit images of objects in its collection, or copies of such objects – whether commercially or not – must therefore in most

---

[25]   Copyright, Designs and Patents Act 1988, section 30(1).

[26]   Copyright, Designs and Patents Act 1988, sections 32 et seq.

[27]   See the Copyright (Educational Establishments) (No 2) Order 1989 (SI 1989 No 1068) and the Copyright, Designs and Patents Act 1988, section 174.

[28]   Copyright and Rights in Databases Regulations 1997, regulation 20(1).

[29]   Copyright, Designs and Patents Act 1988, sections 37 et seq.; see also the Copyright (Librarians and Archivists) (Copying of Copyright Material) Regulations 1989 (SI 1989 No 1212).

[30]   Copyright, Designs and Patents Act 1988, section 62.

cases either make sure that it owns the relevant copyrights, or get the permission of the copyright holders. There is no exception to this rule. copyright offers no option on public access without control of the copyright.

Museums are therefore on the horns of a dilemma. They are under a duty to disseminate information about their collections as widely as possible; yet UK copyright law currently recognizes no public benefit gateway to enable them to achieve this objective without substantial investment in copyright fees and royalties. This seems an unjust position on policy grounds in a situation where, for example, UK law currently allows commercial sale-rooms, galleries and auction houses to copy an artistic work for the purpose of advertising the sale of the work.[31]

III. The Proposed EU Directive

A. *General Background to the Proposals*

The application of the copyright laws of member states of the European Union to digitized images, and the activities of museums and galleries, will be affected by a proposal for a directive on the harmonization of copyright and related rights in the Information Society,[32] which was published by the European Commission in January 1998. The proposal is primarily designed to adjust the law of copyright at a fundamental level to meet the challenges of the new digital technologies. In particular, it seeks to address the use of copyright works, including images, on on-line networks such as the Internet.

In 1995 the European Commission published a Green Paper[33] on the future of copyright, which was followed by a consultation process, the results of which were summarized in the 'follow-up to the Green Paper'.[34] This identified a number of issues requiring legislation, all of which have general relevance to the activities of museums and galleries:

● the need to harmonize the right of reproduction, the basic right at the heart of copyright;
● the need to protect digital 'on-demand' transmissions by creating a new right of communication to the public (the European Commission's proposals for a new right of communication to the public received international approval and were embodied in the WIPO Copyright Treaty adopted in Geneva at the end of 1996[35]);

---

[31] Copyright, Designs and Patents Act 1988, section 63.
[32] 'Proposal for a European Parliament and Council Directive on the harmonization of certain aspects of copyright and related rights in the Information Society': COM (97) 628.
[33] 'Intellectual Property in the Information Society' COM (95) 382 final.
[34] 'Follow up to the Green Paper', 20 November 1996, COM (96) final.
[35] Adopted by the Diplomatic Conference on Certain Copyright and Neighbouring Rights Questions on 20 December 1996, convened under the auspices of the World Intellectual Property Organization (WIPO) in Geneva.

- the need to protect the integrity of technical identification and protection schemes, based on electronic tagging of files, encryption etc.;
- the need to harmonize the right of distribution of copies of works so as to make it consistent with European rules on free movement and the single market.

The proposed Directive which was published in January 1998 is the fruit of these recommendations.

B. *Underlying Themes of the Directive*

Before looking at the details of the proposed Directive as they apply to museums and galleries, it is worth just pausing to pick out a fundamental theme that runs through the proposals. It is quite clear that one of the Commission's greatest concerns is to create a legal regime that fosters economic growth in the EU, and to provide incentives to enable the new digital industries to thrive and hold their own against their American and Asian equivalents. The language of the Explanatory Memorandum to the proposed Directive is full of words like investment, growth, competitiveness. It stresses the need to provide a framework which will help rightsholders to protect their investment.[36]

The idea of creation is therefore assimilated broadly with that of investment. Naturally, an investor wants to protect his or her investment – and it is clear that the 350 submissions made during the consultation process following the Green Paper heavily reflected the interest of producers and, to a lesser extent, authors. They voiced 'concern over new uses of protected material in ways that are not authorized or not anticipated under existing laws'.[37] The Commission clearly appreciates their argument that 'the growing availability of intellectual property in on-line digital formats…creates significant new risks for large scale piracy'.[38]

Two groups have not been so well represented, although lip-service is paid to them – users of material, and institutions established for public benefit including museums and galleries. Creating a work is not just a question of making an 'investment' and waiting to see what happens. Artists need access to the works of their predecessors or contemporaries. The same is true of authors and musicians. Creation is part of a cycle where the works of previous generations are commented on, adopted, borrowed, recycled or rejected. This is part of the role played in culture by museums and galleries – they are repositories of the works of previous and even current generations.

This is acknowledged to some extent in most systems of copyright law. The protection from unauthorized copying granted to the creators of works and their successors in title is made subject to exceptions – allowing certain things

---

[36]   For example, 'appropriate measures are critical in order to achieve a favourable environment which stimulates creativity and investment…', Chapter 2, section I,1.

[37]   Explanatory Memorandum to the proposed Directive, Introduction, section 3.

[38]   Explanatory Memorandum to the proposed Directive, Chapter 1, section 10.

to be done with copyright works where this is seen to be in the public interest such as copying for the purposes of research or private study, or for the purposes of criticism or review, or in the context of education. The Commission has recognized that if it is to harmonize the right of reproduction, it could not ignore these exceptions, which vary considerably from one member state to another.

C. *Provisions of the Proposed Directive as they Relate to Museums and Galleries*

1. The Reproduction Right

The reproduction right is dealt with in Article 2: 'Member states shall provide the exclusive right to authorise or prohibit direct or indirect, temporary or permanent reproduction [of copyright works] by any means and in any form, in whole or in part.' This will include digital reproduction, including the digitization of in-copyright works such as photographs or artistic works in a museum or gallery collection. There is not much here that would require a change from, for example, current law in the UK.

2. The Communication to the Public Right

The communication to the public right is dealt with in Article 3, which provides, in language almost identical to that contained in the 1996 WIPO Copyright Treaty, that member states are to provide authors with 'an exclusive right to authorise or prohibit any communication to the public of originals or copies of their works, by wire or wireless means, including the making available to the public of their works in such a way that members of the public may access them from a place and at a time individually chosen by them'.

This addresses the possibility of direct delivery of digital images, recorded music, audio-visual productions and multimedia products via networks to home computers. Anything which involves a communication of a work to the public by wire or wireless means, including making it available in such a way that members of the public may access it from a time and place individually chosen by them (e.g. from a home computer) is covered. The new right will certainly be broad enough to cover both transmission and retrieval of digital images held on museum and gallery databases over networks, most obviously of course, the Internet.

3. The Permitted Exceptions – General Principles

Article 5 sets out a list of the permitted exceptions – acts which are permitted and which do not infringe copyright. This is therefore the part of the proposed Directive that is of most fundamental significance to museums and galleries, and to their freedom to make use of digital images of in-copyright objects in their collections.

The proposed list of exceptions is intended to be exhaustive.[39] The Commission's stated policy here is to strike 'a balance between, on the one hand, providing the strongest possible incentives to encourage the creation of original works...and, on the other, facilitating the dissemination of such works to users'.[40] However, at the same time, the Commission's Comments on the proposed Directive state that, in the digital environment, 'exceptions and limitations must be construed in a more narrow way...'.[41]

All permitted acts, including those that could be carried out by museums and galleries, are supposed to pass the so-called 'three step test' (set out in Article 5(4) of the proposed Directive). This is derived ultimately from virtually identical language in the Berne Convention:[42]

- they may only be allowed in 'certain specific cases', i.e. on a case-by-case basis;
- they may not be interpreted in a way that would unreasonably prejudice the rightsholders' legitimate interests;
- they may not be interpreted in a way that would conflict with 'normal exploitation' of the works copied or of other subject matter.

These concepts of unreasonable prejudice and normal exploitation are not defined. It is left open to member states or the courts to flesh out what these concepts mean. To a UK lawyer, there are undertones of familiarity: the concept of 'fairness' in the fair dealing exceptions is interpreted in some of our cases by reference to what would prejudice the rightsholder's economic interests. This is not surprising as the UK is a signatory to the Berne Convention and so UK law has had to be consistent with these provisions for some time, at least in principle.

Curiously for a Directive that is intended to harmonize the law only one of these exceptions is obligatory (the right of reproduction as part of a technical process and for the sole purpose of executing an otherwise legal use of a work, where the reproduction is of no economic relevance). All the others are optional, though they must be subject to the overriding requirements of the 'three step test'. In other words, they are intended to set the maximum extent of any permissible exceptions to the reproduction right, while leaving member states free to reduce their scope in favour of authors' rights via, for example, remuneration schemes.

4.   Exceptions to the Right of Reproduction

Three exceptions apply to the right of reproduction, and are not available as exceptions to the communication to the public right (Article 5(2) of the draft). The Commission is clearly persuaded that the economic impact of permitted

---

[39]   Commentary on Article 5, section 2.
[40]   Commentary on Article 5, section 1.
[41]   Comments on the Articles, Article 5, section 1.
[42]   Article 9(2), Paris Act, 24 July 1971.

exceptions may be far greater in the digital sphere than the traditional environment, and that they must be construed more narrowly in the digital sphere to prevent 'economic damage to the market of protected works'.[43] Member states may allow for exceptions allowing print copying and home taping but of most significance to museums and galleries is the exception permitting specific acts of reproduction made by 'establishments accessible to the public'.

5.   Copying by 'Establishments Accessible to the Public'

Specific acts of reproduction made by 'establishments accessible to the public' which are not for direct or indirect economic or commercial advantage would be permitted. This is presumably intended to allow libraries, museums and galleries which are accessible to the public to make copies of works for non-profit-making purposes. A superficial reading of this would suggest that libraries would be permitted to do what they are currently permitted to do under UK law,[44] and that museums, which currently may not avail themselves of such an exemption, will be able henceforth to do so. They might, therefore, be permitted to make copies (including digital images) of objects in their collections for conservation or archival purposes. It is also likely that museums and galleries would be able to make one-off copies for research purposes rather as libraries are permitted to do now.

However, the proposed provision is extremely narrowly drawn. Such an institution could not, for example, make copies of works in its collections or archives in connection with any fund-raising or sponsorship activity because this would be for direct or indirect economic or commercial advantage.

It is left unclear whether the mere fact that an act produces no income for the institution concerned means that it would be allowed by the exception. This is most unsatisfactory for museums and galleries which may derive income but little profit from a reproduction. Indeed, even if the museum or gallery derives no income at all it may still be deemed to be deriving an indirect economic or commercial advantage. The three step test requires that the 'normal exploitation' of a work must not be prejudiced. If the rightsholder (e.g. the artist or his or her estate) normally charges a licence fee for reproduction of his or her work then a museum, for example, could on the face of it never make use of the specific exemption because otherwise it would be saving on the fee normally paid to the rightsholder. Therefore any act of reproduction which produces no profit for a museum but may be carried out in fulfilment of the institution's primary objectives of educating and informing

---

43   Commentary on Article 5, section 1.
44   Copyright, Designs and Patents Act 1988 (inclusive), sections 37–44, these apply in the main to 'prescribed libraries' (defined in statutory instruments made under the Act) which include a number of libraries administered by or belonging to museums and galleries.

the public about its collections would not benefit from the exemption. The existing UK library exemptions would also appear to be swept away.

Finally, and most importantly in the present context, it must be noted that this exception does not cover any communication to the public via on-line networks. It is possible that other exceptions might apply (see below), but an establishment accessible to the public, including a museum or gallery, would not, under the current proposal, be able to transmit copyright works in its collection via the Internet without having to pay a fee to the rightsholder. This effectively condemns museums and galleries to paying copyright royalties regardless of whether the works are being transmitted for non-profit purposes or not. As the Memorandum of Understanding on Multimedia Access to Europe's Cultural Heritage,[45] which was signed by, *inter alia*, 297 museums and galleries and 47 governmental organizations, states: museums and galleries are 'centres for the documentation, dissemination and promotion of culture. A direct involvement of museums is therefore needed in order to confer a visible cultural dimension to the information society.' The Memorandum of Understanding went further and stated: 'We, the signatories to this MoU, are committed to working towards the widest possible access to the resources of Museums and Galleries through multimedia communications systems by 2000.'

These sentiments are not reflected in the proposed Directive and the museums sector in the UK is lobbying hard to rectify this. The Conference of Directors of National Museums and Galleries, a UK organization representing those institutions that are in receipt of direct government funding, has responded to the proposed Directive, seeking to point out that the ability of museums and galleries to fulfil their mission within the Information Society will be compromised if the proposed Directive were to be implemented in its current form. The submission has won the support of similar bodies in Ireland.

6. Exceptions to the Right of Reproduction and the Communication to the Public Right

Five exceptions apply both to the right of reproduction and to the communication to the public right (Article 5(3) of the draft). These too are optional (i.e. member states are not obliged to implement these exceptions into national law). Two are of relevance to the exploitation by museums and galleries of digital images.

(i)   Illustration for Teaching or Scientific Research

Use of a work for the sole (non-commercial) purpose of illustration for teaching or scientific research would be permitted. Unlike the current position

---

[45]   Published March 1998.

under UK law[46] this would not operate as a general 'private study and research' exemption (subject to fair dealing). A further oddity arises from the term 'scientific', which has a narrower meaning in English than (say) French. Commercial research would not be permitted. The proposed exemption allowing works to be used for the purpose of illustration for teaching might however allow some educational-type uses by non-teaching establishments such as, for example, the copying and possibly even transmission via closed educational networks of material held in museum or gallery collections. This would go further than current UK educational exemptions, which apply only to acts done by teachers or pupils, or on behalf of 'educational establishments'. It might also apply to the kinds of educational use of works pioneered in such schemes as SCRAN and, in the US, MESL.[47]

(ii) Criticism and Review

Quotations from a work for the purposes of criticism or review would be permitted, provided that it related to a work or other subject matter which has already been lawfully made available to the public, the source is indicated and its making is in accordance with fair practice and to the extent required by the specific purpose. This is akin to the similar provisions under UK law. However, some differences should be noted:

- Article 5 requires the work to have been lawfully made public whereas some English cases[48] suggest that the exception might cover unpublished works, although the reproduction was most unlikely to be fair in such circumstances;
- the requirement under UK law for a sufficient acknowledgment will change to an 'indication of source', which is perhaps less onerous.[49]

There is nothing in the proposed Directive to suggest that the application of the current UK 'fair dealing' provisions would be widened. Indeed, it would appear that the exception may be narrower.

D. *Technical Measures Designed to Protect Copyright*

Article 6 of the proposed Directive requires member states to provide adequate legal protection against any activities which are carried out in the knowledge or with the reasonable belief that they will enable or facilitate the circumvention of technical measures designed to protect copyright. UK law currently gives remedies to a copyright owner against a person who 'makes, imports, sells, or lets for hire, offers or exposes for sale or hire...any device or

---

[46] Copyright, Designs and Patents Act 1988, section 29.
[47] Ibid.
[48] *Hubbard v. Vosper* [1972] 1 All ER 1023 and *Beloff v. Pressdram* [1973] 1 All ER 241.
[49] See *Sillitoe v. McGraw Hill Book Company (UK) Ltd* [1983] FSR 545: an acknowledgment must recognize the 'position and claims' of the author as well as stating the author and title.

means specifically designed or adapted to circumvent' systems of copy protection employed in relation to copies of works in electronic form.[50] The provision in the proposed Directive would be of much wider application. It would apply not to 'devices' but to prohibit acts which get round encryption techniques and the like which protect digital material.

A possible concern here is that this provision is not sufficiently clear in stating that an act which would not otherwise infringe copyright, for example because it is carried out for the purpose of illustration for teaching or scientific research, will also escape sanction under the technical copy protection provisions.

However, the provision is a step in the right direction in addressing the concerns of museums and galleries arising from the difficulties of controlling the use of their digitized images on the Internet. The circumvention of any encryption measures and the like which they employ to prevent the unauthorized retrieval of images held on their databases would become actionable in itself.

E. *Protection of Rights Management Information*

Article 7 of the proposed Directive requires member states to provide adequate legal protection against any activities which remove or alter rights management information, i.e. unique file tagging techniques and the like which allow material in electronic form to be traced and thus the rights in such material to be managed. Distributing copies of works from which such information has been removed would also be prohibited. These techniques are viewed as essential in the digital domain, where multiple perfect copies can be made and retransmitted with ease, in such a way that their source becomes difficult to trace. This provision would therefore have important implications for the many rights management initiatives which are being piloted and which are designed, for example, to tag electronic files consisting of digital images with information about the rightsholder, such as the MENHIR and IMPRIMATUR projects mentioned earlier.

IV. Conclusion

The UK currently enjoys a particular balance between the rights of copyright owners and the interests of users of copyright material which reflects a particular culture and tradition. The proposed Directive will clearly have an impact on this balance. Many acts currently permitted under UK law would apparently not be permitted under the proposed Directive in its current form. At the same time, some lacunae in UK law such as the absence of any provisions allowing museums and galleries to do certain things in pursuance of

---

[50]   Copyright, Designs and Patents Act 1988, section 296.

their statutory or charitable objectives, may not be addressed or, if they are, not adequately.

The balance currently contemplated in the proposed Directive appears to favour protection with the result that, if it were adopted in its current form, the freedom to use copyright works, albeit in situations deemed acceptable on public interest grounds, would be reduced in scope.

In the circumstances it is unsurprising that the proposed Directive is being hotly debated. Following scrutiny by the European Parliament in late 1998, it will be revised to take into account the many submissions made and the position adopted by the Parliament. The final text of the Directive may not be agreed until late 1999 or even 2000, whereupon it will have to be implemented by member states of the European Union. Museums and galleries therefore still have an opportunity over the next year or two to influence the debate.

Interactive Access and Images – Can Copyright Adapt?

John Rubinstein
Manches & Co., Solicitors, London, England

I. Introduction

As with the introduction to a film dealing with the Carboniferous Age, the mental camera performs a cursory pan over the steaming jungle and swampy marsh in which consumers are having to pick their lumbering way; and with particular emphasis on the landscape, well enough charted, but inadequately drained and cleared, a survey of visual rights and copyrights in the twenty-first century presents a spectre of lagoons in which ferocious reptiles await the unwary landlubber, and the occasional thickets are full of spiky and poisonous fruits which consumers would do well to avoid. The advent of digital technology and its challenge to conventional analogue data and information storage media has given the international legal community its most exciting challenge of the twentieth century.

Digital storage of databases and archival material has enabled owners of such material to offer international point of access to PC users worldwide for the expenditure of a few keystrokes and in some cases service provider subscription fees. Interactive programming has also enabled an unprecedented combination of different media for the presentation of information and ideas; rapid combinations of visual and auditory material which can be adapted and mutated to the needs of the individual accessor of the stored material. Compression technologies enable vast amounts of digitized information to be squirted by radio signal to satellites for simultaneous onward transmission transitionally to decoders many thousands of miles apart. Electricity grids are being pressed into service to carry rivers of information in comparison to which the use of conventional telephone cabling represents a mere trickle. Domestic electric cabling is being considered for extra bandwidth to enable additional telecommunication signals to be received and to provide television viewers with an ever increasing number of channels; whilst also providing for a far greater capacity for the individual to interact with information providers. Enter copyright, a 500-year-old dinosaur, standing on the verge of the twenty-first century.

Copyright, a system which developed in the wake of printing, both of the written word and of images, and which has developed organically since the Guttenberg press first thumped out a press copy, is now straining the seams of a jurisprudence which is presently too inflexible to meet practically the demands of the digital- and Internet-served community.

The jurisprudence assumed the existence of the need for and creation of physical copies of the means of expressing information; it had traditionally two limitations which threaten to prove fatal: copyright has never protected ideas, as opposed to their means of expression, and for copyright to have effect, it requires a physically ascertainable medium upon which the expression of an idea is recorded.

Territoriality has also been challenged by the digital revolution; the ability to transmit stored data in a variety of adaptable formats at speed to all parts of the globe has resulted in the redundancy of traditional territorial markets, dictated by linguistic as well as politico-national considerations. Anti-competitive trading blocks and the insistence on the free availability of competing goods and services has also undermined the concept of territoriality.

The speed of development and adaptation of pre-existing intellectual property, especially that which would traditionally have been protected by copyright, is also putting pressure on the temporal affectations of international copyright law; how long should a work need to be protected, when it is, by its nature, more and more a transient stage in a stream of intellectual development?

Everyone who originates a work wants his or her slice of the action; now there may be multiple contributors to a single work, and the sheer number of competing interests in the work risks making the work unmarketable and/or uneconomic. This is because copyright is by its nature a negative right; it confers upon the rightsholder the right to forbid copying of what the rightsholder has produced. As a corollary of its jurisprudential base, each owner of a copyright in a work which consists of more than one copyright, has the ability to refuse to agree to the copying of that work; and without the consent of each of the interested parties, none of the others can lawfully agree to the copying of that work.

Copyright has given rise to a thriving clearances industry; a large and cumbersome structure spread across many jurisdictions in which each representative fights its own corner having heed to its domestic laws, harmonization of which is progressing at far too slow a pace for the rapid advances of the technological community. Joe Public can do things with his keyboard which are already leaving many traditionally trained communications experts in his wake.

As is the case with many businesses, this sector of human endeavour suffers from the conundrum that creation and development outstrips the marketing of them, which in turn, outstrips the collection of payments for the labours which have been expended on the technologies being used to convey information and data around the world.

Perhaps of most importance to the legal community, the colourful variety and individuality of national legal systems, and the courts which maintain them, provide inconsistent and uncertain fora in which to address the problems and competing interests which the technological revolution has generated. The Virtual Reality Court is still a dream; a court, in which all those exploiting the digital revolution and the randomly regulated Internet would encounter a level playing field of uniform international trading practices and a universal set of standards against which to parade and test problems affecting twenty-first century intercourse – a New York court had to adjudicate on a claim that a service provider was responsible for one of its employees infecting a user of the service with AIDS after a whirlwind cyber-romance blossomed into physical reality.[1]

As director of this scenario, I am now parachuting into the landscape, artists, authors, photographers, musicians, models, muses, agents, database accumulators and creators, collection societies, publishers, merchandisers, scientists, collectors, programmers, service providers, telecommunications companies, broadcasters, charities and patrons of the arts and humanities, museum curators, civil servants, ministers of state, the public, and, last but not least, lawyers – in brief all those who have complementary or competing interests in open or closed accessibility and expression of information, data and ideas.

II. Imagining Accessibility Virtually Speaking

A great deal of the topic to be addressed requires a massive leap of the imagination. Few amongst us have the necessary technical education to have more than an inkling of the processes and causes of how a chip the size of a pinky fingernail can interact with electricity, aluminium and tapping on a keyboard, or the feeding of images on a scanner can store and recall more information on a 3.5 inch floppy disk, than could a roomful of tape spools operating on a 100 spoolwhirring 7-foot high cabinets some 30 years ago.

Lawyers have traditionally been empirical and conservative; this is a handicap when having to confront new technologies. And this trait has been nowhere better demonstrated than in the field of protecting the exploitation of ideas, data and information; instead of creating from scratch a new series of rules to meet new technologies, lawyers have stretched, with increasing lack of success, existing doctrines of law to try to match the technological realities. The response has been heavy-handed; the prophylactic measures some software

---

[1] *Barbara Haybeck v. Prodigy Services Co. and Ors*, US DC (SDNY) 95 Civ 9612, (ackn. David Jacoby – Phillips Nizer Benjamin Krim & Ballon).

manufacturers have adopted when distributing shareware or freeware over the Internet provide interesting reading for the masochist. Some such programs are preceded by reams and reams of legal clauses which I suspect only lawyers ever bother to read.

Those who have produced the freeware and shareware assume that every person who accesses the program in question has a perfect understanding of English – this excludes a majority of those Internet using inhabitants of the planet whose first language is not English. If the terms of exploitation of software are not understood before downloading, or clicking into, the program it is hard to see how the terms for exploitation set out in English will be regarded as binding on the downloader, in a court in which the first language is a language other than English!

The jurisprudential basis for many of the terms is often unclear and confused. A particular favourite of those who programme such terms is the blanket exclusion of liability and warranty clause which is unlikely to be upheld if push comes to shove and the plaintiff is a consumer suing an English corporate defendant in an Ohio court. Of course the practical result might be different if the corporation is an Ohio corporation and the complainant is out of state – Compuserve Limited, based in Columbus Ohio, sought to abort claims of trademark infringement by Patterson, by asserting that the Ohio courts had jurisdiction over Patterson to entertain a declaration of non-infringement of Patterson's trademarks, even though Patterson (a resident of Texas) had never been to Ohio, and all the dealings between him and Compuserve had been conducted over the Internet.[2]

III. International Treaties and Copyright in the UK

There has been a great deal of comment about the passage of the Agreement on Trade Related Aspects of Intellectual Property Rights (TRIPs) (pursuant to the Uruguay Round of GATT) and the WIPO Copyright Treaty. Insofar as the UK is concerned, the passage of these Treaties is unlikely to have a significant impact, as most of the measures prescribed in them are already provided for by the Copyright Designs and Patents Act 1988 (CDPA) as amended, particularly by the Copyright Term Directive, which came into force on 1 January 1996, and which extended the posthumous term of copyright in literary, artistic, dramatic and musical works to 70 years, and the Copyright and Related Rights Regulations 1996 (SI 1996 No 2967) which has introduced as from 1 December 1996, an extended 'distribution' right, a 'rental

---

[2]   *Compuserve Ltd v. Patterson*, 89 F3d 1257 (CA 6th Cir.) USA. See also *The Hearst Corporation v. Ari Goldberger*, US DC (SDNY) 96 Civ 3620 (26 February 1997); *Blake Hall v. Brad Laronde*, 56 Cal. App. 4th 1342 (7 August 1997).

and lending right', and a brand new 'publication right'. I return to the last of those later in this chapter.

In fact TRIPs has generated confusion rather than clarity in the UK as illustrated by *Azrak-Hamway International Inc's Licence of Right Application* [1997] RPC 134. This was a copyright case involving an application to the Comptroller of the Patents Office to settle licences of rights in design drawings belonging to Meccano SA, the well-known construction toy manufacturer. Meccano SA did not wish to grant licences of right to the applicant, and argued that the TRIPs Treaty was directly applicable in the UK, with the result that the licence of right provisions in the CDPA 1988 were null and void, because they contravened the TRIPs Treaty.

It emerged during the case that the Treaty had been signed both by the member states of the EU, and by the Commission of the European Community. Further argument resulted in the Comptroller deciding that the European Commission only had authority from member states to sign those parts of TRIPs on behalf of member states in respect of which harmonization directives had been agreed between the member states and implemented by the European Commission; in the absence of any statutory enactment by Parliament in the UK TRIPs could not be considered in the courts in the UK. Also, even though the European Communities Act 1972 had imported EC law into the laws of the constituent parts of the UK, it only extended to measures which had been expressly acceded to by the member states of the European Community.

IV. Some Matters Affecting Digital Exploitation of Visual Material – Legal Snakes and Ladders from an English Perspective

A. *The Database Right*

1. Copyright and Rights in Databases Regulations 1997: SI 1997 No 3032

Of more importance, however, has been the question of the protection of databases, an issue specifically ducked by the participants at the Diplomatic Conference which took place in December 1996.

The European Community on 11 March 1996 adopted the Database Directive 96/9/EC (OJ, L77, 27 March 1996, pp. 20–28) and pursuant to that adoption, member states are required to introduce substantive legislation to harmonize copyright treatment for databases and to implement a new, *sui generis*, right to protect databases. This was embodied into English law on 1 January 1998. This has had the bizarre result, in the UK, of actually reducing the pre-existing protection afforded to databases by the CDPA 1988, which by section 3(1)(a) specifically protected tables and compilations; the content threshold of the tables or compilations was minimal.[3]

The new regulations add the term 'database' as a new section 3(1)(d) of the CDPA 1988. 'Database' is defined by a new section 3A(1) as: '... a collection of independent works, data or other material which – (a) are arranged in a systematic or methodical way, and (b) are individually accessible by electronic or other means.' New section 3A(2) adds: 'For the purposes of this Part, a literary work consisting of a database is original if, and only if, by reason of the selection or arrangement of the contents of the database the database constitutes the author's own intellectual creation.' If the database does not pass muster under section 3A(2) of the CDPA 1988, it will not attract copyright, but it will be protected by the new *sui generis* right. The regulations are not retroactive, but for databases which are merely 'sweat of the brow' assemblages, with no inherent creativity of the author, as distinct from assembly and listing in conventional manner, and which are created after the implementation of the regulations, they will only qualify for the *sui generis* right.

Regulation 13(1) states: 'A property right ("database right") subsists...in a database if there has been a substantial investment in obtaining, verifying or presenting the contents of a database.' Regulation 13(2) states: 'For the purposes of Paragraph (13)(1) it is immaterial whether or not the database or any of its contents are copyright works, within the meaning of Part 1 of the 1988 Act.'

The *sui generis* right is stated to have a duration of 15 years from the end of the year in which the making of the database is completed; interestingly, the provisions of regulation 17(2) state that if the database is published before the end of 15 years from the end of the year in which the database was completed, the database will be protected for a further 15 years from the end of the year when the database was first made available to the public. This differed from the consultation paper circulated with the draft regulations, which stated at paragraph 4.12: 'The Sui Generis right will last for 15 years from the end of the year in which the database is made *or* published' (emphasis supplied).

However, there is no mistake about the additional provision in regulation 17(3) which states that where a database is updated through substantial investment the period of protection starts anew after completion of updating of the database; as other commentators have remarked already, the result of the EC Database Directive is that databases which are updated will attract an indefinite protection under the new Database Right, which may prove longer than existing copyright protection of the life of author and 70 years!

The database right has been shoehorned into the CDPA 1988 and adds little to the existing UK laws; it will however impact much more positively, for example, in France, which has no protection for databases *per se* other than that

---

[3]   See *Ladbroke (Football) Ltd v. William Hill (Football) Ltd*, 1964 1 All ER 465 (HL); *Waterlow v. Rose* (1989) *The Independent*, 10 November (CA).

provided for in the new Directive. The advent of digitized media of storage and communication has prompted the creation of this unique right for various countries in the EU and the harmonization of EC law in this field will assist substantively the creators of databases in protecting their labours across the EU; the situation whereby, for example, a database created by an English 'maker' could be lifted with impunity in certain member states, whilst a 'maker' of a database in one of those states could bring an action for infringement of copyright in his database in England where the infringer has copied the database or a substantial part of it in England, will be consigned to history.[4] Uniform protection of databases should encourage freer use of databases in the EU as a result.

The database right enacted in the UK is subject to a fair dealing exception for use of a substantial part for teaching or research for non-commercial purposes. It will not be an infringement of the database right to extract or re-utilize an insubstantial part of the database without the consent of the owner of the database right. Infringement by unauthorized extraction or reutilization of a 'substantial' part of the contents of a database poses the question of what is to be understood as a 'substantial' part.

Databases which consist of visual works stored on CD-ROM also attract the database right, and will probably attract copyright protection in the UK. Those rights will be independent of any copyright or publication right which may exist in any visual work included in the database.

B. *The Publication Right*

This discussion is limited to the exploitation of works of art (including photographs), works of artistic craftsmanship, and sculpture (collectively 'artworks').

Regulation 16 of the Copyright and Related Rights Regulations 1996 has introduced a new right into UK laws. This accords a 25-year term of protection by way of a property right equivalent to copyright to 'A person who after the expiry of copyright protection, publishes for the first time a previously unpublished work...a...."Publication right"....'. The publication right necessarily requires a different meaning for the concept of publication to that which applies under the CDPA 1988, as regulation 16(2) cites acts additional to the issue of copies to the public, in respect of artworks, in particular, 'the [authorised] exhibition or showing of the work in public'. It is seminal to note that an unauthorized 'publication' is an act which is done without the consent of the owner of the physical medium in which the artwork is embodied or on which it is recorded. First publication has to take

---

[4]   The maker of the database has to be a community national, resident, company or firm, in order to avail itself of the *sui generis* right.

place in the European Economic Area and has to be published by a publisher who at the time of the first publication is a national of an EEA state.

The significance of this in museological terms is potentially startling; no doubt curators have been dispatched to the subterranean vaults of their institutions to discover which of the old master paintings, drawings and other artwork has been hidden away for years is unpublished and in the public domain. Those works will be dusted down and photographed for digital recording on CD-ROMs, and will provide a handsome source of revenue for the publisher who has the privilege of first access to those works. Others who may be interested in the potential windfall will be owners of photographic archives and unpublished illustrated diaries and manuscripts.

The regulation is a masterpiece of inelegant drafting; the definition of 'publication' is thoroughly ambiguous when considered in the context of regulation 16(1) which provides 'A person who after the expiry of copyright protection, publishes for the first time a previously unpublished work has a property right ("publication right")...'. Regulation 16(2) provides 'For this purpose publication includes any communication to the public, in particular – (a)...(d) the...exhibition or showing of the work in public;...'. Which purpose?

Regulation 16(4) states: 'A work qualifies for publication right protection only if – (a) first publication is in the European Economic Area, and (b) the publisher of the work is at the time of first publication a national of an EEA state.' Does the word 'publication' in the regulation 16(2) refer to the word 'publication' included in the parentheses and quotation marks in regulation 16(1)? Or does it apply to regulation 16(4) – which prescribes the geographic location and the nationality of the publisher – (and regulation 16(5) which deals with expired Crown and parliamentary copyrights)? If this option is the case, every museum and gallery which had hanging on its public gallery walls at midnight on 1 December 1996 a collection of previously unpublished artworks which had passed into the public domain, suddenly had vested in it a publication right in these artworks; since common law copyright was abolished as long ago as 1911 (and there was no saving for an indefinite period of copyright prior to publication for paintings in the 1911 Copyright Act), a substantial number of paintings could be affected by this provision. Or does it define the acts by which a work is to be considered 'published' for the purpose of considering whether a work which is out of copyright is still an 'unpublished' work – for example, a painting which was painted in the seventeenth century, and of which no authorized copies in any medium have previously been made, is an unpublished work as provided for by section 175 of the CDPA 1988; that section does not include the exhibiting of a work in public as an act of publication (section 175(4)(b)), whereas it could be construed that if the work has been exhibited, the act prescribed in regulation 16(2) has occurred and the work is therefore a published work in respect of which a publication right will not arise upon copying.

Further complications are caused by the fact that (for example) anonymous works of art which are exhibited, but unpublished by virtue of section

175(4)(b) of the CDPA 1988, are still protected by copyright at least until 31 December 2039 (see the transitional provisions: CDPA 1988, Schedule 1, section 12(3)(b)).

The requirement of determining whether a work is unpublished in accordance with the provisions of the Copyright Act 1911, the Copyright Act 1956 and the CDPA 1988 is going to impose a monumental legal audit task to establish the situation of each artwork; and the position is further complicated by different rules applying to engravings, and photographs under the particular statutes. Reference will also have to be made to the qualification of the author of the artwork by reason of his or her nationality and the existence of Orders in Council or treaties to establish whether the author's works qualified for copyright protection in the UK. Nevertheless, what is clear is that the intention of the publication right is to put certain artworks back into copyright for a period of 25 years. Was the intention of this section to benefit museums and art galleries to help defray the cost of creating digital databases of their artworks? In the case of those who create the databases for the museums and art galleries and publish those works of art which are in the public domain, they will achieve a windfall by cashing in on the publication right at the expense of cultural heritage, in relation to which it could be argued that the public should not have to pay to obtain copies.

Museums which have studiously refused to permit copying of works in their galleries, and who have not themselves copied such works of art for merchandising purposes (e.g. posters, postcards, jigsaw puzzles etc.), will benefit; but it would be interesting to learn what deal was struck by the National Gallery in London with CORBIS for the digital archiving of the National Gallery's works of art. In whom is vested the publication right for previously uncopied artworks which are out of copyright in the National Gallery? The public has a right to know.

Is it right, especially in the digital age, that artworks which have passed into the public domain should again be subject to restraints on copying? Many jurists have expressed the view that the period of copyright is long enough. And what of the heirs of the authors of such artworks – should not they be allowed to participate in the windfall?

A recent example is worth mentioning here. A London gallery held an exhibition of seventeenth-century paintings it owned and in respect of which an illustrated catalogue of photographs of previously unpublished (in the sense of section 175 of the CDPA 1988) paintings was produced for members of the public attending the gallery exhibition. X, who obtained a copy of the catalogue, sent the catalogue to China and commissioned artists in China to copy in oils some of the illustrated works from the photographs published in the catalogue. The copies of the old masters were then imported into the UK and offered for sale by a gallery in a market town – infringement of the publication right? The market town gallery owner's response: 'what rights – get lost!' The cause of action is there according to the regulations; but it takes a brave litigant to be the first in the field given the lack of precision in the drafting of the regulations.

C. *The Reproduction Communication and Distribution Rights*

Yet another European Communities directive is here – for the harmonization of certain aspects of copyright and related rights in the information society.[5]

This Directive directly recognizes the limitations of copyright in the information society and proposes the harmonized regulation of copyright in the electronic age by the imposition of three newly described rights, the third of which is the most telling. Paragraph 16 of the proposal states:

'...[the Directive] should provide all rightsholders recognized by the Directive with an exclusive right to make available to the public copyright works or any other subject matter by way of interactive on-demand transmissions; whereas such interactive on-demand transmissions are characterized by the fact that members of the public may access them from a place and at a time individually chosen by them; whereas this right does not cover private communications.'

This looks like the access right by the back door!

Paragraph 21 of the proposal emphasizes the problems which copyright and related rightsholders face:

'Whereas a fine balance of rights and interests between the different categories of rightholders, as well as the different categories of rightholders and users of protected subject matter must be safeguarded;....'

A clear recognition of the difficulties posed by multimedia product.

'...whereas the existing exceptions to the rights as set out by the Member States have to be reassessed in the light of the new electronic environment; whereas existing differences in the limitations and exceptions to certain restricted acts have direct negative effects on the functioning of the Internal Market of copyright and related rights....'

For example, the fair dealing exception; the different treatment of moral rights in different jurisdictions; the existence of certain subsidiary rights in certain jurisdictions but not in others.

'...whereas such differences could well become more pronounced in view of the further development of transborder exploitation of works and cross-border activities...'.

A recognition of the effects of televisual and Internet communication and telemarketing of services containing or consisting of copyright material.

The proposal provides an end date of 30 June 2000 for implementation of the proposed Directive. This is going to get in the way of the Millenium celebrations.

---

[5]   (98/C 108/03); COM (97) 628 final, 97/0359; submitted by the Commission on 21 January 1998, published in the OJ on 7 April 1998.

The reproduction right is intended to be 'an exclusive right to authorise or prohibit direct or indirect, temporary or permanent reproduction by any means and in any form, in whole or in part of' original or copy works, fixations of performances, phonograms, first fixations of films, and fixations of broadcasts.

The communication right is provided to authors etc. to authorize or prohibit any communication to the public of their works whether by wire or by wireless means, including through an individual or interactive access site.

The distribution right is intended to confer on authors in respect of the original or copies of their works, the exclusive right to any form of distribution to the public by sale or otherwise.

Recognizing the difficulty of enforcing such rights in cyberspace, the Directive also provides for optional enshrining of exceptions to the reproduction and communication, but not the distribution rights, the most pertinent of which is acts carried on in relation to the above rights 'made by a natural person for private use and for non-commercial ends'. Watch this space!

D. *Moral Rights*

This issue is discussed in the context of artworks. For so long as the US refuses to implement Article 6*bis* of the Berne Convention as amended, digitization of images in interactive CD-ROMs, or transmitted electronically on-line will cause serious difficulties for owners of moral rights, copyright owners (if different from the owners of the moral rights) and publishers of these interactive products.

In the event the copyright owner grants in the US a licence to a licensee which permits the licensee to adapt or amend a visual image in which the author is elsewhere entitled to moral rights, the dispatch of interactive CD-ROMs or on-line electronic transmission of the adaptable image may provoke a claim of infringement of moral rights by the author of the original image.

Moral rights of paternity and integrity are provided for under Chapter IV of the CDPA 1988, whilst the right of paternity has to be asserted by the author – the author has the right to have his or her name accompany their artwork. But if the right of paternity is not asserted, the omission of the author's name does not give rise to liability (section 77 of the CDPA 1988).

In contrast, the right of integrity does not need to be asserted. A derogatory treatment of the artwork (whether by adaptation, addition, deletion or other alteration which distorts or mutilates the work or is otherwise prejudicial to the honour or reputation of the author) is actionable at the behest of authors or their heirs (section 80 of the CDPA 1988).[6]

Use of original artworks created still in copyright should be made only on the basis that the author's moral rights have been waived, or if the author

---

[6]   But note that these moral rights do not accrue in relation to computer programs or computer-generated works.

consents to the use to be made. This can get very complex and expensive, where the heirs of the author, or even of joint authors, have to be consulted to waive the rights, or to consent to the intended treatment.

One further moral right – the right to privacy in photographs commissioned by a person for private and domestic purposes – is also apposite (section 85 of the CDPA 1988). Unlike the laws of say, New York, or France, the law of England contains no specific privacy law. There are however, provisions which give limited privacy entitlements of which section 85 of the CDPA 1988 is one. This provision applies in respect of photographs commissioned after 1 August 1989; just because the photographer owns the copyright, and gives permission for it to be used, that does not obviate the need to get the permission of the commissioner before exploiting the photograph in any manner. This is a particular difficulty for museums, photographic archives and agencies, who may acquire libraries from photographers on their retirement, or take licences of photographic stocks from them, and unbeknownst to the museum, archive or agent, privately commissioned photographs are contained in the stock. Unauthorized use of a photograph protected by the moral right conferred by section 85 of the 1988 Act is treated as a breach of statutory duty, and damages may be exacted or an injunction granted.

An additional difficulty exists in determining when a photograph was actually taken; if taken before 1 August 1989, the first copyright owner of a photograph which was commissioned from a photographer (and paid for), is the commissioner. The same principle applies in the case of a commissioner of a portrait painting or drawing (Copyright Act 1956, section 4(3)). Unauthorized use of such a photograph or portrait is a straightforward infringement of copyright. Extreme care should also be exercised when acquiring a photographic archive from a newspaper publisher.

A different set of rules applied before 1 January 1957 when the Copyright Act 1956 came into force and the Copyright Act 1911 was repealed. That being said, the application of moral rights and privacy law in the UK is relatively relaxed compared to France, which has as a general principle the provisions of Article 9 of the Civil Code which grants every person a generic right of privacy.

E. *Rights of Personality*

Nowhere is the lack of international harmonization of jurisdictional legal systems more cogently demonstrated than in the rights of personality. Having just dwelt briefly on the existence of a generalized right of privacy in France, amongst many other jurisdictions, the creator, and publisher of interactive software may find that material supplied by museums or archives and which are used by them in good faith result in claims being made against them when the work they have created is accessed or marketed in jurisdictions which recognize rights of privacy.

The right of personality extends the right of a person not to have his or her image exploited against their will. In England, the right is limited in two ways;

given the lack of a generalized law of privacy, those who can prevent exploitation of their images are limited to three categories of individuals:

(1)   those who earn monies through endorsement as part of or ancillary to their professional career;
(2)   those who are actionably defamed by the use of their image in a specific context; and
(3)   persons who are protected by statute or court order from having their images reproduced, e.g. children involved in court proceedings, or children under the age of 16 the images of which would be considered by a jury to be indecent.[7]

Again the law in England is considerably more relaxed than in many other jurisdictions, but the lack of harmonization and the sheer expense of obtaining legal clearance in all the jurisdictions into which a digital product may be transmitted through on-line accessing has substantially increased the risk of complaint by any person who considers himself or herself traduced by the unauthorized appearance of that person's image in a product.

F.   *A Strategic Hint*

Lack of harmonization of laws poses a serious problem for exploiters of copyrightable material in digital or electronic media of dissemination or storage systems. In many civil law jurisdictions (such as Germany and Belgium) those who assign their *droits d'auteur* (not exactly parallel with common law jurisdictions' copyright entitlements) the rightsholders who assign or grant their rights are protected by law from assigning rights in media which do not yet exist at the time the assignment or grant is effected.

Some jurisdictions in the US have followed suit – not least in the case in which Mrs. Roger Moore who provided the voice-over for Lady in the Walt Disney film of 'Lady and the Tramp', successfully sued to recover compensation when the film was reproduced on video; a medium which was not in contemplation when she originally assigned all her rights in her voice-over several decades previously. This problem threatens to become more widespread with the advent of digitization and compression technologies, thus opening up the possibility of exploiting new media.

In England it is permitted for authors to assign at law all their copyright and rights in the nature of copyright for the full term of copyright throughout the world in all media of expression or reproduction now or hereafter extant. If the law of the contract is stated to be the law of England, and the jurisdiction agreed contractually is that of the English courts, such a provision will be upheld. I have stopped short of suggesting that the territory should be 'the universe', as I imagine that even the English courts might baulk at such a

---

7   Protection of Children Act 1978; *R v. Land* (1997) *The Independent*, 16 October (CA).

provision; it smacks of a contract of adhesion. However, since man has travelled to the moon, perhaps 'the Solar System' might be effective.

Within the EU, it overcomes the difficulties I have highlighted above owing to terms of the Brussels Convention of 1968 dealing with reciprocal enforcement of judgments of member states in the EU.

Accordingly the smoother exploitation of artwork in new media can be anticipated in the future by providing for assignments of those rights under English law and justiciability of the agreements in the English courts.

V. Some Recent Developments on Specific Issues in the UK

Much has been written in a plethora of academic journals about recent cases that is suffices to name the cases and to give a very short summary. It may be of more interest to hear about matters which cannot yet be named, but which are in the course of being litigated or addressed, and these shall be addressed after the named cases.

A. *Creation Records Ltd and Ors v. News Group Newspapers Ltd [1997] EMLR 444 (ChD, Lloyd J)*

This concerned the pop group Oasis, which used a country club swimming pool and its immediate surrounds to set up various artefacts to produce a photograph for the cover of an album which they were to release. The scenario included emptying the swimming pool, erecting scaffolding in the pool, lowering a Rolls Royce onto the scaffolding, and then refilling the pool, so as to show the car emerging from the water. Noel Gallagher, who was apparently in charge of the artwork for the shoot, arranged for various other props to be dotted around the pool and he and his fellow band members then posed amongst the objects whilst photographs were taken.

Whilst the scenario was being constructed, no attempt was made to keep the public out, but when it came to taking photographs by the group's photographer, security guards patrolled the perimeter which was cordoned off. Meanwhile a freelance photographer had been commissioned by *The Sun*, which had learned of the proposed shoot, to see what he could get by attending the shoot. When the official photography began, he (in the view of the judge) surreptitiously took photographs of the complete set from more or less the same angle as that from which the official photographs were taken.

When *The Sun* published a photograph of the scenario coupled with an offer to the public to send in for a poster of the scenario including Oasis, the plaintiff applied to the court for an injunction alleging infringement of copyright and breach of confidence.

The judge ruled that the copyright claim was untenable because:

(a) the objects were static and there was no 'plot', the collocation of objects could not be said to be a dramatic work;

(b) the work was not an artistic work of sculpture or collage as nothing had in fact been sculpted, nor had anything been stuck together;

(c) the work was not a work of artistic craftsmanship as nothing had actually been produced in the nature of items usually associated with artistic craftsmanship.

The judge specifically rejected the plaintiffs' argument that the CDPA 1988 should be construed in such a way as to exclude novel forms of art and the creativity and originality which had been exercised.

Of significant interest however, was the judge's observation that the collocation of the objects was ephemeral and done so to produce a number of photographs; and as soon as that had been done the collocation was disassembled and dispersed. The collocation only remained in place for a few hours.

Of even more interest was the judge's ruling that the plaintiffs had a good arguable case of a breach of confidence on the grounds that the public knew that it was not supposed to take photographs of the scene during the official shoot. On that basis the judge granted the plaintiffs an injunction to restrain *The Sun* from issuing its posters even though it had already published the photograph in its newspaper. This is a novel departure since the area was open to the public. The previous high water mark had been the case of *Shelley Films Ltd v. Rex Features Ltd* [1994] EMLR 134 (in which the photographs had been taken in a closed set inside studios which were locked during the filming and there were specific signs forbidding photography and security guards). Watch this space!

In an interlocutory application for an interdict the operator of a web site providing news services had copied the headlines of stories from a competitor newspaper's web site. If the accessor clicked onto the competitor's headline, a hypertext link routed the accessor directly into the story underlying the headline on the competitor's site and by-passed the competitor newspaper's web site front page and the advertising which it carried on that page. The newspaper complained that the news service was infringing its copyright in the operation of a cable programme under section 7 of the CDPA 1988, by including the newspaper's headlines in breach of section 20 of the CDPA 1988. The newspaper offered readers a chance to send in letters to its web site, so the news service argued that the newspaper was operating an interactive site, which would be excepted from the definition of a cable programme covered by section 7(1) of the CDPA. Whilst there had been no detailed technological explanation as to how the system worked, in presentation of the parties' arguments, the judge granted the interim interdict ruling:

(a) that while an accessor to the newspaper's web site had to access the site, he was satisfied that following the access to the news service's site, the hypertext link actually resulted in the accessor accessing the newspaper's web site from which information was transmitted to the accessor;

(b) he was also satisfied that the mere provision of a facility to return messages in the form of letters to the newspaper's web site was entirely ancillary to the provision electronically of news, and that there was no interactive feature sufficient to invoke the exception to the definition of 'cable programme' under section 7(2) of the CDPA 1988. (Courtesy of Northern Intellectual Property Chambers.)

Despite the fact that the case was going to be considered further at a full hearing, an eleventh-hour settlement deprived legal practitioners of a detailed analysis of the impact of copyright on hypertext links, and the interim ruling that copyright could subsist in an eight-word headline, tackled by reasoned legal argument.[8]

Shrink wrapped software licence was held not to be binding contract terms when buyer (A) opened the shrink wrapper on which the terms were set out, in spite of a course of dealings with the seller (B); the terms were those of the third-party manufacturer (X) who was accepted for the purposes of the action to be the copyright owner in the software. Because the terms of the sale were dependent on the consent of X to the use by A of the software, there was no consensus achieved between B and A. Importantly, X could enforce his copyrights and rights in the nature of copyright against B directly. The Court would not imply a term that B was supplying the goods and the right to copy it on X's terms as to user with the sale suspended until A accepted those terms.[9]

The English courts would assert jurisdiction over a copyright infringement claim which occurred in Holland to be determined by reference to Dutch law.[10] The English plaintiff asserted the English High Court's jurisdiction on the basis of one of the defendants being domiciled in England, even though other defendants were domiciled in Holland: the plaintiff had begun the cause of action under the Civil Jurisdiction and Judgments Act 1982, which implemented the Brussels Convention 1968 in the UK.

Mr. Justice Lloyd observed:

'In the circumstances of increasingly international dealings as regards intellectual property rights and articles created using them, including the dramatic potential effects of the Internet and other transnational communications systems, and the possible supply of articles in breach of copyright in a Contracting State by a person who does not establish a place of business there, it might be said to be convenient to be able to sue a person who is said to have infringed such rights in two or more Contracting States by one action in the court of domicile (unless Article 16(4) [of the Brussels Convention] requires otherwise) instead of proceeding separately in each relevant jurisdiction: this might result in an economic and efficient resolution of a dispute of an international character and avoid inconsistent results....'

---

[8]   *The Shetland Times v. Wills and Another* [1997] EMLR 277 (Court of Session, Outer House; Lord Hamilton) [1997] FSR 604.

[9]   *Beta Computers (Europe) Ltd v. Adobe Systems (Europe) Ltd* [1996] FSR 367 (Court of Session, Outer House, Lord Penrose).

[10]   *Pearce v. Ove Arup Partnership* [1997] FSR 641 (ChD, Lloyd J).

VI. What's in the Pipeline?

A. *Digital Image Manipulation and Historical Veracity*

Is a digital duplicate negative as valuable as a chemically produced colour negative? X offered Y a duplicate negative of a digitally manipulated image created from images reproduced from original colour negatives. Y did not want the digitally manipulated image and asked to use one of the original negatives which recorded an actual event. X handed over a strip of negatives containing the image of that event and *inter alia* two other negatives of photographs taken at the same time in sequence. The agreement was for Y to publish one image in a newspaper coupled with an outright assignment of copyright worldwide for a period of three months. Is was also a term of the agreement that Y would procure the withdrawal of the image from circulation at the expiry of the three-month term. Y in fact published two of the images contained on the strip of negatives from digitized copies of the original negatives and syndicated the digitized copies of all the negatives on the strip electronically to other publications.

The compression of the images on the original negatives was carried out at great speed. The compression factor used by Y when digitizing the images was barely adequate for reproduction on newspaper but insufficient for other uses including the reproduction of fine art prints. Y lost the strip containing the original negatives and failed to return them to Y.

Proceedings were commenced and Y consented to judgment being entered against it for breach of contract with damages to be assessed following Z's (X's principal) rejection of the offer of a disk containing digitized copies of the images downloaded from Y's computer.

The issues which are to be considered in the assessment of damages are:

(a)   what loss has Z suffered by having to accept inadequately compressed digitally generated duplicate negatives instead of the original chemically produced negatives?

(b)   what loss has Z suffered by only having digitally generated copies bearing in mind that Y originally had refused to accept a digitally manipulated duplicate negative on the ground that the veracity of the event portrayed in the image could not be guaranteed?

(c)   what loss has Z suffered though the unavailability to offer original chemically produced negatives with the copyright in the images bearing in mind that digitally generated copies, of equal quality to those now available to Z, were electronically transmitted to many other countries and Y failed to secure their withdrawal from the market-place?

The parties settled the action with the photographer receiving a £50,000 plus costs settlement, and the inadequately compressed digital images stored on a disk.

B. *Fair Dealing on Academic Networks on the Internet*

A, an academic botanist at an English university obtains lawfully a report prepared by an American oil prospecting company, O, which depends and reports on botanical surveys and information concerning plant life. A, not realizing the value of the report from the point of view of competitors to O, scans the report into his computer, in the interests of the botanical science community, which is linked to an academic network, for free access to fellow botanists. The report is accessed by a very large number of accessors, including competitors of O.

(a)   O insists that the report is withdrawn from the site;
(b)   O requires the identity of all accessors who have accessed the university site;
(c)   O threatens proceedings in one of the states of the US where the fair use rules differ from the fair dealing rules in the UK.

Luckily O had mercy on A and the university.

C. *Internet Copyright Piracy*

E, a CD-ROM games publisher, has exclusively licensed to it a PC computer game ('the game') from world exclusive licensee, F, for publication in the EU. U, without any licence, downloads a freeware version of the game (containing some levels and a build editor program) from the Internet and sells in the EU freeware demo of the game licensed to E in a compilation of other freeware samplers and shareware samplers of games downloaded from the Internet.

Copyright owner A's terms of licence for the freeware version of the game licensed to E is copied onto the compilation. Those terms forbid the unauthorized selling of the freeware version of the game. The compilation as a whole contains a large amount of rubbish as well as the freeware version of the game.

U says because the version of the game which it has downloaded from the Internet is freeware available on the Internet, it is in the public domain and U is entitled to sell, and recoup the cost of manufacturing and distributing, the CD-ROM on which the compilation appears. Neither A nor F, both of whom are based in the US, is willing to spend the money to chase U in the EU. Advise E!

D. *Originality, Equitable Copyrights and Joint Copyright Interests*

C licenses E to exploit a digitally generated character of which C is copyright owner. E asks F if it will carry out fashion promotion of the character in its publication. F agrees orally. Nothing is said with regard to copyright, but F is given 30 days for exclusive use of the images to be used in its publication after which E can use the images for promotion.

C supplies specimen illustrations of the character to F but F says it wants different sketches. To illustrate what it wants F sends rough pose sketches in which it has utilized features of the cartoon character, for C to work up different poses for the character and to add specimen fashion fabrics in the form of clothing. The fashion fabrics are designed by X, Y and Z, but they have licensed F to carry out this project.

C manipulates pre-existing images of the character into poses which are similar but not identical to those proposed by F in its sketches and applies the fabric patterns onto the character using digital image manipulation to do so. C sends the images back to F which publishes the images supplied in its publication.

After the 30-day period E uses the images of the character for other purposes and gives credit to designers X, Y and Z, but not to F. F claims copyright infringement alleging that it is the copyright owner in the images alternatively entitled to a joint copyright and asserts that it did not agree to the subsequent promotional use; it threatens an injunction, but then seeks damages.

F is too unsure of its ground to commence proceedings. E continues to use under licence from C the images on the basis that any work done by F was under an implied licence from C to exploit the character solely for the purposes of the joint venture. Next time E will be getting a written agreement executed making the position clear that any incidental artwork derived from the character images will vest at law, as opposed to equity, in C.

VII. Summary

The electronic age and digitization has produced the most exciting challenge for lawyers this century. There is a mountain of problems to tackle while legislatures and treaty organizations seek to assert harmonization. Satisfactory harmonization is still decades off, in spite of the efforts of the European Commission for the EEA.

This chapter has not even touched on problems posed by national encryption bans – the impact on intranet systems for businesses with branches in the US and France is still to be assessed and dealt with. It has also only addressed in passing the fair dealing and fair use issues; the wide variety of what constitutes fair dealing, and the lack of uniform judicial approach will cause frustration for rightsholders and legitimate fair dealers alike. Freedom of expression issues have not been addressed at all; these have met an impasse in countries such as Singapore, and many of the Islamic countries.

There is enough work to keep an army of legislators, conventionists and legal-eagles engaged to sort out these issues well into the next century; it is up to the lawyers not to stifle the development of free movement and exploitation of information, especially visual information, whilst trying to ensure fairly that those who express original information are fairly rewarded.

Finally the impact of *Zeran v. America Online Inc. US DC (ED Va.) Civ* 1:96cv1564 (21 March 1997) will be addressed briefly. AOL's victory has been upheld in the US Court of Appeals and *certiorari* has been denied by the US

Supreme Court. It could be said to be outside the remit of the UK; however it is not. Section 230(c)(1) of the Communications Decency Act 1996 provides:

'Protection for "Good Samaritan" Blocking and screening of offensive material. – (1) Treatment of Publisher or Speaker. – No provider or user of an interactive computer service shall be treated as the publisher or speaker of any information provided by another information content provider.'

The impact of that provision is to excuse any service provider who provides hypertext links with other sites. The whole issue of potential liability, in respect of copyright, and the ability of 'innocent' ISPs or BBOs in the US to avoid responsibility for infringement of copyright is at the time of writing subject to scrutiny in the US Congress. The signs are, however, that Congress is unlikely to give a blanket immunity to copyright infringers in the same manner that ISP or BBO publishers have been given blanket immunity from libel suits.[11]

---

[11]   *Sidney Blumenthal and Ors v. Drudge and America Online Inc.,* Civ Act No 97 - 1968 (D DC: 22 April 1998). In this case AOL was able to obtain summary judgment dismissing the plaintiffs' claims against it, but Drudge was left in the case on his own.

Copyright and Other Intellectual Property Issues in the Use of Motion Picture Archives, Photo Archives and Museum Collections in the New Media: A Museum Perspective

Christine Steiner
The J. Paul Getty Trust
Los Angeles, California, US

I. Introduction

Museums publish, use, and license images of works in their collections and make the same uses of images owned by third parties. As producers, consumers, and publishers of intellectual property, museums balance the tension between protecting the integrity of reproductions of works of art and encouraging wide access to those images for educational purposes. This chapter presents a defensive perspective; that is, it will not focus on how museums and cultural institutions enforce their rights against infringers, but rather how museums can and must comply with copyright laws both for the use of their own materials and the materials of others. It will also touch on collective licensing.

A grounded understanding of copyright law becomes more urgent with the growth of the Internet. Museums are being pressured, internally and externally, to publish catalogues, collections, and digital archives on-line. Simultaneously, museums are challenged to manage intellectual property, facilitate transactions, and prevent the unauthorized use of images. Recent cases in the US hint at potential liability if visitors to museum web sites download images for which the museum has not cleared the copyright. The museum, regardless of knowledge, could be adjudged to be a primary (or contributory) infringer by virtue of having facilitated the infringement. Museums can avoid liability exposure by explicitly obtaining the right to place an image on-line, either by assuring that they own the copyright or by obtaining a licence from the copyright owner for the use of the work.

A settled body of case law specific to fine art has not yet developed, and the electronic media present new challenges in general. Issues raised by the transition to an on-line environment include, among others, who is liable for third-party infringement; how to assess (and compensate) the copyright components of a multimedia project; whether a digitized image of a work in the public domain can gain a separate copyright; and whether a digital image is a reproduction, or whether it differs sufficiently from an original image to garner its own copyright.

For a work to be protected by copyright, it must be original and contain an expression of the author's creativity. Under US case law, the amount of originality or creativity needed to pass this threshold is not high. A change in colour or medium is not enough originality or creativity to pass the threshold, but a change in angle or lighting might be. These distinctions become more complex when images are digitized; some maintain that digitization creates a separate copyrightable interest because the myriad decisions about colour, lighting, definition, shading, resolution etc., provide originality and creativity; others hold that the process creates a mere reproduction and the faithful reproduction of the work itself or of an earlier reproduction (by photograph, transparency, etc.) is a derivative work. For images of works of art in the public domain – where the copyright has expired or never existed – some hold that there cannot be a separate copyright interest because the underlying work is not in copyright and consequently the derivative cannot be copyrighted.

Museums take the strong position that the reproduced image is separately copyrightable. For museum images, the 'value-added' creative elements include curatorial accuracy and intellectual judgment; these professional elements represent authority and authorship. The steps in the museum approval process assure that the image represents a faithful depiction of what it purports to be. This is important for research, education, presentation, and other purposes. This is the truest application of what the US Copyright Office terms 'human judgment', the elements of creativity an examiner looks for in determining whether a work is copyrightable.

Is this distinction valid for digitazation activities of commercial publishers? There appears to be an emerging trend toward layered assertions of copyright; a museum asserts the copyright to the image and the publisher asserts the copyright to the digitized image. For example, in certain works, the copyright may read: '© A Museum of Art; Digital © The Publisher'. While recognizing the technical skill, it must be queried whether the digitization process, in and of itself, provides a sufficient basis upon which an electronic publisher can assert a separate copyright in the digitized image. While there are certain practical reasons to assert separate copyrights (e.g. providing the publisher with certainty in prosecuting third-party infringement) this objective would be achieved equally by structuring a licensing deal in which the licensee is obligated, by contract, to prosecute infringement. This author views the assertion of a publisher's 'digital copyright' as a troubling trend in which museums are unwitting participants; museums must examine these issues and separately consider the significance of permitting a separate ownership interest in the publisher, recognizing that a copyright interest is an ownership interest that exists for a long duration.

In order to assist museums in efforts to place on-line a large number of images, licensing schemes and rights management systems are being explored. In managing museums' intellectual property, these systems have as their objectives the ability to widely transmit images, while simultaneously limiting access to the images to the proper audiences, transmitting royalty data, and billing customers. These rights management systems will encourage these activities; the public gains access to artistic, educational content, while museums avoid infringement complications and, in appropriate circumstances, receive the much-needed revenue. There are certain initiatives taking shape in the US, which are discussed below.

A. *MESL*

Believing that the development of museum imaging would be hampered without a common framework of rights, permissions, and restrictions, the Getty Information Institute co-sponsored the Museum Educational Site Licensing Project (MESL), launched in 1995. This initiative examined the educational benefits of digital access to museum collections by bringing together museums and universities in a two-year pilot project that explored mechanisms for providing, digitizing, using, and administering museum images for university curricular purposes. A publication detailing the process and results of the pilot project is in the final phase of completion.

B. *AMICO*

Under the auspices of the American Art Museum Directors (AAMD) the Art Museum Image consortium (AMICO) is in formation as a non-profit corporation that will serve the museum and educational communities. AMICO is a consortium of North American art museums that will provide a large library of digital documentation (images, text, etc.) for licensing to educational users. The goals of this non-profit entity include the following: creating a collective library of art for all levels of educational use, providing members' access to collective holdings; negotiating digitized rights with artists, artists' rights societies, artists' estates, and other rightsholders; providing members' access to collective funding to preserve educational holdings; and enhancing the information infrastructure and documentation practices of members. In short, the goals are creating the database, negotiating rights, preparing agreements, transacting the deal, returning revenue, and enhancing technological and administrative standards of all members through a collective approach.

C. *MDLC*

The American Association of Museums (AAM) is assisting a similar licensing effort for museum images, called the Museum Digital Licensing Collective (MDLC). The body of images available for licensing will be more comprehensive than art images: the data bank will include images and text from natural history museums, science museums, as well as historic materials and cultural artefacts. The collective is expected to license more broadly than to the educational community, and it is anticipated that it will engage in commercial licensing activities.

In addition to collective initiatives, museums continue to undertake licensing activities just as they have done for years. Some museums charge on a sliding scale, depending on whether the use is commercial or non-commercial. Some museums grant all requests, some deny all requests, but most decide on a case-by-case basis, a time-consuming and inefficient process. Museums can, through a cost-effective means, offer access to previously inaccessible images, increase revenue in electronic formats, provide education, publications, information, and promotional materials. However museums must balance the goals of increased access against the risks of decreasing security because increasing and simplifying access to images may often conflict with the goals of protecting the economic and integrity rights of the copyrighted images.

D. *Sample Agreements*

In preparing the museum community for avoiding inappropriate exploitation by commercial interests, occasional papers and sample agreements are prepared and distributed within the museum community. One publication, currently distributed by AAM, is a booklet containing two sample licensing agreements for CD-ROM projects, with extensive commentary. The publication addresses, in sample agreements, the terms and conditions required for complex agreements as well as essential terms for shorter simple deals. The first edition is reproduced in full in the appendix. It can be obtained at a modest cost by contacting the American Association of Museums, 1575 Eye Street, NW, Suite 400, Washington, DC, 20005. An upcoming publication, a primer for museums on copyright and trademark issues, is in the planning stages.

Difficulties of Managing Copyrights, Image and Property Rights to Digitized Works Under French Law

Bruno Grégoire Sainte-Marie and Pierre Gioux

Avocats au Barreau de Paris, FG Associés, Paris, France

I. Introduction

The creation and exploitation of a bank of digitized images poses real difficulties when examined pursuant to the provisions of French law on the management of author's rights. France is a remains a country with a strong tradition of protecting the author's monoploy; the following examples allow us to appreciate the legal constraints which weigh on the company which commercializes a base of fixed or (animated) images in France.

A television report had as its subject the Tuileries, a garden situated in Paris. Views of the garden taken from the Champs Elysées included statues of the sculptor Maillol. The report gave rise to a legal action before the French Supreme Court on the grounds that the camera lingered on Maillol's statues, and that no royalties had been paid to the artist's beneficiaries in consideration for the reproduction in the film of the said sculptures. While it is true that French legislation provides for derogations from author's rights, in particular for extracts or short citations, this case sanctioned the most protectionist tendency of author's rights, by holding that film or photographic work could not give rise to extracts or short citations.[1]

Protection of digital images is not limited to intellectual property law, it also benefits real estate owners. Brittany is the most westerly province in France located on the English Channel and the Atlantic Ocean. On these windswept lands small white houses typical of the region have been built. One of these, very isolated and visible from the sea, was photographed to illustrate a promotional campaign for tourism in Brittany. The Court of Appeals which

---

[1] Cass Civ 4 July 1995, Antenne 2/SPADEM n 295.

heard the matter confirmed the judgment of the court of first instance by holding that, in the absence of authorization of the owner, subsequent compensation was due to him.[2]

Such decisions, based on the so-called 'intangible principle' of the law of property, concern houses, those places where people live and where the rights in question are tinged in addition with a 'personality right' that is the right of every person to the protection of his or her address, lodging, privacy, and related elements.

However, in a matter where the law of property in no way concerned a dwelling, French case law has recently achieved notoriety by the protection that it has given the law of property as against the right to information. In December 1995, a speleologist in charge of guarding the caves at Ardéche, made an exceptional discovery by finding a cave decorated with paintings over 30,000 years old. Photographs and films were made of these magnificent paintings, and were disseminated by the international press. However, the owners of the fields under which this cave was to be found instituted legal proceedings to forbid the diffusion of the images taken in the ground under their property without their authorization. The Tribunal de Grande Instance in Paris held on appeal that it was justifiable to forbid the diffusion of images and films unless the prior consent of the property owners has been obtained.[3] The French courts have also held that the colouring of a film can constitute a breach of the moral rights of its author.[4]

In France the protection of the right to image of a person (whether a public figure or not) also imposes the strictest limits. French courts have been equally protective with respect to additional author's rights created by new technology such as the Internet. In early 1998, the Court in Strasbourg decided to forbid the company which published the newspaper Les Derniéres Nouvelles d'Alsace from continuing the diffusion of its paper on-line on the Internet without having reached prior agreement with the journalists regarding additional remuneration for the reuse of their articles on the network.[5]

These few examples illustrate the difficulty that exists in France in creating a base of fixed or animated images which may benefit from legal security in its exploitation. Thus, the subject of a photograph, whether this be a person or real estate is capable of benefiting from protection by way of rights of personality (droit de la personnalité) or property law. Of course, the photographic or film representation of the people or of the property can benefit from the protection of droits d'auteur (copyright) when the photographer or the film-maker has imbued the work with the 'imprint of his personality'. Finally, the

---

[2]   TGI Paris, 26 May 1993 de Kerguezec/CLM BBDG Philip Plisson et Comité Régional du Tourisme.
[3]   TGI Paris, 21 June 1995.
[4]   Cass. 1er Civil, 28 May 1991, Colorisation consorts Huston/Turner Entertainment et autres.
[5]   TFI de Strasbourg, 3 February 1998, USJF, SNJ/PLURIMEDIA.

digitization and the exploitation of the photograph or the film must benefit from authorizations of all of the rightsholders.

The scope of this discussion will be limited to databases of fixed images. In this context only, one may distinguish the following rightsholders:

(a) the owner of the database;
(b) the author of the database;
(c) the author of a work integrated into the database;
(d) the owner of the media of the work integrated into the base;
(e) the author of works *represented* in the work integrated into the base;
(f) the owner of property – whether constituting original work or not – represented in the work integrated in the base;
(g) the person whose image is *represented on the work integrated in the base.*

In order to eliminate any repetition, a chronological approach distinguishing the period of creation of the database and the period of its exploitation will be avoided; instead, an approach will be adopted according to the nature of the rights, i.e. *droits d'auteur* (copyright), property law, and rights of personality.

II. Authors' Rights: The Difficult Management of Authors' Rights Relating to a Bank of Digitized Images

A. *Image versus Work*

To begin with, must a photograph necessarily be considered a work protected by the provisions of the French Intellectual Property Code? Some photographs exist which do not justify being protected. However, it being virtually impossible for the lawyer to say whether all the conditions of the protection are effectively present or not, it is prudent to consider that any image is the subject of protection by *droits d'auteur*. It is however possible to state that the taking of a photograph of an immobile object on precise instructions and without particular lighting by a photographer does not give rise to protection.

In order to be protected by *droits d'auteur*, an intellectual creation must correspond to two distinct criteria: it must manifest itself in a tangible expression or form, that is fixed in a medium (photographic, magnetic, digitized, paper etc.) and it must bear the imprint of the personality of the author. This last criteria, which can appear very subjective, is absolutely *not* synonymous with inventiveness or novelty. If this were the case, we would find ourselves in effect in a situation of absolute arbitrariness.

According to French case law, any creation is original which is not the simple reproduction of an existing work, and which expresses the tastes, intelligence and know-how of its author, in other words, his or her personality, in its composition and expression. We will therefore keep this definition in mind as a basis for a certain degree of legal security that an intellectual creation is *a priori* a protected work.

According to the Intellectual Property Code, creations of the mind are considered as works protected by copyright, as for example literary and scientific writings, choreographic works, musical compositions, films, drawings, paintings, photographs, etc. These works are protected regardless of their utilization, the merit of the author, their artistic quality, or their usefulness.

A database is constituted or created from images which are pre-existing or specially ordered and realized for this purpose.

B. *Pre-existing Images*

The integration of pre-existing images into a database is the starting-point of a genuine obstacle course for whoever seeks to obtain the authorizations necessary for their exploitation. Several hypotheses are possible:

(a)   the works in question have fallen into the public domain;
(b)   they originate from catalogues containing freely usable works;
(c)   they are privately funded;
(d)   they have come from an author's property or estate.

1.   Works in the Public Domain

A work protected by *droits d'auteur* (copyright) is said to have fallen in the public domain when the inheritance rights of all the rightsholders have expired, that is 50 or 70 years after the death of the author, with years of war being added to this legal duration. However, the fact that a work is in the public domain does not signify for all purposes that it is free of all rights and thus that one can use it without restriction. Indeed, the moral rights of the author must be respected in any case. The producer of the base will therefore have to respect the author's paternity right (*droit de paternité*) and the right to the integrity of his or her work. These rights are in effect perpetual, inalienable and tansferable to heirs. Authors' societies, moreover, have the capacity to institute legal proceedings to defend the moral rights of authors, even if the latter have been deceased for several centuries.

2.   The So-called 'Free Use' Works

We are seeing the birth today of catalogues of images, most often on high definition CD-ROMs, which are sold 'free of rights'. These compact disks are for the most part pressed overseas where the copyright regime such as we know it does not exist. Often the use of these images is restricted to a certain type of commercial purpose.

That being the case, a risk nevertheless remains: in effect nothing prevents an author, who has surrendered his or her rights for the realization of such a product overseas, from commencing a legal action in France directly against the user of his or her work, on the grounds that the commercialization of the work in France was not agreed to pursuant to the terms of the Intellectual

Property Code. In effect, the only applicable law in France in the domain of copyright is French law, and its application is a matter of public order, which implies that one may not derogate from it in any fashion by agreements to the contrary.

3. Privately Funded work

The term 'private funds' is not entirely exact. This expression concerns in fact works the rights to which have already been transferred to companies or organizations for prior exploitation. For example, these may be literary works which have been assigned by an author to a publisher for their publication, photographs which have been sold to a tourist office for the promotion of a region, a musical piece written by a composer for a live performance by an orchestra, a video film commissioned specially for the promotion of a company or an organization. The above types of transferees contribute the elements to integrate into the database, that is, the texts, photographs, films, music of which they are in possession.

C. *Specially Realized Images*

The person who creates the database can in this case either ask purely and simply for the creation of images and acquire the rights for them, or participate in the production of these images and have the patrimonial rights assigned to them. Here, the question is no longer so much to discover those parties which are the holders of the rights, as to organize the assignment of the latter for the profit of the database operator.

We may here note that according to the provisions of Article L. 111-1 of the French Intellectual Property Code, the author of a work enjoys, by the sole fact of creation, an intangible property right which is exclusive and enforceable against all other parties. The Code also specifies that the entering into of an employment contract does not effect any derogation to the principle just described, and thus, except in special cases, it is generally admitted that an employment contract must expressly provide for the transmission of patrimonial rights.

D. *Digitized Images*

At this stage, it also appears useful to tackle the question of digitization. Without doubt, more and more photographs will be taken by means of digital cameras, and thus the question of rights to photos which are taken in the future will effectively become moot. Nevertheless, for the next few years, existing photos or those which will not have been taken by a digital camera, will have to undergo a transformation at the time of their digitization by a change in media.

The date of the first law on copyright, in particular covering photographs, was 1957. This forces us to reason in terms of the anteriority or lack of anteriority of the image in relation to this date. Any assignment of rights to an image before this date will certainly not include digitization without the authorization of the rightsholder, unless an assignment was specifically provided for by contract for any *unknown mode* of commercialization. If the assignment was to take effect after 1957, doctrine and case law demand that all modes of commercialization be specified by contract. It is therefore prudent to verify whether digitization was contractually envisaged and, if not, to request the necessary authorization.

It has been stated by an important number of French legal writers and judges that digitization is likely to violate the moral rights of an author, and that in this respect, the act of digitizing a work should have been the subject of an authorization. The Berne Convention confers upon authors the exclusive right to authorize the reproduction of their work 'in whatever manner and in whatever form this may be' and it also provides that 'any sound or visual recording is considered as a reproduction within the meaning of the present convention'. This application of author's rights, which has been long affirmed by French and foreign doctrine, whether of the *droits d'auteur* or copyright tradition, has been recently reinstituted by the French courts. It is confirmed by Article 1.4 of the Common Declarations adopted at Geneva in December 1996 specifying that the right of reproduction applies 'fully in the digital environment, in particular to the use of works in digital form' and 'that the storage of a protected work in digitized form on an electronic support constitutes a reproduction'.

Article 9 of the OMPI Treaty of December 1996, yet to be ratified by the requisite number of countries, has also reinforced the right of authors of photographic works by allowing them to benefit from now on from the common law duration of protection of the Berne Convention, which grants to the author a protection for life and for 50 years after his or her death.

E. *Circumstances of Limitation on Protection*

Article 10 of the OMPI Treaty of December 1996 places certain restrictions on the monopoly of the author in 'special cases where there has been no injury to the normal exploitation of the work, nor any unjustified prejudice caused to the legitimate interests of the author'. The states adhering to the Treaty will have the possibility of providing for new limitations or exceptions adapted to the digital network environment. However the provisions in question are not of such a nature as to create, under French law, the possibility of an exception comparable to that of 'fair use'. The exceptions laid down in Article L. 122-5 of the Intellectual Property Code only concern copies or reproductions strictly reserved for the private use of the copier, and not intended for collective uses. In addition, analyses and short citations cannot concern images, at least, not under current law.

III. Right to Image

The right to image constitutes a source of legal difficulty for whoever wishes to use photographs of a documentary or commercial nature. Under French law, any person possesses a right regarding the representation and reproduction of their image, as well as their property. In addition, artists, sculptors, painters, architects, film and theatre directors possess author's rights on the works of which they are the creators. The reproduction and the publication of their works without their consent constitutes an infringement of copyright. It is therefore advisable to obtain this consent, usually granted in consideration of payment of a royalty, before any publication.

A. *The Principle of Prohibition*

1. Civil Liability

The right to exploit an image in France is governed by a general principle: 'each person has an exclusive right relative to his image and may authorize the reproduction of it at his own discretion'. The general rule is therefore, other than for limited exceptions, a prohibition against capturing and reproducing the image of a person without his or her authorization. The exclusive right recognized as belonging to each person constitutes an aspect of the law of personality (*droit de la personnalité*), and aims to protect each individual against any invasion of physical, intellectual or moral integrity.

2. Criminal Liability

French legislation and case law has as its purpose the guaranteed protection of private life. We have seen earlier in this chapter that potential invasion of private life in effect renders the image of another unavailable for publication without his or her express consent. The protection of private life is reinforced by new provisions of the Criminal Code, which severely sanction violations of private life. Article 226-1 states that:

'The act, by any means, of willingly violating the intimate private life of another: in capturing, recording, or transmitting, without the consent of their author's word pronounced privately and confidentially: in fixing, recording or transmitting, without his consent, the image of a person who is in a private place will be punished by one year of imprisonment and 300 000 Francs fine.

When the acts in the present article are accomplished within the sight and knowledge of the person affected, without him opposing it, when he was in a position to do so, the consent of that person is presumed.'

This Article is completed by Article 226-2 which states:

'The act of conserving, bringing or allowing to be brought to the public awareness or to that of a third party, or of using in any manner whatsoever, any recording or document obtained with the assistance of one of the acts defined by Article 226-1, will be punished by the same penalties.

When the offence provided for by the previous paragraph is committed by means of the written or audiovisual press, the particular provisions of the laws which govern these matters are applicable in relation to the determination of the responsible parties.'

This implies that capturing another's image when one is located on a public thoroughfare and is aiming directly toward a private place, with a view to publication, without the authorization of the person photographed, is illegal. The conservation (in archives), or the publication, and the representation thereby realized, is punished by the same penalties.

In order to bring to the public awareness an image realized in a private place, it is necessary to obtain from the person in question an authorization of diffusion. Otherwise, the photographed person will be able to sue the person responsible for the publication (i.e. the diffusion to the public) that is, the photographer or the publisher. It is not because a model has given consent to a series of poses (this consent can be implicit) that he or she has explicitly authorized the diffusion of his or her image. This consent *can never be implicit*. It is therefore advisable to obtain a signed and dated written agreement.

In a judgment dated 25 May 1983, of the TGI of Paris, an organ of the press had published a photograph of a person taken in a police station. It did not have the authorization of the person. The judges held first that a search room of a police station is not a public place; then affirmed that any person has an exclusive right to his or her image and to the use of such image, and may oppose its diffusion without *express and special* consent.

B. *The Exceptions*

The exceptions to the rule of authorization are very limited; they can be regrouped into three categories.

1. An Image Taken in a Public Place

By way of derogation to the general principle prohibiting publication without authorization, it is considered that regarding street scenes or groups of people in a public place, it is not necessary to obtain the consent of the people photographed in order to publish their image. This derogation must nevertheless fulfil the following conditions:

(a)   it must concern a public place;
(b)   it must not have restrictive framing;
(c)   it must not invade private life.

(i)   *Definition of Public Place*

In relation to the right to image, the following is the definition of a public place according to the French Supreme Court: 'a place accessible to all without anyone's special authorization, (and) that the access be permanent or subject to certain conditions, hours or pre-determined causes'. The public thoroughfare and the street are naturally public places, however it has been judged as follows:

(i)   that a private beach, even if paying, can be a public place (the entry fee is only a condition of its access, which remains open to all);
(ii)   that places of worship are considered as public places;
(iii) that, on the other hand, a prison is a private place.

The current case law on this notion leaves room for a great deal of imprecision, if not ambiguity.

(ii) Restrictive Framing

Restrictive framing is the framing which individualizes one, or even several, person(s) in a photograph taken in a public place. The criteria of individualization is once again subjective and difficult to appreciate. It may nevertheless be considered that a person is individualized in a photograph when the two following conditions are cumulatively fulfilled.

(i)   If the figure constitutes the principal subject of the shot. The case law uses the term of 'restrictive framing'. It is therefore necessary, in order to avoid 'restrictive framing', that a person does not stand out too clearly in the photograph;
(ii)   if the figure is identifiable without much difficulty by a normally attentive spectator, even if it concerns close relatives.

In this regard one decision is quite notable: that of the Court of Appeals of Paris of 11 July 1987. In this case a person was photographed in a public place; the person did not pose for the photo, but the photo was not clandestine. There was publication of the photo without authorization, and the framing of this photo was found to be restrictive.

The court judged that the publisher was guilty of an indiscretion which constituted a 'fault' within the meaning of Article 1382 of the Civil Code, in framing the photograph on the sole image of this person, with a view to its publication, without having obtained prior authorization and also because it had captured the features of a private individual, solely for its own profit and at its own will.

There will therefore be no 'individualization' of the figure if one needs to take a magnifying glass in order to recognize the subject. On the other hand, even if the face does not appear clearly, but the silhouette allows the model to be identified at a glance, there will be individualization of the person. In the case where the model is individualized, and his or her image is captured in a public place, the publication will require the authorization of the person concerned.

(iii) Invasion of Private Life

The rule is based on Article 9 of the Civil Code, which states:

'Each person has the right to have his private life respected. Judges may, independently of the question of compensation for damages suffered, prescribe any proper measures, such as sequestration and seizure among others, to prevent or end an invasion of the intimacy of private life; these measures may be taken, in urgent cases, by way of interlocutory relief.'

The case law applies Article 9 of the Civil Code strictly.

In a judgment of 4 July 1984 of the TGI of Paris,[6] the Tribunal held that there had been an invasion of private life in the sense of Article 9 of the Civil Code. This case concerned the publication of a photo of a participant in a demonstration which had taken place during a homosexual summer school in the South of France. A person had been photographed during this demonstration, and quite obviously there had not been any authorization of publication. The publication of this photograph had as its consequence the revelation of the sexuality of the person photographed, when in fact the person kept this side of his personality a secret from his family and his work colleagues.

The judges held that the personal rights (*droit de la personnalité*) of an individual can be in conflict with freedom of information. The publication without authorization of this photograph was held to violate the right to image and the intimacy of the private life of the party in question.

In a judgment of 19 March 1986 of the TGI of Paris, *Perrot v. Filipacchi Editions*, a photographic shot had been taken following a bombing at the exit of the infirmary of Galeries Lafayette. The photographed person was recognizable, and the publisher did not possess authorization of publication. Referring to Article 9 of the Civil Code, the judges affirmed that: 'a person wounded in a terrorist attack has the right to oppose, or not consent to, the reproduction of the identifiable image of his body'.

In another case of 2 November 1989 of the TGI of Paris, *Tamarat v. Journal l'Humanité*, an identical solution was adopted. This case concerned a photograph of an exchange agent clerk who was placing two fingers in his nostrils during a session at the Paris Stock Exchange. Mr. Tamarat alleged that there had been a violation of his right to image. The newspaper *l'Humanité* contested the exercise of the clerk's right in relation to the right to information.

The judges held that the violation was effectively established. However, they allowed only limited compensation because of the risk that Mr. Tamarat was exposing himself to ridicule in adopting comportment within public view which was both perfectly ridiculous and contrary to commonly accepted rules of hygiene and decorum.

---

[6]   V...vs Cogedipresse.

Similarly, a public figure has the right to insist that his or her private life be respected, even a monarch. In a case of 13 February 1988 of the Cass. Civ. 1 ere *Jour de France v. Farah Diba*, the court recognized that a monarch may oppose any divulgation of his or her image which does not present him or her in the course of life.

The diffusion on the Internet of a photograph of a person, captured in a public place, will follow the regime just stated, with respect to its diffusion in France. This implies, therefore, that a foreign national will have the ability to commence an action against a defendant before a French jurisdiction to enforce his or her rights, on condition that the diffuser (in the broadest sense of the term) of his or her image is domiciled on French soil. On the other hand, such an action brought by a French national overseas will not, most of the time, result in the same solution. Indeed, in relation to the case law of other western countries, it is advisable to conclude that the current status of such rights in France is extremely protective.

C. *Images Illustrating Current Events*

When photographs are taken during current events or public demonstrations, they can be published without the authorization of the persons photographed, in application of the principle of a recognized right to information. This rule is, however, not absolute:

(a)   it must concern the illustration of *present* current events;
(b)   it must not invade the intimacy of one's private life.

1. Immediate Current Events

Case law requires that the publication be in relation to current events, and that in addition, it take place within a period close to the event. Two judgments are noteworthy in this respect, since they concern the same person and were rendered by the same judges. The cases involved the publication of photographs of a primary school teacher in Neuilly whose class was taken hostage by HB.

In the first case[7] *Moulard Dreyfus v. Ste VSD*, a photograph was published which represented the teacher, in the exercise of her functions at a school party. The judges considered that violation of the right to image was not established on the grounds that the publication had been realized to illustrate *immediate* current events and that it did not violate the intimacy of her private life, since the shot published was showing her in her professional activity, i.e. in a domain necessarily accessible to third parties, and because of this fact removed from her private life.

---

[7]   TGI Paris, 5 January 1994 1ére Chamber, 1ére Section.

In the second case[8] *Moulard Dreyfus v. Publiprint France Soir* the same court considered that the publication without the consent of the teacher, of photographs taken in the street, which showed her on the occasion of the beginning of the school year in another school, violated her right to image, since even if these photos were intended to illustrate an article which concerned her, they were not justified at this date by the need to inform the public, as they had been at the time of the taking of the hostages.

2. Invasion of Privacy

The case law notion of 'immediate news event' loses a part of its meaning on the international level. Though some events may have repercussions on a global scale (wars, natural catastrophes, airplane crashes, etc.), it is difficult to qualify the immediacy of 'local' information when its international diffusion will take place only after first being diffused in the country of origin. The diffusion via Internet of a photograph illustrating a news event would have to be, in our opinion, legally permissible according to current French law on this subject, even if such publication goes beyond the scope of 'immediate current affairs' within the meaning of French case law.

This analysis is based on the provisions of Article 19 of the Universal Declaration of Human Rights, adopted 10 December 1948 by the General Assembly of the UN which states:

'all individuals have the right to liberty of opinion and expression, which implies the right to not suffer for one's opinions, and to seek, receive and spread without consideration of country boundaries, information and ideas by any means of expression whatsoever.'

In the same way the second paragraph of Article 19 of the International Pact related to Civil and Political Rights (text annexed to the resolution adopted 16 December 1966 by the General Assembly of the UN, in force since 23 March 1976 and ratified by France in June 1980) states that:

'every person has the right to liberty of expression; this right includes the liberty to research, receive and transmit information and ideas, of any kind, without consideration of country borders, in an oral, written, printed or artistic form or by any other means of his choice.'

The only limit to this right to information can be created only by an identical legal norm or by international police laws. This is the case for example for the provisions of Article 10 of the Convention for the Safeguard of Human Rights which states:

---

[8]   TGI Paris, 17 November 1993 1ére Chamber, 1ére Section.

'10.1 all persons have the right to liberty of expression...this right includes...the liberty to receive and to communicate information...without distinction as to borders.

10.2 the exercise of these liberties, which entails duties and responsibilities, can be subject to certain formalities, conditions, restrictions or sanctions established by law; such measures constitute the means necessary, in a democratic society, for national security, territorial integrity or public safety, defense of the public order and the prevention of crime, to the protection of health or morals, *to the protection of reputation of reputation and the rights of others*, in order to prevent the disclosure of confidential information or to guarantee the authority or the impartiality of judicial power.'

French case law on the notion of 'immediate news event' is not necessarily compatible with the right to information set forth in the above conventions.

D. *The Image of a Public in the Exercise of his Functions*

The possibility of publishing the image of a public figure without authorization requires that the person be in the exercise of his or public life and not in the domain of his or her private life. Here again the image must not violate the intimacy of private life. The boundary of the latter is determined differently for public figures than for people who are not famous.

A recent decision[9] deserves to be cited insofar as it reveals the degree to which any party may be subject to the reaction of a photographed person. This case concerned the publication of a photograph of a television personality as he could appear in the course of his television show on the screen, in order to illustrate an article on the subject of the emission in question. The Tribunal recognized that the publication of this photograph, which had no character apart from the subject treated, did not violate the right that the presenter possessed on his image.

IV. Rights in Property

A. *The Image as Asset*

In all cases of promotional or commercial use, the authorization of the person photographed is required. The case law in this sense is constant.

The TGI of Paris judged on 7 July 1980 the following case: commercial advertisements for a giant poster reproduced some images of a football match and of players. The court found:

'members of a football team are public figures, photographed in a public place in the exercise of their functions, and they can therefore not oppose the diffusion of their photographs for informational purposes; however they nonetheless conserve the right

---

[9]   TGI Paris, 25 May 1994.

to commercialize their image and thus to authorize the use of (such an image) for advertising purposes.'

In the same sense and based on identical grounds, on 17 December 1980 the TGI of Lyon considered the case of a photograph of a basketball player printed on an advertising billboard for a company selling cameras. The court held that there was no 'violation of the non-commercial right to this image…but a violation of the commercial right to this image'. In other words, the judges considered that the right of the photographed player to commercialize his image had been violated, and that such a fault resulted in pecuniary damages. The ground for the award of damages is the prejudice to image of a person individualized in a group, and used commercially.

The above represents without doubt the principal source of difficulty related to the diffusion of photographs on the Internet. The public availability of photographs on various web sites allows any person connected to download images and reuse them for their own purposes. This reuse can take place either outside the network or within the network itself. One can therefore imagine all sorts of possible reuse, thanks to digitized software and image manipulation (photo editing, misappropriation etc.).

The persons mainly targeted are professional fashion models who live from the commercial use of their image; nothing is easier today than to digitize the face of a top model and to integrate it in a web page for the promotion of a server, a product or a virtual fashion parade to promote a *prêt-à-porter* collection created in a south-east Asian country, for example. Any efficient protection against such acts seems illusory today when they are committed in countries with weak legal protection.

B. *Rights in Other Assets*

The rule is different from that concerning the image of a person. There is no longer protection of a right of personality but rather protection pursuant to the law of property and/or the protection against invasion of privacy. The consent of the owner to the taking of a picture in no case implies consent to reproduction.

1. The Image of an Asset of a Person

When one wishes to reproduce the photograph of an asset belonging to another, the authorization of the owner is often required. This is the case particularly when it concerns a residence (house, castle, etc.), whose originality risks attracting the curiosity of the public. If the photograph was published without the authorization of the owner of the asset and the publication or its representation harms this person in one way or another, it will be possible for this person to take legal action for damages. The proof of the injury will be demonstrated if the owner of the asset manages to show that the publication has invaded the intimacy of his or her private life under Article 9 of the Civil Code, or that is has deprived him or her of the proceeds of the exploitation of the image of the asset photographed. This protection is based on two grounds: the violation, simultaneous or otherwise, of the *law of property* and/or of the *right to the intimacy of private life*.

In a judgment of 26 September 1993, the TGI of Paris condemned a photographer, a communication company, and the Regional Tourism Committee of Brittany, to pay joint and several damages following the use for advertising purposes of the photograph of a house situated at Plougrescant, without the authorization of its owner, on the following grounds:

'That by virtue of the absolute character of the law of property defined under Article 544 of the Civil Code, any owner has the right, though such right may not be abused, to forbid the reproduction for commercial purposes of all his assets, real or otherwise... A great number of people were prompted to identify the house photographed and to visit it (considerably disturbing Madame X).

In this case, the photograph of the house occupied the entirety of an advertising poster.

Similarly, the TGI of Bordeaux, on 19 April 1988, judged regarding the taking and the diffusion of the image of a terrace (a private place) forming an integral part of the home of its owner, that the right of the owner confers on him in the most absolute manner, the enjoyment and the use of the thing which is the subject of that right.

If the photograph of the asset is taken at the time of a news event and for the needs of information, or of a street scene, the applicable legal rules are identical to those for private individuals. This right prevents any third person from capturing and reproducing the image of an asset, whether it is real or personal property, without authorization, since the right to image is a component of the law of property.

2. The Image of a Work

The principle of obtaining the authorization of the owner of a work to its reproduction must be respected in the same manner as previously described. In addition, the consent of the artist or rightsholders is necessary if the work has not fallen into the public domain.

In the absence of the consent of the work's rightsholder, the publication of a photograph of the said work constitutes a copyright infringement within the meaning of Article 335-2 of the Intellectual Property Code. The rule applies to works of art in general, to performances, and to buildings or constructions imprinted with the personality of their author. Thus, a building or a fountain, even though open to the view of the public, cannot be reproduced in image without the authorization of their author, when they constitute the central subject of the shot, for the duration of their protection under author's rights principles.

V. Conclusion

The commercial use of images, today facilitated by their digitization and diffusion through networks, involves high risks of a legal nature under French law. In fact, the activities necessary in order to eliminate such risks are quite costly, as they involve verification of rights assignments, obtaining authorizations to use, and compiling of databases, among other constraints. In a market where competition takes place essentially through pricing, it is regrettable that the above evolution favours the commercialization of stolen images (that is, images which are unauthorized) and therefore, by way of commercial backlash, penalizes the reputable companies which exploit as best they can the photographic archives that they hold.

The Protection of Museum Collections of Film and Photo Archives in Germany after the Implementation of the European Database Directive into German Law

Professor Dr. Mathias Schwarz and Norbert Klinger
Attorneys-at-Law in Munich, Germany

I. Introduction

The following chapter focuses on the protection of film and photo archives under German law, including the protection of multimedia works[1] in analogue as well as in digital form. The discussion will have to differentiate between the protection of the individual film work or photograph and the collection of these works in a digital or analogue archive.

II. The Protection of Films and Photographs under the German Copyright Act in a Digital Environment

Films and photographs have long been protected under the German Copyright Act (section 2, paragraph 1(5) and (6)). The only requirement for copyright protection is that such works can be seen as original creations. This standard is not very difficult to meet. Even mere scientific or documentary films and photographs enjoy copyright protection.

To the extent that these creations do not meet the originality test they are protected by a neighbouring right as so-called *Lichtbilder* (simple photos) (German Copyright Act, section 72) or *Laufbilder* (moving images) (German Copyright Act, section 95). Film and photographic works enjoy copyright protection for a period of 70 years *post mortem autoris*. This protection period

---

[1]   E.g. archives for documentaries, scientific films and topical reports.

has been adopted throughout Europe following the implementation of the EU Term Directive. Section 65, paragraph 2 of the German Copyright Act provides that in establishing the duration of the copyright protection the relevant authors of a film work are the main director, the authors of the script and the dialogues, and the composer of any music especially composed for such film work. By comparison the protection period of the neighbouring right granted to moving images and simple photographs missing originality is 50 years after publication or, if no publication has occurred, 50 years after creation. These protection periods have been continuously extended in the course of the various revisions of the German Copyright Act. It therefore has to be reviewed carefully whether older photographs are still protected under copyright or by a neighbouring right.

In addition to the copyright protection available to authors the German Copyright Act grants a neighbouring right to the producer of a film work (German Copyright Act, section 94). This neighbouring right is again granted for a period of 50 years after publication or, in the absence of such publication, of 50 years after a creation of the film.

The mere digitalization of a film work or a photographic work, whether protected under copyright or in the public domain, under German copyright law will not lead to copyright protection for the digitized work. Nor can the digitized work be seen as a work enjoying derivative copyright protection. The same holds true even if some flaws of the original work are corrected in the course of the digitization process. Only if major changes showing originality in themselves are made, will a derivative work have been created. This may be assumed, for example, for the synchronized version of a film work or for a colourized version of a former black and white film. Whether or not the author of such new version had a licence to create such new versions is irrelevant for establishing whether or not these works enjoy copyright protection.

Multimedia works are not listed as a specific category protected under the German Copyright Act (while a list of protected works is provided in section 2 of the German Copyright Act this list, however, is not exhaustive). Accordingly, multimedia works showing originality will either be protected as works of speech, as film works (if consisting of moving images) or as a new category of its own.

The authors of film works and photographic works as well as the creators of moving images and simple photos and the producer of a film work are all vested with exclusive duplication, distribution and exhibition rights as well as with an exclusive right of presentation of the works to the public including the broadcast right. It is generally accepted that the digitalization of films and photographs in analogue form requires the duplication right irrespective of whether the work in its new digital form is incorporated in a tangible off-line medium (such as a CD-ROM) or an intangible on-line medium (such as the Internet or a large database stored on a hard disk). There is much debate, however, whether the process of digitalization, in addition to the duplication right, also requires the right of alteration or modification provided for by section 23 of the German Copyright Act. According to the prevailing view this is not the case as the works as such are not being modified but only represented in a different technology.

Even more uncertainty accompanies the question which rights are needed if the works are transmitted to an unspecified number of recipients or individual users either on demand or by push technologies. Whereas any distribution to an undefined number of users may qualify as falling under the broadcast right (German Copyright Act, section 20) even if it occurs not simultaneously but in a sequential form, it is disputed whether any individual on demand access to a digitized work should be qualified as falling under either the distribution right or the intangible right of presentation to the public. Whereas the latter view seems to be shared by the majority in the copyright community it is generally accepted that in any event any such act of on-line distribution is protected under copyright. Nevertheless, the German Government seems determined to incorporate the concept of a new right of 'making-available-to-the-public' which has been suggested by the WIPO Protocols of December 1996 as quickly as possible and has therefore published a first draft for a further revision of the German Copyright Act implementing this new right.

German copyright law provides for a fairly extensive protection of moral rights (German Copyright Act, section 12 – publication right; section 13 – right of paternity; section 14 – protection against distortions). Although these rights primarily protect authors they will to a large extent also be available to the creators of simple photographs protected by the neighbouring right and to film producers. The protection against distortion in connection with film productions and other moving images, however, is limited. Section 93 of the German Copyright Act provides that only gross distortions can be prohibited and that the author alleging such a gross distortion has also to take into account the interests of the other authors and the producer of the film work. Cases involving a distortion of the contribution of an author to a film work are therefore almost non-existent. It should be noted, however, that this restriction does not apply to photographs and it is therefore significantly easier to establish than an amalgamation of various photographs or the morphing or other modification of a photograph is in fact a distortion of the original photographic work. To date there are no precedents as to the right of paternity in the digital world, but it seems likely that, absent any specific circumstances, the author of a photographic work will have a course of action if he or she is not given a credit in connection with photographs which are being stored in a digital database. If such credit is 'buried' in a credit section of the database which a normal user would be unlikely to access this may be seen as an inappropriate credit.

The acquisition of rights in films and photographs for inclusion in a digital database creates specific problems under German copyright law, as section 31, paragraph 4 of the German Copyright Act provides that a grant of rights for uses unknown at the time of the respective grant is invalid and that the same shall apply for any obligation to grant any rights for such unknown uses in the future. On the basis of this provision of the German Copyright Act it has been established by the courts, for example, that no rights for a videogram use of a film work could be granted in contracts that pre-date 1976. The question whether the digitization as such of works originally created as analogue works, their inclusion in databases, the on-line access to such works and their distribution over the Internet is to be seen as such a separate new use, has been going on for a number of years without any authoritative court decision having been rendered so far. On the basis of a specific provision applying to labour contracts (German Copyright Act, section 53) some lower courts have held that at least in relationships which are to be seen as labour contracts or contracts for permanent services the author may be obligated to grant the rights for such new uses even if these should be considered new within the meaning of section 31, paragraph 4 of the German Copyright Act. The Federal Supreme Civil Court (*Bundesgerichtshof*) in recent years has been inclined to reduce the scope of this paragraph of the German Copyright Act but it remains to be seen whether it will follow this route when deciding on the use of analogue works in a digital environment.

The German copyright law does not provide for a general fair use principle. There are, however, a number of exceptions which allow for the use of copyrighted works and other contributions protected by neighbouring rights. Section 53 of the German Copyright Act, for example, provides for a right to make copies for private and other specific uses including educational and scientific uses. Furthermore section 58 allows the duplication and distribution of works of performing arts that are being published in catalogues in connection with an exhibition or auction. It is conceivable that this exception would also extend to CD-ROMs of digital photographs of works forming a part of an exhibition. Notwithstanding a number of further exemptions to copyright protection, film works, photographic works and works created in a similar way are broadly under German copyright law.

III. Dual Protection of Databases

Not only individual film works or photographic works may enjoy copyright protection but such protection may also be available to collections of such works or other individual contributions and even to mere compilations of facts. With the growing use of computers and the availability of huge storage capacities the economic risks for such collections of data and other elements have become considerably larger as they can easily be accessed and reproduced in a fraction of the time needed for such tasks only a few years ago. On the other hand the digital media today allow for the marketing of such collections, e.g. in the form of CD-ROMs comprising the collections of institutions like the Tate Gallery or the Guggenheim Museum. On-line access to film works and photographic works made available in such databases may eventually develop into a major business. Bill Gates' company Corbis is said to have compiled a collection of some 25 million images, up from around 100,000 in 1994. So far, 1.3 million of these images have been converted to digital form and some 100,000 pictures are being scanned in every year. Whereas many of these pictures may be protected under copyright as individual works, this need not be the case for all of them as older ones may have fallen into public domain and others may not be protected under copyright given their lack of originality. This is specifically true for jurisdictions which do not provide for additional neighbouring rights. Therefore, the protection of the database as such as opposed to the individual elements forming such database is of vital importance.

In 1992, the EC Commission therefore adopted a proposal for a directive harmonizing the protection of the law on databases in Europe.[2] In addition to earlier directives, the Database Directive was another step towards the implementation of a broader basis for a uniform standard for copyright protection in Europe. This harmonization process is to be welcomed not only in the sense of a Europe-wide adjustment of nationally differing regulations in the field of traditional copyright protection, but also because the specific issues of digital technologies in the field of copyright protection are dealt with, in most cases for the first time, on a European level, thereby anticipating national regulations.[3] In the context of potential on-line access, the necessity for an international protection of databases is obvious, given the fact that such databases often can be accessed from anywhere in the world. The considerable investment necessary to create such databases furthermore requires a stable and uniform legal environment, which will permit the recoupment of such investments through a potential commercial exploitation. This is also true for digital museum archives of films and photographs.

Prior to the passing of the Database Directive and its implementation into German law, traditional analogue archives of museums as well as electronic collections were only protected under certain circumstances. The first possibility legally to protect such archives was based on section 1 of the Law Against Unfair Competition (UWG) under the caption of 'direct adoption of third party's achievements'. A direct adoption of achievements is deemed to have occurred if specific achievements, such as a collection of data researched and compiled by a competitor, are appropriated by another competitor in an almost unchanged form.[4] For example, the Hamburg Regional Court ruled that such a 'direct adoption of achievements' existed in a case where a competitor distributed an electronic address database on CD-ROM which had been produced by simply copying a collection of addresses which had originally been put together by its competitor.[5] This decision could also be applied in respect to museum archives.

---

2   Database Directive 96/9/EC, http://www2.echo.lu/legal/en/ipr/database/text.htme.
3   Refer to EU Database Directive Recitals (1), http://www2.echo.lu/legal/en/ipr/database/recitals.html.
4   BGH GRUR 1988, 308 – Information Service.
5   Regional Court Hamburg CR 1994, 476-, Regional Court Mannheim NJW 1996, 1829.

Apart from a protection under these unfair competition rules, archives under certain circumstances were already protected by German copyright law even prior to the Database Directive becoming effective. For electronic archives copyright protection of the software used to operate the database was and is available pursuant to sections 69(a) ff. of the German Copyright Act, to the extent that the operation of the electronic databases is based on the utilization of software programs specifically developed for this purpose.[6] This protection, however, is limited to the software operating the archive and does not extend to the content of the archive itself.

The archives themselves, whether in the form of electronic databases or of traditional archive collections, could enjoy the protection of section 4 of the German Copyright Act as compilations, provided that they showed the required degree of originality.[7] A pre-condition for the protection under section 4 was, however, that in order to be protected the compilations needed to be a collection of 'works' or other 'contributions' which as such did not require copyright protection of their own. The collection, however, has to meet the standard of constituting a personal intellectual creation within the meaning of section 2, paragraph 2 of the German Copyright Act as regards the selection and arrangement of the respective contributions. Protection in the sense of section 4 of the German Copyright Act may thus exist for museum archives for which the selection and arrangement are vital characteristics. Collections of pure facts or data which could not be construed as 'contributions' such as directories or telephone books or other complete listings did not fall under compilations protected by section 4 of the German Copyright Act.

Under the old law there existed, therefore, a certain gap of protection, as the individual data and facts could not be protected due to their lack of originality, whereas the combination, selection and arrangement of data and facts, even if a specifically created achievement and thus in principle worth protecting, did not qualify for such protection under section 4. This gap of protection has now been bridged by the Database Directive and its implementation into German law.

The Database Directive is intended to protect works, data or other elements for which compilation, storage and access is provided via electronic, electro-magnetic, electro-optical or similar techniques.[8] The term 'database' is defined very broadly to cover collections of works of literature, art or music and other works as well as collections of other materials such as texts, sounds, images, figures, facts and data. The collection of works, data and other independent elements must be systematically or methodically arranged and individually accessible. This means that mere recordings of audio-visual, literary,

[6]   Berger, GRUR 1997, 170 ff.
[7]   Schricker and Löwenheim, *Copyright Act* (1987), section 4, marginal note 8; Fromm and Nordemann, *Copyright Law* (8th ed., 1994), section 4, marginal note 1.
[8]   Cf. Database Directive Recital (13).

photographic or musical works as such are not covered by the Database Directive.[9]

The Database Directive introduces two levels of protection. First, databases are protected by an extended copyright protection for the authors of such databases. In addition hereto, a so-called *sui generis* right is introduced for the purpose of protecting the producer of a database. With respect to a given database both rights may coexist (Article 7, paragraph 4 of the Database Directive).[10]

The copyright protection of databases is based on Article 3, paragraph 1 of the Directive. It provides that databases which, as a result of the selection or arrangement of the material, are their authors' own intellectual property, shall be protected under copyright law. Whether or not the collected material can be regarded as a contribution or whether it consists of a mere compilation of data and facts is therefore no longer relevant. It is also irrelevant whether the material included in the database is in an analogue or in a digital form. On the contrary, the protection under the Database Directive has been expanded to cover non-electronic databases.[11]

The additional so-called *sui generis* right under Article 7 of the Directive provides that the producer of a database shall be entitled to prohibit the extraction and reutilization of the material contained in a database. This right is in many respects different from the usual copyright protection, since it does not require the 'creator's own intellectual achievement', but rather that the producer of the database made an 'essential investment' when creating the database. The *sui generis* protection thus serves to protect the creator of the database from an erosion of its investment by extraction and reutilization.[12]

According to Article 7 of the Database Directive, 'extraction' shall mean the permanent or temporary transfer of all or a substantial part of the contents of a database to another medium by any means or any form. 'Reutilization' shall mean any form of making available to the public all or a substantial part of the contents of the database by way of distribution of copies, rental, on-line or through forms of transmission.

The *sui generis* right in many respects is similar to the neighbouring rights available to film producers and the producers of phonograms pursuant to German copyright law. Similar to the database producer they are being granted a right of their own pursuant to sections 85 and 94 of the German Copyright Act, in view of their specific investments, in particular the financial risk incurred by them, although these producers do not actually have any creative input.

---

9   Cf. Database Directive Recital (17).
10   See no 1 above.
11   Cf. Database Directive Recital (14).
12   Cf. Database Directive Recital (27).

The recent revision of the German Copyright Act which entered into effect on 1 January 1998, implemented into German law both forms of protections for databases, i.e. the protection of the database work itself and the *sui generis* protection for the producer of a database into German law.

The protection of database works has now been added as a separate second paragraph in section 4 of the German Copyright Act. According to this amendment the author of database works which contain systematically or methodically structured elements and which can be accessed individually via electronic media or otherwise is protected by the German Copyright Act.

It is of particular importance in this context that the new section 4, paragraph 2 of the German Copyright Act only refers to a compilation of 'elements'. This wording in contrast to the previous version of section 4 means that not only compilations of works, parts of such works or other contributions may be protected, but that the compilation of other elements, data and facts which are not protected as such can be protected as well. The implementation of the Database Directive by section 4, paragraph 2 thus satisfies the conditions of Article 3 of the Directive which only requires a personal creation in the compilation of elements, but forgoes any requirements as to the contents of the compilation.

Section 4, paragraph 1 of the German Copyright Act was modified accordingly, so that traditional collections may also now contain 'works, data or other independent elements'. This is in contrast to the previous wording 'works or contributions'. Protection is expressly provided irrespective of whether or not the elements constituting the collection as such enjoy protection.

It should further be emphasized that database works under the new German Copyright Act will be covered by the Database Directive which does not require that they be accessible by electronic media but any other means of access will suffice to qualify for a database work.

The *sui generis* protection can be found in sections 84(a) *et seq.* of the German Copyright Act. In principle the definition of a database protected by *sui generis* right complies with the definition in section 4, paragraph 2. Whereas copyright protection requires a creative achievement in assembling the database, the *sui generis* right is already available if the assembling, inspection or representation of the independent elements of the database needed 'considerable investments'[13] by the producer.

This means that in Germany traditional museum archives now enjoy protection irrespective of the content of the material collected in the archive as long as the selection and arrangement of the collection constitutes either a 'personal creation' by the author (section 4, paragraph 1 or 2) or a 'considerable investment' by the producers. The same applies therefore for film

---

[13]   For the definition of 'considerable investment' cf. Vogel, ZUM 1997, 596.

archives which do not contain film works protected by copyright and photographic multimedia works stored on CD-ROM or CDI.[14]

The scope of protection of the *sui generis* right is contained in section 87(b) of the German Copyright Act. According to this section, the producer of a database has the exclusive right to duplicate, disseminate and publish the entire database or significant parts thereof. This right shall apply correspondingly to insignificant parts in terms of nature or scope, provided that these parts are repeatedly and systematically duplicated, disseminated or published and if this duplication, dissemination or publication fails to be in conformity with an ordinary use of the database or if the justified interests of the producer would otherwise be affected in an intolerable manner.

Article 9 of the Database Directive states a number of exceptions from the protection by the *sui generis* right. These exceptions have now been implemented in section 87(c) of the German Copyright Act. According to this section, significant parts of a database may be duplicated to the extent that this duplication is only for private or scientific use or educational purposes.

A. *Term of Protection*

Another relevant restriction of these rights is the term of protection. As opposed to the protection of database works which lasts for 70 years after the author's death, the rights of the database producer will lapse 15 years after publication or within 15 years from its creation if it was not published within this period (German Copyright Act, section 87(d)).

According to Article 10, paragraph 3 of the Database Directive, significant qualitative or quantitative changes in or amendments to the contents which require a considerable amount of new investments will lead to renewed protection. This regulation of the Directive in Article 10, paragraph 3 as well as its implementation in section 87(a), paragraph 1, sentence 2 of the German Copyright Act again do not require the database to be a 'personal creation' but a 'considerable new investment as regards kind or quantity'.

Many archives which, as mere compilations of data and facts, have not been protected so far, now may enjoy independent protection under the German Copyright Act. Under the new *sui generis* right, the museums will be in addition hereto or by the virtue of this new right alone entitled to protection as producers of archives constituting databases.

---

[14]   Cf. Database Directive Recital (22).

The Law of Webcasting and Digital Music Delivery

Bob Kohn, esq.

GoodNoise Corp., Los Angeles, California

This chapter is dedicated to the memory of Frank Sinatra, whose life of music followed its own laws.

The passing away of Francis Albert Sinatra in 1998 marked the end of an era, but he remained with us long enough to witness the dawn of a new age, one that is being hailed as the digital millennium. For several years now, copies of Frank Sinatra's most popular recordings have been transmitted, mostly illegally, over the Internet, passing through cyberspace, like 'Strangers in the Night', to and from destinations unknown to the societies and collection agencies responsible for licensing these transmissions.

These recordings, and the musical works which underlie them, are being transmitted over the Internet in two basic ways:

(a)   by transmissions that are akin to radio broadcasts over the Internet, whether to the public at large or directly to individuals upon request – a method called webcasting; and

(b)   by the delivery of computer files, much like word processing files or a spreadsheet files, that contain sound recordings that can be played on personal computers and other devices equipped with the necessary decoding and audio software and hardware. These I will refer to as downloadable music files or by the name of the file format which made them popular, MP3.

The webcasting of sound recordings and the proliferation of downloadable MP3 files have caused those who create and distribute recorded entertainment to question whether the laws designed to protect their copyrighted content, such as musical works and sound recordings, will effectively be enforceable in the digital world. To address the concerns of those who have answered this question in the negative, lawmakers have proposed and enacted new legislation.

The Digital Performance Rights in Sound Recordings Act of 1995 (the 1995 Act) was enacted specifically to address the concerns raised by copyright owners of musical works and sound recordings. This important legislation made two significant, but distinct, changes affecting the licensing of musical works under US copyright law, one to address the questions raised by webcasting, and the other to address the questions raised by downloadable music files.

Because the 1995 Act fell short of addressing many of the questions raised by the application of digital technology to entertainment content, Congress recently proposed the Digital Millennium Copyright Act (the DM Act). The proposed DM Act is primarily intended to implement the recent World Intellectual Property Organization (WIPO) Copyright Treaty and WIPO Performances and Phonograms Treaty, both concluded at Geneva, Switzerland on 20 December 1996.

However, by a last-minute amendment proposed in the House version of the bill, the proposed DM Act would appear to reverse certain provisions of the 1995 Act relating to webcasting, provisions which also appear to have originally been a negotiation error by the record industry. At the time of this writing, the DM Act was approved by the House of Representatives and was awaiting action by the Congressional Conference Committee for reconciliation with the Senate version of the proposed Act.

This chapter will discuss the application of the 1995 Act, and the relevant provisions of the proposed DM Act, to webcasting and downloadable music delivery.[1]

I. Issues

A brief outline of forms of copyright protection that Congress provided the music industry when it enacted the 1995 Act is summarized in the following Table.

The Table describes ten different potential licensing questions facing webcasters and suppliers of downloadable files as they begin making plans to effect their digital audio transmissions containing copyrighted music. The answer to most of these questions is straightforward. The answers to Questions 1 and 3, however, are likely to remain the subject of some debate in the coming months, and the answer to Question 10 will depend entirely on whether the DM Act (in the form proposed by the House) is passed into law.

II. Two Copyrights Involved

Before addressing the questions presented in the Table, it should be helpful to first review several important concepts, the first of which involves the difference between a song and a sound recording of a song.

---

[1]   The Digital Millennium Copyright Act, Title IV, Miscellaneous Provisions, includes provisions that deal with webcaster licensing (available on the Internet at http://cweb.loc. qov/copyright).

Table of Licensing Questions		
Type of Digital Audio Transmission	Licence for Transmission of Musical Works (Music Publishers)	Licence for Transmission of Sound Recordings (Record Companies)
Digital Phonorecord Delivery	1. Compulsory ($.071) [ASCAP/BMI/SESAC?]	2. Voluntary
Not a Digital Phonorecord Delivery Interactive	3. ASCAP/BMI/SESAC [Compulsory ($.071)?]	4. Voluntary
Non-interactive Subscription		
Non-compliant	5. ASCAP/BMI/SESAC	6. Voluntary
Compliant	7. ASCAP/BMI/SESAC	8. Compulsory
Non-subscription	9. ASCAP/BMI/SESAC No Licence DM ACT: Compulsory if 'eligible'	10. 1995 Act

Anyone seeking to obtain a license (i.e. permission) to use a recording of a song must first understand that his or her use will normally involve not one, but two copyrights:

(a) the copyright in the sound recording; and
(b) the copyright in the underlying song, or musical work.

The copyright in a sound recording, in particular a series of sounds, is completely separate from the copyright in the underlying song featured in the sound recording.

For example, there exists a valid copyright in the song 'I've Got You Under My Skin' by Cole Porter and the copyright is owned by Warner/Chappell Music, Inc., a music publishing company. At the same time, several records of 'I've Got You Under My Skin' have been recorded by numerous recording artists over the years. A completely separate copyright exist for each particular recording – the sequence of sounds that make up the performance of the song by a singer and orchestra. These recordings are owned by the respective record companies that commissioned their creation. For example, the 1956 version of Frank Sinatra's recording of 'I've Got You Under My Skin' is owned by Capitol Records.

Thus, if you wished to obtain permission to use Sinatra's 1956 recording of 'I've Got You Under My Skin', you would require the permission of Capitol to use the recording and the permission of Warner/Chappell to use the underlying song. You could not use the recording without permission from both companies. If you wished to make a new recording of the song, you would require permission from Warner/Chappell, but you would not require permission from Capitol Records or any other record company who happens to own a recording of the song.

III. Performance Right versus Reproduction Right

The second important concept underlying this debate involves the difference between what is known as the reproduction right and the public performance right. The copyright law provides an owner of copyright several exclusive rights, including the exclusive right 'to reproduce the work' (e.g. to make physical copies, such as CDs and sheet music) and 'to publicly perform' the work (e.g. rendering a live performance of a song in a night-club, or playing a recording of a song on the radio).

This exclusive right to reproduce copyrighted works applies to both musical works (e.g. the Cole Porter song) and sound recordings (e.g. the particular recording of it owned by Capitol Records). By contrast, however, the right of public performance under the US copyright law only applies to songs, not to sound recordings. The owners of copyrights in songs have always had a general right of public performance in their musical works. As a result, the copyright owner of the song 'I've Got You Under My Skin' (in this case, Warner/Chappell, through its performance rights representative, ASCAP) will collect money from radio broadcasts of Sinatra's 1956 recording.

By contrast, the record company (in this example, Capitol Records) is not entitled to collect money from such radio broadcasts, because, at least in the US owners of sound recordings do not have a general public performance right.

IV. Digital Performance Rights in Sound Recordings Act 1995

As mentioned above, the 1995 Act made two significant, but distinct, changes affecting the licensing of musical works under US copyright law: to address the questions raised by webcasting, it created a new, but limited, digital public performance right for sound recordings, and to address the questions raised by downloadable music files, it broadened the Copyright Act's existing compulsory mechanical licence provision to include the reproduction and delivery of musical works in sound recordings by digital transmission.

A. *Sound Recordings*

Section 106 of the US Copyright Act sets forth the exclusive rights of a copyright owner, which includes the exclusive right of reproduction and the exclusive right of public performance discussed in the previous section. However, the exclusive right of public performance, set forth in section 106(4), only applies to the following specific types of copyrighted works: 'literary, musical, dramatic, and choreographic works, pantomimes, and motion pictures and other audiovisual works.' Note that sound recordings are not on the list.

Partially to address this omission, the 1995 Act added a new section 106(6), which provided the owner of copyrights in sound recordings an exclusive right in the public performance, but only when such performance is 'by means of a digital audio transmission'. This new limited right of public performance does not apply at all to analogue transmissions and was severely limited by the exemptions and other conditions set forth in section 114 of the Copyright Act, entitled 'Scope of Exclusive rights in sound Recordings', which will be discussed below.

B. *Musical Works*

Under section 106(1) of the Copyright Act, a copyright owner of a musical work has an exclusive right to reproduce the song in copies and phonorecords. This right, however, is subject to section 115 of the Copyright Act, which is often referred to as the 'compulsory licence provision'. Briefly, as long as records of a song were previously distributed in the US, the compulsory licence provision allows anyone else to compel the copyright owner of a song (e.g. a music publisher) to licence the song at a licence fee that is established by law – this fee is called the 'statutory rate'. The statutory rate, as of January 1998, is 7.1 cents, or 1.35 cents per minute of playing time.

The 1995 Act broadened section 115 so that the existing compulsory mechanical licence now covers downloadable music files, something which the 1995 Act calls 'digital phonorecord deliveries' (which are explained in more detail below). In other words, if someone wants to effect digital phonorecord deliveries of other people's songs, they may obtain a licence at the statutory rate. The 1995 Act established a procedure by which the statutory rate for these digital phonorecord deliveries would be set, but as of the time of this writing, such rate has not been announced. (For purposes of this chapter, it is assumed that the statutory rates for the reproduction and distribution of phonorecords in physical form and that of digital phonorecord deliveries will be the same.)

V. The Players

The final concepts underlying this debate concern knowing who the various music industry players are and who they represent. While this may be second nature to music industry veterans, webcasters who earnestly try to discern who it is they have to pay, and what it is they have to pay for, can find this to be a most intimidating endeavour. With apologies for the entertainment law buffs for the following superfluity and to foreign nationals for omitting all but the relevant US industry players in our wonderfully complex industry, I offer the following simplified descriptions.

A. *Record Company*

Record Companies are entities who enter into contractual relationships with recording artists for the financing, promotion, and distribution of sound and video recordings featuring artists' performances. In return, the artist is paid a royalty, which is typically in the form of some percentage of the revenues earned by the record company in connection with the various kinds of commercial exploitation of the artist's recorded performances.

B. *Music Publisher*

Music publishers are entities who enter into contractual relationships with songwriters, often the same person as the recording artist, for the commercial exploitation of the songs written by the songwriters. Publishers may license the song for use in recordings made and distributed by record companies, for use in printed editions, such as sheet music and songbooks, and for live and recorded performances of the songs in night-clubs, restaurants, hotels and similar establishments and on radio, television and other kinds of broadcasts.

C. *ASCAP/BMI/SESAC*

These organizations, commonly known as 'performance rights societies', represent music publishers and songwriters solely with respect to the performances of the songs. Music publishers and songwriters use these organizations to collect money from night-clubs, restaurants, hotels, and other venues, and radio and television stations for the public performance of all the songs they represent in their respective catalogues. They may charge the venues an annual flat fee and charge the radio and television stations a percentage of advertising revenues in exchange for a 'blanket licence' to use all of the songs the particular performance rights society controls or represents. After collecting the money on a blanket basis, each organization then takes surveys of what songs are played during the year, they then allocate the total collected revenue among the particular songs performed and pay each respective music songwriter and corresponding music publisher an amount representing what the song earned in performance royalties during the year. The performance rights societies only deal with the songs, not the recordings of songs, and as previously mentioned, only deal with performances of songs, not with the making or distribution of records or other copies containing songs.

D. *Harry Fox Agency*

This is an organization that specializes in issuing licences to record companies for the reproduction of songs in CDs and other kinds of records. The fees they charge for these uses is limited by the 'statutory rate' specified in the US Copyright Act. After retaining a small percentage for its services, the Harry

Fox Agency pays these fees to music publishers (which then typically pays half of that to the songwriter). Some music publishers issue their own mechanical licences directly to record companies, but many find the economies of scale offered by the Harry Fox Agency to be worth the services fee charged. Though the Harry Fox Agency performs other kinds of licensing services for music publishers, they do not licence performance of songs or engage in any form of licensing services for record companies.

E. *Recording Industry Association of America*

The RIAA headquartered in Washington, DC, is a trade association which represents record companies. The RIAA's stated mission is to promote the mutual interests of record companies, as well as the betterment of the industry overall through government relations, intellectual property protection, and international activities. The association also operates an aggressive anti-piracy unit, conducts extensive consumer and industry research, and provides ongoing communications support.

VI. Terms of Art

With these important concepts in mind, the ten basic licensing questions raised by the digital transmission of recorded music can be answered. Before exploring these questions two key terms of art will be reviewed: that of 'digital audio transmission' and 'digital phonorecord delivery'.

A. *Digital Audio Transmission*

First, as mentioned above, the 1995 Act provided to owners of sound recordings an exclusive right to perform them publicly by digital audio transmission. Essentially, to qualify for the exclusive right, the transmission must be in digital form, audio only, and a transmission.

A 'digital transmission' is a transmission that is in a digital or other non-analogue format. Thus, AM and FM broadcasts in analogue form are not covered. Next, it must be audio only, not audio-visual, because audio-visual works already have a public performance right under section 106(4). As a result, audio-visual works, such as music videos, are not subject to any of the limitations to which section 106(6) is subject, even if only the soundtrack of the video is transmitted. Finally, it must be a transmission. To 'transmit' a work is to communicate it by any process or device whereby sounds or images are received beyond the place from which they are sent. Thus, rendering a live performance, even with the use of a megaphone or loudspeakers, does not itself involve a transmission.

B. *Digital Phonorecord Delivery*

Second, there are two basic kinds of digital audio transmissions: those that result in a specifically identifiable reproduction of a phonorecord by or for any transmission recipient and those that do not. Transmissions that do are called 'digital phonorecord deliveries'. The detailed definition of which is set forth in the next section. An example of a digital phonorecord delivery would be the commercial sale from a web site of an 'MP3 file' – that is, a sound recording saved as computer data file using the compression techniques of an MPEG layer-3 software encoder – downloaded from a web site directly over the Internet to the home computer of a consumer.

C. *Digital Audio Transmissions that Result in Digital Phonorecord Deliveries*

Question 1: What licences are required from the owner of a song to permit a digital phonorecord delivery of a sound recording containing the song – that is, the digital transmission that results in the recipient winding up with a phonorecord containing the song?

1. Reproduction Right

Recall that a copyright owner of a musical work has an exclusive right to reproduce the song in copies and phonorecords. This right is subject to section 115 of the Copyright Act, which is often referred to as the 'compulsory licence provision.' Briefly, as long as records of a song were previously distributed in the US, the compulsory licence provision allows anyone else to compel the copyright owner of a song (e.g. a music publisher) to license the song at a licence fee that is established by law – this fee is called the 'statutory rate'.

As mentioned above, the statutory rate, as of January 1998, is (assumed to be) 7.1 cents, or 1.35 cents per minute of playing time. In other words, if someone wants to effect digital phonorecord deliveries of other people's songs, they may obtain a licence at the statutory rate. The licence which authorizes these transmissions is called a 'mechanical license'; and the organization in the US that issues most of them is the Harry Fox Agency. The nice thing about these licences is that you know you can always get one, and the statutory rate serves as a ceiling to what the music publishers or the Harry Fox Agency can charge you. In addition, the Harry Fox Agency is currently negotiating an agreement with its international counterparts that would make it clear that mechanical licences will be collected from the source of the transmission – that is, the web site offering the digital phonorecord deliveres – regardless of where in the world the transmission recipient receives his or her copy of the recording. Mechanical licences are easy to get, and God bless them.

2. Performance Right

There is a little controversy brewing here. The performance rights societies (e.g. ASCAP, BMI, SESAC) appear to be taking the position that a performance licence is required to effect a digital phonorecord delivery, even though a statutory mechanical reproduction licence has already been obtained for the same delivery. In their view, all transmissions of songs constitute performances of songs, whether or not they result in a specifically identifiable phonorecord made by or for the transmission recipient, and therefore, they say, you must also pay a public performance fee for these transmissions.

The performance rights societies have not yet disclosed how much they intend to charge for these transmissions. They are likely to seek something less than what they charge for transmissions that do not constitute digital phonorecord deliveries, such as 'streaming' audio transmissions (see below).

A webcaster may legitimately ask: if I am paying 7.1 cents for the digital phonorecord delivery, why must I also pay for its transmission, particularly if the phonorecord is not truly performed or in any way rendered during the transmission? Is this a form of 'double-dipping' by the music industry?

I have yet to take a position on this particular controversy, but, at the risk of being branded a pirate by the music industry and a music industry lackey by the web community, I will venture to point out briefly various positions that have been, or may be, made to support each side in this debate.

The performance rights societies could point to the definition of 'digital phonorecord delivery' to support its position. The complete definition of that term, which was added to the Copyright Act by the 1995 Act, is as follows:

'A "digital phonorecord delivery", is each individual delivery of a phonorecord by digital transmission of a sound recording which results in a specifically identifiable reproduction by or for any transmission recipient of a phonorecord of that sound recording, regardless of whether the digital transmission is also a public performance of the sound recording or any nondramatic musical work embodied therein.'

One could certainly infer from the quoted language that a digital phonorecord delivery may involve the public performance of the musical work embodied in the sound recording; but only that it may do so is the best you can say about it. If Congress intended to answer definitely the question, it certainly could have done so in unambiguous terms, such as 'A digital transmission containing a sound recording that results in a digital phonorecord delivery, constitutes a performance of any musical work embodied in that sound recording.' But it did not.

Quite possibly, Congress recognized that some digital phonorecord deliveries may be performed or 'streamed' for listening by the user while they are being downloaded; hence, the quoted language may have been needed to make certain that a digital phonorecord delivery will still be deemed such, even if the digital transmission happens also to constitute a public performance.

The performance rights societies could point to the definition of public performance:

'To perform...a work publicly means –
(1) to perform or display it at a place open to the public or at any place where a substantial number of persons outside of a normal circle of a family and its social acquaintances is gathered; or
(2) to transmit or otherwise communicate a performance or display of the work to a place specified by clause (1) or to the public, by means of any device or process, whether the members of the public capable of receiving the performance or display receive it in the same place or in separate places and at the same time or at different times.'

It appears, from the quoted language, that it does not matter whether you hear the performance at the same time as you download the file. Certainly, when a recording is being streamed to you, it is first buffered in your computer's temporary memory, before the recording is actually played so that you can hear it. What is the difference between storing the recording in temporary memory and storing it on your hard disk (which is typically the case with a digital phonorecord delivery) prior to your hearing the recording?

The problem with these arguments is that the above definition concerns not what a performance is, but what it means to perform a work publicly (as opposed to privately). Nevertheless, even if the transmission of a work is considered a public one, it may still not constitute a performance. According to the Copyright Act 'To perform a work means to recite, render, play, dance, or act it, either directly or by means of any device or process...'. It may well be asked, where, for purposes of the definition of 'perform', is the 'rendering' or the 'playing' of the work in a transmission of a downloaded music file? The performance rights societies could take the position that a sound recording of a work is itself a 'rendering' (i.e. a performance, albeit a recorded one) of the work. This is as opposed to sheet music where the musical notations only are listed. When one digitally transmits the sound file, one is engaged in a transmission of the recorded performance, when, it may be said, the requisite 'rendering' is taking place.

This argument would be plausible but not for the definition of 'sound recordings', which is defined in the Copyright Act as 'works that result from the fixation of a series of sounds'. Thus, by definition, a sound recording is a fixation of sounds, not a rendering of sounds. Arguably, then, by transmitting a sound recording, a fixation of sounds is being transmitted, not a performance or rendering of them.

A better argument, from the performance rights societies' perspective, would be to say that the downloading of a digital file is part of a process that results in a rendering or playing of the work at the recipient's end. Recall that to perform a work means to render or play the work, 'either directly or by means of a device or process'. Thus, arguably, the process of transmitting the bits constituting a digital sound recording file, the recipient's buffering those bits or saving them to his or her hard disk or other storage media, and playing of the bits, either as the bits are being downloaded or later, even after the entire file has been saved to disk, constitutes a playing or rendering of the sound recording 'either directly or by means of a device or process'.

Because technology now permits the playing of the bits either as the bits are being downloaded or after all the bits in the file have been received, the distinction between a digital phonorecord delivery (DPD) and a non-DPD (i.e. a purely 'streaming' digital audio transmission) is being blurred. The performance rights societies may argue that all of these transmissions should be considered performances, merely because it is too impractical, on a case-by-case basis, to make a distinction between them.

In addition, the performance rights societies have argued that a digital phonorecord delivery provides an added value to the consumer – that is, with the advent of digital deliveries, the consumer no longer has to schlep down to a record store to buy a CD; he or she can just order it on-line and receive it in minutes. Consequently, that added value should be paid for. This argument, however, was first made before the success of companies like Amazon.com, from whom you can now order a CD and have it sent to you by overnight courier. What practical difference does it make whether the tracks constituting a record album come to you overnight or several minutes or hours after you have requested them to be downloaded?

Moreover, it may be reasonable to assume that if Congress made digital phonorecord deliveries subject to a compulsory licence under section 115, and set the fee for such licences at the statutory rate, then, arguably, it should be unnecessary for anyone to pay more than the statutory rate to effect the delivery, 'regardless of whether the digital transmission is also a public performance of... any musical work embodied therein'. Again, the quoted language is from the Act's definition of digital phonorecord delivery, and one could infer from it that Congress wanted to make certain that a digital download of a sound recording will be deemed a digital phonorecord delivery, subject to the compulsory licence, with no one having to pay more than the statutory rate, even if the digital transmission happens also to constitute a public performance.

If the performance rights societies are not successful in persuading the industry, or a court, that all digital phonorecord deliveries constitute performances, one might think that the practical result will be this: if the statutory rate for a mechanical reproduction licence is paid with respect to a transmission, then, a performance royalty is not due for the same transmission. Payment of the statutory fee for a mechanical licence is intended to cover the sale of a copy (i.e. a physical phonorecord or a digital phonorecord delivery) and, theoretically, all private performances of the song arising from the use of such copy – and this would include the first performance or rendering that occurs concurrently with the transmission of the digital phonorecord delivery or some time after the digital phonorecord delivery is completed.

This, however, is complicated by the following problem as will be discussed below in connection with Question 3, the Harry Fox Agency, on behalf of the music publishers which it represents, appears to be taking the position that a digital audio transmission of a musical work that is effected by means of an 'interactive service' (discussed below) constitutes a digital phonorecord delivery, even though there is no assurance that the recipient will end up with a reusable copy of the recording. As such, the transmission will require payment of the statutory compulsory licence fee, currently 7.1 cents. As pointed out below, no one disputes that a transmission that is a mere 'streaming' of a recording is a public performance of the song underlying the recording, entitling the performance rights society legitimately to collect performance royalties for them. But, here again, the industry may be open to the accusation of 'double-dipping'.

It would seem that this sticky problem is something that should be worked out between the performance rights societies, which are largely controlled by songwriters and music publishers, and the Harry Fox Agency (or directly by their music publisher members and the songwriters who they represent). The problem is that neither group is likely to welcome the prospect of giving up their side of the revenues to avoid the perceived 'double-dipping' problem.

Be that as it may, other arguments, of varying degrees of persuasiveness, have been put forth by both proponents and detractors on this question, but I thought it wise to reserve my views on the subject until such time as I have formulated them.

Question 2: What licences are required from the owner of a recording to permit a digital phonorecord delivery containing the song – that is, the digital transmission that results in the recipient receiving a phonorecord containing the recording?

There is no controversy about the answer to this question: persons desiring to make digital phonorecord deliveries of sound recordings must obtain a licence from the person who owns the recording, which is typically a record company. Further, unlike for the use of the underlying song, there is no compulsory licence for these kinds of digital audio transmissions. In other words, you must obtain permission from the record company and the record company can charge whatever it likes or even refuse to grant you permission to make the transmission.

The reason for this is simple: digital phonorecord deliveries directly replace sales of records. Without such sales, the purpose of the copyright law will be defeated: record companies would be unable to finance, promote and distribute new recordings, and artists would be unable to earn royalties to support professional recording careers. As a result, there will be an economically insufficient supply of quality musical recordings for the buying public. It is the very purpose of the copyright law to ensure that artists and their record companies receive economic remuneration for their undertakings, so that an efficient supply of quality musical works and sound recordings will be produced and distributed to the listening public.

This theme of the extent to which digital audio transmissions would replace the sale of records played an important role in the development of the 1995 Act and is an important concept in understanding the distinctions among the various kinds of transmissions identified in the 1995 Act discussed below. For example, there is a great distinction between what licences are required for digital audio transmissions that constitute digital phonorecords and transmissions that do not. As shall be seen, the law extends stronger and more flexible performance rights to the owners of sound recordings in instances where the digital audio transmission poses a greater risk of replacing a record sale.

D. *Digital Audio Transmissions that Do Not Result in Digital Phonorecord Deliveries*

Of transmissions that do not result in digital phonorecord deliveries, there are two basic types: transmissions that are part of an interactive service and those that are not.

Under the US Copyright Act:

'An "interactive service" is one that enables a member of the public to receive, on request, a transmission of a particular sound recording chosen by or on behalf of the recipient. The ability of individuals to request that particular sound recordings be performed for reception by the public at large does make a service interactive'.

Clearly, even if the digital audio transmission does not result in a copy at the recipient's end of the transmission, if the recipient can choose, on request, 'a particular recording'. Then there is a high risk that the recipient will never need to purchase a copy of the recording or purchase a digital phonorecord delivery. If the interactive transmission is cheap enough, and the sound quality good enough, members of the public may choose to listen to interactive transmissions instead. Thus, to serve the purpose of the Copyright Act, a licence for interactive transmissions is required. What does this specifically mean in terms of the song and the sound recording?

Question 3: What licences are required from the owner of a song to permit a digital transmission that is part of an interactive service, but does not result in a digital phonorecord delivery of the song?

1. Performance Rights

Clearly, a digital transmission of a song that is part of an interactive service, but does not result in a digital phonorecord delivery of the song – for example, the mere 'streaming' of a song after a user clicks on an icon or link to receive a transmission of a particular sound recording – constitutes a public performance of the song. Hence, the performance rights societies (e.g. ASCAP, BMI, SESAC) are entitled to collect performance royalties under their 'blanket' licences to web sites that offer these interactive transmissions.

2. Reproduction Rights

Here is the second open controversy. As mentioned above, the Harry Fox Agency, on behalf of its music publisher members, is taking the position that songs digitally streamed from interactive services constitute digital phonorecord deliveries, even if no digital copy is, or can be, made by or for the intended recipient of the transmission. Accordingly, interactive transmissions of purely streamed music would require payment of the statutory compulsory licence fee of 7.1 cents each.

As with the other potential 'double-dipping' issue discussed in connection with the answer to Question 2 above, I have not formulated any definitive view on this subject, but the music publishers can take solace from a very specific provision that was in the DRPA and is now part of the compulsory licence provision at section 115(c)(3)(L): 'The provisions of this section concerning digital phonorecord deliveries shall not apply to any exempt transmissions or retransmissions under section 114(d)(1).'

In the view of the Harry Fox Agency, the above language implies that the provisions concerning digital phonorecord deliveries, while not applying to any exempt transmissions under section 114(d)(1) – which will be discussed below – does in fact apply to those transmissions that are not exempt under section 114, which would include all transmissions made as part of interactive services. Thus, according to the argument, the transmitter must pay 7.1 cents per interactive digital audio transmission, whether or not a copy results in the recipient. Regardless of whether one may agree with this result, the argument that the law, as written, requires this result, is a strong one.

Nevertheless, the Harry Fox Agency has recognized that an interactive transmission of a song that is of a short duration and which does not result in a copy being made for the intended recipient, is not likely to have an effect on the sale of a record or a full digital phonorecord delivery of the song. Accordingly, the Harry Fox Agency (and presumably the music publishers it represents) will allow such interactive transmissions without requiring payment of the statutory fee if no more than 30 seconds of the song is transmitted and the transmission is effected by or with the permission of the owner of the sound recording embodying the song. Note, this does not allow anyone to make such 30-second transmissions, only the record company that owns the recording, or its licensees.

Question 4: What licences are required from the owner of a recording to permit a digital transmission that is part of an interactive service, but does not result in a digital phonorecord delivery of the recording?

As mentioned above, even if the digital audio transmission does not result in a copy at the recipient's end of the transmission, if the recipient can choose, on request, 'a particular recording', then there is a high risk that the recipient will never need to purchase a copy of the recording or purchase a digital phonorecord delivery. For this reason, the law specifically gives owners of sound recordings, typically record companies, an exclusive right to license digital audio transmissions that are part of interactive services. This means the record company can charge what it wishes for these transmissions or refuse to provide a licence at all.

E. *Non-Interactive Services*

As mentioned above, there are two kinds of digital audio transmissions that do not result in digital phonorecord deliveries: those that are part of an interactive service and those not part of an interactive service. Of those transmissions that are not part of an interactive service, there are two types: subscription transmissions and non-subscription transmissions.

The former requires a licence, in one form or another, and the latter, under the 1995 Act, does not require a licence. Why? Returning to our recurrent theme, the distinction between subscription and non-subscription transmissions was made because it was felt that the risk of a music service which consumers pay for on a subscription basis poses a moderate to high risk of replacing the sales of records (either physical CDs or digital phonorecord deliveries), while those which are on a non-subscription basis, like traditional, advertising-supported radio broadcasts, and the like, pose only a low risk of replacing record sales.

Here are the relevant definitions:

'A "subscription transmission" is a transmission that is controlled and limited to particular recipients, and for which consideration is required to be paid or otherwise given by or on behalf of the recipient to receive the transmission or a package of transmissions including the transmission.

A "nonsubscription transmission" is any transmission that is not a subscription transmission.'

Let us first turn to subscription transmissions.

F. *Subscription Transmissions*

I would have liked to report that the distinction between subscription and non-subscription transmissions ends there, but it does not. Keeping in the theme of providing greater rights where there is a higher risk of replacing record sales, it was thought that some transmissions are less likely to replace record sales than others. Accordingly, certain subscription transmissions would be treated like any interactive service, giving the record companies full flexibility to negotiate whatever licence fees they like or refuse to license these forms of subscription transmissions. Other forms of subscription transmissions, those which pose a lower threat of replacing the sales of records, would fall within an area of the law which would allow transmitting organizations, like webcasters, to compel the record companies to grant a licence and to pay a fee set not by the record companies, but by a federal arbitration panel.

Thus, the 1995 Act established two types of subscription transmissions of sound recordings: voluntary subscription transmissions and compulsory subscription transmissions. Both require licences from the sound recording owners, typically record companies. However, the former may be licensed by the record companies on a voluntary basis, meaning the record companies can set any licensee fee they wish, or refuse to license these transmissions. With respect to compulsory subscription transmissions, the record companies can be compelled to grant licences and the licence fees are subject to a statutory fee, which will effectively serve as a maximum amount that will be charged for such licences. The licensing questions arising from voluntary subscription transmissions – that is, those which are not subject to compulsory licensing – will be reviewed first.

Question 5: What licences are required from the owner of a song to permit a digital transmission that does not result in a digital phonorecord delivery of the song, is not part of an interactive service, but is part of a subscription transmission that does not comply with compulsory licence provision?

As with the distinction between subscription and non-subscription transmissions, the distinction between subscription transmissions that qualify for compulsory licensing and those that do not is not relevant to the question of what licence is required from the owner of the song embodied in a particular sound recording. (The distinction is only relevant to the question of what licences are required from record companies for the transmission of these recordings.) Thus, to transmit the song (as opposed to the sound recording) a public performance licence from the applicable performance rights society (e.g. ASCAP, BMI, or SESAC) is always required.

This is because, unlike with the general public performance rights which owners of songs have always enjoyed, owners of sound recordings do not have a general public performance right. The owners of sound recordings were only recently given a public performance right for digital audio transmissions of their recordings, and only after a period of prolonged negotiations which resulted in the limitations reflected in section 114, including these fine distinctions between interactive and non-interactive services, subscription and non-subscription transmissions, and subscription transmissions that are subject to a compulsory licence and those which are not. As shall be seen, recognizing this licensing regime which Congress established is the key to unlocking the answers to the questions raised by the recording industry with respect to non-subscription transmissions under the 1995 Act.

Question 6: What licences are required from the owner of a recording to permit a digital transmission that does not result in a digital phonorecord delivery of the recording, is not part of an interactive service, but is part of a subscription transmission that does not comply with compulsory licence provision?

Leaving aside for the moment the criteria necessary to qualify for a compulsory licence to make digital audio transmissions of sound recordings on a subscription basis, the person making a non-qualifying subscription transmission of a recording must obtain a licence from the record company who owns the recording. Moreover, given that the licence is voluntary, the fee charged by the record company for this licence is completely subject to negotiation, meaning the record company may charge what it wants and is free even to refuse to provide a licence for these transmissions.

Question 7: What licences are required from the owner of a song to permit a digital transmission that does not result in a digital phonorecord delivery of the song, is not part of an interactive service, but is part of a subscription transmission that does comply with compulsory licence provision?

As mentioned above, the distinction between subscription transmissions that qualify for a compulsory licence and those that do not is not relevant to the question of what licence is required from the owner of the song. The person making such a digital transmission must obtain a blanket licence from the applicable performance rights society.

Question 8: What licences are required from the owner of a recording to permit a digital transmission that does not result in a digital phonorecord delivery of the recording, is not part of an interactive service, but is part of a subscription transmission that does comply with compulsory licence provision?

Recall that a transmitting entity that wishes to operate a subscription service has available one of two forms of licensing mechanisms: a 'voluntary licence' or a 'compulsory licence'. Under a 'voluntary licence', the record companies in a free market can charge whatever they wish or refuse to license your transmissions at all. Under the 'compulsory licence', the record companies can be compelled to license the transmissions under licence fees set by a governmental body, fees called the statutory rate, which effectively becomes a maximum fee that the record companies can charge for the transmitting entity's use.

To qualify for a compulsory licence to make a subscription transmission, a transmitting organization must meet the conditions set forth in section 114(d)(2) of the Copyright Act. To complicate matters, however, the proposed DM Act would replace the provisions of section 114(d)(2) with a new set of conditions that are in many respects more restrictive than those found under the Copyright Act amendments made under the 1995 Act. Accordingly, the applicable conditions will be briefly reviewed, first under the current law and then under the proposed DM Act.

1. Subscription Transmissions Under the 1995 Act

To qualify, under the law currently in effect, for a compulsory licence to make a subscription transmission, the following conditions must be met by the transmitting entity:

(a) the transmission is not part of an interactive service (defined above);
(b) the transmission does not exceed the 'sound recording performance complement' (see below);
(c) the transmitting entity does not publish an advance program schedule or prior announcement of the titles of the specific sound recordings to be transmitted;
(d) the transmitting entity does not automatically and intentionally cause any device receiving the transmission to switch from one program channel to another; and

(e) the transmission of the sound recording is accompanied by any copyright management information encoded in that sound recording by the copyright owner.

The overall purpose of these conditions is to provide webcasters and other transmitting organizations with a guarantee that if the subscription transmissions which they desire to make have a low risk of being used by consumers to replace sales of records, then the transmitting entity will be allowed to compel the record companies to grant them a licence to make such transmissions at a special rate that is established by law.

The lower risk of these transmissions being used to replace record sales is reflected in the conditions. For example, the transmission cannot be part of an interactive service. If the consumer were permitted to click on an icon or web link (or issue a voice command) and receive a particular recording on demand, he or she could be prepared to record each transmission and use such recordings for future private performances, which are not subject to payment to the sound recording owners. Similarly, the transmitting entity must not publish any advance program schedule or make any prior announcement of the titles of the specific recordings to be transmitted. Again, having access to the playlist in advance would allow the consumer to cherry-pick which sound recordings he or she would like to record at home.

Further, the transmission must not exceed the 'sound recording performance complement'. The sound recording performance complement, which is defined below, is designed to prevent a transmitter from obtaining a compulsory licence at the preferred statutory rate for transmissions, such as an all Beatles channel or transmissions of all the songs from the same album.

'The "sound recording performance complement", is the transmission during any 3-hour period, on a particular channel used by a transmitting entity, of no more than –
(A) 3 different selections of sound recordings from any one phonorecord lawfully distributed for public performance or sale in the United States, if no more than 2 such selections are transmitted consecutively; or
(B) 4 different selections of sound recordings –
   (i)   by the same featured recording artist; or
   (ii) from any set or compilation of phonorecords lawfully distributed together as a unit for public performance or sale in the United States, if no more than three such selections are transmitted consecutively: Provided, that the transmission of selections in excess of the numerical limits provided for in clauses (A) and (B) from multiple phonorecords shall nonetheless qualify as a sound recording performance complement if the programming of the multiple phonorecords was not willfully intended to avoid the numerical limitations prescribed in such clauses.'

Again, the purpose of the sound recording performance complement was to help define a category of transmissions that pose only a moderate risk that consumers will make home recordings of the transmission for the purpose of avoiding having to purchase records for later private performances.

If the subscription transmission meets all of the above conditions, it will qualify for a compulsory licence. In other words, the transmitting organization, under the law, can compel the record companies to provide it with a licence to make these transmissions and the licence fee will be limited to the fee established by law.

Subscription transmission services will be required to provide detailed reports, and maintain extensive records, of their use of sound recordings under the licence. The organizations participating in the US Copyright Office's development of these procedures included the Recording Industry Association of America (RIAA), and three digital music subscription services operating in the US: DMX, Inc. (DMX); Muzak, Inc., and Digital Cable Radio Associates/Music Choice (DCR). Further, after the licence fees for these transmissions have been paid, the money collected will be allocated to the record companies and recording artists, subject to provisions set forth in the 1995 Act.[2]

2. Subscription Transmissions Under the Proposed DM Act

If the proposed DM Act is enacted in the form currently proposed by the House, the conditions necessary for a transmitting organization to effect subscription transmissions would change.[3]

Briefly, the applicability of the restrictions upon a transmitting organization depends upon whether the transmitting organization had been offering its webcasts on or before 31 July 1998 using the same medium of transmission after that date that it was using before. If that is the case, then a compulsory licence for a subscription transmission would be available at a rate set under the auspices of the US Librarian of Congress if:

'(i)   the transmission is not part of an interactive service;

(ii) except in the case of a transmission to a business establishment, the transmitting entity does not automatically and intentionally cause any device receiving the transmission to switch from one program channel to another;

(iii) the transmission of the sound recording is accompanied by the information encoded in that sound recording, if any, by or under the authority of the copyright owner of that sound recording, that identifies the title of the sound recording, the featured recording artist who performs on the sound recording, and related information, including information concerning the underlying musical work and its writer;

(iv) the transmission does not exceed the sound recording performance complement; and

---

[2]   Procedures relating to the compulsory licence for subscription transmissions is set forth in Interim Regulations on Notice and Recordkeeping for Digital Subscription Transmissions Docket No. RM 96-3B, 63 Fed.Register 34289 (24 June 1998) (on the web at http://lcweb.loc.gov/copyright/fedreg/96-3b.html).

[3]   The new conditions proposed under the DM Act are set forth on the web at http://thomas.loc.gov/cgi-bin/query/D?c105:20:./temp/~c105AmWsxV:e99622:.

(v)   the transmitting entity does not cause to be published by means of an advance program schedule or prior announcement the titles of the specific sound recordings or phonorecords embodying such sound recordings to be transmitted;....'

If, however, the transmitting organization had not been offering webcasts on or before 31 July 1998 or had been using a medium of transmission before that date different from that which it was using after that time, then a compulsory licence for a subscription transmission would be available at a rate set under the auspices of the US Librarian of Congress if the transmissions meet the same conditions as those required for anyone desiring to make 'eligible nonsubscription transmissions'. The conditions necessary for eligible non-subscription transmissions to qualify for a compulsory licence under the proposed DM Act are set forth below.

G. *Non-Subscription Transmissions*

Question 9: What licences are required from the owner of a song to permit a digital transmission that does not result in a digital phonorecord delivery of the song, is not part of an interactive service, and constitutes a non-subscription transmission?

Again, the distinction between subscription and non-subscription services is not relevant to licensing the underlying song. The person making such digital transmissions must obtain a blanket licence from the applicable performance rights society (e.g. ASCAP, BMI or SESAC).

It is worth noting, at this juncture, that if the DM Act is passed in the form currently proposed by the House (i.e. eliminating the exemption for non-interactive, non-subscription transmissions), then the performance rights societies, and their music publisher and songwriter members, could suffer a significant reduction in performance royalty income, arising from the fewer number of web radio stations engaging in non-interactive, non-subscription web transmissions.

Question 10: What licences are required from the owner of a recording to permit a digital transmission that does not result in a digital phonorecord delivery of the recording, is not part of an interactive service, and is not part of a subscription service?

As noted above, the answer to this question depends entirely on whether the DM Act is passed in the form currently proposed by the House, a form which eliminates the exemption currently enjoyed by non-interactive, non-subscription transmissions and replaces it with a compulsory licence in favour of a limited class of webcasters.

Music: Licences, Permission Forms, and Releases in the Digital Age

Rachelle V. Browne

Smithsonian Institution, Washington, DC, USA

I. General Background

An owner of a copyrighted work has and controls exclusive rights to display, perform, reproduce, distribute, and adapt the work and to permit others to do so.[1] In the case of a song or music, this means that the copyright owner controls the right to: print lyrics or musical scores or display them on a web page; perform the song or music in public either live or through recordings; reproduce and distribute sound recordings or music sheets; or sample or otherwise adapt protected works for derivative uses as, for example, background for a film or for a new musical work or recording.

Without proper authorization, many uses of music and sound recordings of music are illegal because they infringe on one of the exclusive rights of the copyright owners. Consider the following examples.

An author begins her research of blues legacies by transcribing lyrics from her personal record collection. The lyrics make up over half of here 200-page tome. The author soon discovers that to stay within her budget, she must, in at least one instance, ask the sons of the now deceased writer of the lyrics to intervene in her negotiations with a publishing company that owns the rights for the lyrics.

---

[1]   Subject to several statutory limitations, a copyright owner has a *bundle* of divisible and exclusive rights. In addition to an exclusive performance right, a copyright owner has the exclusive right to do and authorize anyone to: reproduce the work; prepare derivative works based upon the work; distribute copies of the work to the public by sale or other transfer of ownership, or by rental, lease, or lending; and display the work publicly. 17 USC section 106.

A group of music publishers sues Compuserve for the unauthorized reproduction and distribution of copyrighted musical compositions on its bulletin board service. The dispute revolves around the unauthorized uploading and downloading by Compuserve's subscribers of musical compositions like 'Unchained Melody'.

Museums use music in traditional ways, such as for exhibition kiosks, record compilations or documentary films or videotapes, and more recently in computer disks, web pages and other emerging digital formats. Generally, the process of obtaining permission to use copyrighted materials in digital works does not differ from the process for clearing rights for any work that is derived or incorporates elements from pre-existing materials. In both instances, the greatest challenge for the user of copyrighted music is that the owner of the recording containing the song may be different from the owner of the copyrighted lyrics or, for that matter, the owner of the music for the song.

II. Obtaining Permissions

To secure permission, the user must: identify who owns or controls the various elements of the copyrighted musical work; decide on the market and media for which permission is needed; negotiate any other restrictions on the use of the music; obtain a written licence; and pay any necessary fees to the copyright owner. Permission may be sought directly from the individual copyright owner or through an organization representing a voluntary collective of owners.

Terms and conditions that may be addressed in seeking permissions are listed below.

(a) Contemplated market: is the work being designed for exhibition, theatrical, home video or non-profit educational use?

(b) Fee: will the licensor charge a flat fee or a royalty? What is the basis for computing the royalty? Will the licensor waive all or part of the fee if the use if for a non-profit educational purpose?

(c) Exclusivity: will a third party be able to use the same material for a similar purpose?

(d) Future use: does the licence give the museum the right 'to reproduce and electronically publish the work in digital form' or the broader right to use the material in 'all other media and technologies now known or hereinafter developed'? What restrictions does the licensor impose on subsequent reuse?

(e) Term: is the licence for the full term of copyright or a specific number of years?

(f) Credits and disclosures: what affirmative disclosure about ownership or reuse does the licensor want placed on the product?

Obtaining rights to use pre-existing music may be costly and time-consuming. For this reason, the music for many projects have been created with original works.

III. Fair Use of Music

In 1975, Congress invited a group of music educators and publishers to develop guidelines for teachers and students on the fair use of music, as described under section 107 of the Copyright Act.[2] Consistent with the fair use exception in section 107, the guidelines[3] permit copyrighted music to be used without the copyright owner's permission in teaching (including photocopying for classroom use) and scholarly research. The guidelines, although not part of the Copyright Act, help to clarify the minimum standards of educational fair use under that law.

The guidelines state that the following are permissible fair uses of copyrighted music:

(a) emergency copying for a performance;
(b) multiple copying of excerpts (but not more than 10 per cent of the original) for non-performance purposes;
(c) making a single copy of a recording of student performances for evaluation or rehearsal; and
(d) making a single copy of a recording owned by the school or a teacher to construct aural exercises or examinations.

The guidelines do not address specifically the use of music in multimedia products.[4] However, a museum should consider obtaining the copyright owner's permission to use the music or other materials whenever including pre-existing music in a multimedia product for commercial reproduction and distribution or posting it over an electronic network to which access is

---

[2]   Section 107 – Limitations on Exclusive Rights: Fair use. Notwithstanding the provisions of section 106, the fair use of a copyrighted work, including such use by reproduction in copies or *phonorecords* or by any other means specified in that section, for purposes such as criticism, comment, news reporting, teaching (including multiple copies for classroom use), scholarship, or research, is not an infringement of copyright. In determining whether the use made of a work in any particular case is a fair use, the factors to be considered shall include:
  (a) the purpose and character of the use, including *whether such use is of a commercial nature or is for non-profit educational purpose*;
  (b) the nature of the copyrighted work;
  (c) the amount and substantiality of the portion used in relation to the copyrighted work as a whole; and
  (d) the effect of the use upon the potential market for or value of the copyrighted work.

[3]   *Guidelines for Educational Use of Music*, HR Rep. No. 1476, 94th Cong., 2d Sess. 47 (1976), reprinted in 17 USC section 107.

[4]   Representatives of non-profit music education and music publishing met on 26 April 1996, in New York to discuss whether the guidelines need revision in the digital environment. The participants concluded that no change is needed but noted that guidelines considered by others might include the uses of music in digital form. See The Conference on Fair Use: Report to the Commissioner on the Conclusion of the First Phase of the Conference on Fair Use (1997) at http://www.uspto.gov.

uncontrolled and the use may not be deemed a 'fair use' under the general statutory standards.

IV. Museum's Use of Recorded Music for Exhibition Purposes

The 'fair use' standards in section 107 and the guidelines for educational use of music address some permissible uses of music in possible museum settings. In addition, there are other related or independent exemptions, under the federal copyright law, that allow for the non-profit, educational use of copyrighted music without the owner's permission.

For example, suppose a museum wants to play, as background music from a collection of recordings on 'The Love Songs of World War II' in an exhibit about World War II. The recordings, on compact disc, also would be sold in the museum shop, next to the exhibit, where a label would indicate the source of the music and its availability in the shop.

Under federal copyright law, the owner of a copyrighted musical work enjoys the exclusive right, subject to certain limitations, to perform or to authorize the performance of the work publicly.[5] 'To perform' means not only playing the work live but also playing a recording embodying the work. Generally, anyone performing copyrighted musical works in public must obtain a licence from a music performing rights organization, like ASCAP or BMI, or the owner, unless the performance is specifically exempted under the copyright law.

The museum's contemplated use of the recording clearly is a public performance. However, the use falls within one of the statutory exemptions that limit a copyright owner's otherwise exclusive performance right. The copyright law allows for the royalty-free and unlicensed performance of a non-dramatic musical work when the performance is made:

'without any purpose of direct or indirect commercial advantage and without payment of any fee or other compensation for the performance to any performers, promoters or organizers, if there is no direct or indirect admission or charge...'[6]

This limitation means that the museum may be required to pay performance royalties to ASCAP or BMI for performances of copyrighted music in connection with an exhibition only when there is an admission charge[7] or performers are paid. In this instance, there is no admission charge for the

---

[5]   17 USC section 106(4).
[6]   17 USC section 110(4).
[7]   If there is an admission charge, an unlicensed performance may be permissible if 'the proceeds, after deducting the reasonable costs of producing the performance, are used exclusively for educational...or charitable purposes and not for financial gain'. The copyright owner, however, has the right to object, at least seven days before the performance date, to the charge, in which case the performance would have to be licensed and any royalties paid.

exhibition, or the museum, and no performers are being paid. Further, the museum plans to use the music, which is thematically and conceptually related to the exhibition topic, for a non-profit and primarily educational purpose rather than as an inducement offered to the public to patronize a for-profit enterprise, such as a restaurant.[8] Thus, the contemplated use is also, arguably, a fair use within the meaning of section 107.

However, the museum's contemplated sale of the recording in its shop raises the issue of the applicability of another statutory exemption as a possible basis for avoiding payment of a performance right royalty. That exemption allows for the royalty-free use of a non-dramatic musical work by a 'vending establishment' that is:

'open to the public at large without any direct or indirect admission charge, where the sole purpose of the performance is to promote the retail sales of copies or phono records of the work and the performance is not transmitted beyond the place where the establishment is located and is within the immediate area where the sale is occurring'.[9]

This statutory exemption may not apply to the museum's contemplated use of the recording in the exhibition because, among other reasons, the performance of the work would have to be limited to the immediate area where sales of the work take place. The exemption would apply to the museum's playing the recording within the museum shop.

Finally, the above discussion assumes that the museum would play the CD in its entirety in connection with the exhibition. However, if the museum plans to adapt or reproduce the CD, in part, to produce a derivative product, such as a tape embodying excerpts from the CD and other recordings, the museum should confirm the copyright status of the works and obtain any required permissions. Permission for mechanical and synchronization rights may be obtained from the composers or their music publishers.

Under pre-1978 law, copyright protection in musical works lasted for an initial period of 28 years, with a 28-year renewal period. For musical works published during World War II, this may mean that the copyright terms would have expired initially by at least 1985 or will expire by 2013 if the copyrights had been renewed. However, if the works are still copyrighted, and not in the public domain, then permissions may be needed for any derivative uses of the music from the recording. Although the use of brief excerpts from a copyrighted work may be permissible, on a case-by-case basis, as fair use, it is recommended that permission be obtained prior to any derivative use of a copyrighted work.

---

[8] The exemption at section 110(4) is narrowly drawn and may not extend to the use of the recording as background music in the museum's café for the enjoyment of restaurant patrons.

[9] 17 USC section 110(7).

V. New Performance Right for Sound Recordings

Sound recordings were first protected under federal copyright law in 1971. The 1971 law was intended to provide limited copyright protection for the owners of copyrighted song recordings. In 1971, Congress wanted to stop the unauthorized duplication, or 'bootlegging', of phono records, cassettes, compact discs and other sound recordings. Consistent with this narrow objective, copyright owners of sound recordings were given the exclusive right to control the reproduction, distribution and adaption of the sound recordings. However, they were not given the right to control the transmission or playing of the recording in public, unlike the copyright owners of the songs, music or other sound embodied in the sound recordings.

Today, the Internet allows for music and other pre-recorded sound to be performed, without any physical copy of the recording being reproduced, distributed or adapted. An increasing number of digital transmission services on the Internet, also known as 'celestial jukebox', 'pay-per-listen' or 'audio-on-demand' services, allows members of the public to receive, on request, digital transmissions of particular recordings that persons want to hear. These transmissions of pre-recorded music are public performance under copyright law.

Songwriters, music publishers or other copyright owners of songs that are embodied in sound recordings can demand and have demanded that those offering music on the Internet pay a licence fee for the performance of the copyrighted works. But until recently, owners of the copyrights in sound recordings had no control over the mere transmission or performance of the recordings on the Internet.

In November 1995, Congress passed the Digital Performance Right in Sound Recording Act. This Act created a new digital public performance right for sound recordings. Owners of copyrighted sound recordings now enjoy the right to control, and collect fees for, the performance of recordings on the Internet. There are several broad exceptions to copyright owners' otherwise exclusive digital performance rights in sound recordings. For example, certain digital transmissions or pre-recorded music, like radio broadcasts, that are not controlled or limited to particular recipients or for which no consideration is required to be paid are not subject to the Act.

VI. Other Legislative Developments

On 13 November 1997, the President signed the Copyright Technical Amendments Act. In addition to clarifying several aspects of the federal copyright law, this law corrected a loophole through which many songs and compositions recorded in the US between 1901 and 1976 may have fallen into the public domain.

In 1976 in *Rosette v. Rainbo Mfg. Corp.*, 546 F. 2d 461 (2d Cir. 1976), an appellate court decided that the sale of a recording was not a 'publication' of the works contained within the recording for purposes of the 1909 Copyright Act. Based upon that decision, songwriters and music publishers frequently did not require that the cover of a recording that contained one of their works have printed upon it a statutory notice of ownership of their individual copyrighted work(s). Twenty years later in *La Cienega Music Co. v. ZZ Top*, 44 F. 3d 813 (9th Cir. 1995), another appellate court rejected the *Rossette* decision. That court held that the selling of a recording constituted a 'publication' of any of the underlying works, requiring compliance with the notice requirements and thereby effectively placing all pre-1978 works (the 1909 Act applies to pre-1978 works) in the public domain, and making them available for use by any person, without the writer's or music publisher's permission. The 1997 technical amendments to the federal copyright law reversed the decision in *La Cienega*.

VII. Conclusion

Depending on a museum's planned use of a song, music or a sound recording, one or more parties generally would have to be contacted to use the song or the recording of the song. Those parties range from the songwriter, his or her attorney, heir, publisher or other representative to a performing rights organization, such as American Society of Composers, Authors and Publishers or Broadcast Music Inc. Passage of the 1995 Act means that a recording company's permission, often with the performer's approval, or payment of a fee, now is required if that recording is transmitted as part of an interactive paid subscription service on the Internet.

Intellectual Property and Recorded Sound: Goldmine and Minefield

Anthony Seeger, PhD[1]

Smithsonian Folkways Recordings, Washington, DC, USA

I. Introduction

Audio recordings – and by extension video and film – are extremely important media for documenting the events of the past century. They are also significant in themselves, as music and speech have moved audiences deeply and sometimes stimulated them to action. Many people retain a strong emotional bond to certain sounds, images, and events. Digital technologies have made it easier to copy audio, and CD-ROM and other multimedia formats have made audio and video recordings a particularly desirable supplement to printed texts.

One of the difficulties of audio recordings is that both ethical and legal constraints on the dissemination of these materials have become increasingly stringent over the years. The changes are partly a reaction to changes in technology, partly the result of the increasingly litigious tenor of our times, and partly a healthy change in ethical stance.

From 1982–1988 I directed the Indiana University Archives of Traditional Music. This is a large audio archive the collections of which include not only commercially recorded music, but also hundreds of field collections made around the world on everything from wax cylinder to digital audio tape, and now video. The frustration I experienced there was that although we had remarkable collections they were difficult to use. Copyright law prevented me from providing copies of the commercial recordings and restrictions placed by depositors on field collections prevented me from easily disseminating the field collections. As part of an accessibility programme, I not only introduced OCLC computer cataloguing of the archives collections, but I also tried to

---

renegotiate the 1,200 contracts with the depositors to make parts of their collections available, while giving them the option to continue to restrict those parts that – for political, ethical, or other reasons – should not be made widely available. Although this definitely improved access, I continued to be frustrated by the expense and difficulty of managing a huge collection in a fairly small and somewhat remote city – to which patrons still had to come in order to use the collections.

The Smithsonian Institution acquired the Folkways Record Company from its founder, Moses Asch, in 1987. Opinion within the Smithsonian was mixed as to whether the Institution should acquire a record company, especially one with a stipulation that all the recordings issued by Folkways be kept available to the public in some form. One of the conditions of the acquisition on the part of the Smithsonian was that the collection pay for its own acquisition and be essentially self-supporting. I was hired in 1988 to be its first curator and to figure out how to meet the various institutional, collection-level, and contractual obligations of the company. The interest for me was that this collection, unlike most archival collections, was established for the purpose of dissemination as far and as widely possible, through commercial markets. Folkways had several strengths:

(a) a very large catalogue covering many genres of music, speech, and sounds – over 2,100 albums on Folkways, over 30,000 items;
(b) a reputation for quality and dedication to ideology over profit;
(c) most, but not all, recordings had contracts as well as master tapes – about half of these contracts required payment of artist royalties, the other half were one-time buy-outs of rights;
(d) it has been a commercially viable company for nearly 40 years (founded 1 May 1948).

Folkways also had some liabilities:

(i)   Folkways did not have contracts for everything, and some materials were clearly pirated;
(ii)   some materials were appropriate to publish in 1950, but changing attitudes made them inappropriate in the 1980s;
(iii) Folkways had a very bad reputation for paying royalties to artists – mostly not paid;
(iv)   Folkways often did not pay songwriter royalties (called 'mechanical' royalties);
(v)   a somewhat obscure history of publishing companies.

I arrived with the determination to keep the collection available, to place it on a firm ethical footing, and to use new technologies to increase and disseminate knowledge through audio recordings. Here are some of the steps I took.

(1) I raised royalties to a percentage of the list price of the recordings, rather than pennies per album which lost out to inflation. This virtually doubled most artist royalties.

(2) I began to pay royalties on sales and licensing in a systematic way and timely fashion. This required a huge amount of research, paperwork, locating of performers, and staff time. After the first cheques went out I received a lot of letters of the sort 'This is the first cheque I have received in 18 years, where's the rest?'

(3) I divided the operation in three parts: commercial distribution through record stores, mail order, and licensing/royalties.

Smithsonian Folkways Recordings was founded to reissue earlier projects and to formulate new ones. All the earlier collection was kept available by making small runs on audio cassette, and soon on CD-R (recordable compact discs), and selling them through mail order. An office for licensing and royalty payments was established and the responsibility given to a single employee. This person processes all the contracts, knows the terms, and licenses material out (to outside sources), as well as taking out mechanical licences and occasionally taking out licences from other companies.

Our returns on each unit sold through commercial distribution are fairly small, but the numbers are fairly large: about 140,000 units last year, but the differential of income over expense is low. Our returns on each recording sold through mail order are higher (fewer middle 'men' or institutions) and the unit sales significant (about 40,000 units). But it is our master tape licensing that has been the most lucrative, with relatively little effort and expense.

We license the limited term, non-exclusive use of our master tapes' usage to museums, record companies, feature films, and other sources on a sliding fee scale. Our policy is one of collaboration with projects, because the Smithsonian's mission is the increase and diffusion of knowledge. We expect to collaborate on the same terms as the other providers, however. Because we have so much material, we are often a single-source provider. Over half of our licences are free use permissions for educational use (graduate student video projects to be shown in class). At the other extreme, a minute of music in a feature film may bring in $10,000, of which we receive $5,000. Our contracts specify that half of any money we receive by sub-licensing our recordings must be paid to the artist; Folkways keeps the rest. Last year we licensed about $120,000 worth of music, and kept $60,000. Income from licensing has kept Folkways' balance positive every one of the eight years I have been Director.

Licensing is not automatically lucrative.

(a) It must have a clear paper trail demonstrating the possession of sub-licensing rights to the music.

(b) It should have a way to reach artists in order to consult them on uses that might be controversial. For example, Perot's campaign contacted us and asked if they could use Woody Guthrie's 'This Land Is Your Land' as an election song. We contacted the manager of Wood Guthrie's estate.

(c) The sliding scale must be realistic and negotiable.

(d) The original artists should, whenever possible, share in the benefits of the licensing.

(e)   I recommend that one person, someone very familiar with the idiosyncracies of the collection, be placed in charge of this area.

Here are a few examples of our licensing.

- *Where In the World is Carmen Sandiego* CD-ROM version. Brøderbund Software approached us and asked us to license them music from around the world that would play as the player rode a plane from country to country chasing spies. We agreed, with the stipulation that the original recording be cited, that a paragraph on each type of music be included in a database, and a few other things. Payment came in the form of a payment for our labour (used for cataloguing the collection) and a per item flat fee (shared with the artists).
- *Blues CD-I.* We collaborated in a two-CD-I set on blues, prepared by the Smithsonian with the support of Philips Interactive, by providing all of the rural blues for the projects and some curatorial input. Our terms on this project were an up-front fee per item, and a percentage of the overall royalty paid to the Smithsonian on the project.
- We provided 1 minute 20 seconds of a Lithuanian lullaby for a feature film for $10,000.
- We have provided free use of South American Indian recordings to the National Museum of American History for an exhibit – one among many museums to which we have licensed sounds.
- An artist wanted to reissue some Folkways material with other material on a recording published by another company: we licensed the sound to the other company, and split the royalty income from those tracks with the artist. It is my position that Folkways deserves some income for its efforts in the preservation and dissemination of the original recording. It also allows us to keep the rights for further sub-licensing in the future.

So far the overall operation of Smithsonian Folkways has made small amounts of money. In 1994 our gross sales were around $2 million our artists received about $190,000, and the difference between income and expenses was about $120,000. This is split three ways: one-third to my curatorial discretionary fund for archival expenses (mostly put into equipment and setting up a web site), the Center for Folklife Programs & Cultural Studies (of which Folkways is a part) receives another one-third, and the Smithsonian General Fund receives the final one-third, plus 18 per cent overhead on many of our expenses which it has withheld during the year. Folkways pays its own rent, salaries, manufacturing, distribution, and all other costs associated with the commercial dissemination of recorded sound.

Based on our success with Folkways we have acquired five other record companies by gift – Paredon, Cook, Dyer-Bennet Records, Monitor Records, and Fast Folk Music Magazine. All of these strengthen our coverage of folk and traditional music from around the world.

It would be much easier, in some ways, to run just a licensing operation. It could be done with many fewer staff and a higher ratio of income to expenses.

It would, however, relegate the museum to only maintaining an existing collection, rather than increasing as well as disseminating knowledge.

II. Advice on Audio Licensing

Even in a simple licensing operation some elementary things need to be considered.

A. *First Steps*

1. Establish all those who might have rights to a body of materials before making them available for licensing.
2. Establish credits and contact those who should share in any income derived.
3. Establish a series of appropriate forms, approved by a lawyer, for licensing.
4. Begin small, and then grow.

B. *Licensing Agreements*

1. License to others non-exclusively and for a limited period of time, with renewal periods allowed if appropriate.
2. In most projects, payment in advance is the best way to ensure profitability – many projects do not generate much in the way of profits to share. If royalties are to be received, ask for an advance on the first 'x' number of copies, to ensure some income.

C. *Payments*

1. Share royalties with appropriate artists.

III. Primary Audio Rights

A. *Performers' Rights, or Master Tape Rights*

1. Record companies generally own the master tapes, and the use of the performances on those tapes. These rights may or may not include sub-licensing rights (to third parties).
2. Performers usually receive a royalty from sales and sub-licensing from record companies.
3. Sometimes there are several performers, a producer, and others who have to be consulted or have to receive payments.

B. *Songwriter's or Composer's Rights*

1. A performer may perform something composed by a third party. The composer or songwriter may have copyrighted the song and have rights to the music.
2. These are often paid to the songwriter or composer through the Harry Fox Agency, a large collection agency for music publishers.

IV. Further Reading

Mark Halloran, *The Musician's Business & Legal Guide* (Prentice Hall, New York, 1996).

Diane Sward Rappaport, *How To Make and Sell Your Own Recordings: A Guide for the Nineties* (Prentice Hall, New York, 1992)

Anthony Seeger, 'The Role of Sound Archives in Ethnomusicology Today', (1986) 30 *Ethnomusicology*, pp. 261–276. This article focuses on the difficulties of audio archives and ways ethnomusicologists can reduce those difficulties.

Anthony Seeger, 'Ethnomusicology and Music Law', (1992) 36 *Ethnomusicology* 3, pp. 345–360. This article focuses on the ambiguities of music law as it relates to the traditional music of non-literate societies, and the work of ethnomusicologists, archivists, and others who deal with collections of these materials.

Sydney Shemel and M. William Kraisovsky, *This Business of Music* (5th ed. Billboard Publications, Inc., New York, 1985).

The Whole Folkways Catalogue. Washington, DC: Smithsonian Folkways Recordings. To order: leave message at 202-286-3262; fax 202-287-3699; e-mail folkways@aol.com. Consult on World Wide Web: http://www.si. edu/folkways.

SOURCE MATERIAL

Editor's Note

The United States Copyright Office in connection with the proposed legislation to resolve a variety of issues arising from the uses and abuses of copyrighted works in the new media and to implement the WIPO treaties prepared reports on the United States House of Representatives Administration bill H.R. 2180 (Appendix 7) and a compilation of cases dealing with on line copyright infringement (Appendix 8).

In October 1998, President Clinton signed the Digital Millennium Copyright Act, Pub. L. No. 105-304 (1998). The interim regulations (63 Fed. Reg. 59233, 3 November 1998) may be downloaded from the Copyright Office web site at http://lcweb.locgov. Pertinent provisions on the DMCA are provided in Appendix 9. The provisions dealing with on line copyright liability adopt the judicial analysis of Religious Technology Center.

Appendix 1

WIPO COPYRIGHT TREATY

adopted by the Diplomatic Conference on 20 December 1996

Contents

Preamble

The Contracting Parties,

Desiring to develop and maintain the protection of the rights of authors in their literary and artistic works in a manner as effective and uniform as possible,

Recognizing the need to introduce new international rules and clarify the interpretation of certain existing rules in order to provide adequate solutions to the questions raised by new economic, social, cultural and technological developments,

Recognizing the profound impact of the development and convergence of information and communication technologies on the creation and use of literary and artistic works,

Emphasizing the outstanding significance of copyright protection as an incentive for literary and artistic creation,

Recognizing the need to maintain a balance between the rights of authors and the larger public interest, particularly education, research and access to information, as reflected in the Berne Convention,

Have agreed as follows:

Article 1

Relation to the Berne Convention

(1) This Treaty is a special agreement within the meaning of Article 20 of the Berne Convention for the Protection of Literary and Artistic Works, as regards Contracting Parties that are countries of the Union established by that

Convention. This Treaty shall not have any connection with treaties other than the Berne Convention, nor shall it prejudice any rights and obligations under any other treaties.

(2) Nothing in this Treaty shall derogate from existing obligations that Contracting Parties have to each other under the Berne Convention for the Protection of Literary and Artistic Works.

(3) Hereinafter, 'Berne Convention' shall refer to the Paris Act of July 24, 1971 of the Berne Convention for the Protection of Literary and Artistic Works.

(4) Contracting Parties shall comply with Articles 1 to 21 and the Appendix of the Berne Convention.

Article 2

Scope of Copyright Protection

Copyright protection extends to expressions and not to ideas, procedures, methods of operation or mathematical concepts as such.

Article 3

Application of Articles 2 to 6 of the Berne Convention

Contracting Parties shall apply *mutatis mutandis* the provisions of Articles 2 to 6 of the Berne Convention in respect of the protection provided for in this Treaty.

Article 4

Computer Programs

Computer programs are protected as literary works within the meaning of Article 2 of the Berne Convention. Such protection applies to computer programs, whatever may be the mode or form of their expression.

Article 5

Compilations of Data (Databases)

Compilations of data or other material, in any form, which by reason of the selection or arrangement of their contents constitute intellectual creations, are protected as such. This protection does not extend to the data or the material itself and is without prejudice to any copyright subsisting in the data or material contained in the compilation.

Article 6

Right of Distribution

(1) Authors of literary and artistic works shall enjoy the exclusive right of authorizing the making available to the public of the original and copies of their works through sale or other transfer of ownership.

(2) Nothing in this Treaty shall affect the freedom of Contracting Parties to determine the conditions, if any, under which the exhaustion of the right in paragraph (1) applies after the first sale or other transfer of ownership of the original or a copy of the work with the authorization of the author.

Article 7

Right of Rental

(1) Authors of:

(i) computer programs;

(ii) cinematographic works; and

(iii) works embodied in phonograms as determined in the national law of Contracting Parties,

shall enjoy the exclusive right of authorizing commercial rental to the public of the originals or copies of their works.

(2) Paragraph (1) shall not apply:

(i) in the case of computer programs where the program itself is not the essential object of the rental; and

(ii) in the case of cinematographic works, unless such commercial rental has led to widespread copying of such works materially impairing the exclusive right of reproduction.

(3) Notwithstanding the provisions of paragraph (1), a Contracting Party that, on 15 April 1994, had and continues to have in force a system of equitable remuneration of authors for the rental of copies of their works embodied in phonograms may maintain that system provided that the commercial rental of works embodied in phonograms is not giving rise to the material impairment of the exclusive rights of reproduction of authors.

Article 8

Right of Communication to the Public

Without prejudice to the provisions of Articles 11(1)(ii), 11*bis*(1)(i) and (ii), 11*ter*(1)(ii), 14(1)(ii) and 14*bis*(1) of the Berne Convention, authors of literary and artistic works shall enjoy the exclusive right of authorizing any communication to the public of their works, by wire or wireless means, including the making available to the public of their works in such a way that members of the public may access these works from a place and at a time individually chosen by them.

Article 9

Duration of the Protection of Photographic Works

In respect of photographic works, the Contracting Parties shall not apply the provisions of Article 7(4) of the Berne Convention.

Article 10

Limitations and Exceptions

(1) Contracting Parties may, in their national legislation, provide for limitations of or exceptions to the rights granted to authors of literary and artistic works under this Treaty in certain special cases that do not conflict with a normal exploitation of the work and do not unreasonably prejudice the legitimate interests of the author.

(2) Contracting Parties shall, when applying the Berne Convention, confine any limitations of or exceptions to rights provided for therein to certain special cases that do not conflict with a normal exploitation of the work and do not unreasonably prejudice the legitimate interests of the author.

Article 11

Obligations concerning Technological Measures

Contracting Parties shall provide adequate legal protection and effective legal remedies against the circumvention of effective technological measures that are used by authors in connection with the exercise of their rights under this Treaty or the Berne Convention and that restrict acts, in respect of their works, which are not authorized by the authors concerned or permitted by law.

Article 12

Obligations concerning Rights Management Information

(1) Contracting Parties shall provide adequate and effective legal remedies against any person knowingly performing any of the following acts knowing or, with respect to civil remedies having reasonable grounds to know, that it will induce, enable, facilitate or conceal an infringement of any right covered by this Treaty or the Berne Convention:

(i) to remove or alter any electronic rights management information without authority;

(ii) to distribute, import for distribution, broadcast or communicate to the public, without authority, works or copies of works knowing that electronic rights management information has been removed or altered without authority.

(2) As used in this Article, 'rights management information' means information which identifies the work, the author of the work, the owner of any right in the work, or information about the terms and conditions of use of the work, and any numbers or codes that represent such information, when any of these items of information is attached to a copy of a work or appears in connection with the communication of a work to the public.

Article 13

Application in Time

Contracting Parties shall apply the provisions of Article 18 of the Berne Convention to all protection provided for in this Treaty.

Article 14

Provisions on Enforcement of Rights

(1) Contracting Parties undertake to adopt in accordance with their legal systems, the measures necessary to ensure the application of this Treaty.

(2) Contracting Parties shall ensure that enforcement procedures are available under their law so as to permit effective action against any act of infringement of rights covered by this Treaty, including expeditious remedies to prevent infringements and remedies which constitute a deterrent to further infringements.

Article 15

Assembly

(1)(a) The Contracting Parties shall have an Assembly.

(b) Each Contracting Party shall be represented by one delegate who may be assisted by alternate delegates, advisors and experts.

(c) The expenses of each delegation shall be borne by the Contracting Party that has appointed the delegation. The Assembly may ask the World Intellectual Property Organization (hereinafter referred to as 'WIPO') to grant financial assistance to facilitate the participation of delegations of Contracting Parties that are regarded as developing countries in conformity with the established practice of the General Assembly of the United Nations or that are countries in transition to a market economy.

(2)(a) The Assembly shall deal with matters concerning the maintenance and development of this Treaty and the application and operation of this Treaty.

(b) The Assembly shall perform the function allocated to it under Article 17(2) in respect of the admission of certain intergovernmental organizations to become party to this Treaty.

(c) The Assembly shall decide the convocation of any diplomatic conference for the revision of this Treaty and give the necessary instructions to the Director General of WIPO for the preparation of such diplomatic conference.

(3)(a) Each Contracting Party that is a State shall have one vote and shall vote only in its own name.

(b) Any Contracting Party that is an intergovernmental organization may participate in the vote, in place of its Member States, with a number of votes equal to the number of its Member States which are party to this Treaty. No such intergovernmental organization shall participate in the vote if any one of its Member States exercises its right to vote and vice versa.

(4) The Assembly shall meet in ordinary session once every two years upon convocation by the Director General of WIPO.

(5) The Assembly shall establish its own rules of procedure, including the convocation of extraordinary sessions, the requirements of a quorum and, subject to the provisions of this Treaty, the required majority for various kinds of decisions.

Article 16

International Bureau

The International Bureau of WIPO shall perform the administrative tasks concerning the Treaty.

Article 17

Eligibility for Becoming Party to the Treaty

(1) Any Member State of WIPO may become party to this Treaty.

(2) The Assembly may decide to admit any intergovernmental organization to become party to this Treaty which declares that it is competent in respect of, and has its own legislation binding on all its Member States on, matters covered by this Treaty and that it has been duly authorized, in accordance with its internal procedures, to become party to this Treaty.

(3) The European Community, having made the declaration referred to in the preceding paragraph in the Diplomatic Conference that has adopted this Treaty, may become party to this Treaty.

Article 18

Rights and Obligations under the Treaty

Subject to any specific provisions to the contrary in this Treaty, each Contracting Party shall enjoy all of the rights and assume all of the obligations under this Treaty.

Article 19

Signature of the Treaty

This Treaty shall be open for signature until 31 December 1997, by any Member State of WIPO and by the European Community.

Article 20

Entry into Force of the Treaty

This Treaty shall enter into force three months after 30 instruments of ratification or accession by States have been deposited with the Director General of WIPO.

Article 21

Effective Date of Becoming Party to the Treaty

This Treaty shall bind

(i) the 30 States referred to in Article 20, from the date on which this Treaty has entered into force;

(ii) each other State from the expiration of three months from the date on which the State has deposited its instrument with the Director General of WIPO;

(iii) the European Community, from the expiration of three months after the deposit of its instrument of ratification of accession if such instrument has been deposited after the entry into force of this Treaty according to Article 20, or, three months after the entry into force of this Treaty if such instrument has been deposited before the entry into force of this Treaty.

(iv) any other intergovernmental organization that is admitted to become party to this Treaty, from the expiration of three months after the deposit of its instrument of accession.

Article 22

No Reservations to the Treaty

No reservation to this Treaty shall be admitted.

Article 23

Denunciation of the Treaty

This Treaty may be denounced by any Contracting Party by notification addressed to the Director General of WIPO. Any denunciation shall take effect one year from the date on which the Director General of WIPO received the notification.

Article 24

Languages of the Treaty

(1) This Treaty is signed in a single original in English, Arabic, Chinese, French, Russian and Spanish languages, the versions in all these languages being equally authentic.

(2) An official text in any language other than those referred to in paragraph (1) shall be established by the Director General of WIPO on the request of an interested party, after consultation with all the interested parties. For the purposes of this paragraph, 'interested party' means any Member State of WIPO whose official language, or one of whose official languages, is involved and the European Community, and any other intergovernmental organization that may become party to this Treaty, if one of its official languages is involved.

Article 25

Depositary

The Director General of WIPO is the depositary of this Treaty.

Appendix 2

WIPO DIPLOMATIC CONFERENCE ON CERTAIN COPYRIGHT AND NEIGHBORING RIGHTS QUESTIONS

Geneva, 2 to 20 December 1996

AGREED STATEMENTS CONCERNING THE WIPO
PERFORMANCES AND PHONOGRAMS TREATY

adopted by the Diplomatic Conference on 20 December 1996

Concerning Article 1

It is understood that Article 1(2) clarifies the relationship between rights in phonograms under this Treaty and copyright in works embodied in the phonograms. In cases where authorization is needed from both the author of a work embodied in the phonogram and a performer or producer owning rights in the phonogram, the need for the authorization of the author does not cease to exist because the authorization of the performer or producer is also required, and vice versa.

It is further understood that nothing in Article 1(2) precludes a Contracting Party from providing exclusive rights to a performer or producer of phonograms beyond those required to be provided under this Treaty.

Concerning Article 2(b)

It is understood that the definition of phonogram provided in Article 2(b) does not suggest that rights in the phonogram are in any way affected through their incorporation into a cinematographic or other audiovisual work.

Concerning Articles 2(e), 8, 9, 12, and 13

As used in these Articles, the expressions 'copies' and 'original and copies', being subject to the right of distribution and the right of rental under the said Articles, refer exclusively to fixed copies that can be put into circulation as tangible objects.

Concerning Article 3

It is understood that the reference in Articles 5(a) and 16(a)(iv) of the Rome Convention to 'national of another Contracting State' will, when applied to this Treaty, mean, in regard to an intergovernmental organization that is a Contracting Party to this Treaty, a national of one of the countries that is a member of that organization.

Concerning Article 3(2)

For the application of Article 3(2), it is understood that fixation means the finalization of the master tape ('bande-mère').

Concerning Articles 7, 11 and 16

The reproduction right, as set out in Articles 7 and 11, and the exceptions permitted thereunder through Article 16, fully apply in the digital environment, in particular to the use of performances and phonograms in digital form. It is understood that the storage of a protected performance or phonogram in digital form in an electronic medium constitutes a reproduction within the meaning of these Articles.

Concerning Article 15

It is understood that Article 15 does not represent a complete resolution of the level of rights of broadcasting and communication to the public that should be enjoyed by performers and phonogram producers in the digital age. Delegations were unable to achieve consensus on differing proposals for aspects of exclusivity to be provided in certain circumstances or for rights to be provided without the possibility of reservations, and have therefore left the issue to future resolution.

Concerning Article 15

It is understood that Article 15 does not prevent the granting of the right conferred by this Article to performers of folklore and producers of phonograms recording folklore where such phonograms have not been published for commercial gain.

Concerning Article 16

The agreed statement concerning Article 10 (on Limitations and Exceptions) of the WIPO Copyright Treaty is applicable *mutatis mutandis* also to Article 16 (on Limitations and Exceptions) of the WIPO Performances and Phonograms Treaty.

Concerning Article 19

The agreed statement concerning Article 12 (on Obligations concerning Rights Management Information) of the WIPO Copyright Treaty is applicable *mutatis mutandis* also to Article 19 (on Obligations concerning Rights Management Information) of the WIPO Performances and Phonograms Treaty.

RESOLUTION CONCERNING AUDIOVISUAL PERFORMANCES

adopted by the Diplomatic Conference on 20 December 1996

The Delegations participating in the Diplomatic Conference on Certain Copyright and Neighboring Rights Questions in Geneva,

Noting that the development of technologies will allow for a rapid growth of audiovisual services and that this will increase the opportunities for performing artists to exploit their audiovisual performances that will be transmitted by these services;

Recognizing the great importance of ensuring an adequate level of protection for these performances, in particular when they are exploited in the new digital environment, and that sound and audiovisual performances are increasingly related;

Stressing the urgent need to agree on new norms for the adequate legal international protection of audiovisual performances;

Regretting that, in spite of the efforts of most Delegations, the WIPO Performances and Phonograms Treaty does not cover the rights of performers in the audiovisual fixations of their performance;

Call for the convocation of an extraordinary session of the competent WIPO Governing Bodies during the first quarter of 1997 to decide on the schedule of the preparatory work on a protocol to the WIPO Performances and Phonograms Treaty, concerning audiovisual performances, with a view to the adoption of such a protocol not later than in 1998.

RECOMMENDATION CONCERNING DATABASES

adopted by the Diplomatic Conference on 20 December 1996

The Delegations participating in the Diplomatic Conference on Certain Copyright and Neighboring Rights Questions in Geneva,

Recognizing that databases are a vital element in the development of a global information infrastructure;

Conscious of the importance of encouraging further development of databases;

Aware of the need to strike a balance between the interests of the producers of databases in protection from unfair copying and the interests of users in having appropriate access to the benefits of a global information infrastructure;

Expressing interest in examining further the possible implications and benefits of a *sui generis* system of protection of databases at the international level;

Noting that a treaty on such a *sui generis* system was not negotiated or adopted at the Conference;

Recommend the convocation of an extraordinary session of the competent WIPO Governing Bodies during the first quarter of 1997 to decide on the schedule of further preparatory work on a Treaty on Intellectual Property in Respect of Databases.

AGREED STATEMENTS CONCERNING THE WIPO COPYRIGHT TREATY

adopted by the Diplomatic Conference on 20 December 1996

Concerning Article 1(4)

The reproduction right, as set out in Article 9 of the Berne Convention, and the exceptions permitted thereunder, fully apply in the digital environment, in particular to the use of works in digital form. It is understood that the storage of a protected work in digital form in an electronic medium constitutes a reproduction within the meaning of Article 9 of the Berne Convention.

Concerning Article 3

It is understood that in applying Article 3 of this Treaty, the expression 'country of the Union' in Articles 2 to 6 of the Berne Convention will be read as if it were a reference to a Contracting Party to this Treaty, in the application of those Berne Articles in respect of protection provided for in this Treaty. It is also understood that the expression 'country outside the Union' in those Articles in the Berne Convention will, in the same circumstances, be read as if it were a reference to a country that is not a Contracting Party to this Treaty, and that 'this Convention' in Articles 2(8), 2bis(2), 3, 4 and 5 of the Berne Convention will be read as if it were a reference to the Berne Convention and this Treaty. Finally, it is understood that a reference in Articles 3 to 6 of the Berne Convention to a 'national of one of the countries of the Union' will, when these Articles are applied to this Treaty, mean, in regard to an intergovernmental organization that is a Contracting Party to this Treaty, a national of one of the countries that is member of that organization.

Concerning Article 4

The scope of protection for computer programs under Article 4 of this Treaty, read with Article 2, is consistent with Article 2 of the Berne Convention and on a par with the relevant provisions of the TRIPS Agreement.

Concerning Article 5

The scope of protection for compilations of data (databases) under Article 5 of this Treaty, read with Article 2, is consistent with Article 2 of the Berne Convention and on a par with the relevant provisions of the TRIPS Agreement.

Concerning Articles 6 and 7

As used in these Articles, the expressions 'copies' and 'original and copies' being subject to the right of distribution and the right of rental under the said Articles, refer exclusively to fixed copies that can be put into circulation as tangible objects.

Concerning Article 7

It is understood that the obligation under Article 7(1) does not require a Contracting Party to provide an exclusive right of commercial rental to authors who, under that Contracting Party's law, are not granted rights in respect of phonograms. It is understood that this obligation is consistent with Article 14(4) of the TRIPS Agreement.

Concerning Article 8

It is understood that the mere provision of physical facilities for enabling or making a communication does not in itself amount to communication within the meaning of this Treaty or the Berne Convention. It is further understood that nothing in Article 8 precludes a Contracting Party from applying Article 11*bis*(2).

Concerning Article 10

It is understood that the provisions of Article 10 permit Contracting Parties to carry forward and appropriately extend into the digital environment limitations and exceptions in their national laws which have been considered acceptable under the Berne Convention. Similarly, these provisions should be understood to permit Contracting Parties to devise new exceptions and limitations that are appropriate in the digital network environment.

It is also understood that Article 10(2) neither reduces nor extends the scope of applicability of the limitations and exceptions permitted by the Berne Convention.

Concerning Article 12

It is understood that the reference to 'infringement of any right covered by this Treaty or the Berne Convention' includes both exclusive rights and rights of remuneration.

It is further understood that Contracting Parties will not rely on this Article to devise or implement rights management systems that would have the effect of imposing formalities which are not permitted under the Berne Convention or this Treaty, prohibiting the free movement of goods or impeding the enjoyment of rights under this Treaty.

Appendix 3

WIPO PERFORMANCES AND PHONOGRAMS TREATY

Adopted by the Diplomatic Conference on 20 December 1996

Contents

Preamble

CHAPTER 1: GENERAL PROVISIONS

CHAPTER II: RIGHTS OF PERFORMERS

CHAPTER III: RIGHTS OF PRODUCERS OF PHONOGRAMS

Article 11: Right of Reproduction

Article 12: Right of Distribution

Article 13: Right of Rental

Article 14: Right of Making Available of Phonograms

CHAPTER IV: COMMON PROVISIONS

Article 15: Right to Remuneration for Broadcasting and Communication to the Public

Article 16: Limitations and Exceptions

Article 17: Term of Protection

Article 18: Obligations concerning Technological Measures

Article 19: Obligations concerning Rights Management Information

Article 20: Formalities

Article 21: Reservations

Article 22: Application in Time

Article 23: Provisions on Enforcement of Rights

CHAPTER V: ADMINISTRATIVE AND FINANCIAL CLAUSES

Article 24: Assembly

Article 25: International Bureau

Article 26: Eligibility for Becoming Party to the Treaty

Article 27: Rights and Obligations under the Treaty

Article 28: Signature of the Treaty

Article 29: Entry into Force of the Treaty

Article 30: Effective Date of Becoming Party to the Treaty

Article 31: Denunciation of the Treaty

Article 32: Languages of the Treaty

Article 33: Depositary

Preamble

The Contracting Parties,

Desiring to develop and maintain the protection of the rights of performers and producers of phonograms in a manner as effective and uniform as possible,

Recognizing the need to introduce new international rules in order to provide adequate solutions to the questions raised by economic, social, cultural and technological developments,

Recognizing the profound impact of the development and convergence of information and communication technologies on the production and use of performances and phonograms,

Recognizing the need to maintain a balance between the rights of the performers and producers of phonograms and the larger public interest, particularly education, research and access to information,

Have agreed as follows:

CHAPTER I

GENERAL PROVISIONS

Article 1

Relation to Other Conventions

(1) Nothing in this Treaty shall derogate from existing obligations that Contracting Parties have to each other under the International Convention for the Protection of Performers, Producers of Phonograms and Broadcasting Organizations done in Rome, 26 October 1961 (hereinafter the 'Rome Convention').

(2) Protection granted under this Treaty shall leave intact and shall in no way affect the protection of copyright in literary and artistic works. Consequently, no provision of this Treaty may be interpreted as prejudicing such protection.

(3) This Treaty shall not have any connection with, not shall it prejudice any rights and obligations under, any other treaties.

Article 2

Definitions

For the purposes of this Treaty:

(a) 'performers' are actors, singers, musicians, dancers, and other persons who act, sing, deliver, declaim, play in, interpret, or otherwise perform literary or artistic works or expressions of folklore;

(b) 'phonogram' means the fixation of the sounds of a performance or of other sounds, or of a representation of sounds other than in the form of a fixation incorporated in a cinematographic or other audiovisual work;

(c) 'fixation' means the embodiment of sounds, or of the representations thereof, from which they can be perceived, reproduced or communicated through a device;

(d) 'producer of a phonogram' means the person, or the legal entity, who or which takes the initiative and has the responsibility for the first fixation of the sounds of a performance or other sounds, or the representations of sounds;

(e) 'publication' of a fixed performance or a phonogram means the offering or copies of the fixed performance or the phonogram to the public, with the consent of the rightholder, and provided that copies are offered to the public in reasonable quantity;

(f) 'broadcasting' means the transmission by wireless means for public reception of sounds or of images and sounds or of the representations thereof; such transmission by satellite is also "broadcasting"; transmission of encrypted signals is "broadcasting" where the means for decrypting are provided to the public by the broadcasting organization or with its consent;

(g) 'communication to the public' of a performance or a phonogram means the transmission to the public by any medium, otherwise than by broadcasting, of sounds of a performance or the sounds or the representations of sounds fixed in a phonogram. For the purposes of Article 15, 'communication to the public' includes making the sounds or representations of sounds fixed in a phonogram audible to the public.

Article 3

Beneficiaries of Protection under this Treaty

(1) Contracting Parties shall accord the protection provided under this Treaty to the performers and producers of phonograms who are nationals of other Contracting Parties.

(2) The nationals of other Contracting Parties shall be understood to be those performers or producers of phonograms who would meet the criteria for eligibility for protection provided under the Rome Convention, were all the Contracting Parties to this Treaty Contracting States of that Convention. In respect of these criteria of eligibility, Contracting Parties shall apply the relevant definitions in Article 2 of this Treaty.

(3) Any Contracting Party availing itself of the possibilities provided in Article 5(3) of the Rome Conventions or, for the purposes of Article 5 of the same Convention, Article thereof 17 shall make a notification as foreseen in those provisions to the Director General of the World Intellectual Property Organization (WIPO).

Article 4

National Treatment

(1) Each Contracting Party shall accord to nationals of other Contracting Parties, as defined in Article 3(2), the treatment it accords to its own nationals with regard to the exclusive rights specifically granted in this Treaty and to the right to equitable remuneration provided for in Article 15 of this Treaty.

(2) The obligation provided for in paragraph (1) does not apply to the extent that another Contracting Party makes use of the reservations permitted by Article 15(3) of this Treaty.

CHAPTER II

RIGHTS OF PERFORMERS

Article 5

Moral Rights of Performers

(1) Independently of a performer's economic rights, and even after the transfer of those rights, the performer shall, as regards his live aural performances or performances fixed in phonograms have the right to claim to be identified as the

performer of his performances, except where omission is dictated by the manner of the use of the performance, and to object to any distortion, mutilation or other modification of his performances that would be prejudicial to his reputation.

(2) The rights granted to a performer in accordance with paragraph (1) shall, after his death, be maintained, at least until the expiry of the economic rights, and shall be exercisable by the persons or institutions authorized by the legislation of the Contracting Party where protection is claimed. However, those Contracting Parties whose legislation, at the moment of their ratification of or accession to this Treaty, does not provide for protection after the death of the performer of all rights set out in the preceding paragraph may provide that some of these rights will, after his death, cease to be maintained.

(3) The means of redress for safeguarding the rights granted under this Article shall be governed by the legislation of the Contracting Party where protection is claimed.

Article 6

Economic Rights of Performers in their Unfixed Performances

Performers shall enjoy the exclusive right of authorizing, as regards their performances:

(i) the broadcasting and communication to the public of their unfixed performances except where the performance is already a broadcast; performance and

(ii) the fixation of their unfixed performances.

Article 7

Right of Reproduction

Performers shall enjoy the exclusive right of authorizing the direct or indirect reproduction of their performances fixed in phonograms, in any manner or form.

Article 8

Right of Distribution

(1) Performers shall enjoy the exclusive right of authorizing the making available to the public of the original and copies of their performances fixed in phonograms through sale or other transfer of ownership.

(2) Nothing in this Treaty shall affect the freedom of Contracting Parties to determine the conditions, if any, under which the exhaustion of the right in paragraph (1) applies after the first sale or other transfer of ownership of the original or a copy of the fixed performance with the authorization of the performer.

Article 9

Right of Rental

(1) Performers shall enjoy the exclusive right of authorizing the commercial rental to the public of the original and copies of their performances fixed in phonograms as determined in the national law of Contracting Parties, even after distribution of them by, or pursuant to, authorization by the performer.

(2) Notwithstanding the provisions of paragraph (1), a Contracting Party that, on 15 April 1994, had and continues to have in force a system of equitable remuneration of performers for the rental of copies of their performances fixed in phonograms, may maintain that system provided that the commercial rental of phonograms is not giving rise to the material impairment of the exclusive rights of reproduction of performers

Article 10

Right of Making Available of Fixed Performances

Performers shall enjoy the exclusive right of authorizing the making available to the public of their performances fixed in phonograms, by wire or wireless means, in such a way that members of the public may access them from a place and at a time individually chosen by them.

CHAPER III

RIGHTS OF PRODUCERS OF PHONOGRAMS

Article 11

Right of Reproduction

Producers of phonograms shall enjoy the exclusive right of authorizing the direct or indirect reproduction of their phonograms, in any manner or form.

Article 12

Right of Distribution

(1) Producers of phonograms shall enjoy the exclusive right of authorizing the making available to the public of the original and copies of their phonograms through sale or other transfer of ownership.

(2) Nothing in this Treaty shall affect the freedom of Contracting Parties to determine the conditions, if any, under which the exhaustion of the right in paragraph (1) applies after the first sale or transfer of ownership of the original or a copy of the phonogram with the authorization of the producer of phonograms.

Article 13

Right of Rental

(1) Producers of phonograms shall enjoy the exclusive right of authorizing the commercial rental to the public of the original and copies of their phonograms, even after distribution of them by or pursuant to authorization by the producer.

(2) Notwithstanding the provisions of paragraph (1), a Contracting Party that, on 15 April 1994, had and continues to have in force a system of equitable remuneration of producers of phonograms for the rental of copies of their phonograms, may maintain that system provided that the commercial rental of phonograms is not giving rise to the material impairment of the exclusive rights of reproduction of producers of phonograms.

Article 14

Right of Making Available of Phonograms

Producers of phonograms shall enjoy the exclusive right of authorizing the making available to the public of their phonograms, by wire or wireless means, in such a way that members of the public may access them from a place and at a time individually chosen by them.

CHAPTER IV

COMMON PROVISIONS

Article 15

Right to Remuneration for Broadcasting and Communication to the Public

(1) Performers and producers of phonograms shall enjoy the right to a single equitable remuneration for the direct or indirect use of phonograms published for commercial purposes for broadcasting or for any communication to the public.

(2) Contracting Parties may establish in their national legislation that the single equitable remuneration shall be claimed from the user by the performer or by the producer of a phonogram or by both. Contracting Parties may enact national legislation that, in the absence of an agreement between the performer and the producer of a phonogram, sets the terms according to which performers and producers of phonograms shall share the single equitable remuneration.

(3) Any Contracting Party may in a notification deposited with the Director General of WIPO, declare that it will apply the provisions of paragraph (1) only in respect of certain uses, or that it will limit their application in some other way, or that it will not apply these provisions at all.

(4) For the purposes of this Article, phonograms made available to the public by wire or wireless means in such a way that members of the public may access them from a place and at a time individually chosen by them shall be considered as if they had been published for commercial purposes.

Article 16

Limitations and Exceptions

(1) Contracting Parties may, in their national legislation, provide for the same kinds of limitations or exceptions with regard to the protection of performers and producers of phonograms as they provide for, in their national legislation, in connection with the protection of copyright in literary and artistic works.

(2) Contracting Parties shall confine any limitations of or exceptions to rights provided for in this Treaty to certain special cases which do not conflict with a normal exploitation of the performance or phonogram and do not

unreasonably prejudice the legitimate interests of the performer or of the producer of phonograms.

Article 17

Term of Protection

(1) The term of protection to be granted to performers under this Treaty shall last, at least, until the end of a period of 50 years computed from the end of the year in which the performance was fixed in a phonogram.

(2) The term of protection to be granted to producers of phonograms under this Treaty shall last, at least, until the end of a period of 50 years computed from the end of the year in which the phonogram was published, or failing such publication within 50 years from fixation of the phonogram, 50 years from the end of the year in which the fixation was made.

Article 18

Obligations concerning Technological Measures

Contracting Parties shall provide adequate legal protection and effective legal remedies against the circumvention of effective technological measures that are used by performers or producers of phonograms in connection with the exercise of their rights under this Treaty and that restrict acts, in respect of their performances or phonograms, which are not authorized by the performers or the producers of phonograms concerned or permitted by law.

Article 19

Obligations concerning Rights Management Information

(1) Contracting Parties shall provide adequate and effective legal remedies against any person knowingly performing any of the following acts knowing or, with respect to civil remedies, having reasonable grounds to know that it will induce, enable, facilitate or conceal an infringement of any right covered by this Treaty:

(i) to remove or alter any electronic rights management information without authority;

(ii) to distribute, import for distribution, broadcast, communicate or make available to the public, without authority, performances, copies of fixed performances or phonograms knowing that electronic rights management information has been removed or altered without authority.

(2) As used in this Article, 'rights management information' means information which identifies the performer, the performance of the performer, the producer of the phonogram, the phonogram, the owner of any right in the performance or phonogram, or information about the terms and conditions of use of the performance or phonogram, and any numbers or codes that represent such information, when any of these items of information is attached to a copy of a fixed performance or a phonogram or appears in connection with the communication or making available of a fixed performance or a phonogram to the public.

Article 20

Formalities

The enjoyment and exercise of the rights provided for in this Treaty shall not be subject to any formality.

Article 21

Reservations

Subject to the provisions of Article 15(3), no reservations to this Treaty shall be permitted.

Article 22

Application in Time

(1) Contracting Parties shall apply the provisions of Article 18 of the Berne Convention, *mutatis mutandis*, to the rights of performers and producers of phonograms provided for in this Treaty.

(2) Notwithstanding paragraph (1), a Contracting Party may limit the application of Article 5 of this Treaty to performances which occurred after the entry into force of this Treaty for that Party.

Article 23

Provisions of Enforcement of Rights

(1) Contracting Parties undertake to adopt, in accordance with their legal systems, the measures necessary to ensure the application of this Treaty.

(2) Contracting Parties shall ensure that enforcement procedures are available under their law so as to permit effective action against any act of infringement

of rights covered by this Treaty, including expeditious remedies to prevent infringements and remedies which constitute a deterrent to further infringements.

CHAPTER V

ADMINISTRATIVE AND FINAL CLAUSES

Article 24

Assembly

(1)(a) The Contracting Parties shall have an Assembly.

(b) Each Contracting Party shall be represented by one delegate who may be assisted by alternate delegates, advisors and experts.

(c) The expenses of each delegation shall be borne by the Contracting Party that has appointed the delegation. The Assembly may ask WIPO to grant financial assistance to facilitate the participation of delegations of Contracting Parties that are regarded as developing countries in conformity with the established practice of the General Assembly of the United Nations or that are countries in transition to a market economy.

(2)(a) The Assembly shall deal with matters concerning the maintenance and development of this Treaty and the application and operation of this Treaty.

(b) The Assembly shall perform the function allocated to it under Article 26(2) in respect of the admission of certain intergovernmental organizations to become party to this Treaty.

(c) The Assembly shall decide the convocation of any diplomatic conference for the revision of this Treaty and give the necessary instructions to the Director General of WIPO for the preparation of such diplomatic conference.

(3)(a) Each Contracting Party that is a State shall have one vote and shall vote only in its own name.

(b) Any Contracting Party that is an intergovernmental organization may participate in the vote, in place of its Member States, with a number of votes equal to the number of its Member States which are party to this Treaty. No such intergovernmental organization shall participate in the vote if any one of its Member States exercises its right to vote and vice versa.

(4) The Assembly shall meet in ordinary session once every two years upon convocation by the Director General of WIPO.

(5) The Assembly shall establish its own rules of procedure, including the convocation of extraordinary sessions, the requirements of a quorum and, subject to the provisions of this Treaty, the required majority for various kinds of decisions.

Article 25

International Bureau

The International Bureau of WPIO shall perform the administrative tasks concerning the Treaty.

Article 26

Eligibility for Becoming Party to the Treaty

(1) Any Member State of WIPO may become party to this Treaty.

(2) The Assembly may decide to admit any intergovernmental organization to become party to this Treaty which declares that it is competent in respect of, and has its own legislation binding on all its Member States on, matters covered by this Treaty and that it has been duly authorized, in accordance with its internal procedures, to become party to this Treaty.

(3) The European Community, having made the declaration referred to in the preceding paragraph in the Diplomatic Conference that has adopted this Treaty, may become party to this Treaty.

Article 27

Rights and Obligations under the Treaty

Subject to any specific provisions to the contrary in this Treaty, each Contracting Party shall enjoy all of the rights and assume all of the obligations under this Treaty.

Article 28

Signature of the Treaty

This Treaty shall be open for signature until 31 December 1997, by any Member State of WIPO and by the European Community.

Article 29

Entry into Force of the Treaty

This Treaty shall enter into force three months after 30 instruments of ratification or accession by States have been deposited with the Director General of WIPO.

Article 30

Effective Date of Becoming Party to the Treaty

This Treaty shall bind

(i) the 30 States referred to in Article 29, from the date on which this Treaty has entered into force;

(ii) each other State from the expiration of three months from the date on which the State has deposited its instrument with the Director General of WIPO;

(ii) the European Community, from the expiration of three months after the deposit of its instrument of ratification or accession if such instrument has been deposited after the entry into force of this Treaty according to Article 29, or, three months after the entry into force of this Treaty if such instrument has been deposited before the entry into force of this Treaty;

(iv) any other intergovernmental organization that is admitted to become party to the Treaty, from the expiration of three months after the deposit of its instrument of accession.

Article 31

Denunciation of the Treaty

This Treaty may be denounced by any Contracting Party by notification addressed to the Director General of WIPO. Any denunciation shall take effect one year from the date on which the Director General of WIPO received the notification.

Article 32

Languages of the Treaty

(1) This Treaty is signed in a single original in English, Arabic, Chinese, French, Russian and Spanish languages, the versions in all these languages being equally authentic.

(2) An official text in any language other than those referred to in paragraph (1) shall be established by the Director General of WIPO on the request of an interested party, after consultation with all the interested parties. For the purposes of this paragraph, 'interested party' means any Member State of WIPO whose official language, or one of whose official languages, is involved and the European Community, and any other intergovernmental organization that may become party to this Treaty, if one of its official languages is involved.

Article 32

Depositary

The Director General of WIPO is the depositary of this Treaty.

Appendix 4

STATEMENT OF MARYBETH PETERS REGISTER OF COPYRIGHTS BEFORE THE HOUSE SUBCOMMITTEE ON COURTS AND INTELLECTUAL PROPERTY

ON H.R. 2180 AND H.R. 2281

105th CONGRESS, 1st SESSION

16 September 1997

Mr Chairman, members of the subcommittee, I appreciate the opportunity to testify today on H.R. 2281, the 'WIPO Copyright Treaties Implementation Act' and H.R. 2180, the 'On-Line Copyright Liability Limitation Act.' H.R. 2281 would make the changes to US law that are necessary to allow the United States to join the two World Intellectual Property Organization treaties concluded in Geneva in December of 1996. H.R. 2180 would add a new section 512 to the Copyright Act, creating an exemption from infringement liability for certain acts of transmitting or providing access to material on-line, that are typically engaged in by providers of on-line services and Internet access.

H.R. 2281 — The WIPO Copyright Treaties Implementation Act

The changes that would be made by H.R. 2281 are significant but few in number. The nature and scope of copyright rights and exceptions would not be affected, continuing the substantive balance of interests embodied in today's Copyright Act. The bill's primary effect would be to add to the law two technological adjuncts to copyright, intended to ensure that rights can be meaningfully enforced and licensed in the digital environment. In addition, several minor technical changes would be made to provisions of the Copyright Act to provide the protection required by the treaties to works from other countries that join the treaties.

The Copyright Office supports the bill generally. In our view, it fully and adequately implements the obligations of the new WIPO treaties, without amending the law in areas where a change is not required for implementation. While other issues relating to how copyright law applies to the use of copyrighted works in digital form, such as the liability issues addressed by H.R. 2180, are important and should be fully debated and carefully considered by Congress, they do not need to be dealt with in order to make US law compatible with the treaty obligations.

The treaties are extremely valuable for the United States, as they will require other countries to adopt a copyright system that comports with the balance already struck in US law, and ensure that US works are adequately protected abroad in the digital age. They have been widely hailed as fair and balanced by copyright owner and user groups alike. The sooner the treaties become effective, and the more countries that join them, the less piracy there will be of US works around the world. This process may take some time, however, since the treaties will not take effect until thirty countries have joined. The United States' approach will be influential, and our prompt ratification is likely to encourage others to do the same.

In addition to satisfying our treaty obligations, the Copyright Office believes that the proposed additions to US law further valuable goals domestically in and of themselves. Prior versions of the technological adjuncts were proposed in the 104th Congress as part of the National Information Infrastructure Copyright Protection Act. At that time, the Copyright Office expressed support for the goals of these provisions, but raised certain concerns about their formulation. The versions contained in H.R. 2281 represent a refinement of those prior proposals, which we view as substantially improved.

This does not mean that we see the language of these provisions as perfect. Rather, it represents a reasonable effort to achieve compromise on several difficult issues. The anti-circumvention provision in particular has raised concerns as to its scope and impact, and may need further refinement. On this and other issues, the Copyright Office has some questions and suggestions, which are described below. We look forward to working with the Subcommittee in the weeks ahead.

A. Technical Amendments

The two WIPO treaties obligate each member country to protect works from other member countries, including works in existence on the date each treaty becomes effective for that country, without imposing any formalities as conditions for the enjoyment or enforcement of rights. In order to implement these obligations, the bill would make several technical amendments to three sections of the Copyright Act: section 104, which specifies the conditions on which works from other countries are protected in the United States; section 104A, which provides protection to preexisting works form other countries; and section 411(a), which makes copyright registration a precondition to bringing suit for infringement for some works. These amendments in turn require some additions and changes in the definitional section of the Copyright Act, section 101.

The Copyright Office prepared the initial drafts of these sections of the bill, and fully supports them in their current form. These sections make those changes that are necessary to fulfill future US obligations to other WIPO treaty members, and do so in a simple and efficient way.

1. Section 104: Subject matter of copyright: National origin.

Section 104 of the Copyright Act sets out the criteria making foreign works eligible for US copyright protection. In its current form, it contains separate but overlapping sections relating to particular treaties. The bill would amend section 104 to add the new WIPO treaties, and re-organize its structure by listing all of the relevant factual 'points of attachment', and applying them to all countries with which the United States has an appropriate treaty relationship. Thus, all countries that have copyright relations with the United States would be referred to collectively by a new defined term in section 101: 'treaty party'. The amended section 104 would then extend protection to foreign works from any treaty party based on the following four 'points of attachment': nationality of the author, place of first publication of the work, place of fixation of the sounds embodied in sound recording, and the situs of a constructed architectural work. The amendment implements the treaty obligation in a manner that simplifies and clarifies section 104, as well as making it more easily adaptable to future changes is US treaty membership. If we join any future treaties, they can simply be added to the list of 'international agreements' without detailed amendments repeating the criteria for eligibility for purposes of each treaty.

2. Section 104A. Copyright in restored works.

As to retroactive protection for existing works from treaty parties, the approach is straight-forward. The amendment adds to section 104A's definition of 'eligible countries' whose works are subject to restoration those countries that are parties to treaties that require such retroactivity, including the new WIPO treaties.

3. Section 411(a). Registration and infringement actions.

The WIPO treaties prohibit formalities from being imposed on the enjoyment or exercise of rights. Under current law, all works other than Berne Convention works whose country of origin is not the United States must be registered with the Copyright Office before suit can be brought for their infringement. 17 U.S.C. § 411(a). The bill would amend this provision to exempt works from members of the two WIPO treaties.

It does so in the simplest way possible, by reframing the registration requirement in the affirmative, as the converse of the current statute. In other words, the provision states affirmatively that 'United States works' must be registered before suit, with 'United States works' defined as the converse of the current definition of works whose country of origin is not the United States. This approach avoids the need to change several complex technical provisions of the Copyright Act each time the United States joins another treaty.

B. Technological Adjuncts to Copyright

Each of the WIPO treaties includes two provisions that require member countries to provide technological adjuncts to copyright protection. These technological adjuncts are intended to further the development of digital networks by making them a safe environment for copyrighted works to be disseminated and exploited. One provision protects against circumvention of the technology that copyright owners may use to protect their works against infringement. It is phrased in very general terms, leaving up to each country precisely how to define the prohibited conduct. The other provision prohibits the deliberate alteration or deletion of information that copyright owners may choose to provide over the Internet to identify their works and the terms and conditions of their use.

The bill would create a new Chapter 12 Title 17 to implement these obligations. The prohibitions themselves are contained in new sections 1201 and 1202; sections 1203 and 1204 set out civil remedies and criminal penalties, respectively.

1. Anti-circumvention

a. Background and purpose

New section 1201 would implement Article 11 of the WIPO Copyright Treaty and Article 18 of the WIPO Performances and Phonograms Treaty, which require treaty members to

'provide adequate legal protection and effective legal remedies against the circumvention of effective technological measures that are used by authors in connection with the exercise of their rights...and that restrict acts, in respect of their works, which are not authorized by the authors concerned or permitted by law.'

This language was deliberately written to be broad and general, and to leave to individual countries considerable flexibility in determining precisely how to formulate the prohibition. There are likely to be different methods adopted in different countries to satisfy this obligation. The ultimate test of treaty compliance for any of them will be whether the language chosen 'provide[s] adequate legal protection and effective legal remedies.'

After an extensive analysis, the Copyright Office has concluded that existing protections under US law are insufficient to satisfy the treaty obligation. In making this determination, the Copyright Office examined a number of existing bodies of law. These include the doctrine of contributory infringement under copyright law, and a variety of federal statutes including the Audio Home Recording Act, 17 U.S.C. § 1002, the Communications Act, 47 U.S.C. §§ 553 and 605, the National Stolen Property Act, 18 U.S.C. § 2314, the Electronic Communications Privacy Act, 18 U.S.C. §§ 2510 *et seq.*, and the Computer Fraud and Abuse Act, 18 U.S.C. § 1030.

We do not believe that the doctrine of contributory infringement provides sufficient protection to fulfill the treaty obligation to provide 'adequate legal protection and effective legal remedies' against circumvention. As the Supreme Court interpreted that doctrine in *Sony Corp. v. Universal City Studios, Inc.*, 464 US 417 (1984), the manufacturer or distributor of a copying device is not liable if the device is 'merely capable of substantial noninfringing uses.' *Id.* at 442. Most devices for circumventing technological measures, even those designed or entirely used for infringing purposes, will be *capable* of substantial noninfringing uses since they could potentially be employed in the course of a fair use, or in the use of a public domain work. It is therefore not surprising that the *Sony* standard, in practice, has been ineffective in addressing the circumvention problem. *See Vault Corp. v. Quaid Software Ltd.*, 847 F.2d 255 (5th Cir 1983). Copyright, moreover, may not afford any recourse against those who engage in acts of circumvention alone.

Some of the other laws we considered address particular aspects of circumvention of particular types of technological protection measures such as the scrambling of broadcast signals. In the aggregate, however, they fail to provide the general coverage required by the treaties.

The anti-circumvention issue is without doubt the most difficult of the issues presented in treaty implementation. The challenge is how to formulate a prohibition that provides meaningful protection to copyright owners, while avoiding chilling the development of legitimate consumer technology and lawful uses of copyrighted works and public domain materials. While a perfect solution may not be possible, we believe that an appropriate compromise can be found. Section 1201 or H.R. 2281 represents a reasonable attempt to reach such a compromise. It reflects the lengthy debate that took place in the United States and Geneva over the course of the past two years, and is narrower and more carefully tailored than prior proposals.

In the Copyright Office's November 1995 testimony on the NII Copyright Protection Act, we noted the importance of providing legal protection for technological measures used by copyright owners to protect their works against unauthorized use on the Internet. Unless copyright owners have confidence that their works can be secured against loss, they will not be willing to utilize this promising new means of exploitation to its full potential. As I stated then,

'One of the most serious challenges to effective enforcement of copyright in the digital environment is the ease, speed and accuracy of copying at multiple, anonymous locations. In order to meet this challenge, copyright owners must rely on technology to protect their works against widespread infringement. But every technological device that can be devised for this purpose can in turn be defeated by someone else's ingenuity. Meaningful protection for copyrighted works must therefore proceed on two fronts: the property rights themselves, supplemented by legal assurances that those rights can be technologically safeguarded.'

It was for these reasons that the countries meeting in Geneva to negotiate the WIPO treaties agreed unanimously on the need for such a legal prohibition.

At the same time, the Copyright Office expressed concern about the breadth of the language used in the NII bill. Our chief concern related to various problems we saw with the 'primary purpose of effect' test used to determine the legality of a device or service used to circumvent technological protection. We noted that 'primary purpose' could be difficult to prove, and that a device intended for entirely legitimate purposes might be put to use primarily to circumvent.

The language of H.R. 2281 addresses these concerns, and a number of concerns that were expressed by others, in a manner which represents a substantial improvement over the prior bill. It aims more precisely at culpable conduct, and more clearly excludes circumvention engaged in to access or use material that is not protected by copyright. The bill also adopts a new two-tier approach, separating out technological measures that control access to copyrighted material and technological measures that prevent infringing uses of that material, and providing stronger protection for the former. Finally, it contains for the first time a savings clause stating explicitly that the substance and scope of copyright rights and exceptions, including fair use, are not affected.

b. The coverage of the bill

The substance of section 1201's prohibition is set out in paragraphs (1) and (2). Paragraph (1) deals with the circumvention of technological measures that control access to a copyrighted work, for example through encryption. This provision is similar to existing legislation prohibiting the decryption of cable programming signals transmitted by satellite, which protects the ability of broadcasters to secure a market for pay cable by scrambling signals and allowing only paying subscribers to view them.

Not every technological measure that controls access would be covered by this language. The prohibition would apply only to those measures that operate by requiring the application of information, or a process or a treatment, that is authorized by the copyright owner. Moreover, the measure must do so 'in the ordinary course of its operation.' This would exclude technologies that may have the incidental or unintended effect of controlling access, or do so only when used in an unusual way.

Subparagraph (a) prohibits the act itself of circumventing a technological measure that effectively controls access to a copyrighted work. Subparagraph (b) relates to the means or technologies that may be used in order to circumvent. It prohibits the manufacture or sale of products or services that meet three criteria meant to distinguish legitimate business activities from the illegitimate. Thus, the provision covers circumstances where the products or services are primarily designed or produced to perform the prohibited acts, or are marketed by advertising their capability of doing so. It also covers those products or services that have only limited commercially significant purpose or use other than to perform the prohibited acts.

Paragraph (2) of section 1201 deals with measures that prevent acts of infringement, rather than access. Such measures might include a technology that blocks users from downloading copies. The treatment of these infringement prevention measures differs from the treatment of access prevention measures in paragraph (1) in that it does not include a prohibition on the act of circumvention itself. It covers only the manufacture or sale of products or services, utilizing the same approach of focusing on how the product or service is marketed, designed or produced, and the nature and extent of its commercially significant purposes or uses.

Paragraph (2) is limited to measures that protect rights of a copyright owner under Title 17.

Paragraph (4) specifies that section 1201 cannot be read to alter existing rights, defences limitations or remedies under Title 17.

c. Issues and concerns

Two main areas of concern have been identified with respect to section 1201: its coverage of products used to circumvent, such as consumer electronics and software, and its potential impact on fair use interests.[1]

Some have urged that the legislation not address the provision of products or services, but focus solely on acts of circumvention. They state that the treaties do not require such coverage, and argue that devices themselves are neutral, and can be used for either legitimate or illegitimate purposes.

It is true that the treaties do not specifically refer to the provision of products or services, but merely require adequate protection and effective remedies against circumvention. As discussed above, however, the treaty language gives leeway to member countries to determine what protection is appropriate, with the question being whether it is adequate and effective. Because of the difficulty involved in discovering and obtaining meaningful

---

1. These concerns relate not only to fair use, but to all permitted uses under the Copyright Act, including those made possible by the idea-expression dichotomy and the first sale doctrine. For purposes of our discussion here, we will refer to all of these user privileges collectively as fair use interests.

relief from individuals who engage in acts of circumvention, a broader prohibition extending to those in the business of providing the means for circumvention appears to be necessary to make the protection adequate and effective. It is the conduct of commercial suppliers that will enable and result in large-scale circumvention.

The bill's approach to manufacturing, importing and selling is essentially an application of the familiar concept that those who participate in or assist in a prohibited act may themselves be culpable. There is ample precedent for the approach. So-called 'black boxes' for descrambling cable and satellite signals are banned under federal law, as are devices for thwarting serial copy management systems in digital audio recording devices. See 47 U.S.C. §§ 553(a)(2) and 605(c)(4); 17 U.S.C. § 1002(c).

The challenge is how to limit the coverage of such activities sufficiently, so as not to chill legitimate development activities. There appears to be general agreement on two basic propositions: (1) People should not be able to engage in profit-making activities intentionally aimed at circumventing protection for copyrighted material; (2) the development and sale of multi-purpose products with substantial lawful uses should not be prevented. The difficulty lies in the grey area in between.

The NII Copyright Protection Act sought to draw the line between permissible and impermissible products and services by looking to their 'primary purpose or effect.' The Copyright Office and others raised concerns about the potential overbreadth of this standard. H.R. 2281 is significantly more restrictive in its coverage; it imposes three limitations on circumstances where liability may be found. The provider would have to deliberately design the product to circumvent or advertise it as doing so, or the product would have to be essentially a circumvention device with only limited use for other purposes. In contrast, those items that have significant legitimate purposes or functions, such as general purpose computers, would not be covered despite the fact that they may also be used on occasion to circumvent.

The 'only limited commercially significant purpose or use' test appears to build on, but tighten, the *Sony* standard. It makes the standard more meaningful by referring to the extent to which the product is actually used for legitimate purposes, rather than its capability to be used for such purposes. At the same time, it is consistent with *Sony* in that it does not prohibit products with a substantial non-circumventing use, only those with merely limited commercially significant non-circumventing use.

These limitations improve on prior versions of anti-circumvention legislation, and aim more precisely at bad actors—those who deliberately facilitate unlawful activity. The limitations would rule out, for example, devices produced for a legitimate purpose that unexpectedly turn out to be used by consumers primarily to circumvent (as long as they were also used for their intended purpose to a commercially significant extent). It might be possible, however, to refine the approach even further, and we would be happy to work with any who have such suggestions.

The other major area of controversy relates to the impact of section 1201 on fair use and other user privileges under the Copyright Act. The Copyright Office firmly believes that the fair use doctrine is a fundamental element of the copyright law, and that its continued role in striking an appropriate balance of rights and exceptions should not be diminished. We also believe that it is possible to provide effective protection against circumvention without undermining this goal.

Section 1201 seeks to accomplish this result in several ways. First, it treats access-prevention technology separately from infringement-prevention technology, and does not contain a prohibition against individual acts of circumvention of the latter. As a result, an individual would not be able to circumvent in order to gain unauthorized access to a work, but would be able to do so in order to make fair use of a work which she has lawfully acquired. Second, it contains a savings clause that explicitly preserves fair use and other exceptions to rights in the Copyright Act.

Some argue, however, that these attempts do not go far enough and will not avoid damage to fair use interests. As a practical matter, they are concerned that access will not be made available for fair use purposes, and that there may be technological control over each occasion of use. They are also concerned that section 1201 will prevent the development of products that enable individuals to bypass such continued access controls, or infringement-prevention technology under paragraph (2), in order to make fair use. These are important issues that deserve careful consideration.

Some background may be helpful inconsidering the topic of access controls. It has long been accepted in US law that the copyright owner has the right to control access to his work, and may choose not to make it available to others or to do so only on set terms. This means not only that a copyright owner may keep a work forever unpublished, but also that he can publish it while controlling the conditions under which others are allowed to see it–such as charging a fee or imposing restrictions on how the work may be used.[2] Users generally pay for access and then, depending on the form in which the work is embodied, may accept the copyright owner's terms or negotiate for other terms. Libraries, for example, typically purchase a physical copy such as a book to make available on-site, or in obtaining access to works in electronic form, accept the terms presented or negotiate terms for use by their patrons.

The bill would continue this basic premise, allowing the copyright owner to keep a work under lock and key and to show it to others selectively. Section 1201 has therefore been analogized to the equivalent of a law against breaking and entering. Under existing law, it is not permissible to break into a locked room in order to make fair use of a manuscript kept inside.

---

2. The extent to which restrictions can be imposed by contract on uses that would otherwise be permissible under copyright law has also become a controversial issue. See, e.g., *ProCD, Inc. v. Zeidenberg*, 86 F.3d 1447 (7th Cir. 1996) (holding that the Copyright Act does not generally preempt contract rights).

In this area too, the treaties do not specifically require protection for access controls in themselves. Again, the determination to be made by Congress is how best to ensure adequate and effective protection for technological measures used by copyright owners to prevent infringement. It is our understanding that access controls such as encryption will be the primary and most effective measures that copyright owners are likely to use in the on-line environment.

One key issue is the type of access involved. Once a person has lawfully acquired access to a work, will he or she be able to make fair use? Or will such strong technological controls be imposed that each use will require additional authorization? If the former, users could be required to pay for access as they are today, and then subsequent uses might be permissible under Copyright Act exemptions. (Some have noted, however, that the existence of legal protection itself may change bargaining power in negotiating terms of use.) If the latter, it might not be possible ever to engage in such exempted conduct without payment of a new access fee.

Other critical questions are whether, as a practical matter, copyright owners will adopt reasonable terms for granting lawful access, including recognition of fair use interests; whether copyrighted works will remain available in formats other than electronic, encrypted form to be used for fair use purposes; and whether any technological means will be developed to allow individuals to circumvent for lawful purposes. The Copyright Office agrees that it would be extremely undesirable to end up with a world where fair use interests were not accommodated in an optimal manner. We share the concerns as to how these questions will be answered. If the fair use community's fears were realized, the risk would be high. If access for such purposes becomes unduly restricted, with fees charged for each use, unreasonable costs imposed, and copies not available in non-electronic form, a legislative solution would be called for.

Finally, questions have been raised about the meaning and effect of the savings clause. In the view of the Copyright Office, this clause serves two functions: (1) It constitutes a recognition of the importance of the existing balance built into the Copyright Act, including the fair use doctrine; (2) it may eliminate the possibility of an unclean hands-type argument in an infringement case. In other words, a copyright owner would not be able to defeat a fair use claim by pointing to the fact that the defendant had circumvented a technological protection measure. Cf. Harper & Row, Publishers v. Nation Enters., 471 U.S. 539, 563 (1985) (weighing in the fair use balance the bad faith of the defendant in gaining unauthorized access to the plaintiff's work); Atari Games Corp. v. Nintendo, 975 F.2d 832, 843 (Fed. Cir 1992).

As drafted, however, the clause does not establish fair use as a defense to the violation of section 1201 in itself. It refers only to 'rights, remedies, limitations, or defenses to copyright infringement, including fair use,' and the fair use provision in section 107 by its terms applies only to infringement of copyright rights. While the clause might be read by a court as a signal to extend the concept of fair use as a judge-made defence, it does not provide clear legislative authority to do so.

2. Copyright management information

a. Background and purpose

New section 1202 would ensure the accuracy and reliability of copyright management information provided to users of copyrighted works.

The Internet offers tremendous potential to develop as a marketplace for copyrighted works. Electronic licensing should prove to be easier and less expensive than traditional methods of obtaining permissions. Users could agree with a keystroke to a particular price for a particular type of use, with transaction costs minimized.

If the system is to work, however, users need to be able to trust its integrity. Information must be easily available that identifies works, their owners, and their licensing terms—and the information must be reliable. If authorizations can turn out to be defective because someone changed the name of the copyright owner or misrepresented the material as available for free, consumers will not be will to rely on the system. It is therefore critical to protect the integrity of the electronic marketplace.

In order to do so, the treaties oblige countries to make it unlawful to knowingly remove or alter such information when provided by the copyright owner in connection with a copy or communication of the work in electronic form, or to distribute, import, broadcast or communicate to the public works or copies of works knowing that such information has been removed or altered. Article 12 of WIPO Copyright Treaty; Article 19 of WIPO Performances and Phonograms Treaty. The treaties define the relevant information as 'information which identifies the work, the author of the work, the owner of any right in the work, or information about the terms and conditions of use of the work, and any numbers or codes that represent such information, when any of these items of information is attached to a copy of a work or appears in connection with the communication of a work to the public.'

Again, the Copyright Office has examined a number of bodies of law to determine whether implementing legislation is necessary. We considered trademark law, the National Stolen Property Act, 18 U.S.C. § 2318, the prohibitions concerning copyright notice n the Copyright Act, 17 U.S.C. § 506, federal and state laws regarding unfair competition, false advertising and consumer protection, state law regarding rights of publicity, and common law fraud. We have concluded that these laws in the aggregate provide less coverage than is required by the treaty. In particular, with the exception of 17 U.S.C. § 506(d) with respect to the fraudulent removal of a copyright notice, they address the alteration, but not the removal, of only a small subset of rights management information.

Apart from the treaty requirements, we believe that such a law is good domestic policy. In the Copyright Office's testimony on the NII Copyright Protection Act, we supported the adoption of similar protection into US law.

We pointed out that '[i]t is in everyone's interest, both owners and users of copyrighted material, to be able to rely on the information provided to facilitate identification and licensing.' Again, however, we raised a few questions about the relevant provision as drafted, with regard to both the scope of its coverage and its interaction with provisions of existing law. We believe that the proposed section 1202 in this bill adequately and appropriately implements the treaty obligation, and does so in a manner that resolves many of the questions we had raised about the prior version. It goes beyond the bare minimum obligation in several respects, mainly in covering the provision of false information and information not in electronic form. In our view, these extensions are useful and appropriate.

b. The coverage of the bill

Section 1202 contains three paragraphs. The third paragraph defines 'copyright management information', the first two deal with, respectively, the provision of such information that is false, and the deletion or alteration of such information. Paragraph (a) prohibits the knowing provision, public distribution, or importation for public distribution, of false copyright management information. Paragraph (b) prohibits the following acts when done without the authority of the copyright owner or the law: the knowing removal or alteration of copyright management information, or the distribution or importation for distribution of copyright management information that has been altered without the authority of the copyright owner or the law, or copies or phonorecords from which copyright management information has been removed without the authority of the copyright owner or the law.

Paragraph (c) defines 'copyright management information' as the following items, when conveyed in connection with copies, phonorecords, performances or displays of a work: identifying information about the work, its author,[3] or the copyright owner (including title and names); terms and conditions for use of the work; identifying numbers or symbols referring to such information or links to such information; or such other information as the Register of Copyrights may prescribe by regulation.

c. Issues and concerns

The issue has been raised as to this provision's impact on the privacy interests of consumers. Because section 1202 does not *require* the provision of any

3. Section 1202 implement the relevant obligation under both WIPO treaties. Since performers whose performances are fixed in sound recordings may qualify as authors under US copyright law, the reference in the definition of 'copyright management information' to identifying information about the 'author of a work' covers such performers as well as other categories of authors.

information over the Internet or elsewhere, it will not lead to the collection or dissemination of information about users and therefore should not affect their privacy. The provision simply makes it unlawful for someone to provide false information with bad intent, or deliberately to delete or alter such information, once it has already been provided. Nor could it be used to prevent consumers from taking steps to remove private information from the Internet, since the definition of 'copyright management information' does not include information about users, and since the prohibited acts require an element of knowledge or intent tied to infringement.

While the clause explicitly stating that 'the Register of Copyrights may not require the provision of any information concerning the user of a copyrighted work' therefore does not appear to be necessary, if such language will assuage any lingering concerns, the Copyright Office certainly has no objections to its inclusion. We recommend, however, that the wording be changed to eliminate the implication that the Office *does* have authority to require the provision of any other information. As noted above, section 1202 does not mandate that any particular information be provided, but simply protects whatever information is in fact provided.

The provisions in section 1202 do not apply to those who act innocently. The acts covered all must have been performed knowingly. In addition, the provision of false information is only unlawful where it is done 'with the intent to induce, enable, facilitate, or conceal infringement.' Liability for the removal or alteration of information requires the actor to know or have reason to know that his acts 'will induce, enable, facilitate or conceal' infringement.

Some copyright owners have expressed concern that this standard will be too difficult to meet, requiring proof of an ultimate infringement in order to find a violation. The Copyright Office believes that it is important to make clear, possibly in legislative history, that the reference to infringement does not mean that the actor must have intended to further any particular act of infringement—just to make infringement generally possible or easier to accomplish.

We believe that the knowledge and intent standards resolve the concerns we expressed in 1995 about the prohibition's scope of coverage. They ensure that no one will be liable who deletes, alters or provides inaccurate information for legitimate reasons, such as technological constraints or a good faith belief that he or she has the right to do so. For example, a broadcaster who interrupts a broadcast of a motion picture for a news bulletin, thereby deleting part of the motion picture's credits, would not fall within the prohibition. Nor would the provision apply to an individual who believed she was entitled to claim authorship in a work, based on a dispute over the work's status as a joint work or work made for hire. Similarly, de minimis alteration, or clarification or supplementation of information, would be ruled out. As to the provision of false information, the provision as drafted would ensure that a film distributor who distributes an old copy of a motion picture containing outdated information about the ownership of rights in the motion picture would not be liable simply because it knew the information was false. Nor could it be argued that the use of a pseudonym constituted a violation.

The bill also improves on the prior versions in other respects. It limits the context in which information is protected to information 'conveyed in connection with' copies, performances or displays of a work. This provides a link between the information and a particular manifestation of the copyrighted work, and avoids any application of the provision to such information that may happen to be contained on a piece of paper in a file somewhere. In addition, the coverage of 'identifying number or symbols' will allow the development of voluntary coding systems which can refer users to a complete and up-to-date database of licensing information.

We do note a few remaining concerns about the provision's interaction with other provisions of existing law, and a few minor drafting issues. In its current form, section 1202 still overlaps with and renders redundant at least some of the provisions of section 506(c)-(d). These sections require careful analysis to determine whether they should be deleted or amended to accommodate the new prohibitions. In paragraph (b)(3), we would propose adding a reference to 'public display' of works or phonorecords, in addition to the coverage of distribution, importation and public performance. Finally, we suggest making parallel the acts covered by paragraphs (a) and (b), adding an equivalent to subparagraph (3) to paragraph (a) to cover the distribution, importation, public performance or public display of copies of works knowing that they contain false information.

Conclusion

The Copyright Office urges prompt ratification of the WIPO treaties, and supports H.R. 2281 as a reasonable implementation of the treaties' obligations. To that end, we would be pleased to assist Congress to resolve the questions raised in this statement as well as any other concerns.

Appendix 5

THE CONFERENCE ON FAIR USE – REPORT TO THE COMMISSIONER ON THE CONCLUSION OF THE FIRST PHASE OF THE CONFERENCE ON FAIR USE

BRUCE A. LEHMAN

Assistant Secretary of Commerce and Commissioner of Patents and Trademarks and Chair, Working Group on Intellectual Property Rights of the Information Infrastructure Task Force

SEPTEMBER 1997

Single copies of this Report, as well as the Interim Report of December 1996, may be obtained, free of charge, by sending or faxing a written request to:

CONFU Report
c/o Richard Maulsby, Director
Office of Public Affairs
US Patent and Trademark Office
Washington, DC 20231
Fax: (703) 308-5258

INTRODUCTION

In 1993, President Clinton formed the Information Infrastructure Task Force (IITF) to articulate and implement the Administration's vision for the National Information Infrastructure (NII), and established the US Advisory Council on the National Information Infrastructure within the Department of Commerce to advise the Secretary of Commerce on a national strategy for promoting the development of the NII.[1] The IITF is chaired by the Secretary of Commerce

---

[1] See Exec. Order No 12864, 3 C.F.R. 634 (1993).

and consists of high-level representatives of the Federal agencies that play a role in advancing the development and application of information technologies. Guided by the principles for government action described in *NII Agenda for Action*[2] *and GII Agenda for Cooperation*,[3] the participating agencies worked with the private sector, public interest groups, Congress, and State and local governments to develop comprehensive telecommunications and information policies and programs that will promote the development of the NII and best meet the needs of the country.

The IITF is organized into three committees: the Telecommunications Policy Committee, the Committee on Applications and Technology, and the Information Policy Committee. The Working Group on Intellectual Property Rights (hereinafter 'Working Group'), chaired by Assistant Secretary of Commerce and Commissioner of Patents and Trademarks Bruce A. Lehman, was established within the Information Policy Committee to examine the intellectual property implications of the NII and to make recommendations on any appropriate changes to US intellectual property law and policy.[4]

Following a public hearing in November 1993,[5] and review and analysis of both the solicited written comments and the extensive number of public comments that were submitted, the Working Group released a preliminary draft of its report (hereinafter 'Green Paper') on 7 July 1994.[6] Following release of the Green Paper, the Working Group heard testimony from the public in four days of hearings in Chicago, Los Angeles, and Washington, DC, in September 1994.[7]

The Green Paper expressed significant concerns with the ability of the limitations on copyright owners' exclusive rights, particularly those contained in the fair use provisions of the Copyright Act, to provide the public with adequate access to copyrighted works transmitted digitally.[8] While recognizing that those principles underlying the guidelines for library and educational use

---

[2]   Information Infrastructure Task Force, National Telecommunications and Information Administration, *National Information Infrastructure: Agenda for Action* (1993).

[3]   Information Infrastructure Task Force, *Global Information Infrastructure: Agenda for Cooperation* (1995).

[4]   For a list of participating agencies, see Information Infrastructure Task Force, Working Group on Intellectual Property Rights, *Intellectual Property and the National Information Infrastructure: The Report of the Working Group on Intellectual Property Rights* (1995) [hereinafter 'WHITE PAPER'] at App. 3.

[5]   See Request for Comments on Intellectual Property Issues Involved in the National Information Infrastructure Initiative, 58 Fed. Reg. 53,917 (1993).

[6]   See Information Infrastructure Task Force, Working Group on Intellectual Property Rights, *Intellectual Property and the National Information Infrastructure: A Preliminary Draft of the Report of the Working Group on Intellectual Property Rights* (1994) [hereinafter 'GREEN PAPER'].

[7]   See Notice of Hearings and Request for comments on Preliminary Draft of the Report of the Working Group on Intellectual Property Rights, 59 Fed. Reg. 42,819 (1994); Extension of Deadline for Comments on Preliminary Draft of the Report of the Working Group on Intellectual Property Rights, 59 Fed. Reg. 50,222 (1994).

[8]   See 'GREEN PAPER' *supra* note 6, at 133.

of printed matter and music should still apply, the Working Group believed it would be 'difficult and, perhaps, inappropriate, to apply the specific language of some of those guidelines in the context of digital works and on-line services.'[9]

The Working Group decided to convene a Conference on Fair Use (CONFU) to bring together copyright owner and user interests to discuss fair use issues and, if appropriate and feasible, to develop guidelines for fair uses of copyrighted works by librarians and educators.[10] At the time of issuance of the Report of the Working Group on Intellectual Property Rights (hereinafter 'White Paper'),[11] in September 1995, CONFU was still meeting and had not concluded its work.

Meeting regularly in public sessions, CONFU grew from the forty groups which were invited to participate in the first meeting on 21 September 1994, to the approximately one hundred organizations participating as of May 1997.[12] Since 1994, the Working Group has facilitated plenary session meetings and coordinated the flow of information for CONFU.[13] A five-person Steering Committee, selected in September 1994 by all CONFU participants, acted as the formal structure guiding the CONFU process.[14]

BACKGROUND

As the White Paper noted, 'intellectual property is a subtle and esoteric area of the law that evolves in response to technological change.'[15] The Copyright Act[16] was enacted in response to 'significant changes in technology [that had]

---

[9] *Id.* at 134.
[10] See Notice of First Meeting of Conference on 'Fair Use' and the National Information Infrastructure (NII), 59 Fed. Reg. 46,823 (1994).
[11] See WHITE PAPER *supra* note 4, at 83.
[12] See CONFERENCE ON FAIR USE PARTICIPANTS *infra* Appendix A.
[13] This was accomplished by having an attorney-advisor in the Office of Legislative and International Affairs of the Patent and Trademark Office act as an executive secretary for the Conference on Fair Use. From September 1994 to July 1995, Christopher A. Meyer served in this capacity; from September 1995 to the present, Peter N. Fowler has served in that capacity and authored both this Report and the CONFU Interim Report in December 1996.
[14] The initial Steering Committee members were: Stan Cahill, Public Broadcasting System; Carol C. Henderson, American Library Association; Mary B. Levering, US Copyright Office, Library of Congress; Carol A. Risher, Association of American Publishers; and Mark Traphagen, Software Publishers Association. In late 1995, Carol Henderson designated Adam M. Eisgrau as her replacement, and Stan Cahill ceased being an active participant on the Steering Committee.
[15] See WHITE PAPER, *supra* note 4, at 7.
[16] The Copyright Act of 1976, as amended, is codified at 17 U.S.C. '101 *et seq.* (1994). Hereinafter, the Act is cited as "17U.S.C. '_____" or "17.U.S.C.A. '__(WEST SUPP. 1996)."

affected the operation of the copyright law.'[17] It specifies that certain uses of copyrighted works are outside the control of the copyright owner, and it provides a number of exceptions to the 'exclusive' rights of copyright owners. While many regard these exceptions as rights of users, they are, technically, outright exemptions from liability or affirmative defenses to what would otherwise be acts of infringement.

The most significant and, perhaps, murky of the limitations on a copyright owner's exclusive rights is the doctrine of fair use.[18] Though now embodied in statutory language, the doctrine of fair use is rooted in more than 200 years of judicial decisions. Fair use is an affirmative defense to an action for copyright infringement. It is potentially available with respect to all manner of unauthorized uses of all types of works in all media. When the fair use doctrine applies to a specific use of a work, the person making fair use of the work does not need to seek permission from the copyright owner or to compensate the copyright owner for the use of the work.

Before examining the work of CONFU, it is useful to examine the statutory language concerning fair use. Section 107 of the Copyright Act provides:

'Notwithstanding the provisions of sections 106 and 106A, the fair use of a copyrighted work, including such use by reproduction in copies or phonorecords or by any other means specified by that section [sic], for purposes such as criticism, comment, news reporting, teaching (including multiple copies for classroom use), scholarship, or research, is not an infringement of copyright. In determining whether the use made of a work in any particular case is a fair use the factors to be considered shall include—

(1)   the purpose and character of the use, including whether such use is of a commercial nature or is for nonprofit educational purposes;
(2)   the nature of the copyrighted work;
(3)   the amount and substantiality of the portion used in relation to the copyrighted work as a whole; and
(4)   the effect of the use upon the potential market for or value of the copyrighted work.'

The fact that a work is unpublished shall not itself bar a finding of fair use if such finding is made upon consideration of all the above factors.[19]

---

[17]   See H.R. REP. NO. 1476, 94th Cong., 2d Sess. 47 (1976), *reprinted in* 1976 U.S.C.C.A.N. 5659 [hereinafter HOUSE REPORT].
[18]   See 17 U.S.C.A. '107 (WEST SUPP. 1996); see also, 3 NIMMER ON COPYRIGHT' 13 (1993). There are a number of websites devoted to copyright and fair use issues, see e.g., Stanford University Copyright and Fair Use Site (http://www.fairuse.stanford.edu) or University of Virginia Law Library Copyright and Fair Use Site (http//www.gopher.lib.virginia.edu).
[19]   17 U.S.C. '107 (1994).

The copyright law allows copyright owners to exercise the rights granted to them, to license their rights, or to give them away. Some copyright owners are not motivated by any commercial considerations. Those creators and authors who wish to dedicate their works to the public domain may, of course, do so notwithstanding the availability of protection under the Copyright Act. Nothing in the law prevents those who do not wish to claim copyright from waiving their rights and allowing unrestricted reproduction, distribution and other uses of their works. As the White Paper notes, '[c]opyright protection is not an obstacle in the way of the success of the NII; it is an essential component. Effective copyright protection is a fundamental way to promote the availability of works to the public.'[20]

While the NII and other digital technology present myriad opportunities for fair uses of works,

'[i]t is reasonable to expect that courts would approach claims of fair use in the context of the NII just as they do in "traditional" environments. Commercial uses that involve no "transformation" by users and harm actual or potential markets will likely always be infringing, while non-profit educational transformative uses will likely often be fair. Between these two extremes, courts will have to engage in the same type of fact-intensive analysis that typifies fair use litigation and frustrates those who seek a "bright line" clearly separating the lawful from the unlawful.'[21]

Given the lack of such 'bright lines', interested parties, including the user communities, copyright owners, and those who act in an intermediary role, such as libraries, educators, and publishers, have over the years developed voluntary guidelines to address practical use situations. The fair use,[22] library copying,[23] and educational use[24] provisions of the Copyright Act have been the subject of four sets of guidelines for libraries and educational institutions, to which affected parties have agreed. These various guidelines, while having no force of law, are contained at different places in legislative history. The current guidelines cover certain copying by and for teachers in the classroom context,[25] the copying of music for educational purposes,[26] the copying of relatively recent journal articles by one library for a patron of another,[27] and the off-air

---

[20]   See WHITE PAPER, *supra* note 4, at 16.
[21]   See WHITE PAPER, *supra* note 4, at 80.
[22]   17 U.S.C.A. '107 (WEST SUPP. 1996).
[23]   17 U.S.C. '108 (WEST SUPP. 1996).
[24]   17 U.S.C. '110 (WEST SUPP. 1996).
[25]   See *Agreement on Guidelines for Classroom Copying in Not-for-Profit Educational Institutions* [hereinafter 'CLASSROOM GUIDELINES'], contained in HOUSE REPORT, *supra* note 17, at 68-74, *reprinted in* 1976 U.S.C.C.A.N. 5681-88.
[26]   See *Guidelines for Educational Use of Music*, contained in HOUSE REPORT, *supra* note 17, at 70-71, *reprinted in* 1976 U.S.C.C.A.N. 5684-85.
[27]   See CONTU *Guidelines on Photocopying Under Interlibrary Loan Arrangements*, contained in REPORT OF THE CONFERENCE COMMITTEE ON THE NEW COPYRIGHT LAW (H.R. No. 1733, 94th Cong., 2d Sess., at 71-73) *reprinted* in 1976 U.S.C.C.A.N. 5812-14.

videotaping of educational broadcast materials.[28] The result has been, in certain circumstances, a quantitative gloss on the construction of fair use and library copying privileges.

I. THE CONFU PROCESS

The genesis of CONFU was the Green Paper's call for a 'conference to bring together copyright owner and user interests to develop guidelines for fair uses of copyrighted works by and in public libraries and schools.'[29] Some forty organizations representing copyright owners, educators, and librarians were invited to submit statements that identified the issues that they believed CONFU should address, and that set out no more than three principles that participants believed should apply to educational and library fair use in the digital context.[30] These statements were distributed to all participants and discussion of the proposed principles occurred at the first session of CONFU on 21 September 1994. The participants' proposed principles were subsequently grouped into several categories: fair use in general, policy concerns, media application, marketplace, licensing/transaction tracking, new guideline concerns, and browsing.[31]

Participants were encouraged to follow the example of previous successful efforts to develop voluntary fair use guidelines – the Classroom Guidelines in 1976,[32] and the National Commission on New Technological Uses of Copyrighted Works (hereinafter 'CONFU'), which dealt with the issues raised by photocopiers and computers in 1978.[33]

In addition, there was a recognition that the Consortium of College and University Media Centers (CCUMC), which had convened a working group composed of many of the same participants as CONFU, and begun in June 1994 a process to develop fair use guidelines for educational multimedia uses. While a parallel effort, the CCUMC multimedia working group was open to all CONFU participants, its progress reported at CONFU meetings, and its results, ultimately considered part of the CONFU process, were added to the Report on the Conclusion of the First Phase of CONFU.

At three half-day meetings on 21, 24 and 26 October 1994, there was an initial effort to organize the discussion and work of CONFU by means of

---

[28] See *Guidelines for Off-Air Recording of Broadcast Programming For Educational Purposes*, contained in HOUSE REPORT ON PIRACY AND COUNTERFEITING AMENDMENTS (H.R. No. 495, 97th Cong., 1st Sess. at 8-9), *reprinted* in U.S. COPYRIGHT OFFICE, *Reproduction of Copyrighted Works by Educators and Librarians (Circular 21)* (1992) p. 26.

[29] See GREEN PAPER, *supra* note 7, at 134.

[30] See WRITTEN STATEMENTS SUBMITTED TO CONFU *infra* Appendix B.

[31] See SUMMARY OF INITIAL PROPOSED PRINCIPLES *infra* Appendix C.

[32] See CLASSROOM GUIDELINES contained in HOUSE REPORT, *supra* note 17, at 68-74, *reprinted in* 1976 U.S.C.C.A.N. 5681-88.

[33] See note 27 *supra* and accompanying text.

subgroupings of participants into library, elementary-secondary, and higher education subcommittees. These meetings identified a variety of new uses and issues for discussion. However, because they reflected the same copyright owner and user concerns, they crossed all organizational subgroupings; hence, this approach did not prove to be a useful organizing structure. Since individuals had volunteered to present short papers or reports on these discussion issues at future meetings, it was decided, rather, to meet in plenary sessions to hear and discuss the topic presentations. This process began in early December 1994.

The presentation and discussion of these topics laid the foundation for informed discussions prior to participants turning to the subject of drafting various scenarios, and, further, allowed participants to decide which topics should be explored as scenarios and which were useful only as background information. The scenario presentations and discussions allowed participants to decide which topics were appropriate for guidelines, and how to deal with such topics, if at all, in the process of drafting guidelines.

Following presentations on twenty-one different topics,[34] certain topics were selected for discussion of specific scenarios which would provide concrete examples of how schools and libraries might use copyrighted works under fair use and whether such uses were covered by current law. These scenarios, which included distance learning, multimedia, electronic reserves, visually impaired, transient copying, use of software in libraries, preservation, visual image archives, interlibrary loan/document delivery, downloading for personal use, and browsing,[35] provided a range of examples of what, in the opinions of the drafters of the scenarios, may or may not be considered fair use or, in the case of interlibrary loans, guidelines for Section 108. Subsequently, following further sessions devoted to topic and scenario discussions, and as a result of the extensive background discussions at monthly sessions, six working groups,[36] with various representatives of rightsholders and educational and library users as participants, emerged to draft and negotiate fair use guidelines in five specific areas. A Statement of Scenarios on the use of copyrighted computer software in libraries was also created.

These working groups met and negotiated throughout 1995 and most of 1996, running contemporaneously with monthly plenary sessions to discuss issues and drafts of voluntary guidelines with the entire group of participants. In addition, a number of individuals and organizations interested in nonprofit music education and music publishing met on 26 April 1996, at Columbia University, under the auspices of CONFU, to discuss whether current guidelines for educational uses of music needed revision in the digital

[34] See TOPIC AND ISSUE PAPER PRESENTERS *infra* Appendix D.
[35] See TOPIC GRID *infra* Appendix E.
[36] The Working Groups were: DIGITAL IMAGES, DISTANCE LEARNING, EDUCATIONAL MULTIMEDIA, ELECTRONIC RESERVE SYSTEMS, INTERLIBRARY LOAN/DOCUMENT DELIVERY, and SOFTWARE USE IN LIBRARIES.

environment.[37] The general consensus was that no change was needed at that time, but that music publishers, music educators, and music librarians would need to be aware of the guidelines being developed by CONFU, which might include uses of music in digital form.

As progress was being made in some areas and not in others, it was decided at the plenary session meeting on 30 May 1996, that a concerted effort would be made by all working groups to complete, if possible, the drafting of widely acceptable guidelines in light of a general consensus to end the CONFU plenary process by 30 November 1996. The multimedia working group stated at that time that should it reach agreement on fair use multimedia guidelines sooner, it would seek to have such voluntary guidelines included in legislative history.[38]

On 30 May 1996, participants agreed to adopt for all sets of guidelines a Uniform Preamble,[39] which had been drafted and coordinated by Mary Levering, Associate Register for National Copyright Programs in the US Copyright Office. On 6 September 1996, participants agreed that a brief factual report of the CONFU process, including any resultant guidelines, should be prepared with advice and comment from the CONFU Steering Committee. A draft of such a report was circulated by the Steering Committee for comment prior to a plenary session on 25 November 1996. At the meeting on 25 November 1996, a number of revisions to the draft report were suggested and discussed, and it was agreed by the participants that the three sets of guidelines dealing with digital images, distance learning, and educational multimedia, would be attached as appendices to what would now be called an Interim Report. It was agreed that the Interim Report would be circulated as a useful background for those who would now consider the endorsement or non-endorsement of the three sets of guidelines during an agreed to six-month endorsement period, recognizing that the proposed guidelines for digital images and distance learning, unlike those for educational multimedia, were completed only a short time prior to the meeting and might possibly be revised at some point in the future as the working groups may determine appropriate.

The Interim Report was published in early January 1997, in both hard copy and electronic form, and it was made available on numerous websites, including the official US Patent and Trademark Office website.[40] Following an

---

[37] See PARTICIPANTS IN THE MEETING ON THE FAIR USE OF MUSIC MATERIALS IN A DIGITAL ENVIRONMENT, *infra* Appendix F.

[38] Inasmuch as no copyright legislation was under active consideration at that time by Congress, the CCUMC Working Group on Educational Multimedia sought the endorsement of the guidelines by the Subcommittee on Courts and Intellectual Property, Committee on the Judiciary, US House of Representatives, which adopted a Non-legislative Report Relating to the Fair Use Guidelines for Educational Multimedia (27 September 1996).

[39] See UNIFORM PREAMBLE FOR FAIR USE GUIDELINES *infra* Appendix G.

[40] The official US Patent and Trademark Office website is available at: http://www.uspto.gov.

extended period for discussion and consideration of the proposals for guidelines, CONFU participants met on 19 May 1997, to consider the degree to which the three proposals for guidelines had gained acceptance and endorsement among the copyright owner and user communities as reflected in comments and statements received by the CONFU facilitator. It was determined that a report, which would update the Interim Report as to the status of CONFU and the results achieved to date, be drafted and published in recognition of what was viewed by many as the conclusion of the first phase of the Conference of Fair Use. Participants were given until 30 June 1997, to submit to the facilitator any formal or revised statements or comments of their position on the three sets of guidelines, with such submissions to be included in the aforementioned report, as well as, posted on the US Patent and Trademark Office website.[41]

In recognition of the need for continued work and discussion on some of the guidelines, as well as the desire of most participants to continue a forum for dialogue on other fair use issues, it was the consensus of the participants that CONFU would reconvene a meeting on 18 May 1998. The purpose of the meeting would be to assess the status of the three sets of guidelines, to take reports on the work of the remaining working groups on digital images and distance learning, and to assess the progress, if any, toward achieving greater acceptance, endorsement, and implementation of the various sets of guidelines within the copyright owner and user communities.

II. STATUS OF THE GUIDELINES

Following what amounted to an intensive self-education process by CONFU participants, the various working groups, where it proved possible, began the task of discussing and drafting proposed guidelines, often taking months of negotiation on both concepts and language. Some working groups succeeded in drafting proposals for guidelines which were acceptable to a broad range of participants. Others were not as successful in drafting proposals for guidelines acceptable to a broad cross-representative number of CONFU participants. In some areas, participants felt that the time was not yet ripe to write actual guidelines since the technology was still evolving and the marketplace was still experimenting with how to deal with these issues. In other areas, there was no clear consensus on how to draft guidelines, or whether, in some cases, guidelines were even necessary. Some institutions and organizations which participated in CONFU are opposed to one or more of the proposals for guidelines, while others have endorsed some or all of the guidelines. Indeed, at the end of Phase One of the process, some organizations concluded that it was

---

[41] See NOTIFICATIONS RECEIVED FROM ORGANIZATIONS AND INSTITUTIONS CONCERNING THE PROPOSALS FOR FAIR USE GUIDELINES *infra* VOLUME TWO.

premature to adopt any guidelines at this time. Finally, it was a matter of general agreement by all CONFU participants that the participation by such institutions and organizations in the process of drafting these proposals for guidelines does not assume the endorsement by any of the participating institutions and organizations.

What follows is a summary of the work of the respective working groups on the various proposals for guidelines.

A. DIGITAL IMAGES

It was recognized at the outset of CONFU that digital images collections raise issues different from text issues; that these considerations and concerns were not addressed by text norms and understandings (e.g. quality/distortion/accuracy issues, commercial exploitation potential, and the critical mass necessary for educational uses). Moreover, print issues were well represented within the CONFU process, and, because not much attention had been paid to the issues regarding images in the old technologies, it was even more difficult to grapple with the issues in the new technologies. These issues were discussed at early CONFU plenary sessions and separately at a College Art Association meeting in April 1995, in New York, convened by Barbara Hoffman, counsel to the College Art Association.

Subsequently, various versions of scenarios and drafts of proposed guidelines were prepared and presented by Barbara Hoffman and discussed at several CONFU plenary sessions. Recognizing the scope of the issues, and the disagreements on threshold understandings of copyright issues relating to digital images, it was recommended at the CONFU plenary session in December 1995, that a more formal CONFU working group, representing both educational users and copyright owners, was needed to review and negotiate the working drafts. After a few sessions in early 1996, it became clear that, in order to make significant progress on the drafting of widely acceptable guidelines, other disciplines, in addition to art history and art scholarship, needed to be represented in the working group in order to represent broader interests and concerns regarding educational fair use of digital images.

Drawing also on representative parties from the scientific, biomedical, and mathematics communities, the Digital Images Working Group was reorganized under the leadership of Patricia Williams, Vice President of Policy and Program of the American Association of Museums, with the assistance of Anita DiFanis, Director of Government Affairs of the Association of Art Museum Directors, and others, including, Mary B. Levering, Associate Register for National Copyright Programs of the US Copyright Office, Library of Congress, Hope O'Keeffe, Deputy General Counsel of the National Endowment for the Arts, and Victor S. Perlman, General Counsel of the American Society of Media Photographers, with more than twenty participating organizations providing support and guidance to this expanded process. This expanded effort led to new Educational Fair Use Guidelines for

Digital Images being drafted with input from the copyright owner and user communities. The purpose of the Guidelines is to clarify the application of the fair use doctrine as it relates to the creation of digital archives, digital images and their use, for eductional purposes, including the digitizing of pre-existing analog image collections and newly acquired analog visual images.

Having completed the drafting process in November 1996, the working group concluded that, while there was no consensus within the working group as to recommending the guidelines for endorsement, there was consensus that the draft guidelines could be disseminated to organizations for review, discussion, and possible endorsement over the next several months. As with other sets of guidelines, participation in the process of drafting these guidelines does not assume the endorsement by any of the participating organizations, and organizations may or may not choose to endorse the digital images guidelines. On 25 November 1996, it was decided that this proposal would be submitted for consideration as a completed proposal for fair use guidelines for digital images.[42]

Following extensive national discussion and consideration of the proposal for guidelines by many organizations concerned with art education, art history and art preservation, it was apparent at the CONFU meeting on 19 May 1997, that while a number of organizations had endorsed the proposed guidelines and were willing to implement them in order to see if they worked, there was a significant number of organizations that opposed endorsement of the guidelines at this time on the basis that the proposed guidelines were viewed as unworkable. Given that most participants supported the goal of achieving workable guidelines, but acknowledging the lack of consensus on the proposed guidelines, it was proposed that a monitored use period be instituted for at least one year, during which institutions could implement the proposed guidelines and use them in practical classroom and institutional situations.

During this use period, those institutions and organizations which voluntarily implement the guidelines will be asked to provide their observations, comments, and criticisms of the guidelines to the Digital Images Working Group, whose membership has been expanded to include a greater number of educational and academic organizations. The working group will continue to meet periodically to discuss specific problems reported in using the guidelines and to reevaluate the guidelines based on specific concerns expressed. The working group will consider revising the guidelines with the goal of gaining wider support and endorsement of them. A report on the experiences of those institutions and organizations that implement the guidelines during the use period, together with a summary of other activities of the working group, will be made at a meeting on 18 May 1998.

---

[42] See PROPOSED EDUCATIONAL FAIR USE GUIDELINES FOR DIGITAL IMAGES *infra* Appendix H.

B. DISTANCE LEARNING

The Distance Learning Working Group met under the leadership of Laura Gasaway, Professor of Law and Director of the Law Library at the University of North Carolina, who represented the Association of American Universities, to discuss the issues involved in distance learning activities and to draft guidelines.

The purpose of the Educational Fair Use Guidelines for Distance Learning is to provide guidance on the application of the performance and display of copyrighted works in some of the distance learning environments that have developed since the enactment of Section 110 and that may not meet the specific conditions of Section 110(2). It is the belief of the working group that these Guidelines basically extend the face-to-face teaching exemptions in Section 110 of the Copyright Act to distance learning but with certain restrictions.

After considerable discussion, the working group had determined that it was feasible to draft guidelines which only apply to the real time performance and display of a lawfully acquired copyrighted work not covered under Section 110(2) of the Copyright Act, but that it was not feasible at this time to draft guidelines that apply to asynchronous delivery of distance learning over a computer network.

Although participants in the working group believed that fair use applies in some aspects of such instruction, they did not develop fair use guidelines to cover these situations because, among other things, they felt that the area was still unsettled, that in the face of rapidly developing technology, educational institutions are only now beginning to experiment with such distance learning courses, and publishers and other content creators are in the early stages of developing materials and marketing strategies for publisher-produced computer network delivery of distance learning materials. The working group suggested that the issue of fair use guidelines for asynchronous computer network delivery of distance learning courses be revisited within three to five years.

As with other sets of guidelines, the participation by organizations in the process of drafting these guidelines does not assume the endorsement by any of the participating organizations. On 25 November 1996, it was decided to submit the guidelines to CONFU participants for consideration as a proposal for fair use guidelines for distance learning.[43]

Following extensive national discussion and consideration of the proposal for guidelines by many organizations concerned with distance education issues, it was apparent at the CONFU plenary session meeting 19 May 1997, that while numerous organizations had endorsed the proposed guidelines, there was a significant number of organizations that opposed endorsement of the

---

[43] See PROPOSED EDUCATIONAL FAIR USE GUIDELINES FOR DISTANCE LEARNING *infra* Appendix I.

guidelines for a variety of reasons. Among the various reasons put forward by individual organizations was the commonly viewed belief that the proposed guidelines did not go far enough in addressing concerns about fair use of asynchronous computer network delivery of distance learning courses.

Given that most participants supported the goal of adopting workable guidelines, yet acknowledging the lack of consensus among CONFU participants on the proposed guidelines, it was agreed that the working group be expanded to include additional representatives from the educational community in order to attempt to resolve some of the concerns and reservations expressed by participants about the proposed guidelines.

This expanded working group would continue to meet periodically to address the concerns raised about the proposed guidelines, and would now additionally pursue the development of fair use guidelines for asynchronous network delivery of distance learning courses. A report on the efforts of the Distance Learning Working Group to draft further guidelines will be made at a meeting on 18 May 1998.

C. EDUCATIONAL MULTIMEDIA

The Consortium of College and University Media Centers (CCUMC), which convened a large group of representatives of both copyright owners and educational institutions which became the Educational Multimedia Working Group, had begun its process of discussing and drafting possible educational multimedia fair use guidelines four months prior to the convening of CONFU. This working group acted under the leadership of the late Ivan Bender, counsel to CCUMC, and Lisa Livingston, Director of Instructional Media, City College/City University of New York, and chair of the CCUMC Government Relations Committee.

The purpose of the Fair Use Guidelines for Educational Multimedia, which were drafted by copyright owners and users after considerable discussion and negotiation, is to clarify the application of fair use of copyrighted works as teaching methods are adapted to new learning environments. The Guidelines apply to the fair use of portions of lawfully acquired copyrighted works in educational multimedia projects which are created by educators or students as part of a systematic learning activity at nonprofit educational institutions. Such institutions are defined as nonprofit organizations whose primary focus is supporting research and instructional activities of educators and students for noncommercial purposes.

On 6 September 1996, CONFU accepted the Educational Multimedia Fair Use Guidelines developed by the organizations participating in the CCUMC working group, and, further, indicated that such guidelines could be included in any resulting CONFU report. On 25 November 1996, it was agreed by CONFU participants, at the urging of a large number of CCUMC working group members who were also participants in CONFU, that the Educational

Multimedia Fair Use Guidelines be included in the CONFU Interim Report.[44]

Following extensive national discussion and consideration of the guidelines by numerous organizations concerned with multimedia and education issues, it was apparent at the CONFU meeting on 19 May 1997, that a substantial number of CONFU participants, as well as, other institutions and organizations in both the copyright owner and user communities, supported or had endorsed the guidelines. However, there was not a consensus in support of the guidelines among those organizations participating in CONFU that represent academic and educational institutions and library concerns.

Since many CONFU participants voiced support for the guidelines, and the guidelines were already being implemented in several educational institutions around the country, it was decided that the Educational Multimedia Fair Use Guidelines would be released in their present and final form. It was suggested that the implementation of the guidelines be observed over the course of the next year, and it was further agreed that a report on the implementation of the guidelines would be made at a meeting on 18 May 1998.

D. ELECTRONIC RESERVE SYSTEMS

The working group met under the leadership of Dr. Kenneth D. Crews, Director of the Copyright Management Center at Indiana University-Purdue University at Indianapolis, who represented the Indiana Partnership for Statewide Education, Laura Gasaway, Professor of Law and Director of the Law Library at the University of North Carolina, who represented the Association of American Universities, Dr. Douglas C. Bennett, Vice President of the American Council of Learned Societies, Carol A. Risher, Vice President of Copyright and New Technology, Association of American Publishers, and Mary E. Jackson, consultant to the Association of Research Libraries. The focus of the working group's attention was to discuss the issues involved in the application of fair use to the creation of electronic reserve systems that allow storage, access, display and downloading of electronic versions of materials that support the instructional requirements of a specific course within a nonprofit educational institution.

After considerable discussion, the working group reached an impasse in late 1995 over the proposed scope and language of possible guidelines. This disagreement among the representatives of the copyright owner, educational institution, and library communities led all parties involved to conclude that it was not possible to draft fair use guidelines capable of gaining wide acceptance at this time. Some members of the working group, however, continued to meet and discuss these issues, which culminated in their drafting and circulating

[44] See FAIR USE GUIDELINES FOR EDUCATIONAL MULTIMEDIA *infra* Appendix J.

for comment proposed guidelines in March 1996, in the hope of finding a middle ground position which could gain acceptance.

During a CONFU plenary session meeting in May 1996, all parties interested in electronic reserve systems were encouraged to discuss the proposed guidelines in an effort to explore whether widely acceptable guidelines were achievable. Subsequent discussions, however, again revealed significant differences of opinion among the working group's participants about the draft guidelines 5 March 1996.

During the CONFU plenary session on 6 September 1996, there was a general consensus that the proffered Fair Use Guidelines for Electronic Reserve Systems had not received widespread acceptance at that time. While some participants expressed a willingness to endorse or adopt them,[45] other participants expressed their opposition to the proffered guidelines.[46] In discussion of whether the draft guidelines could be characterized as being an understanding of fair use by those organizations that endorsed them, there was a consensus that they were not widely supported at that time within CONFU. While acknowledging that some institutions may feel free to adopt and implement them, it was decided on 25 November 1996, that the proffered guidelines for electronic reserve systems would not be disseminated as a formal work product of CONFU.

At the CONFU plenary session meeting on 19 May 1997, it was concluded that, while the previously proffered guidelines for electronic reserve systems would not be included in a report on the conclusion of Phase One of CONFU, the issue of developing guidelines for electronic reserve systems could still be part of the discussion within the framework of CONFU should there appear to be substantial support among CONFU participants for reactivating the working group on this issue. The Steering Committee will monitor this issue during the next year and will coordinate with those participants who may wish to renew such discussions within the context of a working group.

---

[45] The following organizations are on record as endorsing or supporting the proffered Fair Use Guidelines for Electronic Reserve Systems: American Association of Law Libraries, American Council of Learned Societies, Association of American University Presses, Inc., Indiana Partnership for Statewide Education, Music Library Association, National Education Association, National School Boards Association, and Special Libraries Association.

[46] The following organizations are on record as opposed to the proffered Fair Use Guidelines for Electronic Reserve Systems: American Society of Composers, Authors and Publishers, American Society of Journalists and Authors, American Society of Media Photographers, Association of American Publishers, Association of Research Libraries, Authors Guild/ Authors Registry, Recording Industry Association of America, and Software Publishers Association.

E. INTERLIBRARY LOAN AND DOCUMENT DELIVERY

The working group met under the leadership of Mary E. Jackson, Consultant to the Association of Research Libraries, and Dr. Douglas C. Bennett, Vice President of the American Council of Learned Societies, to discuss the issues involved both in digital interlibrary loan and document delivery activities and to attempt to draft guidelines. After considerable discussion, the working group unanimously agreed on 27 March 1996, that it was premature to draft guidelines for digital transmission of digital documents.

Subsequent discussions throughout the spring and summer of 1996, failed to achieve agreement on guidelines for digital delivery of print originals under interlibrary loan arrangements. After considerable discussion within the working group and in general plenary sessions, it was agreed by both the copyright owner and user communities that it was not possible, at this time, to draft widely acceptable guidelines for digital delivery of print materials by libraries.

At the CONFU plenary session meeting on 19 May 1997, it was decided that, while there had been agreement that it was not possible at this time to draft guidelines for digital delivery of print materials by libraries, the issue of developing guidelines for the digital delivery of print materials by libraries could still be part of the discussion within the framework of CONFU should there appear to be substantial support among CONFU participants for reactivating the working group on this issue. The Steering Committee will monitor this issue during the next year and will coordinate with those participants who may wish to renew such discussions within the context of a working group.

F. USE OF COMPUTER SOFTWARE IN LIBRARIES

After plenary discussions of the scenarios developed by Sarah K. Wiant, the Director of the Law Library at Washington and Lee University, who represented the Special Libraries Association, and Mark Trpahagen, Vice President and Counsel for Intellectual Property and Trade Policy of the Software Publishers Association, it was generally agreed by CONFU participants that, since the scenarios developed by the working group clearly illustrated the general rules and how particular uses of computer program software in libraries either complied with or violated the Copyright Act, there was no need to draft guidelines.

Following several presentations of the statement and scenarios on the use of copyrighted computer programs (software) in libraries, and a thorough discussion and slight revision of the statement, the Statement on Use of Copyrighted Computer Programs (Software) in Libraries − Scenarios[47] was adopted by CONFU participants on 6 September 1996.

---

[47]   See STATEMENT ON USE OF COPYRIGHTED COMPUTER PROGRAMS (SOFTWARE) IN LIBRARIES − SCENARIOS *infra* Appendix K.

During the plenary session meeting on 25 November 1996, participants agreed by consensus that the Statement and Scenarios should be appended to the Interim Report. Subsequently, during the CONFU plenary session meeting on 19 May 1997, it was agreed by consensus that the Statement and Scenarios be included in a report on the conclusion of the first phase of CONFU.

G. SUMMARY

In summary, the CONFU process resulted in the development of proposed fair use guidelines for digital images, some aspects of fair use guidelines for distance learning, fair use guidelines for educational multimedia, and the adoption of a statement of scenarios dealing with the use of computer software in libraries. The proposed guidelines proffered by a minority of the working group on electronic reserve systems were not supported widely by CONFU participants. As for the digital transmission of documents in the context of interlibrary loan and document delivery activities by libraries, it was determined by the interested parties involved in the working group that it was premature to draft guidelines addressing this issue.

Copies of all notifications or statements of endorsement or opposition to the three sets of proposals for guidelines, together with all comments from individuals, received by this facilitator, are appended to this report. As additional notifications or comments on the guidelines are received by the facilitator, they will be posted on the U.S. Patent and Trademark Office website.

III. RESULTS

1. It was agreed by the participants at the CONFU plenary session meeting held on 19 May 1997, that a Report to the Commissioner on the Conclusion of the First Phase of the Conference on Fair Use will be written by the facilitator, that said Report will include the three sets of guidelines for digital images, distance learning, and educational multimedia and all statements and comments received concerning them, and that said Report would be made available and published in both hard copy and electronic form to all CONFU participants and the public.

2. It was agreed by the participants at the CONFU plenary session meeting held on 19 May 1997, that in connection with the Proposed Educational Fair Use Guidelines for Digital Images, a use period of at least one year will be instituted for their voluntary adoption, implementation, and review by interested institutions. During this use period the Digital Images Working Group will meet periodically to address the various concerns, observations, and criticisms received in connection with the proposed guidelines, and to discuss and negotiate possible refinements of the guidelines with the goal of achieving broad-based support and endorsement of the guidelines. A report by the Working Group on its activities and the results of the use period will be made at a meeting on 18 May 1998.

3. It was agreed by the participants at the CONFU plenary session meeting held on 19 May 1997, that in connection with the Proposed Educational Fair Use Guidelines for Distance Learning, the membership of the current Distance Learning Working Group would be expanded to include academic and educational institutions directly involved in distance learning activities. During the next year, the Distance Learning Working Group will continue to meet periodically to address the various concerns, observations, and criticisms received in connection with the proposed guidelines, to discuss and negotiate the development of guidelines for asynchronous network delivery of distance learning courses, and to discuss and negotiate possible refinements of the proposed guidelines with the goal of achieving broad-based support and endorsement of the guidelines. A report on the working group's activities will be made at a meeting on 18 May 1998.

4. It was agreed by the participants at the CONFU plenary session meeting held on 19 May 1997, that the Steering Committee be expanded to eleven members. Following a discussion on the need to expand the Steering committee in such a way as to make it more representative of both the copyright owner and user communities, the following individuals were elected by consensus to serve on the expanded Steering Committee: Christine Dalziel, American Association of Community Colleges and the Instructional Communications Council; Adam M. Eisgrau, American Library Association; Mary B. Levering, US Copyright Office, Library of Congress; Lisa Livingston, Consortium of College and University Media Centers; Victor S. Perlman, American Society of Media Photographers; Carol Risher, Association of American Publishers; Judith M. Saffer, Broadcast Music, Inc.; Mark Traphagen, Software Publishers Association; Laila van Eyck, National Association of State Universities and Land-Grant Colleges; John C. Vaughn, Association of American Universities; and Patricia Williams, American Association of Museums.

5. It was agreed by the participants at the CONFU plenary session meeting held on 19 May 1997, that CONFU remains committed to fostering a dialogue on all fair use issues, including browsing, electronic reserves, interlibrary loan and document delivery, even though proposals concerning these issues have not been developed fully to date nor been widely accepted by participants.

6. It was agreed by the participants at the CONFU plenary session meeting held on 19 May 1997, that a meeting would be convened on 18 May 1998, to receive reports from the continuing working groups on their activities, to receive a report from the Digital Images Working Group on the voluntary use period initiated in connection with the proposed fair use guidelines for digital images, to review the experiences of institutions that have implemented the fair use guidelines for educational multimedia, and to assess the progress, if any, in drafting more comprehensive fair use guidelines for distance learning, as well as toward achieving greater acceptance in the copyright owner and use communities for the three sets of fair use guidelines.

IV. CONCLUSION

CONFU is an extraordinary public-private effort, requiring many days of meetings and travel since its inception in September 1994. Many organizations, from both the public and private sector, and especially a large number of nonprofit organizations, have devoted substantial human and financial resources and have made significant sacrifices to participate in the CONFU effort to develop fair use guidelines for educational and library uses of copyrighted works in a digital environment. The total investment of time, resources, and sustained participation by those involved cannot be measured fully.

Some organizations approached CONFU initially in the belief that there was little chance of reaching agreement on guidelines. Others expressed their misgivings and skepticism as to whether such a negotiating process could yield substantial and meaningful results. Yet, most participants feel that it is both a beneficial forum for discussion and an instructive and productive endeavor for those interested in fair use issues, even when the good faith efforts and best intentions of the participants have not always resulted in a meeting of minds.

Now the CONFU has concluded its first phase of activity, and has placed three sets of guidelines in the world for public debate, discussion, endorsement, and implementation, as institutions and organizations see fit, it now necessarily moves into a new phase of existence. Much the way an engineer, after spending time and energy to build a model of his or her invention, must now use it to see if it works, making refinements or changes where necessary to improve its functioning, so, too, does CONFU now need to encourage the implementation and use – the experimentation, if you will – of the guidelines to see how they work in the classrooms, libraries, and media centers where they are needed, and, ultimately, where their value as workable guidelines will be assessed.

It is true that not all CONFU participants support the three sets of guidelines. Indeed, some CONFU participants strongly oppose them, while others strongly support them. It can fairly be said that the CONFU process of developing fair use guidelines has amply proven the truth of the old adage that reasonable minds can disagree. That is why this Report, therefore, contains all statements and comments received in connection with the three sets of guidelines, so that such information and opinions may be included in one's own assessment of the value of the guidelines.

As CONFU moves into its next phase, there may not be agreement among all participants as to the value and viability of the guidelines so far produced, but there does appear to be wide-spread support among participants for continuing a dialogue on fair use issues with an ultimate goal of developing broad-based agreement, at the very least, on principles and practices, if not guidelines, in the copyright owner and user communities. Should this happen, this accomplishment alone will have proven the worth of CONFU as a valuable and important contribution to the appreciation of fair use in the rapidly expanding digital environment in which we live.

Appendix 6

FINAL CONFU REPORT ON FAIR USE FOR DIGITAL AGE*

The Conference on Fair Use (CONFU), created in 1994, on 24 November issued its final report on fair use issues in the digital environment. While a few of the CONFU working groups succeeded in drafting fair use guidelines for their areas of interest, there was no general consensus on any of the proposals when the CONFU sessions terminated last May.

Four Years of Meetings

CONFU initially convened in 1994 as an off-shoot of Clinton Administration's Information Infrastructure Task Force (IITF).

In July of that year, the IITF's Working Group on Intellectual Property issued a preliminary 'green paper' recommending a variety of changes to the copyright law to accommodate the new electronic information technologies (48 PTCJ 233, 7/14/94). A final 'white paper' on the subject was issued in September of 1995 (50 PTCJ 552, 567, 9/14/95).

Meanwhile, some members of the Working Group in September of 1994 narrowed their attention to the development of fair use guidelines for library and educational uses of copyrighted works in the digital environment (48 PTCJ 511, 523, 9/15/94). The group held public hearings (48 PTCJ 567, 9/29/94) and began meeting (48 PTCJ 685, 10/20/94) to discuss fair use issues and formulate guidelines.

Ultimately, six CONFU working groups emerged to draft a statement on the use of software in libraries, as well as fair use guidelines in five specific areas: (1) digital images; (2) distance learning; (3) educational multimedia; (4) electronic reserve systems; and (5) interlibrary loan and document delivery.

*   *Patent, Trademark & Copyright Journal*, Volume 57 Number 1403 Thursday, 3 December 1998 ISSN 1522-4325.

Two other topics of interest to CONFU participants–the concerns of the visually impaired and the need for digital preservation of material–were eventually addressed by legislation. One bill (H.R. 3794, Pub. L. No. 104-197) added a new Section 121 to the Copyright Act allowing reproduction of copyrighted works in specialized formats for the blind, and another (S. 505, Pub. L. No. 105-298) expanded the library reproduction rights at Section 108 to include digital reproductions.

The CONFU plenary and working group meetings were on-going for the next few years. An interim report containing proposed guidelines on digital images, distance learning and educational multimedia, as well as a statement on library uses of computer programs was published in December 1996 (53 PTCJ 115, 125, 12/19/96).

The three proposed guidelines were discussed at CONFU's plenary meeting in May 1997. However, in a September 1997 report to the Commissioner of Patents and Trademarks, CONFU concluded that the guidelines and other fair use issues needed more work, and that CONFU would reconvene in May 1998 to assess the status of its activities.

Consensus Lacking in Working Groups

The working groups' reports at CONFU's final plenary session on 18 May 1998, revealed continued discord among the interested parties on the issues they were charged with addressing. Working groups in several of the targeted areas succeeded in drafting proposed guidelines, while other working groups concluded that fair use guidelines for their areas were premature or unnecessary.

The CONFU's 24 November final report outlines the status of the working groups' proposed guidelines as follows:

- *Digital Images:* This working group hoped to clarify the application of the fair use doctrine to the creation and use of digital image archives for educational purposes, including the digitizing of pre-existing analog image collections and newly acquired analog visual images.

  Following extensive national discussion of the working group's 1996 draft guidelines on digital images, it was apparent at the 19 May 1997 CONFU meeting that a significant number of organizations opposed endorsement of the guidelines. Consequently, it was agreed that a one-year period for voluntary adoption be instituted, during which the working group would address any criticisms of the guidelines it received, with the goal of refining the guidelines for endorsement at CONFU's May 1998 meeting. However, the working group ceased to meet after an initial meeting in the fall of 1997, and no further action was taken on the guidelines.

- *Distance Learning:* The aim of this working group was to provide guidance on the application of fair use principles to 'real-time' performance and display of copyrighted works in distance learning environments.

  Like the Digital Images working group, the Distance Learning working group in May 1997 failed to win CONFU endorsement of its 1996 proposed guidelines.

The working group was accordingly reconstituted and expanded in part to address concerns about fair use for 'asynchronic' (vs. real-time) computer network delivery of distance learning courses. However, strong opposition among the participating organizations led to the demise of the working group. This development was reported at CONFU's final 8 May 1998 session, as was a since-enacted bill (H.R. 2281, Pub. L. No. 105-304) that directs the Copyright Office to provide Congress with a report on ways to promote distance learning through digital technologies.

- *Educational Multimedia:* Guidelines for the fair use of copyrighted works in educational multimedia projects which were drafted by the Consortium of College and University Media Centers (52 PTCJ 723, 730, 10/31/96) won the initial support of CONFU. However, the same lack of consensus that impeded CONFU's adoption of the proposed Digital Images and Distance Learning guidelines led CONFU participants in May 1997 to implement a two to three-year monitoring period for voluntary adoption of its proposed guidelines in practical classroom and institutional settings. A status report was made at CONFU's final session on 18 May 1998.

- *Electronic Reserve Systems:* The application of fair use to the creation of electronic reserve systems that allow storage, access, display and downloading of electronic versions of materials that support the instructional requirements of a specific course within a non-profit educational institution was the focus of this working group. The working group began circulating proposed guidelines in March 1996, but by November of that year it was decided that the guidelines would not be disseminated as the formal work product of CONFU.

- *Interlibrary Loan and Document Delivery:* A CONFU working group to consider fair use issues regarding the digital delivery of print originals under interlibrary loan arrangements met several times in 1996, but concluded that it was premature to draft guidelines in this area.

- *Use of Computer Software in Libraries:* After early plenary sessions to address use of computer programs in libraries, the CONFU participants ultimately decided that there was no need to develop fair use guidelines that were separate from the 1996 Statement on Use of Copyrighted Computer Programs in Libraries which was adopted by CONFU participants.

Assessment

The CONFU report acknowledged the unachieved goals of the project, but called the discussions on the unresolved issues 'extremely valuable if not immediately fruitful'. Most CONFU participants, according to the report, concluded that CONFU had been an 'instructive, if not always productive, endeavor.'

The report praised the 'extraordinary public-private effort' made by CONFU participants. 'Many organizations, especially non profit organizations, devoted substantial human and financial resources and made substantial sacrifices to participate in the CONFU effort,' the report noted. 'As CONFU concluded,' the report summed up, 'it was clear that fair use was alive and well in the digital age, and that attempts to draft widely supported guidelines will be complicated by the often competing interests of the copyright owner and user communities.'

Appendix 7

H.R. 2180 — The 'On-Line Copyright Liability Limitation Act'

H.R. 2180, the 'On-Line Copyright Liability Limitation Act,' would add a new section 512 to the Copyright Act, creating a new exemption from infringement liability for certain acts of transmitting or providing access to material on-line that are typically engaged in by providers of on-line services and internet access.

As the Copyright Office has stated, existing doctrines of copyright law have so far been applied by the courts to such acts in a generally appropriate way. If a statutory structure is established to provide greater certainty for service providers, we view H.R. 2180 as a useful starting point for a fresh beginning in achieving a resolution to this important and controversial issue. This bill builds on the concepts that were developed in last year's negotiations chaired by Congressman Goodlatte. However, the bill is simpler in its approach in various respects. Notably, it provides a single exemption that is available to any person engaging in certain acts, which were dealt with in several separate exemptions in prior proposals. In determining eligibility for the exemption, the bill avoids terms that are specific to particular business models or technologies, and focuses instead on general concepts of a person's level of control, participation, and knowledge of the infringement. It also omits detailed notification procedures and industry-specific codes of conduct, leaving such matters to resolution by the affected parties. This approach offers the benefit of flexibility, allowing adaptation to the inevitable rapid changes in technology and business practices.

Background

In addressing the responsibility of those who participate in bringing infringing works to the public, the courts have over the years developed doctrines of contributory infringement and vicarious liability to supplement the potential direct infringement that may occur through acts of distribution and public performance or display. Under current law, a person is liable for direct infringement who engages in an act within section 106 without authorization, regardless of his knowledge or intent. 17 U.S.C. § 501. A person is vicariously liable for the infringement of another if he has the right and ability to control the infringement, and receives a direct financial benefit, with or without knowledge of infringement. *RCA/Ariola Int'l v. Thomas & Grayston Co.*, 845 F.2d 773, 781 (8th Cir. 1988). A person is liable for contributory infringement who induces, causes or materially contributes to another's infringement, knowing or having reason to know of the infringement. *Sony Corp. v. Universal City Studios, Inc.*, 464 U.S. 417, 435 (1984).

A number of courts have applied these doctrines to on-line activities in recent years. The Copyright Office has prepared a summary of the case law, which is attached to our testimony. While the legal analysis has not always been consistent, the outcomes have been appropriate, imposing liability only on parties who clearly should have been held responsible.

The most extensive judicial analysis of the issues to date can be found in *Religious Technology Center v. Netcom On-Line Communications Service, Inc.*, 907 F. Supp. 1361 (N.D. Cal. 1995). The *Netcom* case is in many respects quite favourable to the interests of on-line service providers. The court found that none of the acts committed by the defendant on-line service provider were direct infringements, and that the provider was not vicariously liable for the infringing acts of its subscriber. Although the court did not dispose of the plaintiff's claim of contributory infringement on summary judgment, it declined to grant a preliminary injunction in part because it viewed the plaintiff as unlikely to succeed on the merits of the claim, because of a lack of evidence that the provider should have known of the infringement or substantially contributed to it.

Other courts have imposed liability on the party placing the work on-line, or on an electronic bulletin board (BBS) operator. In those cases that have held BBS operators liable, the facts have generally supported the conclusion that the defendant knew that the infringement was taking place and either actively encouraged the infringing activity or failed to take steps to prevent it. No case has yet held a service provider liable.

Nonetheless, providers of on-line and internet access services remain concerned about the lack of certainty in how courts will develop the application of these doctrines, and their exposure to lawsuits in the interim. H.R. 2180 seeks to provide greater certainty while safeguarding the ability of copyright owners to protect their exclusive rights in an on-line environment.

Discussion

The issue of service provider liability is of great concern to all of the interests involved, and has received tremendous attention both in the United States and at an international level. It is critical to ensure that any new exemption not undermine the ability of copyright owners to enforce their rights and have meaningful recourse to prevent on-line infringement. At the same time, of course, liability should not be imposed inappropriately. The goal is a system where copyright owners and service providers work together to minimize infringement and expand the Internet as a medium for exploiting copyrighted works.

In the past, the Copyright Office has cautioned that any legislation shielding service providers from liability (1) should be calibrated to particular degrees of involvement and responsibility; (2) should not contain mandatory extra-judicial procedural requirements for copyright owners to be able to enforce their rights; and (3) should not create incentives to avoid knowledge of infringement. While we recognize that the particular calibration of the elements in the bill will be subject to negotiation, we believe that the approach of H.R. 2180 essentially meets these criteria.

H.R. 2180 would amend the Copyright Act to create a new section 512. This section exempts any person who transmits or otherwise provides access to material on-line from liability for direct infringement, as well as vicarious liability for the infringing acts of another, if six criteria are met. Anyone who qualifies under these criteria would also be exempt from monetary damages for contributory infringement. The exemption applies only to liability that is based solely on transmitting or otherwise providing access to material on-line; other acts, such as retention and further use of copies of material, are not covered. The exemption would encompass within its scope the specific circumstances covered by separate exemptions in prior proposals: 'mere conduit' transmissions, material residing on a server, and electronic communications.

The six criteria relate to levels of active involvement and knowledge. They are drawn from discussions during last year's negotiations, and from existing case law, with various modifications to take into account issues raised in those discussions.

The first three criteria — that the person seeking the exemption (A) does not initially place the material on-line; (B) does not generate, select, or alter the content of the material; and (C) does not determine the recipients of the material — establish a passive, intermediary role. The remaining criteria relate to the degree of the person's participation, benefit and knowledge. All are phrased in simple language as basic concepts, leaving room for further discussion of their meaning as well as flexibility for application in a wide array of changing circumstances.

We note that the result of the exemption would be to codify some aspects of existing doctrines of contributory infringement and vicarious liability, but to narrow them in certain respects. Some activities that could result in liability under the existing doctrines would qualify for the exemption. Conversely, however, some activities that would not qualify for the exemption, may not be infringing under current liability doctrines.

It is important to understand that failure to qualify for the new exemption would not necessarily lead to liability. The doctrines of existing law would apply, and determine whether liability was appropriate.

Other provisions are helpful in removing possible disincentives to a provider's taking prompt action to limit the effects of an infringement. These include a 'good Samaritan' defence ensuring that a provider cannot be liable for taking down material in response to a notice alleging infringement. Another subsection provides that neither a provider's action in taking down allegedly infringing material, nor its failure to act, will be held against it in considering a defense to a claim of infringement. This eliminates, among other things, a potential Hobson's choice between increasing potential exposure to liability by allowing continued access to infringing material after receiving notice, and prejudicing a defence such as fair use by removing material.

Finally, some deterrence is provided against those who falsely claim infringement. Subsection (d) would make anyone who materially misrepresents that material on-line is infringing liable for damages incurred by those relying on the misrepresentation by taking down the material.

H.R. 2180 contains no formalized notice and takedown procedure or prescription of responsible operating practices for the on-line services industry, as was proposed last year. Such provisions could be negotiated privately by the affected parties. This approach has the benefit of avoiding the codification of industry-specific rules in inflexible statutory language.

Conclusion

In summary, if legislation is enacted to deal with this issue, the Copyright Office favours a simplified approach such as that taken in H.R. 2180. We view the bill as a constructive starting point for further discussion. While we recognize that many of the specifics of the legislation are subject to negotiation, we believe the bill identifies the key concepts of levels of participation and knowledge in a useful way. We believe that progress has been made in clarifying the issues, and would be pleased to work with Congress and the affected parties to assist in finding an acceptable solution.

Appendix 8

CASE LAW ON ONLINE TRANSMISSIONS OF COPYRIGHTED WORKS
United States Copyright Office June 1997

The following is a brief summary of reported US cases as of June 1997 challenging unauthorized online transmissions of copyrighted works. All courts addressing a copyright claim either found infringement or sufficient evidence to support such a finding. The nature of the analysis, however, differed from case to case. Most courts relied on the reproduction right; some found that other rights, such as the rights of distribution and public display, had been implicated. Those courts that discussed the issue of RAM copies took it as settled that a reproduction of a work in a computer's RAM is sufficiently fixed to constitute a copy under the copyright law.

In a number of these cases, the question of which rights were infringed is less than clear. The courts often fail to differentiate among the rights, or to conduct a thorough analysis of each separately. Thus, they may simply find 'copying' in its plain English meaning, or use words like 'transmitted,' 'posted,' 'distributed,' 'uploaded,' or 'downloaded' without clearly indicating what actions were sufficient to constitute a *prima facie* infringement, and of which right.

Despite the consistent determinations on infringement, the courts have not subjected everyone in the chain of distribution to liability. In general, liability was imposed on individuals who placed unauthorized copies of works on the Internet or on operators of bulletin board services (BBSs) dedicated to encouraging piracy, based either on direct infringement or on contributory infringement. In a few cases, a court's imprecise language suggested the possibility of direct infringement by a BBS operator which had not itself engaged in acts within the scope of the copyright owner's rights. In each of these cases, however, the facts appeared sufficient to support a finding of contributory infringement based on knowledge and participation.

Plaintiffs generally did not name Internet access providers or online service providers (together, 'IAP's) as defendants. The sole case indicating potential liability for an IAP was *Religious Technology Center v. Netcom*, where the court held that an IAP would be liable for contributory infringement if it had allowed distribution of infringing material with knowledge of the infringement.

I. Cases holding reproduction right and other rights implicated

Sega Enters. Ltd. v. MAPHIA, 948 F. Supp. 923 (N.D. Cal. 1996)

Action against operator of BBS, whose subscribers uploaded or downloaded unauthorized copies of plaintiff's works.

Citing *MAI v. Peak*, 991 F. 2d 511 (9th Cir. 1993), court found copies were made when works were uploaded to or downloaded from the BBS. Citing Netcom, court held defendant was not directly liable for the reproduction since the subscribers, not defendant, copied the works by uploading or downloading them. Court held defendant liable for contributory infringement, where defendant knew of the infringing activity and contributed to this activity by, among other things, providing the BBS as a central depository site for the unauthorized copies of the game, furnishing facilities for the copying of the game by providing, monitoring, and operating the BBS software, hardware, and phone lines necessary for the users to upload and download games, and allowing the subsequent distribution of the copies by subscriber downloads.

This decision explicitly clarifies and supersedes an earlier decision on a motion for a preliminary injunction, which suggested the possibility of the BBS operator being liable for direct infringement, not just contributory infringement. *Sega Enterprises Ltd. v. MAPHIA*, 857 F. Supp. 679 N.D. Cal. 1994).

Religious Technology Ctr. v. Netcom On-Line Communication Servs., Inc., 907 F. Supp. 1361 (N.D. Cal. 1995)

Action against operator of BBS and Internet access provider (IAP) for copyright infringement where BBS subscriber posted plaintiff's works on BBS.

Court stated that when subscriber posts work on Usenet, it is transmitted and automatically copied from BBS operator's computer onto IAP's computer and other computers on Usenet. Court stated that 'there is no question after *MAI* that "copies" were created,' as the subscriber's act of posting messages caused reproduction of plaintiff's works on both defendants' storage devices.

As to defendants' liability, court held that their storage and re-transmission of infringing copies did not constitute direct infringement of the rights of reproduction, distribution, or public display due to the absence of the necessary 'volitional or causal elements,' where the defendants did not initiate such acts themselves, or take any affirmative action that resulted in such acts. In contrast to the holding of *Playboy v. Frena* (described below) on this point, court stated that only the subscriber should be directly liable for the infringement of these rights, because he uploaded copies onto the computer and caused their distribution.

Defendants were, however, potentially liable for contributory infringement of the distribution right. Court held that defendants would be liable for contributory infringement, if plaintiffs could prove that defendants, with knowledge of the infringing postings, continued to allow the distribution of the works on their systems. Preliminary injunction denied, however, because there was little evidence that defendants knew or should have known of the infringement, and their participation was not substantial. Court found no vicarious liability because though there was an issue of fact as to defendants' right and ability to control, there was no direct financial benefit to them.

Central Point Software, Inc. v. Nugent, 903 F. Supp. 1057 (E.D. Tex. 1995)

Action against operator of BBS, who allowed and encouraged subscribers to upload and download unauthorized copies of plaintiffs' works.

Citing Vault Corp. v. Quaid Software Ltd., 847 F.2d 255 (5th Cir. 1989), court stated that copying of plaintiff's software could be established if it was reproduced in a computer's memory without permission. Court found defendant liable, apparently for direct infringement, based on evidence that plaintiff's works were copied to defendant's hard drive when posted on the BBS, and available for downloading, stating, 'It is uncontroverted that Defendant reproduced these later versions of the copyrighted works.' Opinion unclear as to whether BBS operator did anything other than allow and encourage subscribers to upload and download the software. In its discussion of statutory damages, the court indicated that the distribution right was an additional basis for its finding of infringement, stating that '[d]efendant chose to violate the copyright laws by reproducing and providing distribution of the plaintiffs' copyrighted software.'

Playboy Enters. Inc. v. Frena, 839 F. Supp. 1552 (M.D. Fla. 1993).

Action against operator of a BBS whose subscribers uploaded and downloaded unauthorized copies of plaintiff's works.

Without any further analysis, court found direct infringement of (1) the right of distribution, stating: 'There is no dispute that Defendant Frena supplied a product containing unauthorized copies of a copyrighted work. It does not matter that Defendant Frena claims he did not make the copies himself.' and (2) the right of public display because defendant displayed copyrighted works on the BBS to subscribers.

Brode v. Tax Management, Inc., 1990 U.S. Dist. LEXIS 998 (N.D. Ill. 1990)

Action by author of copyrighted work against its publishers and Mead Data, provider of LEXIS computer assisted research service, alleging infringement based on continued availability of the work on LEXIS after the license to publish it electronically had expired.

Defendant argued that the work's 'mere availability on LEXIS failed to abridge plaintiffs copyright,' and that there was no act of reproduction or distribution since plaintiff had presented no evidence that the work was ever 'called up' or 'printed out.' Court did not address this argument as to the distribution right, but as to the reproduction right, it held that sufficient evidence had been adduced that the database containing plaintiff's work was 'called up' to survive a motion of summary judgment.

II. Cases holding the reproduction right alone implicated

Sega Enterprises v. Sabella, 1996 U.S. Dist. LEXIS 20470 (N.D. Cal. 1996)

Action against operator of BBS, whose subscribers uploaded and downloaded unauthorized copies of plaintiff's works.

Citing MAI, court found copying of works established by the fact that they were uploaded or downloaded from the BBS. Following Netcom, court held that defendant was not directly liable for infringement since she did not herself upload or download the works. The court found that Sabella engaged in acts including providing the BBS as a central depository site for the copies of the works, allowing their subsequent distribution by user downloads, and providing, monitoring, and operating the BBS software, hardware, and phone lines necessary for the users to upload and download the works. Court therefore held defendant liable for contributory infringement where she knew of her subscribers' infringing activity and contributed to this activity by providing facilities, direction, and encouragement for the unauthorized copying. While the court explained that through the operation of a BBS 'video game programs can be distributed,' it focused on the acts of reproduction, rather than distribution.

Religious Technology Ctr. v. Lerma, 1996 U.S. Dist. LEXIS 15454 (E.D. Va. 1996)

Action against defendant who copied plaintiff's works onto his computer and posted them onto the Internet. Initially action included claims against defendant's IAP, but these claims were voluntarily dismissed by plaintiffs.

Defendant admitted copying works by posting segments on the Internet. Rejecting fair use defence, court held that defendant infringed plaintiff's copyrights by 'posting' the material.

Scientist, Inc. v. Lindsey, 1996 U.S. Dist. LEXIS 7099 (E.D. Pa. 1996), *summ. j. denied*, 1996 U.S. Dist. LEXIS 11372 (E.D. Pa. 1996)

Action against publisher of Internet newsletter which contained unauthorized copies of plaintiff's works. IAP not named as a defendant.

Copying of plaintiff's works in defendant's online newsletter not denied; opinion turned on issue of originality of material copied. Court denied summary judgment, finding material issues of fact as to the issue of originality.

III. Other online transmission cases

The following cases do not directly address claims of copyright infringement, but contain relevant assumptions, analogies or dicta.

United States v. Stowe, 1996 U.S. Dist. LEXIS 11911 (N.D. Ill. 1996)

Motion by operator of BBS for the return of computer hardware and software seized by the government in criminal copyright infringement case.

The warrant that authorized the seizure was based on allegations of copyright infringement by a BBS operator, where the BBS had been designed so that users could download copyrighted software only if they had previously uploaded other copyrighted software. Citing the government's continuing criminal investigation, court denied defendant's motion.

ProCD Inc. v. Zeidenberg, 86 F. 3d 1447 (7th Cir. 1996)

Action by producer of computer program and database against purchaser who made the database available on the Internet, and sold access to users. Defendant's actions violated the terms of the shrinkwrap license, which prohibited use of the product for commercial purposes.

Court held that shrinkwrap licenses are binding contracts, and that enforcement under state law did not create rights equivalent to exclusive rights within the scope of copyright, and so was not preempted by the Copyright Act. In dicta, the court stated that copyright law would prohibit an unauthorized individual from 'transmit[ting]' or copying the work.

Playboy Enters v. Chuckleberry Publ., Inc., 939 F. Supp. 1032 (S.D.N.Y 1996), *recons. denied*, 1996 U.S. Dist. LEXIS 9865 (S.D.N.Y. 1996)

Trademark infringement case bearing on the meaning of 'distribution' on the Internet. Defendant had established in Italy an Internet site containing pictorial images under the 'Playmen' name, which were available for downloading by subscribers. IAP not named as a defendant.

Motion for contempt; issue was whether defendant's activities on the Internet violated a 1981 injunction barring it from distributing or selling in the United States a magazine bearing the name 'Playmen.' Relying on the copyright cases *Playboy v. Frena and Religious Technology Center v. Netcom* (discussed above) in its analysis, court concluded that a prohibited distribution occurred when defendants set up an Internet site containing images under the 'Playmen' name that could be downloaded by subscribers. Defendant argued that it had not distributed its magazine in the United States, but merely 'posted' images on a computer in Italy, which was outside of the scope of the injunction. Court held that defendant had distributed its product in the United States, when it solicited United States subscribers to its Internet site and provided them with passwords. In its later opinion denying a motion for reconsideration, the court clarified that its finding that distribution occurred in the United States was based not only on the exchange between defendants and users concerning passwords, but on the fact that by inviting users to download images, defendant 'caused[ed] and contribut[ed] to their distribution within the United States.'

Comedy III Prods. v. Class Publ., Inc. 1996 U.S. Dist. LEXIS 5710 (S.D.N.Y. 1996)

Action under the Lanham Act and related state law causes of action. IAP not named as a defendant.

Defendants had continued to advertise merchandise bearing the names, likenesses, and trademarks of the Three Stooges on its web site after its license to do so had expired. Court held that defendants violated plaintiff's rights to 'the titles, symbols, trademarks, copyrights, designs, advertising, artwork, likenesses and logo of the Three Stooges,' and that their conduct violated Section 43(a) of the Lanham Act.

(1) These concerns relate not only to fair use, but to all permitted uses under the Copyright Act, including those made possible by the idea-expression dichotomy and the first sale doctrine. For purposes of our discussion here, we will refer to all of these user privileges collectively as fair use interests.

(2) The extent to which restrictions can be imposed by contract on uses that would otherwise be permissible under copyright law has also become a controversial issue. See, e.g., *ProCD, Inc. v. Zeidenberg*, 86 F.3d 1447 (7th Cir. 1996) (holding that the Copyright Act does not generally preempt contract rights).

(3) Section 1202 implements the relevant obligation under both WIPO treaties. Since performers whose performances are fixed in sound recordings may qualify as authors under U.S. copyright law, the reference in the definition of 'copyright management information' to identifying information about the 'author of a work' covers such performers as well as other categories of authors.

Appendix 9

SEC. 202. LIMITATIONS ON LIABILITY FOR COPYRIGHT INFRINGEMENT

(a) IN GENERAL - Chapter 5 of the title 17, United States Code, is amended by adding after section 511 the following new section:

Sec. 512. Limitations on liability relating to material online

(a) TRANSITORY DIGITAL NETWORK COMMUNICATIONS - A service provider shall not be liable for monetary relief, or, except as provided in subsection (j), for injunctive or other equitable relief, for infringement of copyright by reason of the provider's transmitting, routing, or providing connections for, material through a system or network controlled or operated by or for the service provider, or by reason of the intermediate and transient storage of that material in the course of such transmitting, routing, or providing connections, if—

(1) the transmission of the material was initiated by or at the direction of a person other than the service provider;

(2) the transmission, routing, provision of connections, or storage is carried out through an automatic technical process without selection of the material by the service provider;

(3) the service provider does not select the recipients of the material except as an automatic response to the request of another person;

(4) no copy of the material made by the service provider in the course of such intermediate or transient storage is maintained on the system or network in a manner ordinarily accessible to anyone other than anticipated recipients, and no such copy is maintained on the system or network in a manner ordinarily accessible to such anticipated recipients for a longer period than is reasonably necessary for the transmission, routing, or provision of connections; and

(5) the material is transmitted through the system or network without modification of its content.

(b) SYSTEM CACHING-

(1) LIMITATION ON LIABILITY – A service provider shall not be liable for monetary relief, or, except as provided in subsection (j), for injunctive or other equitable relief, for infringement of copyright by reason of the intermediate and temporary storage of material on a system or network controlled or operated by or for the service provider in a case in which–

(A) the material is made available online by a person other than the service provider;

(B) the material is transmitted from the person described in subparagraph (A) through the system or network to a person other than the person described in subparagraph (A) at the direction of that other person; and

(C) the storage is carried out through an automatic technical process for the purpose of making the material available to users of the system or network who, after the material is transmitted as described in subparagraph (B), request access to the material from the person described in subparagraph (A),

if the conditions set forth in paragraph (2) are met.

(2) CONDITIONS – The conditions referred to in paragraph (1) are that–

(A) the material described in paragraph (1) is transmitted to the subsequent users described in paragraph (1)(C) without modification to its content from the manner in which the material was transmitted from the person described in paragraph (1)(A);

(B) the service provider described in paragraph (1) complies with rules concerning the refreshing, reloading, or other updating of the material when specified by the person making the material available online in accordance with a generally accepted industry standard data communications protocol for the system or network through which that person makes the material available, except that this subparagraph applies only if those rules are not used by the person described in paragraph (1)(A) to prevent or unreasonably impair the intermediate storage to which this subsection applies;

(C) the service provider does not interfere with the ability of technology associated with the material to return to the person described in paragraph (1)(A) the information that would have been available to that person if the material had been obtained by the subsequent users described in paragraph (1)(C) directly from that person, except that this subparagraph applies only if that technology–

(i) does not significantly interfere with the performance of the provider's system or network or with the intermediate storage of the material;

(ii) is consistent with generally accepted industry standard communications protocols; and

(iii) does not extract information from the provider's system or network other than the information that would have been available to the person described in paragraph (1)(A) if the subsequent users had gained access to the material directly from that person;

(D) if the person described in paragraph (1)(A) had in effect a condition that a person must meet prior to having access to the material, such as a condition based on payment of a fee or provision of a password or other information, the service provider permits access to the stored material in significant part only to users of its system or network that have met those conditions and only in accordance with those conditions; and

(E) if the person described in paragraph (1)(A) makes that material available online without the authorization of the copyright owner of the material, the service provider responds expeditiously to remove, or disable access to, the material that is claimed to be infringing upon notification of claimed infringement as described in subsection (c)(3), except that this subparagraph applies only if–

(i) the material has previously been removed from the originating site or access to it has been disabled, or a court has ordered that the material be removed from the originating site or that access to the material on the originating site be disabled; and

(ii) the party giving the notification includes in the notification a statement confirming that the material has been removed from the originating site or access to it has been disabled or that a court has ordered that the material be removed from the originating site or that access to the material on the originating site be disabled.

(c) INFORMATION RESIDING ON SYSTEMS OR NETWORKS AT DIRECTION OF USERS-

(1) IN GENERAL – A service provider shall not be liable for monetary relief, or, except as provided in subsection (j), for injunctive or other equitable relief, for infringement of copyright by reason of the storage at the direction of a user of material that resides on a system or network controlled or operated by or for the service provider, if the service provider–

(A)(i) does not have actual knowledge that the material or an activity using the material on the system or network is infringing;

(ii) in the absence of such actual knowledge, is not aware of facts or circumstances from which infringing activity is apparent; or

(iii) upon obtaining such knowledge or awareness, acts expeditiously to remove, or disable access to, the material;

(B) does not receive a financial benefit directly attributable to the infringing activity, in a case in which the service provider has the right and ability to control such activity; and

(C) upon notification of claimed infringement as described in paragraph (3), responds expeditiously to remove, or disable access to, the material that is claimed to be infringing or to be the subject of infringing activity.

(2) DESIGNATED AGENT – The limitations on liability established in this subsection apply to a service provider only if the service provider has designated an agent to receive notifications of claimed infringement described in paragraph (3), by making available through its service, including on its website in a location accessible to the public, and by providing to the Copyright Office, substantially the following information:

(A) the name, address, phone number, and electronic mail address of the agent.

(B) other contact information which the Register of Copyrights may deem appropriate.

The Register of Copyrights shall maintain a current directory of agents available to the public for inspection, including through the Internet, in both electronic and hard copy formats, and may require payment of a fee by service providers to cover the costs of maintaining the directory.

(3) ELEMENTS OF NOTIFICATION –

(A) To be effective under this subsection, a notification of claimed infringement must be a written communication provided to the designated agent of a service provider that include substantially the following:

(i) A physical or electronic signature of a person authorized to act on behalf of the owner of an exclusive right that is allegedly infringed.

(ii) Identification of the copyrighted work claimed to have been infringed, or, if multiple copyrighted works at a single online site are covered by a single notification, a representative list of such works at that site.

(iii) Identification of the material that is claimed to be infringing or to be the subject of infringing activity and that is to be removed or access to which is to be disabled, and information reasonably sufficient to permit the service provider to locate the material.

(iv) Information reasonably sufficient to permit the service provider to contact the complaining party, such as an address, telephone number, and, if available, and electronic mail address at which the complaining party may be contacted.

(v) A statement that the complaining party has a good faith belief that use of the material in the manner complained of is not authorized by the copyright owner, its agent, or the law.

(vi) A statement that the information in the notification is accurate, and under penalty of perjury, that the complaining party is authorized to act on behalf of the owner of an exclusive right that is allegedly infringed.

(B)(i) Subject to clause (ii), a notification from a copyright owner or from a person authorized to act on behalf of the copyright owner that fails to comply substantially with the provisions of subparagraph (A) shall not be considered under paragraph (1)(A) in determining whether a service provider has actual knowledge or is aware of facts or circumstances from which infringing activity is apparent.

(ii) In a case in which the notification that is provided to the service provider's designated agent fails to comply substantially with all the provisions of subparagraph (A) but substantially complies with clauses (ii), (iii), and (iv) of subparagraph (A), clause (i) of this subparagraph applies only if the service provider promptly attempts to contact the person making the notification or takes other reasonable steps to assist in the receipt of notification that substantially complies with all the provisions of subparagraph (A).

(d) INFORMATION LOCATION TOOLS – A service provider shall not be liable for monetary relief, or, except as provided in subsection (j), for injunctive or other equitable relief, for infringement of copyright by reason of the provider referring or linking users to an online location containing infringing material or infringing activity, by using information location tools, including a directory, index, reference, pointer, or hypertext link, if the service provider–

(1)(A) does not have actual knowledge that the material or activity is infringing;

(B) in the absence of such actual knowledge, is not aware of facts or circumstances from which infringing activity is apparent; or

(C) upon obtaining such knowledge or awareness, acts expeditiously to remove, or disable access to, the material;

(2) does not receive a financial benefit directly attributable to the infringing activity, in a case in which the service provider has the right and ability to control such activity; and

(3) upon notification of claimed infringement as described in subsection(c)(3), responds expeditiously to remove, or disable access to, the material that is claimed to be infringing or to be the subject of infringing activity, except that, for purposes of this paragraph, the information

described in subsection (c)(3)(A)(iii) shall be identification of the reference or link, to material or activity claimed to be infringing, that is to be removed or access to which is to be disabled, and information reasonably sufficient to permit the service provider to locate that reference or link.

(e) LIMITATION ON LIABILITY OF NONPROFIT EDUCATIONAL INSTITUTIONS – (1) When a public or other nonprofit institution of higher education is a service provider, and when a faculty member or graduate student who is an employee of such institution is performing a teaching or research function, for the purposes of subsections (a) and (b) such faculty member or graduate student shall be considered to be a person other than the institution, and for the purposes of subsections (c) and (d) such faculty member's or graduate student's knowledge or awareness of his or her infringing activities shall not be attributed to the institution, if–

(A) such faculty member's or graduate student's infringing activities do not involve the provision of online access to instructional materials that are or were required or recommended, within the preceding 3-year period, for a course taught at the institution by such faculty member or graduate student;

(B) the institution has not, within the preceding 3-year period, received more than two notifications described in subsection(c)(3) of claimed infringement by such faculty member or graduate student, and such notifications of claimed infringement were not actionable under subsection (f); and

(C) the institution provides to all users of its system or network informational materials that accurately describe, and promote compliance with, the laws of the United States relating to copyright.

(2) INJUNCTIONS – For the purposes of this subsection, the limitations on injunctive relief contained in subsections (j)(2) and (j)(3), but not those in (j)(1), shall apply.

(f) MISREPRESENTATIONS – Any person who knowingly materially misrepresents under this section–

(1) that material or activity is infringing, or

(2) that material or activity was removed or disabled by mistake or misidentification,

shall be liable for any damages, including costs and attorneys' fees, incurred by the alleged infringer, by any copyright owner or copyright owner's authorized licensee, or by a service provider, who is injured by such misrepresentation, as the result of the service provider relying upon such misrepresentation in removing or disabling access to the material or activity claimed to be infringing, or in replacing the removed material or ceasing to disable access to it.

(g) REPLACEMENT OF REMOVED OR DISABLED MATERIAL AND LIMITATION ON OTHER LIABILITY –

(1) NO LIABILITY FOR TAKING DOWN GENERALLY – Subject to paragraph (2), a service provider shall not be liable to any person for any claim based on the service provider's good faith disabling of access to, or removal of, material or activity claimed to be infringing or based on facts or circumstances from which infringing activity is apparent, regardless of whether the material or activity is ultimately determined to be infringing.

(2) EXCEPTION– Paragraph (1) shall not apply with respect to material residing at the direction of a subscriber of the service provider on a system or network controlled or operated by or for the service provider that is removed, or to which access is disabled by the service provider–

(A) takes reasonable steps promptly to notify the subscriber that it has removed or disabled access to the material;

(B) upon receipt of a counter notification described in paragraph (3), promptly provides the person who provided the notification under subsection (c)(1)(C) with a copy of the counter notification, and informs that person that it will replace the removed material or cease disabling access to it in 10 business days; and

(C) replaces the removed material and ceases disabling access to it not less than 10, nor more than 14, business days following receipt of the counter notice, unless its designated agent first receives notice from the person who submitted the notification under subsection (c)(1)(C) that such person has filed an action seeking a court order to restrain the subscriber from engaging in infringing activity relating to the material on the service provider's system or network.

(3) CONTENTS OF COUNTER NOTIFICATION – To be effective under this subsection, a counter notification must be a written communication provided to the service provider's designated agent that includes substantially the following:

(A) A physical or electronic signature of the subscriber.

(B) Identification of the material that has been removed or to which access has been disabled and the location at which the material appeared before it was removed or access to it was disabled.

(C) A statement under penalty of perjury that the subscriber has a good faith belief that the material was removed or disabled as a result of mistake or misidentification of the material to be removed or disabled.

(D) The subscriber's name, address, and telephone number, and a statement that the subscriber consents to the jurisdiction of Federal District Court for the judicial district in which the address is located, or if the subscriber's address is outside of the United States, for any judicial district in which the service provider may be found, and that the subscriber will accept service of process from the person who provided notification under subsection (c)(1)(C) or an agent of such person.

(4) LIMITATION ON OTHER LIABILITY – A service provider's compliance with paragraph (2) shall not subject the service provider to liability for copyright infringement with respect to the material identified in the notice provided under subsection (c)(1)(C).

(h) SUBPOENA TO IDENTIFY INFRINGER-

(1) REQUEST- A copyright owner or a person authorized to act on the owner's behalf may request the clerk of any Untied States district court to issue a subpoena to a service provider for identification of an alleged infringer in accordance with this subsection.

(2) CONTENTS OF REQUEST – The request may be made by filing with the clerk–

(A) a copy of a notification described in subsection (c)(3)(A);

(B) a proposed subpoena; and

(C) a sworn declaration to the effect that the purpose for which the subpoena is sought is to obtain the identity of an alleged infringer and that such information will only be used for the purpose of protecting rights under this title.

(3) CONTENTS OF SUBPOENA – The subpoena shall authorize and order the service provider receiving the notification and the subpoena to expeditiously disclose to the copyright owner or person authorized by the copyright owner information sufficient to identify the alleged infringer of the material described in the notification to the extent such information is available to the service provider.

(4) BASIS FOR GRANTING SUBPOENA – If the notification filed satisfies the provisions of subsection (c)(3)(A), the proposed subpoena is in proper form, and the accompanying declaration is properly executed, the clerk shall expeditiously issue and sign the proposed subpoena and return it to the requester for delivery to the service provider.

(5) ACTIONS OF SERVICE PROVIDER RECEIVING SUBPOENA – Upon receipt of the issued subpoena, either accompanying or subsequent to the receipt of a notification described in subsection (c)(3)(A), the service provider shall expeditiously disclose to the copyright owner or person authorized by the copyright owner the information required by the subpoena, notwithstanding any other provision of law and regardless of whether the service provider responds to the notification.

(6) RULES APPLICABLE TO SUBPOENA – Unless other wise provided by this section or by applicable rules of the court, he procedure for issuance and delivery of the subpoena, and the remedies for noncompliance with the subpoena, shall be governed to the greatest extent practicable by those provisions of the Federal Rules of Civil Procedure governing the issuance, service, and enforcement of a subpoena duces tecum.

(i) CONDITIONS FOR ELIGIBILITY –

(1) ACCOMMODATION OF TECHNOLOGY – The limitations on liability established by this section shall apply to a service provider only if the service provider–

(A) has adopted and reasonably implemented, and informs subscribers and account holders of the service provider's system or network of, a policy that provides for the termination in appropriate circumstances of subscribers and account holders of the service provider's system or network who are repeat infringers; and

(B) accommodates and does not interfere with standard technical measures.

(2) DEFINITION – As used in this subsection, the term 'standard technical measures' means technical measures that are used by copyright owners to identify or protect copyrighted works and–

(A) have been developed pursuant to a broad consensus of copyright owners and service providers in an open, fair, voluntary, multi-industry standard process;

(B) are available to any person on reasonable and nondiscriminatory terms; and

(C) do not impose substantial costs on service providers or substantial burdens on their systems or networks.

(j) INJUNCTIONS – The following rules shall apply in the case of any application for an injunction under section 502 against a service provider that is not subject to monetary remedies under this section:

(1) SCOPE OF RELIEF – (A) With respect to conduct other than that which qualifies for the limitation on remedies set forth in subsection (a), the court may grant injunctive relief with respect to a service provider only in one or more of the following forms:

(i) An order restraining the service provider from providing access to infringing material or activity residing at a particular online site on the provider's system or network.

(ii) An order restraining the service provider from providing access to a subscriber or account holder of the service provider's system or network who is engaging in infringing activity and is identified in the order, by terminating the accounts of the subscriber or account holder that are specified in the order.

(iii) Such other injunctive relief as the court may consider necessary to prevent or restrain infringement of copyrighted material specified in the order of the court at a particular online location, if such relief is the least burdensome to the service provider among the forms of relief comparably effective for that purpose.

(B) If the service provider qualifies for the limitation on remedies described in subsection (a), the court may only grant injunctive relief in one or both of the following forms:

(i) An order restraining the service provider from providing access to a subscriber or account holder of the service provider's system or network who is using the provider's service to engage in infringing activity and is identified in the order, by terminating the accounts of the subscriber or account holder that are specified in the order.

(ii) An order restraining the service provider from providing access, by taking reasonable steps specified in the order to block access, to a specific, identified, online location outside the United States.

(2) CONSIDERATIONS – The court, in considering the relevant criteria for injunctive relief under applicable law, shall consider–

(A) whether such an injunction, either alone or in combination with other such injunctions issued against the same service provider under this subsection, would significantly burden either the provider or the operation of the provider's system or network;

(B) the magnitude of the harm likely to be suffered by the copyright owner in the digital network environment if steps are not taken to prevent or restrain the infringement;

(C) whether implementation of such an injunction would be technically feasible and effective, and would not interfere with access to noninfringing material at other online locations; and

(D) whether other less burdensome and comparably effective means of preventing or restraining access to the infringing material are available.

(3) NOTICE AND EX PARTE ORDERS – Injunctive relief under this subsection shall be available only after notice to the service provider and an opportunity for the service provider to appear are provided, except for orders ensuring the preservation of evidence or other orders having no material adverse effect on the operation of the service provider's communications network.

(k) DEFINITIONS-

(1) SERVICE PROVIDER – (A) As used in subsection(a), the term 'service provider' means an entity offering the transmission, routing, or providing of connections for digital online communications, between or among points specified by a user, of material of the user's choosing, without modification to the content of the material as sent or received.

(B) As used in this section, other than subsection(a), the term 'service provider' means a provider of online services or network access, or the operator of facilities therefor, and includes an entity described in subparagraph (A).

(2) MONETARY RELIEF – As used in this section, the term 'monetary relief' means damages, costs, attorneys' fees, and any other form of monetary payment.

(1) OTHER DEFENSES NOT AFFECTED – The failure of a service provider's conduct to qualify for limitation of liability under this section shall not bear adversely upon the consideration of a defense by the service provider that the service provider's conduct is not infringing under this title or any other defense.

FORMS

Appendix 10

CONTRATO DE LICENCIA PARA USO DEL BANCO DE IMAGENES XX-FLASH

Entre NN S.A., con dimicilio en _____, Buenos Aires, Argentina (en adelante **"Licenciante"**) representada en este acto por el distribuidor autorizado que se identifica al pie del presente contrato y la empresa identificada al pie del presente contrato, (en adelante **"Usuario Final"**) se ha llegado al siguiente contrato:

1. INTRODUCCION - OBJETO

1.1 El **Licenciante** es titular de los derechos de autor sobre las imágenes fotográficas y de diseño (en adelante **"imágenes"**) contenidas en los diferente volúmenes del banco de imágenes (*"clip-art"*) titulado **"XX-Flash"** registrado ante la Dirección Nacional del Derecho de Autor por expediente No. _____ (en adelante **"Obra"**).

1.2 El **Licenciante** es asimismo licenciatario mundial no exclusivo de **ZZ Systems Inc.**, una compañía de California, Estados Unidos de Norteamérica (en adelante **"ZZ"**) con facultades suficientes para sublicenciar su programa de computación **ZZ Dynamic** Retrieval (en adelante **"ZZ-DR"**), cuyos derechos de propiedad intelectual corresponden originariamente o por licencia a **ZZ**.

1.3 Por este contrato, el **Licenciante** concede al **Usuario Final** una licencia para la utilización de las **Imágenes** contenidas en los volúmenes de la **Obra** que se indican al final de contrato y una sublicencia para la utilización de aplicaciones de **ZZ-DR** integradas al soporte que contiene la **Obra**, todo ello con arreglo a las condiciones que siguen.

2. FACULTADES CEDIDAS

En virtud del presente contrato, el **Licenciante** faculta al **Usuario Final** en forma no exclusiva, incesible, e intransferible, para:

2.1. Utilizar las **Imágenes** total o parcialmente, en su estado original o modificadas, tantas veces como el **Usuario Final** lo desee y en la forma que al mismo convenga, <u>únicamente</u> como parte de materiales producidos por el **Usuario final** para su <u>propio uso con destino a su propia publicidad o promoción</u>, tanto en medios impresos como en televisión abierta o por cable, sistemas en línea, páginas en la Web o cualquier otro medio de soporte y transmisión similar.

2.2   Utilizar los programas objeto de **ZZ-DR** con el fin restringido y exclusivo de seleccionar, recuperar, copiar o transferir a otro archivo las imágenes.

3. ACTOS VEDADOS AL LICENCIATARIO

ZZ y el **Licenciante** se reservan todas las facultades autorales no licenciadas explícitamente. Al sólo efecto ejemplificativo, se aclara que:

3.1   La **Obra** no podrá copiarse con otros fines que los indicados, ni utilizarse con destino distinto del expresamente licenciado.

3.2   El **Usuario Final** no podrá ceder ni transferir a ningún título, en todo o en pate, los derechos adquiridos por el presente sin la aprobación   por   escrito   del **Licenciante**.

3.3   El **Usuario Final** no permitirá la copia o utilización de la **Obra** por terceros en ningún caso.

3.4   El **Usuario Final** no podrá usar la **Obra** por cuenta ni en servicio de terceros, sea a título oneroso o gratuito,   ni   explotarla   mediante alquiler, prestación de servicios de tiempo compartido o procesamiento de datos para terceros, ya que es condición de la licencia de utilización que   la   misma   se   restrinja   al cumplimiento de los fines y funciones propias de la publicidad y promoción del **Usuario final**.

3.5   Está expresamente prohibido al **Usuario   Final** realizar ingeniería regresiva o decompilación de la **Obra**, así como modificar la **Obra**, en cualquiera de sus expresiones, excepto que **ZZ** y el **Licenciante** hayan autorizado por escrito en forma   previa   y   expresa   dichas modificaciones.

4 TERMINO DE LA LICENCIA

La   licencia   concedida   por   este contrato es, en principio, perpetua; solo caducará por las siguientes causales:

4.1   Falta de pago por parte del **Usuario   Final**   de   cualquier concepto adeudado al **Licenciante** en virtud del presente contrato.

4.2   Que el **Usuario Final** no respete las restricciones en el uso y la copia de la **Obra** estipuladas en el presente.

4.3   Quiebra o concurso preventivo del **Usuario Final,** o cualquier otra situación que aparte o controle a los órganos normales de dirección del mismo.

4.4 No cumplimiento por parte del **Usuario Final** de la obligación de mantener en reserva los secretos del **Licenciante**, o efectuar ingeniería regresiva de la **Obra**.

4.5 Renuncia voluntaria del **Usuario Final**.

A la terminación del presente por cualquier causa, el Usuario Final deberá proceder a borrar de la/s memoria/s de/los computador/es designado/s los programas objeto de la Obra y a destruir todo y cualquier soporte material de la misma que se encuentre en su poder. Dentro de los treinta (30) días, deberá enviar al Licenciante constancia documentada de haber cumplido estas obligaciones.

5. PAGO DE LOS DERECHOS DE AUTOR

Como precio de la licencia de derechos de propiedad intelectual que involucra este contrato, el **Usuario Final** pagará en concepto de "derechos de autor" el monto indicado en el *Anexo I* según las condiciones estipuladas en el mismo. La mora en el cumplimiento de los pagos será automática y provocará que se devengue un interés compensatorio de un dos por ciento (2%) mensual, a calcularse desde la fecha de la mora hasta la del efectivo pago.

6. RESPONSABILIDADES Y LIMITES

6.1 El **Licenciante** garantiza que es el titular de los derechos de autor sobre las **Imágenes** y que posee la libre disposición de los derechos de propiedad intelectual que por el presente licencia. El **Licenciante** defenderá y manterndrá indemne al **Usuario Final** respecto de cualquier reclamo de un tercero que pretenda cualquier derecho sobre las **Imágenes** o que intente impedir o limitar la explotación de las mismas sobre cualquier base.

6.2 El **Licenciante** garantiza que al ser utilizada con uso de los recursos apropiados a la plataforma indicada al final del presente contrato, la **Obra** funcionará substancialmente de acuerdo con las especificaciones de la documentación técnica de la misma. Ni el **Licenciante** ni **ZZ** garantizan que la **Obra** funcionará ininterrumpidamente ni que estará totalmente libre de errores ni asumen ninguna otra responsabilidad, ni otorgan ninguna otra garantía expresa o implícita distinta que la indicada en este inciso, respecto de las consecuencias dañosas que eventualmente puedan derivar al **Usuario Final** o a terceros del funcionamiento o del no funcionamiento de la **Obra**.

6.3 Por un plazo de ciento veinte (120) días contados a partir de la fecha del presente contrato, el **Licenciante** reemplazará sin cargo el ejemplar que soporta la **Obra** en caso de que el mismo fuera defectuoso.

6.4 A todo evento y para cualquier caso, se estipula que la responsabilidad conjunta del **Licenciante** y de **ZZ** por cualquier concepto relacionado con este contrato, no podrá nunca superar la cantidad abonada por el **Usuario Final** en concepto de "derechos de autor".

7. SECRETOS DEL AUTOR

El **Usuario Final** manifiesta conocer que las ideas, secuencia, estructura, organización, procedimientos, rutinas, algoritmos, programas e interfaces del usuario, a cuyo conocimiento accede con motivo del presente contrato, forman parte del secreto comercial del **Licenciante** y/o de **ZZ**. El **Usuario Final** afirma saber que el mantenimiento de uno absoluta reserva respecto de todas y cada una de estas informaciones, constituye una condición esencial para la firma del presente contrato, dado que el conocimiento por terceros de los secretos de **ZZ** y/o del **Licenciante**, los privaría de la posibilidad de usufructuar pacifica y exclusivamente de sus informaciones reservadas y derechos de propiedad intelectual.

En razón de lo anterior, el **Usuario Final** se obliga a preservar los secretos del **Licenciante** y de **ZZ** con el cuidado de un buen hombre de negocios y a notificar formalmente y por escrito la existencia del secreto y la obligacion de mantenerlo en estricta confidencialidad a cualquier miembro de su personal que con motivo del cumplimiento de sus funcions tenga acceso permanente o eventual a la información referente a la **Obra**.

El **Usuario Final** se obliga a mantener en los soportes o archivos en los que se copie la **Obra** o cualquier parte de las **Imágenes**, así como en las salidas escritas y o por pantalla donde se reproduzcan total o parcialmente las **Imágenes**, las frases y signos de *copyright* y/o de reserva de propiedad intelectual, confidencialidad y restricción de uso introducidas por **ZZ** y/o el **Licenciante.**

8. DISPOSICIONES GENERALES

8.1   Los títulos de las cláusulas de este contrato no forman parte del convenio, su finalidad es exclusivamente para comodidad de lectura y no limitan ni amplían lo convenido en el texto que encabezan.

8.2   Si alguna de las previsiones de este contrato resultara inválida, tal invalidez no acarreará la del resto de lo convenido, que permanecerá con plena fuerza y efecto.

8.3   Cualquier renuncia de derechos o tolerancia respecto del cumplimiento de los términos de este contrato tendrá efectos obligatorios solamente si ha sido concedida por escrito, se aplicará únicamente a los casos especificados, y no afectara la exigibilidad de los términos y condiciones convenidas en el presente.

8.4   Este contrato expresa todos los términos convenidos entre las partes, y reemplaza toda y cualquier previa provisión, compromiso o propuesta no incluida en él.

8.5   Todas las notificaciones requeridas o permitidas por este contrato, se efectuarán por escrito y se remitirán por carta certificada o telegrama colacionado a los domicilios constituidos.

8.6 Todas las acciones derivadas del presente, con la excepción de las que tiendan al cobro de derechos de autor o de otros conceptos adeudados por el **Usuario Final** al **Licenciante** y de las relacionadas con el reclamo por el **Licenciante** de obligaciones derivadas de la propiedad intelectual y del secreto, caducarán al año de la firma del presente.

9. LEY, JURISDICCION Y DOMICILIO

Este contrato se interpretará y ejecutará de conformidad con las leyes de la República Argentina. Las partes se someten a la jurisdicción de los tribunales de la justicia ordinaria de la Ciudad de Buenos Aires, conviniendo que en cualquier supuesto se aplique en lo pertinente el procedimiento especial establecido por los arts. 80 y siguientes de la ley 11.733.

A los efectos del contrato, las partes constituyen sus domicilios en los lugares indicados al pie del presente.

En prueba de conformidad, las partes firman tres (3) ejemplares del presente y de su *Anexo I*, uno para cada una de ellas y el tercero para constancia del Distribuidor firmante, en Buenos Aires, a __ de _____ de 199__.

Volúmenes de **XX-Flash** licenciados por la presente:	
Plataforma:	N° de esta licencia:

Distribuidor autorizado del Licenciante:	Usuario Final:
_____	_____
Dirección: _____	Dirección: _____
Firmado por: _____	Firmado por: _____
Cargo: _____	Cargo: _____

Appendix 11

SASKIA, LTD.
SITE LICENSE AGREEMENT

Number _____

This Software License Agreement (hereinafter referred to as the 'Agreement') is entered into as of _____ between Saskia, Ltd., Cultural Documentation, an Oregon Corporation, located in Portland, Oregon, USA (hereinafter referred to as 'Saskia') and _____, located in _____ (hereinafter referred to as 'Licensee').

DEFINITIONS AND CLARIFICATIONS:

(a) Software shall refer to any electronically readable information provided by Saskia or such information resulting from actions by the Licensee upon items to which Saskia administers copyright, specifically computer or electronically readable versions ('digital images') of photography, including any modifications or variations thereof.

(b) Saskia administers copyright to Software listed in Appendix B ('Licensed Software'). Dr. Ronald V. Wiendenhoeft, as the photographer, is the owner of the copyright.

(c) Licensee desires to obtain a license to copy, install and use the Software on multiple computers located at the Site specified in Appendix C ('Site').

(d) Licensee agrees that all rights to digital representations of photography by Saskia are owned by, and remain with Saskia unless specifically granted in writing to Licensee.

NOW THEREFORE, the parties hereby agree as follows:

313

1. GRANT OF RIGHTS

(a) **License to Use Software**. Saskia grants Licensee a non-exclusive, non-transferable, license to install and use the software identified in Appendix B ('Licensed Software') on all computer systems now or in Appendix C ('Site'), and to use the associated catalog information provided by Saskia.

(b) **Right to Copy Software**. Licensee may copy the Software to the extent necessary to exercise the foregoing License, and for backup and archival purposes. All copies of the Software shall be subject to all terms, conditions and obligations of this Agreement. All copies of the Software shall be identifiable by Licensee and Saskia at least by means of the Saskia Catalog Number System.

(c) **Restrictions on Use**. The foregoing rights to copy, install, and use the Software shall be subject to the following restrictions:

(1) Licensee shall not copy or allow copies of the Software to be made, except as specifically allowed under this Agreement;
(2) Licensee shall not use the software in, or allow others to use the software in, a network, multiple CPU or multiple-user arrangement, except within the confines of the Site, as defined in Appendix C ('Site');
(3) Licensee shall not resell, lease, sublicense or distribute the Software to any person, firm or entity.

2. PERMITTED AND PROHIBITED USES

(a) **Permitted Uses**. Saskia licenses the Software covered by this agreement for use specifically in teaching and research only. Licensee may use the Software in any capacity for teaching purposes, so long as those uses are not prohibited by this agreement. Specifically,

(1) Saskia grants permission to use the Software on a multi-user network at the location specified;
(2) Saskia grants permission to modify the Software as needed for use by the Licensee.

(b) **Prohibited Uses**. Saskia reserves all rights regarding publication of software for any purpose outside the scope of the license. Specifically,

(1) Saskia prohibits the Licensee from granting access to the Software to other parties not specifically covered by the location specified in Appendix C ('Site');
(2) Saskia prohibits the Licensee from allowing copies of the Software to be made by students or any other persons not bound by confidentiality agreements protecting the Software;
(3) Saskia prohibits use of the Software for use in any publication, scholarly or otherwise; or for any purpose other than teaching or research;
(4) Saskia prohibits Licensee to transfer Software to film or other medium, except for purposes of storage for electronic retrieval as provided in this agreement.

3. OWNERSHIP OF LICENSED SOFTWARE

(a) **Ownership**. Licensee acknowledges that the Software, and all copies and modifications thereof made by the Licensee hereunder, are the exclusive property of Saskia and title to the above shall at all times remain with Saskia or its assignee. Licensee further acknowledges that Licensee has no rights in the Software except those expressly granted by this Agreement.

(b) **Protection**. Licensee will take all reasonable steps to protect the Software from any use, reproduction, publication, disclosure or distribution except as specifically authorized by this Agreement.

(c) **Notices**. Licensee shall not remove, alter, cover or distort any copyright notice, trademark, or other proprietary rights notice placed by Saskia on the Software or in the documentation, and shall ensure that all such notices are reproduced on all copies of the Software made by Licensee. Licensee is permitted to remove 'color bars' displaying the Saskia copyright notice from the Software.

4. CONFIDENTIALITY

Licensee acknowledges that the Software is copyrighted. Though copyrighted, Licensee acknowledges that the Software is unpublished, and therefore subject to all terms and conditions of this License Agreement, above and beyond the protection granted by US and International copyright laws.

5. TERM AND TERMINATION

The License granted under this Agreement shall continue for the duration of the copyright in the software, unless sooner terminated by Saskia in accordance with this agreement. In the event that Licensee breaches any of the terms of this Agreement, and Licensee fails to correct such breaches within thirty days, this Agreement shall terminate.

Upon termination of the license to use the Licensed Software, Licensee shall be obligated to immediately cease using the Licensed Software, to return to Saskia, or destroy, all copies of the Licensed Software, and provide Saskia with written certification of its compliance with the foregoing. Termination of this Agreement shall not relieve Licensee from its obligations arising hereunder before termination, including, but not limited to the responsibility for paying previously accrued fees and the responsibility for not disclosing the Licensed Software.

6. WARRANTY

(a) **Warranty**. Vendor warrants to Licensee that the media containing the Licensed Software delivered to Licensee is free form defects in materials and workmanship under normal use for a period of ninety (90) days from the date of original delivery to Licensee. If a defect in such media appears during this 90 day period, the defective may be returned to Saskia, and Saskia will replace it without charge to Licensee.. This shall constitute Licensee's sole and exclusive remedy for a breach of the warranty set forth in this paragraph.

(b) **DISCLAIMER OF WARRANTY.** EXCEPT AS SPECIFICALLY PROVIDED HEREIN, SASKIA MAKES NO EXPRESS OR IMPLIED WARRANTIES WHATSOEVER, AND EXPRESSLY DISCLAIMS THE IMPLIED WARRANTIES OF MERCHANTABILITY AND FITNESS FOR A PARTICULAR PURPOSE.

7. LIMITATION OF LIABILITY

SASKIA' LIABILITY TO LICENSE SHALL BE LIMITED TO DIRECT DAMAGES, AND SHALL IN NO CASE EXCEED THE AMOUNT OF THE LICENSE FEES PAID BY LICENSEE TO SASKIA HEREUNDER. IN NO EVENT SHALL SASKIA BE LIABLE FOR INCIDENTAL, SPECIAL, OR CONSEQUENTIAL DAMAGES (INCLUDING LOST PROFITS) SUFFERED BY LICENSEE, EVEN IF IT HAS PREVIOUSLY BEEN ADVISED OF THE POSSIBILITY OF SUCH DAMAGES.

8. GENERAL PROVISIONS

(a) **Assignment**. This Agreement may not be assigned by Licensee or by operation of law to any other person, persons, firms, institutions or corporations without the express written approval of Saskia

(b) **Notices**. All notices and demands hereunder shall be in writing and shall be served by personal service or by mail at the address of the receiving party set forth in this Agreement (or at such different address as may be designated by such party by written notice to the other party). All notices or demands by mail shall be by certified or registered mail, return receipt requested, or by nationally recognized private express courier, and shall be deemed complete upon receipt.

(c) **Governing Law**. This Agreement shall be governed by and construed in accordance with the substantive laws of the State of Oregon.

(d) **Survival of Certain Provisions**. The obligation to pay all accrued Licensed Fees, and the confidentiality obligation set forth in the Agreement shall survive the termination of the Agreement by either party for any reason.

(e) **Headings.** The titles and headings of the various sections and paragraphs in this Agreement are intended solely for convenience of reference and are not intended for any other purpose whatsoever, or to explain, modify or place any construction upon or on any of the provisions of this agreement.

(f)   **All Amendments in Writing.** No provisions in either party's purchase orders, or in any other business forms employed by either party will supersede the terms and conditions of this Agreement, and no supplement, modification, or amendment of this Agreement shall be binding, unless executed in writing by a duly authorized representative of each party to this Agreement.

(g)   **Severability.** If any parts of the Agreement should be found to be void, unenforceable or illegal for any reason, it shall in no way affect the validity or enforceability of all remaining provisions of this agreement.

(h)   **Entire Agreement.** The parties have read this Agreement and agree to be bound by its terms, and further agree that it constitutes the complete and entire agreement of the parties and supersedes all previous communications, oral or written, and all other communications between them relating to the license and the subject matter hereof. No representations or statements of any kind made by either party, which are not expressly stated herein, shall be binding on such party.

The Following Appendices are attached and incorporated into this Agreement:

Appendix A: License Fee Structure
Appendix B: Licensed Software
Appendix C: Site
Appendix D: Agreement Covering Scanning by Licensee

IN WITNESS WHEREOF, the parties have caused this Agreement to be executed by their duly authorized representatives as of the date first written above.

Saskia: **Licensee:**

By: _____   By: _____

     _____   _____

For: Saskia, Ltd   For: _____
      2721 NW Cannon Way   _____
      Portland, OR 97229   _____
      (503)520-8855   _____

APPENDIX A:

<u>License Fee Structure</u>
as of December 1, 1993

1.   Software

Software purchased from Saskia

Per-invoice quantities:
1-250 (additional set-up fee applies for delivery)	$4.00/ea.
250-999	$3.50/ea.
1000+	$3.00/ea.

Set Pricing	varies

Scanning Rights for Digitizing by Licensee (as described in Appendix D)

Digitizing rights for slides purchased from Saskia	$2.00/ea

2.   Licensee shall pay license fees due before commencing use of Software, unless prior written arrangements for payment have been made.

3.   Quantity discounts shall be based only on individual purchase orders, and not on cumulative purchase history.

4.   Saskia reserves the right to change these fees by providing written notice to Licensee.

APPENDIX B:

Licensed Software

1.   Software shall consist of an electronically coded format of photography to which Saskia administers copyright.

2.   Software shall be identified by Saskia Catalog Numbers. Licensee agrees that Saskia's numbering system shall remain in use at the site to aid in identification of works. Additional identification may be used as long as a cross-reference to Saskia Catalog Numbers is maintained.

3.   All Software shall be acknowledged in writing by Licensee prior to commencement of use by Licensee.

4.   Licensee shall at all times retain a complete list of Licensed Software, along with documentation demonstrating payment of license fees.

5.   Licensee agrees that Saskia shall have absolute say in identifying works by Saskia Catalog Number.

6.   Licensee agrees that in the case of duplicate Saskia Catalog Numbers, Saskia will provide correct identification for purposes of this agreement.

Complete List of Works Covered by Agreement,
by Saskia Catalog Number
(attach additional pages as needed, marked with License Agreement number):

APPENDIX C:

<u>Site</u>

1.   This agreement specifically permits Software to be used only at the institution and location designated below. Additional locations must license the Software individually.

Designated Site of License:

_____

_____

_____

_____

_____

2.   Communications regarding this agreement should be handled by a designated representative of the Licensee. This representative may change from time to time, provided written notification is delivered to Saskia within thirty days of such change.

Designated Representative for Contact:

_____

_____

_____

_____

_____

APPENDIX D:

Agreement Concerning Scanning by Licensee

This agreement shall be incorporated into the general Agreement when Licensee expresses desire to digitize photography whose copyright is owned by Saskia.

1.   Licensee agrees that permission to digitize photography whose copyright is owned by Dr. Ronald V. Wiendenhoeft, is a right administered exclusively by Saskia.

2.   Licensee agrees that all digitized images (referred to as 'Software' in the Agreement) produced by Licensee shall be identical to those purchased from Saskia for purposes of this License Agreement, and are subject to all restrictions of the Agreement.

3.   Licensee agrees that intent to digitize photography must be presented in writing to Saskia, permission granted, and appropriate fees paid to Saskia, before such digitizing may occur.

4.   Licensee agrees that Saskia has the right to refuse permission to digitize any or all works to which Saskia holds title, for any reason, including, but not limited to, prior agreements with museums.

5.   Licensee agrees that Saskia may grant permission for a limited number of 'test scans,' without requesting payment of appropriate License Fees, but that such Software may not be used for any purpose other than testing or evaluation until appropriate License Fees have been paid, and an appropriate License Agreement with Saskia has been executed.

APPENDIX 12

SAMPLE CD-ROM LICENSING
AGREEMENTS FOR MUSEUMS*

Distributed to the institutional members of: American Association of Museums,
The American Federation of Arts, Association of Art Museum Directors

*We gratefully acknowledge the generous assistance of the Annenberg/CPB Project for
supporting the publication of these booklets.*

Table of Contents

Dedicated to the memory of Jane E. Lytle

* MUSE Educational Media
  1 East 53rd Street, 10th floor
  New York, NY 10022-4201
  212 • 688 • 8280 | fax 212 • 688 • 0409

323

Introduction

The enclosed sample agreements have been prepared by MUSE Educational Media in consultation with attorneys and representative museums. The agreements present contractual language that reflects the views and opinions of museum professionals and legal specialists.

The agreements are not intended to replace the need for a museum to consult with counsel about its multimedia licensing terms and conditions. These sample agreements are based on US law and are intended for the United States.

Multimedia and intellectual property is a complex field undergoing rapid changes. Technology introduces new elements and considerations to copyright and other intellectual property laws, as well as related areas of law. However, the enclosed sample agreements should serve as a helpful base to drafting licensing agreements that can be adapted to meet the specific needs of each museum.

The sample licensing agreements are designed to help museums address distinctly different types of CD-ROM licensing situations. These licensing possibilities are based upon the number of images to be licensed and the museum's degree of participation in developing a CD-ROM.

Two licensing scenarios are discussed through sample agreements and commentary:

1. Long Sample Licensing Agreement – For licensing more than a small number of images, but less than ten to twenty percent of the images in a CD-ROM.
2. Short Sample Licensing Agreement – For licensing a handful of images.

For more complex scenarios in which a museum's collections comprise a major portion or the exclusive subject of a CD-ROM, only some of the important issues are identified by the example of a contract table of contents from a sample agreement. This is because these contracts are lengthy, individualized documents that are negotiated and drafted to meet the unique requirements of particular museums and CD-ROM productions. These scenarios include:

3. Exclusive Museum Collection Profile, Licenser Only – The CD-ROM profiles one museum's collections, but the museum does not participate in producing or developing the CD-ROM.
4. Exclusive Museum Collection Profile, Joint Producer/Developer – The CD-ROM profiles one museum's collections and the museum jointly develops/produces the CD-ROM with the licensee.
5. Major Content Provider – Material from the museum's collections represents a significant portion of the content in the CD-ROM.

Another possible way to produce a CD-ROM is for the museum to hire a producer/developer through a work-for-hire contract.

These agreements are the result of discussions commentary and review by the museums participating in the MUSE Museum Multimedia Study Group. The Study Group, inaugurated in March 1994, is a group of representative museums and leading professional advisors formed to develop access guidelines and licensing standards for the use of museum materials in multimedia applications. The following museums/associations are participating:

American Museum of Natural History	Michael C. Carlos Museum
American Association of Museums	Museum Trustee Association
Brooklyn Museum	The Museum of Modern Art
The Cleveland Museum of Art	National Gallery of Art
Isabella Stewart Gardner Museum	The Pierpont Morgan Library
Erie County Historical Association	Shelburne Museum
The Henry Ford Museum & Greenfield Village	Yale University Art Gallery

The enclosed material was drafted and compiled by MUSE Educational Media, which is solely responsible for any omissions or errors. Legal review and analysis were provided by numerous intellectual property attorneys, law firms and museum counsel. We would like to thank in particular for their helpful comments and suggestions:

Seth H. Dubin, *Satterlee Stephens Burke & Burke*
Brian Kahin, *General Counsel, Interactive Multimedia Association*
Jeffrey D. Neuburger, *Brown Raysman & Millstein*
Gerald R. Singer, *Eckhart, McSwain, Silliman & Sears*
Christine Steiner, *General Counsel, The J. Paul Getty Trust,*
  (prev., Assistant General Counsel, Smithsonian Institution)

Multimedia is a fast-changing medium. It is expected and intended that these agreements will evolve to accommodate the changing needs, practices and experience of museums with CD-ROM technology. It is also anticipated that they will be adapted, in consultation with counsel, to suit the particular needs of each museum. Above all, it is our hope that these agreements will offer a solid, conservative legal framework from which museums can begin to explore CD-ROM's potential to increase public appreciation of their collections.

Geoffrey Samuels
Director, *Museum Multimedia Study Group*
MUSE Educational Media
April, 1995

Long CD-ROM Sample Agreement

This Agreement is made and entered into as of _____, 199__ by and between _____('Museum') located at [address of Museum] and _____('Licensee') located at [address of producer/distributor].

WHERAS, Licensee desires to produce a multimedia Work (the 'Work') that will include digitized images and descriptive text of selected material in the collection of Museum (the 'Images'); and

WHEREAS, Museum desires to encourage the responsible use of the Images; NOW, THEREFORE, in consideration of the mutual covenants and agreements contained herein, the parties agree as follows:

Definitions:

The following terms have the following meanings when used herein:

"First Edition" means the first version of the commercially distributed Work that incorporates the Images specified below, and, subject to the Museum's written agreement not to be unreasonably withheld, any minor revisions restricted to corrections of editorial content of the first version.

"Images" means the photographs, negatives, slides or electronic digitized pictures of the objects specified in Schedule A, appended hereto.

"Documentation" means the artist's or author's name (or object's cultural designation), title and date of object, size, and medium.

"Related Text" means textual commentary about an object, beyond the basic description provided by Documentation.

"Work Element" means that directly relevant portion of the Work that incorporates an Image.

"Work" means the product entitled "_____" in formats compatible with the Platform.

"Territory" means: _____

"Platform" means the following computer and CD-ROM formats: ___

---

1. LICENSE

(a) Museum grants to Licensee a non-exclusive, non-transferable, limited license to use the Images solely in the First Edition of the Work and in accordance with the terms of this Agreement.

(b) Any enhancements or changes to the Work, either editorial or programmatic, constitute a new edition, which will require a new license for the use of the Images.

(c) The Work may only be sold or distributed in the Territory.

(d) The Work will be distributed through the following channel(s) of distribution: _____.

(e)   The Images may be used only as part of the Work and may not be distributed or published in any other form or medium. Satellite, electronic, broadcast, on-line or network access, distribution or transmission of the Images, or the Work, or any part thereof, is expressly prohibited for any purposes.

(f)   Nothing set forth in this Agreement shall restrict the Museum's right to the Image(s), including the right to allow others to use the Images.

(g)   Licensee shall not use the Museum's name in any manner in connection with the Work, except as may be expressly agreed by the Museum in writing.

(h)   Except as expressly set forth herein, the Museum reserves all rights in and to the Images, including without limitation the right to exploit the Images in any work in any future or unknown technology.

Commentary

1. LICENSE

The License should be non-exclusive and limited to one edition of a multimedia Work. The method of distribution, territory and platform (Mac, DOS CDI, etc.) are all potential sources of revenue, and hence negotiating points when the Museum discusses royalties with the Licensee.

The license is only for CD-ROMs that the user inserts into a computer for individual use. On-line access through local or wide-area networks (commercial, non-profit, Internet, or interactive-TV) is prohibited. Such access is beyond the scope of this sample agreement; it requires an entirely different way of calculating royalties, as well as different techniques to protect Museum Images. In addition, all future technologies, anticipated or unknown, should be excluded.

If the Licensee is planning to sell the Work through site, or multiple user, licenses that offer special discount pricing for multiple users at a particular location or organization, such plans should be indicated here in clause (d), as well as in Schedule C (Royalty and Payment Terms). Distribution channels such as trade, direct mail, membership, and computer manufacturer bundling, and other original equipment manufacturer resellers, as well as software bundling, should be identified as they are all potential negotiating points. They are also indications of the Licensee's commitment to promote the Work.

The territory might be limited to the United States, North America, Europe, Japan, or Worldwide. Territory should be valued on the basis of potential customers with computers capable of playing CD-ROMs, rather than conventional political boundaries. The larger the potential market, the greater the compensation. International intellectual property laws should also be considered (which are beyond the scope of this document).

The Agreement could include a clause indicating the Museum will negotiate in good faith to extend the license to other forms of distribution as they appear. However, in a world where technology develops rapidly, it is essential that the Museum not attempt to predict the market by prematurely licensing rights to currently undeveloped or speculative venues. Any known technologies which are to be excluded from the license should be identified explicitly. In addition, if the Museum has some type of pre-existing exclusive relationship, it must be careful to avoid entering into conflicting obligations.

2. TERM

The Term of this Agreement will commence [Alternate 1:] upon first publication of the Work anywhere in the Territory, or ( ) months from the date of this Agreement, whichever comes first [Alternate 2:] upon the date of this Agreement. The Term of this Agreement will expire three (3) years from the commencement of the Term, unless renewed by the parties for a further term to be mutually agreed or terminated earlier pursuant to the terms contained herein. Upon expiration of the Term, Licensee will have a period of six (6) months to sell off any unsold copies of the Work, but Licensee may not manufacture any new copies of the Work during the sell-off period or thereafter.

In the event the Work is unavailable for purchase by the general public at any time during the Term for a period of greater than six (6) months, Licensee's rights will expire and all rights granted hereunder will revert to Museum. Licensee will notify the Museum in writing if the work becomes unavailable, although such notification is not the exclusive determination as to whether the Work is unavailable.

Commentary
2. TERM

A term of three years, after development of the Work, is usually sufficient for a Work, with five years as maximum for most CD-ROM licenses. These terms are most certainly negotiable, and can vary depending upon such factors as the scope and scale of the Work and funds and resources invested by the Licensee. The Museum may also grant the Licensee an option to extend for a second three year term for a supplemental payment. The terms and language for an extended Term should be agreed-upon when negotiating the advance and royalties for the first term. A sell-off period is reasonable to allow the Licensee to sell-off inventory, provided the Licensee continues to account and pay for units sold during the sell-off period.

The Term should start at the date of signing if the Museum does not have an established relationship with the Licensee and wishes to ensure that a "running clock" will encourage the Licensee to proceed with due dispatch in developing the Work. On the other hand, if the Museum has a comfortable working relationship with the Licensee, it might wish to commence the Term when the Work is first distributed for sale. Even then, however, it is worth having some comfort that the agreement does not function solely as an open-ended option for the Licensee. A typical development time for a CD-ROM is nine months, although there are, of course, significant variations in production length due to issues relating to scripting, rights clearance and assembling related materials, as well as on-going technological advances (which may curiously lengthen production time as more features are included in the Work).

Although the Licensee should notify the Museum when the Work becomes unavailable for purchase by the public, the Museum would be prudent to receive free mail order catalogs from several large CD-ROM catalog retailers. An occasional review of the catalogs will help the Museum monitor retail trends and consumer market developments.

3. COMPENSATION

(a) Advance: Upon mutual execution of this Agreement, Licensee will pay to Museum a guaranteed non-refundable, but recoupable advance against royalties in the amount of $_____ . The foregoing advance will be deducted from royalties payable to Museum pursuant to Clause 3 (b) below.

(b) Royalty: Licensee will pay to Museum such royalties as defined and itemized in Schedule C (Royalty and Payment Terms), appended hereto, for each copy of the Work sold by Licensee. The Licensee is granted the right to distribute up to 100 copies of the Work without compensating Museum. Licensee may deduct from such royalty payments the amount of the advance paid to Museum pursuant to Clause 3 (a) above.

(c) Payment and Accounting: Licensee shall render a statement within sixty (60) days after January first and July first [note: these dates might be adapted to the Museum's fiscal year], whichever comes first, and to render semi-annual statements thereafter within sixty (60) days after the end of each semi-annual period. Such statements will state the number of copies of the Work manufactured and sold during the immediately previous semi-annual period, all revenues by category of distribution channel, and cumulative sales from the commencement of the Term. Such accountings will be accompanied by Museum's royalty payment if such payments have been earned and a detailed explanation of how such royalties were calculated.

(d) Examination of Licensee's Records: Museum or its duly authorized representative may examine the books and records of Licensee pertaining to the manufacture and sale of the Work. Such examination will be at the offices of Licensee during normal business hours and not more than twice in any calendar year. Such examination shall be at the expense of Museum, except that in the event such examination discloses a five (5%) percent or more underpayment to Museum during any previous semi-annual period, Licensee will reimburse Museum for the cost of the examination, and shall immediately remit full amount of underpayment plus ten (10%) percent.

Commentary

3. Compensation

(a) **Advance** The amount of the advance will depend upon (i) the number of the images licensed, as well as the importance of the images to the project; (ii) the scope and nature of the project, including such issues as number of images, potential market, distribution, and territory; and (iii) the project budget. The advance should be paid upon the signing of the agreement, 50% on signing and 50% on delivery of the materials to the Licensee. If the Museum has minor reservations about the ability of the Licensee to meet sales projections, the size of the advance should be increased. If the Museum has serious doubts, the Museum should not sign the agreement. In a multiple year deal, it may be appropriate to have an advance at the beginning of each year.

(b) **Royalty** Negotiation of royalties is an art into itself. By way of a general introduction, the royalty can be expressed in terms of fixed amount (e.g., $2.00 per Work sold); a percentage of the most favored wholesale price; and various ratios using sliding scales based upon sales volume. An advantage of the fixed amount is that it discourages discounting and product 'dumping.' If the royalty schedule is contingent upon the Licensee recouping production costs, the definitions of production costs as well as the timing of reimbursement should be clearly expressed. The Museum should recognize that in this early stage of the CD-ROM market, consumers are fickle and the industry experiences relatively high merchandise return rates. The Museum should note the implications of revenue accounting pre-and post-return, as well as the more customary concerns of calculating income on the basis of gross vs. net income (i.e., lower percentage of gross avoids accounting problems typically associated with higher percentage of net). The definition of what comprises the 'net' and what is excluded from the 'net' must be explicit.

(c) **Payment and Accounting** This clause requires semi-annual statements with accompanying royalty payments, as well as an accounting of total sales-to-date.

(d) **Examination of Licensee's Records** This is a standard audit provision. The Licensee may ask that the audit is conducted by a certified public accountant; the Museum, however, should seek to use its own 'duly authorized representative.' The Licensee may request confirmation of the Museum's audit by an independent third party (which presumably the Licensee would only seek should the Museum uncover evidence of underpayment). If the Licensee has not complied with royalty terms during any previous semi-annual accounting period, the Museum should immediately receive the money due plus a 10% fine.

4. DEVELOPMENT OF THE WORK

(a) Licensee will design and develop the Work in accordance with the specifications set forth in Schedule B (Description of the Work) and Schedule D (Production Schedule), appended hereto.

(b) Licensee will pay all costs and assume all liability and responsibility for the development, manufacture, advertising and marketing of the Work, except as otherwise set forth herein.

(c) Museum will be available to provide Related Text describing the Images beyond the basic Documentation for such Images as noted in Schedule A. If Related Text is requested, the Museum may charge for such information at rates to be mutually agreed-upon in advance. Museum will provide Related Text about the requested Images in accordance with the timetable in Schedule D (Production Schedule).

Commentary
4. Development of the Work
This clause links the Agreement to schedules that define the content of the CD-ROM, its 'look and feel,' and how and when the Museum will assist the Licensee in producing the Work. It is crucial that both the Museum and the Licensee clearly understand their mutual obligations. Most difficulties with CD-ROM productions occur when the timetables are not met. In many cases, this is because mutual obligations were not clearly set forth as dates and deadlines for specific tasks. Vague contractual terms requesting material in 'a timely manner' are likely to cause difficulties, as they are open to different reasonable interpretations based upon local practices. Hence, it is highly desirable that the Licensee and Museum agree upon a timetable (Schedule D) for when the Museum will provide images and related text, and the major steps the Licensee will follow in producing the Work.

If the Licensee should wish to include additional written material provided by the Museum, the timing for the delivery of such material and editorial review procedures should be explicitly stated in an accompanying schedule. The Museum may wish to charge additional fees and expenses for such material. If the textual material is supplied by Museum non-employee staff or consultants, the Museum should have such staff or consultant(s) sign a work-for-hire agreement before writing any text to assign the copyright to the Museum. All works created by employees are considered as works made for hire. Obviously, more complex arrangements are possible, such as if the Licensee wishes to draw upon text previously written by a curator and published in a book. All such arrangements should be reviewed by Museum counsel.

5. MUSEUM APPROVALS
(a) Development Approvals: During the development of the Work, Licensee will submit the Work to Museum for its review and approval in accordance with the milestones itemized in Schedule D. Museum will review the Work Elements, defined in Schedule B, and shall:
    i.   Give its approval in writing of the Work Element(s) that incorporate the Image(s), or
    ii.   Provide a written explanation of non-approval to Licensee with sufficient detail to permit Licensee to change or correct the elements so that the Work will obtain approval.

Once Museum has given its written approval for a Work Element, that element will not be modified without the prior written mutual consent of both parties.

Museum will not unreasonably withhold its written approval and will review material submitted to it by Licensee in accordance with the timetable specified in Schedule D.

(b) Documentation and Related Text Approval/Restrictions: Any Documentation and Related Text provided by the Museum will be included in the Work as written. Any changes requested by the Licensee must be approved by the Museum in advance in writing. Such approval review will follow the timetable in Schedule D. The Museum reserves the right to exercise its sole discretion in determining whether to approve any changes to museum-supplied Documentation or Related Text.

(c) Museum Final Approval: The Work and accompanying printed materials shall comply with the Work specifications, standards and quality control procedures as defined in Schedule B. Licensee agrees to undertake the work in accordance with the production schedule appended hereto as Schedule D and to furnish Museum for its inspection and written approval, a prototype and final Work. No Work, printed materials, [or marketing materials including but not limited to advertisements, sell sheets, press releases and other promotional materials] will be manufactured or distributed by Licensee until Museum has given its prior approval in writing, which permission will follow the time frames itemized in Schedule D. Such approval will not be unreasonably withheld.

(d) Use of Name: For use of the Museum's name or logo in the Work or advertising and promotion of the Work, the Licensee must first furnish Museum with a copy of all written materials and obtain Museum's written approval in advance. Except as provided herein, Licensee shall not refer to the Museum in any manner or through any medium whether written, oral, or visual for any purpose whatsoever, but not limited to advertising, marketing, promotion, publicity, solicitation or fundraising.

Commentary

5. MUSEUM APPROVALS

(a) **Development Approvals** The Museum should modify this clause to reflect the level of approvals with which it feels comfortable and the method of giving that approval. The review process could require significant time commitments. It should also specify the appropriate quality criteria to meet its interest. In general, the Museum should preview how its images are used within the context of the Work section that will display the images. However, if the Museum is concerned about the images within the context of the entire Work, then this clause should be amended to indicate wider review of material.

While the color and resolution of an image is a major concern, the ways in which the user sees the image are equally important. The Museum should recognize that its approval criteria should also be reasonable and consistent with production and marketplace realities. If there is any doubt as to the ability of the Licensee to present Museum images in a context and manner the Museum requires, the Museum should request to see prototype screens and sequences before signing the Agreement. Such prototypes should also be made an integral part of the Agreement, with language that assures production meets standards at least equivalent to the prototype.

(b) **Documentation and Related Text Approval and Restrictions** The Museum should insist upon sole discretion in determining how any museum-supplied related textual comments about an image are used. Dropped words or phrases can dramatically alter the sense and meaning of commentary.

(c) **Museum Final Approval** The Licensee must have prior written approval from the Museum before it can press or distribute any CD-ROMs. While this helps insure that the Licensee will be attentive to Museum concerns, it also requires that the Museum is responsive to the Licensee's requests for final approval according to the development timetable schedule. This schedule should be examined closely to assure that it reflects realistic expectations. If the Museum's name will be used in marketing the CD-ROM, additional steps of approval will be required. The Museum should recognize that written approvals will require the attention of appropriate Museum staff and, as such, plan accordingly. The need for a realistic timetable for how and when Museum staff will review Work elements with Museum images cannot be overemphasized.

(d) **Use of Name** The Museum's name is a major goodwill asset and it must be fully understood by the Licensee that the Museum has strict approval rights over how it is to be used.

6. IMAGE RESOLUTION RESTRICTIONS

Each copy of the Work will contain only digital representations of each Image which will be of a resolution at least _____ by _____ pixels with at least _____ bits of color or _____ bits of gray-scale information per pixel, and no greater resolution than _____ by _____ pixels with no more than _____ bits of color and _____ bits of gray-scale information per pixel.

Details of an Image may be included as well, but the resolution of any details must be within these same parameters. No Image may be in any way distorted, whether by rotation, inversion, change of proportion, color alteration, superimposition, animation, cartooning, removal of blemishes or inscriptions, or other method, except as follows: _____

_____

_____

_____

The Image will not be cropped more than _____ percent in any dimension, over-printed, or otherwise altered without Museum's permission. Permission is not required for minor color correction or the removal of technical defects, if both the original digitized image and corrected image are delivered to Museum promptly upon scanning and correction. User selected adjustments, activated by Work program commands, are permitted, providing they conform to the user selected adjustments specified in Schedule B.

Commentary
6. IMAGE RESOLUTION RESTRICTIONS
Technology is evolving rapidly and it seems that every six months, entirely new ways emerge to view images on a computer or television screen (driven by a computer). The Museum community will have to work with the production community in developing imaging resolutions and displays that meet consumer acceptance and the needs of the museums. The first steps will involve individual museums working with individual licensees to work out mutually-acceptable image resolutions. As CD-ROMs are increasingly used by consumers, a general consensus of acceptable image resolution levels will emerge. The Museum should, however, be explicit as to how its images will be viewed in a particular CD-ROM.

The agreement explicitly recognizes that in this new electronic medium, one image is often seen in several different ways, such as a close-up or in another section of the program. As long as the Image conforms to scanning restrictions, the Licensee can use multiple copies of the Image in the Work (assuming this use agrees with Museum practices with respect to presenting image details, portions, etc.).

7. MATERIALS SUPPLIED TO LICENSEE
Museum will deliver to Licensee high quality slide(s), transparency(ies), or digitized image(s) of the Images, and related Documentation in print [or electronic format]. Digitized Image(s) will be provided in the format and media the Museum solely selects. Licensee will return slide(s), transparency(ies) or digitized Image(s) media to Museum within _____ days of delivery by Museum. In the event of loss or damage to such slide(s) or transparency(ies), Licensee will pay the sum of $ _____ to Museum for each slide or transparency lost or damaged. In the event of loss or damage to digitized Image media, Licensee will pay the sum of $_____ to Museum for each digitized Image(s) media lost or damaged. Licensee will be responsible for the slide(s), transparency(ies), digitized Image(s) media until received by Museum, and Licensee shall maintain adequate insurance for loss and damage to the slides,

transparencies, or digitized Image(s) media at all times that such material is in Licensee's possession.

Commentary
7. MATERIALS SUPPLIED TO LICENSEE
The Museum should charge its standard rate for non-return of slides and transparencies. While electronic media, such as floppy disks and CD-ROMs are inexpensive, it is advisable to require comparable penalties for loss and damage as a matter of principle.

8. MATERIALS SUPPLIED TO MUSEUM
In the event that Museum delivers a slide or transparency rather than a digitized Image, Licensee will provide Museum with a copy of each unencoded Image that conforms to the specifications and standards set forth herein promptly upon scanning; and a copy of each encoded Image promptly upon encoding. These copies of the Images will be provided in a _____ format file on _____ media, with appropriate identifying labels and information as suggested by Museum. Museum reserves the right to receive a digitized Image with higher resolution standards for its own use, providing such higher resolutions are possible through generally available production processes.

Commentary
8. MATERIALS SUPPLIED TO MUSEUM
The standard approach to digitizing images is to digitize at a high level of resolution and 'dumb down' the image to the level desired for the CD-ROM, i.e., the screen display limitations defined in this Agreement. The Museum should require a copy of the digitized image with the highest resolution level generally available through commercial imaging houses, such as Kodak Photo CD. High-quality images can then be used by the Museum for various purposes, such as collection management, in-house multimedia productions, and licensing.

The Museum should request adequate information about the image files to help identify the files. At a minimum, the Museum should request a concordance between the image ID number or file name, and the accession number. It would also be useful to have details about the type of scanner, level of color correction, resolution and bit depth for each image, or batch of images if processed in the same manner. This additional information will prove helpful in the future if the files need to be transferred to another format, as well as to other digital applications.

9. INTELLECTUAL PROPERTY COPY PROTECTION
Licensee shall encode the Images using the procedure and image identification codes described in Schedule E (Label Codes and Credit Line), appended hereto.

Commentary
9. INTELLECTUAL PROPERTY COPY PROTECTION
A variety of copyright embedding protection schemes are available. The Museum should identify a copyright encoding process appropriate to its requirements. While no scheme will prevent illegal copying, it can be very useful in tracking the source of the

original, and is therefore an important component in asserting an infringement action. The Museum should require the Licensee to take an active role in instituting steps to protect the Museum's Images.

10. COPY PROTECTION

The Work will be designed so that the Images are not accessible by the user except through the program interface. Specifically, Licensee will insure that it will not be possible to copy any digital Image for further distribution by any method, or to print out any Image except within the range of resolutions specified in Clause 6 above.

Commentary
10. COPY PROTECTION

The Museum should have the Licensee demonstrate the actual copy protection scheme to be used in the Work. If acceptable, the specific copy protection scheme should be identified in Schedule B, which describes the Work's content and quality control. A Licensee may wish to modify this provision so that it applies only to copy/print technologies that exist at the time of signing the Agreement.

11. LIMITATIONS OF USE/COPYRIGHT NOTICE

Licensee shall affix the following notice and legend prominently on the outer package, the front page of the documentation, the optical or magnetic media and the opening screen of the Work:

This multimedia Work and its contents are protected under copyright law. The following is prohibited:

– copying of all or part of the Work for any reason whatsoever;
– any public performance or public display;
– the distribution of the Work, or any part of it, including without limitation the transmission of any image over a network'
– the preparation of any derivative Work, including without limitation the extraction, in whole or in part, of any images;
– any rental, lease, or lending of the Work.

The above notice will be a requirement for any sublicensee.

Each of the Images will be identified as an Image of the Museum with a copyright notice and credit information as specified by the Museum as set forth in Schedule E. The copyright notice will appear in Documentation accompanying the Work at least once in the Work's text, referencing or indexing the Image. Any Image(s) not in the public domain having underlying artist's or author's rights will have a copyright in the name of the underlying artist or author, as well as a separate photograph copyright in the name of the Museum.

Commentary
11. LIMITATIONS OF USE/COPYRIGHT NOTICE

This section is for packaging and Work labeling to inform the user of copyright restrictions. While a general copyright is, of course, in the Licensee's interest, the

Museum should ensure that it includes the limitations and restrictions identified in this clause. It is highly important that the Licensee properly credit the Museum's images. The Museum is responsible for specifying the copyright notice and credit information in Schedule E. This copyright notice does not prohibit the user from printing an image from the CD-ROM, providing such printing is an integral functional component of the Work, as defined in Schedule B.

If a Museum is supplying all the images for a Work, please see the copyright language suggested in 'Sample Table of Contents – CD-ROM Based on Single Museum Collection' on page 27.

12. DOCUMENTATION OF IMAGES

Full documentation as set forth in Schedule A, consisting of the artist's or author's name (or object's cultural designation), the title of the work, date, size, medium and copyright notice when required, must appear exactly as specified by Museum without editing, omissions or use of abbreviations or acronyms, either adjacent to the reproduction on the screen, in a user-accessible credit 'zoom' window, or in a user-accessible list of sources and credits. Documentation may be limited to artist's or author's name (or object's cultural designation), and title and date of the work in the caption accompanying the Image if the full Documentation appears elsewhere within the Work.

Commentary
12. DOCUMENTATION OF IMAGES

In addition to specifying how the Museum's images should be documented, the Museum may wish to see screen samples of documentation. There are many varieties of screen displays and they evolve continually, unlike documentation in print which has a limited number of accepted models. Advance viewing by the Museum may prevent potential disagreements with the Licensee.

13. MUSEUM COPIES OF WORK

Licensee will furnish Museum, free of charge, twenty-five (25) copies of the Work within fifteen (15) days of pressing.

Commentary
13. MUSEUM COPIES OF WORK

The costs of replicating CD-ROMs and packaging are quite low. The Museum should ask for at least 25 free copies of the CD-ROM as a courtesy from the Licensee, assuming that images from the Museum's collection represent a significant portion of the Work's images. Other quantities could be negotiated. It should be noted that in many instances the packaging costs more than the CD-ROM!

14. MUSEUM SALE OF WORK

Licensee will sell copies of the Work to Museum, if Museum so requests, at its actual cost of production for sale in Museum shops, mail order division, or other Museum-affiliated venues. Museum will receive timely delivery of such copies of the Work. Royalties will not be paid on such sales.

Commentary
14. MUSEUM SALE OF WORK
The Museum should be able to purchase CD-ROMs at the actual cost of production for re-sale through Museum shops, catalogs, etc. Museum shops and other member-related venues are prime retail distribution points for CD-ROMs drawing upon the Museum's collections. By re-selling works purchased at the actual cost of production, the Museum will be able to capture more revenue than through purchasing the works at 'most favored wholesale price' – a figure that can vary substantially. If the Licensee refuses to sell at actual cost, the Museum should insist upon receiving royalties from sales through museum-affiliated venues.

15. ASSIGNMENT
Licensee may not assign this Agreement without the prior written consent of Museum. Such consent will not be unreasonably withheld or delayed. This Agreement is binding upon the heirs, successors, administrators and assigns of the parties hereto.

Commentary
15. ASSIGNMENT
This clause restricts the ability of the Licensee to transfer the Agreement to another party without the Museum's prior written approval.

16. INFRINGEMENT
Licensee and Museum shall promptly notify each other of infringements of the Work, the Images, or Related Text, as used in the Work. Museum may bring its own action against infringers of its Images, and Licensee shall cooperate fully.

Commentary
16. INFRINGEMENT
This clause establishes each party's right to protect its respective copyright in the Work and Images. While it is in the Licensee's interest to prosecute infringers of the entire Work, the Licensee may be less inclined to pursue infringers of a particular image. Unless the Museum has the resources to enforce its copyright, it should seek to ensure the active cooperation of the Licensee in bringing actions against infringers.

17. INSURANCE
Licensee will procure Errors and Omissions Insurance in amounts no less than $ ____ per occurrence and $ ____ in the aggregate. Such insurance will name Museum as an additional insured and provide for thirty (30) days advance written notice of any cancellation. Licensee will furnish Museum with a certificate of insurance evidencing such coverage prior to the first public release of the Work.

Commentary
17. INSURANCE

The Licensee should have Errors and Omissions insurance to cover the misuse of the images. This is especially important for smaller production companies. The level of insurance will depend on a variety of factors, such as the capitalization and experience of the Licensee, proposed territory, etc. The Museum should consult with its insurance agent for analysis of acceptable coverage and rationale.

18. RIGHTS

All rights in the Images, and any Documentation and Related Text supplied by the Museum, including without limitation any copyrights, other than the non-exclusive license to Licensee explicitly granted herein, will remain vested in Museum.

Commentary
18. RIGHTS

The Museum should categorically assert all its rights. On the other hand, the Museum should not enumerate those rights, in case certain ones are omitted, as there is substantial controversy about intellectual property in the emerging electronic marketplace.

19. MUSEUM'S WARRANTIES

(a) Museum is acting only as an owner of the physical original. The Museum is not responsible for determining the copyright status of the Image(s), or for securing copyright permission and the payment for any such permissions required. The rights granted under this Agreement do not include any rights that persons other than the Museum may have in the Images or Work, including any artists' rights of attribution or control under the laws of any country or state, moral rights, or the rights of publicity or privacy.

(b) Notwithstanding the above, the Museum warrants and represents that it is a copyright holder of all rights for the Image(s) so identified in Schedule A.

(c) Except as expressly set forth herein, Museum disclaims any warranties, expressed or implied, including warranties of non-infringement or fitness for a particular purpose.

Commentary
19. MUSEUM'S WARRANTIES

The Licensee will reasonably expect the Museum to represent that it has the right to grant the permission to reproduce the image electronically. Unless the Museum has clearly established all rights to an object, the Museum should not make any representations about the rights status of a particular object. The Museum's basic position is its ability to control access to an object in its collection, and ownership of the separate copyright of a photograph of that object which is used to make a derivative work (the digitized image). The Museum should require that all photographs of its objects be produced under work-for-hire contracts.

There may be other rights holders whose permission is required for the Licensee to include the image in the CD-ROM, but the Museum should make no representations as to such other potential rights holders or their rights. The Museum has expressly informed the Licensee of the Licensee's responsibility to secure permissions from any other rights holders. Should legal action be brought by rights holders, this notification will help establish the Museum's position.

The Museum is not offering to 'clear' the rights to the images. The Licensee may request the Museum to help identify other rights holders. If the Museum provides assistance, it should do so in such a way that does not open the Museum to any liability for failing to identify any rights holders. Rights 'clearance' can be a time-consuming process; the Museum should request compensation for such work.

It should be noted that some materials held under deposit arrangements (gifts, bequests, or loans) may be restricted by the terms of such agreements, including limitations on the exploitation of tangible rights (the physical property) and/or the intangible rights (copyright and allied rights).

The Museum is not providing an indemnity, although the Licensee may seek one.

20. LICENSEE'S WARRANTIES AND INDEMNITIES

Licensee warrants and represents that the Work, as distinct from the Images subject to Museum's warranties above, will not violate or infringe upon the rights, including, without limitation, copyrights, or any other intellectual property rights, moral rights or publicity or privacy rights of any other person or entity. Licensee hereby indemnifies and holds Museum harmless against any costs, expenses, losses, damages, judgments and claims (including court costs and attorney fees) that Museum may suffer or incur: (i) as a result of a claim of any third party based on or arising out of the Work; or (ii) arising from Licensee's breach of any provision of this Agreement.

Commentary
20. LICENSEE'S WARRANTIES AND INDEMNITIES

It is advisable for the Museum to receive an indemnity from the Licensee because the images are intrinsic to the very purpose and nature of the Museum. The clause also reinforces the need for the Licensee to seek all necessary permissions from rights holders, as well as avoid infringing upon any rights, or moral rights.

21. TERMINATION

If Licensee defaults in any of its material undertakings, including payment and accounting, or otherwise is in breach of its warranties and representations, and such breach is not cured within fifteen (15) days of receipt of written notice of such breach from Museum, Museum may terminate this Agreement at any time thereafter on further written notice to Licensee. Notwithstanding Museum's termination of this Agreement, Museum shall retain all unrecouped advances, and Licensee shall pay all royalties due and owing to Museum hereunder. Upon a termination under this clause of the Agreement, Licensee shall have no right of sell-off. Upon termination all rights granted to Licensee will revert to Museum. Such termination is without prejudice to any other rights and remedies of Museum in the event of breach by Licensee.

Commentary
21. TERMINATION
The Museum should review carefully with its counsel any requests to alter the substance of this clause.

22. AUTHORIZED REPRESENTATIVES
Museum's Authorized Officer, _____, is the only individual authorized to commit the Museum to this Agreement, as well as provide contractual interpretation, dispute resolution, or modification of this Agreement. For purposes of providing guidance and direction in daily operational matters, granting approvals or withholding same, and for general contract coordination as detailed herein, the Museum's Designated Representative shall be _ _ _ _ _ . However, _ _ _ _ is not empowered to change any of the terms or scope of this Agreement. Museum shall advise the Licensee in writing of any substitution for said representatives.

Commentary
22. AUTHORIZED REPRESENTATIVES
The Museum should identify who will be responsible for coordinating the Museum's activities in supplying material and reviewing work from the Licensee. This position has an importance beyond the written page, because the Museum needs a 'point person' to ensure that it can meet the deadlines set forth in Schedule D (production schedule).

23. NOTICE
All notices hereunder will be given by telefax, overnight courier or certified or registered U.S. mail. Such notice will be given as follows:

If to Museum:

If to Licensee:

24. GENERAL
(a)   This Agreement constitutes the entire agreement between the parties and supersedes all prior agreements with respect to the subject matter hereof.
(b)   This Agreement may be amended or modified only in writing, subscribed to by a duly authorized representative of each party hereto.
(c)   A waiver by either party of a breach or default of any provision of this Agreement by the other party will not constitute a waiver by such party of any succeeding breach of the same or other provision: nor shall any delay or omission on the part of either party to exercise or avail itself of any right, power or privilege that it has or may have hereunder, operate as a waiver of any right, power or privilege by such party.
(d)   This Agreement does not create a partnership, principal/agent relationship or joint venture between the parties, and neither party may bind the other, except as expressly provided herein.

(e)   This Agreement will be interpreted in accordance with the law of the State of [the Museum is located], without regard to that state's choice of law, other than federal laws governing copyright, patent and trademark, and the parties agree to submit to its jurisdiction for the resolution of any dispute that may arise hereunder.

Commentary
(e) JURISDICTION

The choice of laws can be negotiated. Considerations will include adequacy of contract and intellectual property laws in the proposed jurisdiction, the degree of risk and likelihood of litigation arising from this agreement, ability to enforce a judgment in this jurisdiction, etc. Museums should also consider alternative dispute resolution, such as arbitration.

(f)   In any civil action between Museum and Licensee arising from or in connection with this Agreement, the prevailing party shall recover its reasonable costs and attorneys' fees.

The parties hereto indicate their consent to be bound to the terms and conditions herein contained by signing below.

LICENSEE   MUSEUM

By:_____   By:_____

Schedule A – Description of Images
(Image list and documentation)

Commentary
Schedule A – Description of Images

Defines each image to be supplied by the Museum, the method of transmission (slide, transparency, etc.), condition of the image supplied by the Museum and necessary documentation, any related text available about the images, as well as notation of any images for which the Museum holds all copyrights.

Schedule B – Description of the Work
(Content, quality control specifications)

Commentary
Schedule B – Description of Work

Defines the Work's subject matter, context within which image will be used, proposed market, and techniques (Work elements) for the user to access and view the image. Defines resolution restrictions.

Schedule C – Royalty and Payment Terms

Commentary
Schedule C – Royalty and Payments Terms

Defines the compensation structure and revenue source (e.g., sales, rentals, site or multiple-use licenses, etc.), including the basis for calculating royalties.

Schedule D – Production Schedule
(Licensee and Museum obligations, milestones)

Commentary
Schedule D – Production schedule

Defines the timetable for image delivery, major production milestones and Museum reviews and written approvals.

Schedule E – Label Codes and Credit Line

Commentary
Schedule E – Label Codes and Credit Line

Defines the labeling and embedding techniques to be used by the Licensee to protect the Museum's copyright and the credit line format.

Short CD-ROM Sample Agreement

Agreement dated as of [DATE] between [_____] (the 'Museum' and [_____] ('Licensee'):

Definitions:
The following terms have the following meanings when used herein:

'First Edition' means the first version of the commercially distributed Work that incorporates the Image(s) specified below, as well as any minor revisions restricted to corrections of editorial content of the first version.

'Image' means each photograph, negative, slide or electronic digitized picture of the following object(s):

'Work' means the CD-ROM product entitled '_____ .'

1. LICENSE
Museum grants to Licensee a non-exclusive, not-transferable, limited license to use the Images solely in the First Edition of the Work and in accordance with the terms of this Agreement. Any enhancements or changes to the Work, either editorial or programmatic, constitute a new edition, which will require a new license for the use of the Images. The Work may only be sold or distributed in the Territory. The Images may be used only as part of the Work and may not be distributed or published in any other form or medium. Satellite, electronic broadcast, on-line or network access, distribution or transmission of the Images, or the Work, or any part thereof, is expressly prohibited for any purposes. Nothing set forth in this Agreement shall restrict the Museum's right to the Image(s), including the right to allow others to use the Images. Licensee shall not use the Museum's name in any manner in connection with the Work, except as may be expressly agreed by the Museum in writing. Except as expressly set forth herein, the Museum reserves all rights in and to the Images, including without limitation the right to exploit the Images in any work in any future or unknown technology.

Commentary
1. LICENSE
The License should be non-exclusive and limited to one edition of a multimedia Work. The license is only for CD-ROMs that the user inserts into a computer for individual use. On-line access through local of wide-area networks (commercial, non-profit, Internet, or interactive-TV) is prohibited. Such access is beyond the scope of this sample agreement; it requires an entirely different way of calculating royalties, as well as different techniques to protect Museum Images.

2. FEE AND TERRITORY

Licensee will pay to Museum the non-refundable fee for the territory(ies) indicated according to the payment terms stated in the attached Fee and Territory Schedule.

Commentary
2. FEE AND TERRITORY

The accompanying Fee and Territory Schedule identifies the allowed markets and required payment terms.

3. IMAGE RESOLUTION RESTRICTIONS

(a) Each copy of the Work will contain digital representations of each Image that will be of a resolution at least ___ by ___ pixels with at least ___ bits of color or ___ bits of gray-scale information per pixel, and no greater resolution than ___ by ___ pixels with no more than ____ bits of color and ___ bits of gray-scale information per pixel. Details of an Image may be included as well, subject to the prior written approval of the Museum, but the resolution of any details must be within the above parameters.

(b) No Image may be in any way distorted, whether by rotation, inversion, change of proportion, color alteration, superimposition, animation, cartooning, removal of blemishes or inscriptions, or other method, except as follows:

_____
_____
_____

(c) The Image will not be cropped more than _____ percent in any dimension, over-printed, or otherwise altered without Museum's permission. Permission is not required for minor color correction or the removal of technical defects, if both the original digitized Image and corrected Image are delivered to Museum promptly upon scanning and correction. User selected adjustments, activated by Work program commands, are permitted providing they do not affect the Image as described in (a) above.

Commentary
3. IMAGE RESOLUTION RESTRICTIONS

Technology is evolving rapidly and it seems that every six months entirely new ways emerge to view images on a computer or television screen (driven by a computer). The Museum community will have to work with the production community in developing imaging resolutions and displays which meet consumer acceptance and the needs of the museums. The first steps will involve individual museums working with individual licensees to work out mutually-acceptable image resolutions. As CD-ROMs are increasingly used by consumers, a general consensus of acceptable image resolution levels will emerge. The Museum should, however, be explicit as to how its images will be viewed in a particular CD-ROM.

The agreement explicitly recognized that in this new electronic medium one image is often seen in several different ways, such as a close-up or in another section of the program. As long as the Image conforms to scanning restrictions, the Licensee can use multiple copies of the Image in the Work (assuming this use agrees with Museum practices with respect to presenting image details, portions, etc.).

4. DOCUMENTATION OF IMAGES

Full documentation consisting of the artist's name, author's name, or object's cultural designation, the title of the work, date, size, medium and photographic copyright notice, must appear exactly as specified by Museum without editing, omissions or use of abbreviations or acronyms, either adjacent to the reproduction on the screen, in a user-accessible credit 'zoom' window, or in a user-accessible list of sources and credits. Documentation may be limited to artist's name, or author's name, or object's cultural designation, title and date of the work in the caption accompanying the Image if full documentation appears elsewhere within the Work. Full documentation will be supplied by Museum with the Image(s).

Commentary
4. DOCUMENTATION

This is an area where print publishers, with substantial experience working with museums, often make errors. Special attention should be exercised in this new media with new producers.

5. COPY PROTECTION

The Work will be designed so that the Image(s) are not accessible by the user except through the program interface. Specifically, Licensee will insure that it will not be possible to print any Image(s) except within the range of resolutions specified in Clause 3 above, or to copy any digital Image file for further distribution by any electronic method.

Commentary
5. COPY PROTECTION

If the Museum has doubts about a proposed copy protection method, it should request a demonstration.

6. MATERIALS SUPPLIED TO MUSEUM

In the event that Museum delivers a slide or transparency rather than a digitized Image, Licensee will provide Museum with a copy of each unencoded Image that conforms to the specifications and standards set forth herein promptly upon scanning; and a copy of each encoded Image promptly upon encoding. These copies of the Images will be provided in a _____ format file on _____ media, with appropriate identifying labels and information as suggested by Museum. Museum reserves the right to receive a digitized Image with higher resolution standards for its own use, providing such higher resolutions are possible through generally available production processes.

Commentary
6. MATERIAL SUPPLIED TO MUSEUM

The current standard approach to digitizing images is to digitize at a high level of resolution and 'dumb down' the image to the level desired for the CD-ROM, i.e., the screen display limitations defined in this Agreement. The Museum should require a copy of the digitized image with the highest resolution level generally available through commercial imaging houses, such as Kodak Photo CD. High-quality images can then be used by the Museum for various purposes, such as collection management, in-house multimedia productions, and licensing.

The Museum should request adequate information about the image files to help identify the files. At a minimum, the Museum should request a concordance between the image ID number or file name, and the accession number. It would also be useful to have details about the type of scanner, level of color correction, resolution and bit depth for each image, or batch of images if processed in the same manner. This additional information will prove helpful in the future if the files need to be transferred to another format, as well as for other digital applications.

7. RIGHTS

All rights in the Images, and any documentation and related text supplied by the Museum, including without limitation any copyrights, other than the non-exclusive License to Licensee granted herein, will remain vested in Museum.

Commentary
7. RIGHTS

The Museum should categorically assert all its rights. On the other hand, the Museum should not enumerate those rights, in case certain are omitted, as there is substantial controversy about intellectual property in the emerging electronic marketplace.

8. MUSEUM'S WARRANTIES

(a) Museum warrants and represents that to the best of its knowledge [Alternate: so far as it is aware, but without investigation], the rights granted by it hereunder will not infringe the rights of any third party. Notwithstanding the foregoing, Museum is acting only as an owner of the physical original. The Museum is not responsible for determining the copyright status of the Image(s), or for securing copyright permission and the payment for any such permissions required. The rights granted under this Agreement do not include any rights that persons other than the Museum may have in the Images or Work, including any artists' rights of attribution or control under the laws of any country or state, moral rights, or the rights of publicity or privacy.

(b) Notwithstanding the above, the Museum warrants and represents that it is a copyright holder of all rights for the following Image(s):

_____
_____
_____
_____

(c) Except as expressly set forth herein, Museum disclaims any warranties, expressed or implied, including warranties of non-infringement or fitness for a particular purpose.

Commentary
8. MUSEUM'S WARRANTIES

The Licensee will reasonably expect the Museum to represent that it has the right to grant the permission to reproduce the image electronically. Unless the Museum has clearly established all rights to an object, the Museum should not make any representations about the rights status of a particular object. The Museum's basic position is its ability to control access to an object in its collection, and ownership of the separate copyright of a photograph of that object which is used to make a derivative work (the digitized image). The Museum should require that all photographs of its objects be produced under work-for-hire contracts.

There may be other rights holders whose permission is required for the Licensee to include the image in the CD-ROM, but the Museum should make no representations as to such other potential rights holders or their rights. The Museum has expressly informed the Licensee of the Licensee's responsibility to secure permissions from any other rights holders. Should legal action be brought by rights holders, this notification will help establish the Museum's position.

The Museum is not offering to 'clear' the rights to the images. The Licensee may request the Museum to help identify other rights holders. If the Museum provides assistance, it should do so in such a way that does not open the Museum to any liability for failing to identify any rights holders. Rights 'clearance' can be a time-consuming process; the Museum should request compensation for such work.

The Museum is not providing an indemnity, although the Licensee may seek one.

9. LICENSEE'S WARRANTIES AND INDEMNITIES

Licensee warrants and represents that the Work, as distinct from the Images subject to Museum's warranties above, will not violate or infringe upon the rights, including, without limitation, copyrights, or any other intellectual property rights, moral rights or publicity or privacy rights of any other person or entity. Licensee hereby indemnifies and holds Museum harmless against any costs, expenses, losses, damages, judgments and claims (including court costs and attorney fees) that Museum may suffer or incur: (i) as a result of a claim of any third party based on or arising out of the Work; or (ii) arising from Licensee's breach of any provision of this Agreement.

Commentary
9. LICENSEE' WARRANTIES AND INDEMNITIES

It is advisable for the Museum to receive an indemnity from the Licensee because the images are intrinsic to the very purpose and nature of the Museum. The clause also reinforces the need for the Licensee to seek all necessary permissions from rights holders, as well as avoid infringing upon any rights, or moral rights.

10. MUSEUM COMPLIMENTARY COPY OF WORK

Licensee will furnish Museum, free of charge, one copy of the Work within thirty (30) days of pressing.

Commentary
10. MUSEUM COMPLIMENTARY COPY OF WORK
The Museum should receive at least one free copy of the CD-ROM as a courtesy.

11. GOVERNING LAW
The terms of this Agreement shall be governed by and interpreted in accordance with the laws of the State [in which the Museum is located] without regard to that state's choice of law.

FEE AND TERRITORY SCHEDULE
(Sample Payment Criteria)

TERRITORY
North America   Europe   Worldwide   Other

IMAGE FEES
Black & White: Slide   Transparency   Digitized Image (format/media)
Color: Slide   Transparency   Digitized Image (format/media)
Two or More Languages
Standard Service
Expedited Service
New Photography Fees:
   Two-dimensional Object
   Three-dimensional Object
Digitization Fee
Special Handling Fees
Platform
State Sales Tax
Payment Terms:

DAMAGES
Licensee will return slide(s), transparency(ies) or digitized Image(s) media to Museum within _____ days of delivery by Museum. In the event of loss or damage to such slide(s) or transparency(ies), Licensee will pay the sum of $ _____ to Museum for each slide or transparency lost or damaged. In the event of loss or damage to digitized Image media, Licensee will pay the sum of $ _____ to Museum for each digitized Image(s) media lost or damaged. Licensee will be responsible for the slide(s), transparency(ies), digitized Image(s) media until received by Museum.

Sample Table of Contents:
CD-ROM Based on a Single Museum Collection

As an indication of the complexity of contracts when a museum provides a major portion, or all of the content for a CD-ROM, the headings from a typical contract are listed below. These contacts can run from thirty to sixty pages.

Although only sample clause headings are listed below to indicate the customized nature of these contracts, it is important to raise the issue of copyright ownership in these works.

Copyright when Museum supplies substantial portion of Work content

It is now generally understood that the Museum should seek to hold the copyright in Museum-supplied digitized images, documentation and related text, as well as copyright in the work itself, when the Museum significantly assists in developing the work; has supplied a significant portion of work content; and/or associates its name with the work. The long duration of copyright in a work made for hire – a term of 75 years from the year of publication – counsels extreme caution permitting the Licensee to assert copyright (or to share joint copyright in a Museum-oriented product). The contract provisions, including the Term of the License and the Grant of Rights, should prove adequate to allow the Licensee to take the product to market, recoup development costs and to realize the anticipated profit.

Suggested language to be reviewed with counsel for addressing copyright in contracts covering the above-mentioned situations, is as follows:

a) *The copyright in the Work shall be solely owned by the Museum. The Museum shall also solely own all right, title, and interest, including but not limited to any and all intellectual property interest, in and to the digital images of art work, and any related text, photographs video and audio information provide by the Museum as herein warranted [NOTE: If the Museum is co-developer on the project, add the following: The Museum shall also own any graphics, screen, icons, and user interface elements developed by the Museum.]*

b) *All right, title and interest, including but not limited to any and all intellectual property interest, in and to the operating software, its documentation, and specifications (the 'Engine') created by Licensee, as herein warranted, shall be owned and/or remain with Licensee. Licensee grants to Museum the irrevocable and non-exclusive license, for the duration of the copyright, to use, enhance, or modify the Engine for general Museum purposes and to create, distribute, and reproduce noncompetitive products not inconsistent with the Grant of Right to Licensee as herein defined.*

Table of Contents

16. LICENSED TERRITORY
17. TERM
18. DISTRIBUTION
   a. Distribution Channels
   b. Discount Purchase by Museum
   c. Restriction on Uses
   d. No Charge for Samples to Museum
19. WARRANTIES AND INDEMNIFICATION
   a. Mutual Warranties
   b. Museum Warranty
   c. Indemnification by Museum
   d. Producer Warranty
   e. Indemnification by Producer
   f. Notice of Action
20. INSURANCE
   a. Amount of Insurance
   b. Certificate of Insurance
21. COPYRIGHT AND TRADEMARK NOTICES
22. COOPERATION IN DEFENSE OF LAWSUITS
23. GOOD WILL
24. TERMINATION
   a. Immediate Right of Termination
   b. Right to Terminate on Notice
   c. Terminate When No Longer in Print
   d. Excusable Delay
25. POST TERMINATION AND EXPIRATION RIGHTS AND OBLIGATIONS
   a. Stop Trade
   b. Payments
   c. Inventory
   d. Disposition of Remaining Inventory
   e. Discounted Sale of Remaining Inventory
   f. Cessation of Use of Name
   g. Cessation of Use of Property
   h. Injunctive Relief
   i. Producer Election Upon Certain Terminations
26. RESERVATION OF RIGHTS
27. AUTHORIZED REPRESENTATIVES
   a. Museum
      i. Contracting Officer
      ii. Contracting Officer's Representative
   b. Producer
   c. Substitution

Glossary

The following are abbreviated definitions of terms cited in the sample agreements:

Color
The value of each picture element or pixel is described by bits of information. A binary (black and white) image is represented by one bit. More bits allow for more colors and greater accuracy:

2 bits/pixel is equivalent to 4 colors
4 bits/pixel is equivalent to 16 levels of gray or 16 colors
8 bits/pixel is equivalent to 256 levels of gray or 256 colors
24 bits/pixel is equivalent to 8 bits per primary color or more than 16 million colors

On-Line/Network Access
A computer is able to access information from sites outside of itself if it is connected to one of a variety of information transmission technologies, such as the Internet and Local Area Networks (LAN).

Platform
The platform is the device that displays the CD-ROM program to the user. It can refer to the operating system that supports the program, or the hardware as well. For example, the Macintosh refers to the proprietary Apple computer hardware and operating system. Windows is the Microsoft proprietary operating system than runs on PC-compatible computers; UNIX and OS/2 are other operating systems for PC-compatible computers. 3DO is proprietary hardware and software licensed by the 3DO company. As with the weather, platforms can be expected to change over the coming years.

Resolution
Digital resolution expresses the number of pixels (picture elements) represented in an image. Digital resolution usually means the sum of the pixels expressed in terms of horizontal and vertical dimensions, e.g., 3072 x 2320 pixels. Print resolution, on the other hand, is noted in terms of dots per inch (dpi).

Work Element
A particular function/sequence or location of a multimedia program that controls how an image is displayed or accessed.

MUSE Educational Media

MUSE Educational Media, Inc. and MUSE Film and Television, Inc. are jointly a not-for-profit educational organization using television and interactive media to take art and cultural history beyond the walls of museums and into classroom and homes worldwide. MUSE, based in New York City, was founded in 1992 by Karl Katz, previously creator and director of the Office of Film and Television at The Metropolitan Museum of Art.

MUSE initiates projects to:

Reach out to new audiences Working with museums to design media-based outreach programs for under-served populations.

Make exhibitions more widely available Producing documentary films that record and preserve temporary exhibits.

Inspire the experience of art in all its forms Using conventional and interactive technologies to engage children and adults in the exploration and appreciation of art and cultural history.

Engage new technologies CD-ROM and videodisk to communicate in imaginative new ways.

Appendix 13

UK LAW PRE DATABASE DIRECTIVE 'DATABASE CREATION AGREEMENT'

Dated_____1993

(1)   X
– and –
(2)   Y

COLLABORATION AGREEMENT
relating to the paintings of Z

Rubinstein Callingham Polden & Gale
2 Raymond Buildings
Gray's Inn
London WC1R 5BZ

Telephone: 071 242 8404
Fax: 071 831 7413

THIS AGREEMENT is made this   day of   1993

BETWEEN:-

(1) X

(2) Y

WHEREAS:

The parties have agreed that Y will collaborate with X on the creation of a computer generated database upon and subject to the following terms and conditions

NOW IT IS AGREED as follows:-

1.   Definitions

The following terms shall have the following meanings:

1.1   'database': a collection of collated and compiled information (whether or not in the public domain) and data entries organised into records or manifestations in such a way that they can be assessed via related data entries without duplicating them, arranged, stored and accessed by electronic means, together with the electronic materials necessary for the operation of the database, such as its thesaurus, index or system for obtaining or presenting information (but not including any computer program used in the making or operation of the database) and the expression 'database' shall include all data from time to time created by the parties for the purpose of this Agreement whether or not such data have at any particular time been incorporated into the database

1.2   'data': information concerning the landscapes and figure subjects painted in oil and water colour (and, if so determined by the parties, sketches and drawings in any other medium or artistic illustration) by John Singer Sargent

[1.3   'field': specified item of information in a record data entry]

1.4   'media': magnetic tape, disc or other physical material for computer processing used by the data supplier in accessing or supplying the data

[1.5   'file': a collection of records]

1.6   'record': complete unit of related data items organised in named fields

1.7   'integrity': the need for data to be accurate, up-to-date, complete and consistent

1.8   'personal representative': The personal representative or other person entitled to the deceased's estate

1.9.   'rights': All vested contingent and future rights of copyright and all rights in the nature of copyright and all rights to prevent unfair abstraction of material from a database in all languages and all accrued rights of action and all other rights of whatever nature in and to the database and in and to the Work whether such rights are now known or in the future created by virtue of or pursuant to any of the laws in force in each and every part of the Territory

1.10.   'sequel': A new work which is related to and written after the completion [and publication] of the Work and in determining whether a new work is a sequel the factors to be considered shall include (but not be limited to) the extent to which the new work:
        (1) is based on material contained in the Work
        (2) deals with the same subject or subject matter as the Work and/or of the database
        (3) is based fully or in part on research forming the basis of the Work
        (4) is patterned on the style format events theme characters or characterisation of the Work and
        (5) is designed to exploit commercially the appeal popularity or success of the Work

1.11   'term': The full periods of copyright in the database and in the Work respectively and all renewals reversions and extensions of such period subsisting or arising under the laws in each and every part of the Territory and afterwards so far as permissible in perpetuity

1.12.   'territory': The World

1.13.   'Work': A book to be derived from the database to document the landscapes and figure subjects painted in oil and water colour by Z between 1900 and 1914 (provisionally entitled '   ') the general nature of which is set out in the Second Schedule to this Agreement.

2.   Collaboration

2.1   X and Y shall collaborate to create the database which shall contain data covering and concerning the landscapes and figure subjects in oil and water colour (and, if so determined by the parties, sketches and drawings in any other medium of artistic illustration) painted by Z [and shall also collaborate on the writing of the Work]

2.2.   X and Y have agreed on a tentative outline of the database which is set out in the First Schedule and the respective contributions of X and Y to the database are indicated there

[2.3.   X and Y have agreed on a tentative outline of the Work which is set out in the Second Schedule and in which the name of X or of Y has been placed opposite the title of each of the proposed chapters and X and Y agree that each of them shall prepare the first draft of each chapter against which his name is written and to submit the first and subsequent drafts of each such chapter to the other party for comments or suggestions

2.4.   In order to achieve uniformity of style [X] shall write the final draft of the Work in X's own style keeping where appropriate as near as is reasonably possible to the version written by [Y]

2.5.   All decisions affecting the structure, composition, exploitation and integrity of the database shall be discussed between X and Y prior to implementation but X shall have the final say

2.6.   All licences contracts or other agreements relating in any aspect to the database and/or the Work or to any of the Rights in the database and/or the Work (or any part of it or them) shall require only the signature of X in order to be valid or binding

2.7.   As well as being used in the creation of the Work, the database shall be used for the purposes of an accompanying exhibition of the landscape and subject pictures of Z

3.   Rights and Credits

3.1.   All Rights in the database and in the Word shall be held by X exclusively

3.2.1.   To extent that any Rights in the database and/or in the Work might not automatically vest in X, Y hereby assigns his entire right title and interest in the Rights in the database and in the Work to X by the way of present assignment of existing and/or future copyright TO HOLD unto X absolutely throughout the Territory for the entire duration of the Term

3.2.2. Y acknowledges X's unrestricted right throughout the Territory during the Term to license the exploitation of all or any part of the Rights to third parties

3.2.3. Y agrees to do all such things and to sign and execute all and any documents and deeds at such times and in such locations as X may reasonably require in order to perfect protect or enforce any of the Rights assigned to X by this Agreement and Y hereby irrevocably appoints as his attorney in his place to do such things and to sign and execute such documents for and on his behalf in the event that Y shall fail to do so within 14 days of receipt of a request from X to do so, and Y warrants and undertakes that he will confirm and ratify and be bound by any and all of the actions of X pursuant to this clause and this appointment shall take effect as an irrevocable appointment pursuant to section 4 of the Powers of Attorney Act 1971

3.3. X and Y shall receive [equal] authorship credit on the same line or on adjacent lines one directly below the other (the name of X shall precede that of Y whether reading from left to right or from top to bottom as appropriate) in [equal] size type on and in connection with the Work and in all advertising promotion and publicity for the Work

4. Waiver of Moral Rights

Y hereby unconditionally and irrevocably waives all moral rights in respect of the database and of the Work to which he may now or at any time in the future be entitled under the Copyright, Designs and Patents Act 1988 and/or under any similar laws in force from time to time during the Term in any part of the Territory, and WA declares that this waiver shall operate in favour of X, his licensees, assigns and successors in title

5. Proceeds and Expenses

5.1. In consideration of Y's obligations hereunder and the rights assigned by Y to X, X agrees to account and to pay to Y a fee equal to [   ] percent of all monies received by X with respect to the Work and the sale licence or disposition of any of the Rights in the Work

5.2. Within two months of receiving any royalty statement from the publisher of the Work, X shall send to Y a statement of account showing details of all monies due from X to Y together with the monies due to Y

5.3.   Expenses incurred by either of the parties arising out of or relating to the creation of the database shall be borne [equally] by the parties PROVIDED THAT any such expense is only incurred with the prior approval of the other party

6.   Non Disclosure of Materials

6.1.   If the Work is not completed or published X may in any event use or disclose or licence the use or disclosure of any of the material in the database (whether relating to the period 1900 to 1914 or otherwise) for any other purpose whatsoever

6.2.   If the Work is not completed or published, Y may not use or disclose or licence the use or disclosure of any of the material in the database without the prior written approval of X

7.   Ownership of Materials

7.1.   Subject to clause 7.4, all physical or material objects and any tangible or intangible intellectual property rights in such objects utilised or brought into existence by either party in connection with the creation completion or exploitation of the database and of the Work (including but without limitation all files, records, magnetic tapes, magnetic disks, photographs, illustrations and computer printouts and computer software) shall be owned by X exclusively

7.2.   Subject to due operation of the law or as required by order of a duly constituted Court of Law neither party may allow any third party access to the database or to significant portions of the data without the other party's prior written consent

7.3.   The master files containing original documentation and reproductions and material processed into and supporting the database will be held by X and his collaborator. The master files shall be the exclusive property of X

7.4.   Files held by Y (but not any intellectual property rights in such files) shall be deemed to be the property of Y but Y may not sell or pass to any third party this property or the data contained therein without the prior written consent of X

8.   Withdrawal from Collaboration

If Y withdraws from this Collaboration before completion of the database of the Work, the provisions of Clauses 14.4 and 14.5 shall apply.

9.   Warranties

9.1.   Y warrants to X in respect of the material created and to be created by Y for inclusion in the database and/or in the Work that:

9.1.1.   Y is the sole author of all such material

9.1.2.   Y shall not previously have exercised licensed assigned or charged any rights in such material

9.1.3.   No such material nor any abridgement, translation or version of it has been published before the date of this Agreement

9.1.4.   No such material contains anything of an obscene, blasphemous or libellous nature or which infringes the copyright or any other rights of any person

9.1.5.   Y will keep X fully indemnified against all actions claims proceedings cost and damages (including any damages or compensation paid by X on the advice of his legal advisers and after consultation with Y to compromise or settle any claim) and all legal costs or other expenses arising out of any breach of any of the above warranties or out of any claim by a third party based on any facts which if substantiated would constitute such a breach

9.2.   X Warrants to Y in request of X's contributions to the Work that:

9.2.1.   such contributions will contain nothing of an obscene blasphemous or libellous nature or which infringes the copyright or any other rights of any person

9.2.2.   X will keep Y fully indemnified against all actions claims proceedings costs and damages (including any damages or compensation paid by Y on the advice of his legal advisers and after consultation with X to compromise or settle any claim) and all legal costs and other expenses arising out of any breach of the above warranty or out of any claim by a third party based on any facts which if substantiated would constitute such a breach

10.   Sequel

During the Term Y shall not write publish or authorise the writing or publication of any Sequel without the prior written consent of X

11.   Death of X or Y

11.1.   If Y dies before the database is completed X shall have the right to immediate possession of all items referred to in clause 7 which at the date of death were in the possession of Y and shall be entitled to complete the database either by himself or (at his discretion) with the assistance of any other person whose terms of engagement (including but not limited to co-authorship of the Work credit and compensation) shall be in the sole discretion of X who may also revise or permit revision of any material previously prepared by Y

11.2   Notwithstanding the provisions of clause 11.1 Y shall retain the right to credit as a co-author of the Work under clause 3.3

11.3.   Y's estate shall continue to be entitled to the share of money proceeds and other consideration received in respect of the Work as mentioned in clause 5.1, subject to the prior deduction from such share of the compensation (if any) payable to any additional co-author engaged by X under clause 11.1

11.4.   In the event of X's disablement or death, any decisions about the future of the database and of the Work and about the exploitation of X's rights in the database and in the Work shall be made by X's wife or personal representatives as the case may be, after consultation with Y

12.   Relationship between the Parties

12.1.   The relationship between X and Y shall be one of collaboration on a single project

12.2.   This Agreement shall not in any way constitute X and Y partners or joint venturers principal and agent or employer and employee

12.3.   This Agreement is not intended to confer on any person, other than X, Y and their respective estates, any express or implied benefit or burden

13. Confidentiality

13.1.   Both X and Y shall treat as confidential all knowledge and information (including all knowledge and information derived or obtained from the creation of the database, notwithstanding that certain matters contained therein will individually be in the public domain relating to the materials necessary to forming the database) which does or may hereafter constitute the database

13.2. Except insofar as Y may be expressly authorised by X to do so, Y shall not during this collaboration or at any time thereafter disclose or communicate to any person any given knowledge or information or permit or suffer any act matter or thing whereby the same may be disclosed or communicated to or ascertained by others

14. Termination

14.1. X may terminate this Agreement by summary notice to Y if Y is in breach of this Agreement and in the case of a breach capable of being remedied fails to remedy that breach within 30 days of receiving notice to do so

14.2. Y may terminate this Agreement by serving notice to X if X is in breach of this Agreement and in the case of a breach capable of being remedied fails to remedy that breach within 30 days of receiving notice to do so

14.3. X may terminate this Agreement by notice to Y if the Work is not to be produced

14.4. On termination of this Agreement for any reason whatsoever:-

14.4.1. all rights in the database and in the Work (on in such part of the database and/or in the Work as has been completed as at the date of termination) shall remain exclusively vested in X; and

14.4.2. all materials referred to in clause 7 that are in the possession of Y shall immediately be delivered up to X

14.5. If termination occurs before the database and/or the Work is completed:-

14.5.1. X may in his absolute discretion make such arrangements for the completion of the database and/or the Work as he thinks fit;

14.5.2. Y shall not be entitled to any authorship credit in respect of the Work but will be entitled to an acknowledgement of his contribution to the Work; and

14.5.3. the other rights and liabilities of the parties shall, in the absence of agreement, be determined by arbitration pursuant to clause 15.5

15. General

15.1. Force Majeure

15.1.1. If either party is prevented from fulfilling his obligations under this Agreement by reason of any supervening event beyond his control (including, but not by way of limitation, accidental damage or destruction of hardware or software, fire, flooding, power failure, air conditioning breakdowns, erasure of data from files, mounting of incorrect discs/tapes or use out of date versions of programmes, read errors, tape breaks, programme errors or data or accidental loss of confidential information, procedural failures in system and/or faulty design) the party unable to fulfil its obligations shall immediately give notice of this to the other party and shall do everything in its power to resume full performance

15.1.2. Subject to the previous sub-clause, neither party shall be deemed to be in breach of its obligations under this Agreement

15.1.3. If the period of incapacity exceeds six months then this Agreement shall automatically terminate unless the Parties expressly agree otherwise in writing

15.2. Whole Agreement

This Agreement contains the whole agreement between the Parties and supersedes any prior written or oral agreement between them in relation to its subject matter and the Parties confirm that they have not entered into this Agreement upon the basis of any representations that are not expressly incorporated into this Agreement

15.3. Headings

Headings contained in this Agreement are for reference purposes only and shall not be incorporated into this Agreement and shall not be deemed to be any indication of the meaning of the clauses and sub-clauses to which they relate

15.4. Proper Law and Jurisdiction

This Agreement shall be governed by English law in every particular including formation and interpretation and shall be deemed to have been made in England and the Parties agree to submit to the exclusive jurisdiction of the English courts

15.5.   Arbitration

Any difference between the Parties concerning the interpretation or validity of this Agreement or the rights and liabilities of either of the Parties shall in the first instance be referred to the arbitration of two persons (one to be nominated by each party) or their mutually agreed umpire in accordance with the provisions of the Arbitration Acts 1950-1979

15.6.   Notices

15.6.1. Any notice, consent or the like (in this clause referred to generally as 'notice') required or permitted to be given under this Agreement shall not be binding unless in writing and may be given personally or sent to the party to be notified by pre-paid first class post or by telex electronic mail or facsimile transmission at its address as set out above or as otherwise notified in accordance with this clause

15.6.2. Notice given personally shall be deemed given at the time of delivery thereof

15.6.3. Notice sent by post in accordance with this sub-clause shall be deemed given at the commencement of business of the recipient on the third business day next following its posting

15.6.4. Notice sent by telex, electronic mail or facsimile transmission in accordance with this sub-clause shall be deemed given at the time of its actual transmission

15.7.   No modification

This Agreement may not be modified except by an instrument in writing signed by both of the Parties or their duly authorised representatives

15.8.   Waiver

The failure by either Party to enforce at any time or for any period any one or more of the terms or conditions of this Agreement shall not be a waiver of them or of the right at any time subsequently to enforce all terms and conditions of this Agreement

15.9.   Interpretation

15.9.1. In this Agreement unless the context requires otherwise:

(a) Words and expressions that are defined in the Copyright Designs and Patents Act 1988 shall bear the same meanings in this Agreement;

(b) Words importing the singular number shall include the plural and vice versa;

(c) Words importing any particular gender shall include all other genders;

(d) References to clauses and to the Schedule are to clauses of and the Schedule to this Agreement

15.9.2. Any reference in this Agreement to any statute or statutory provision shall be construed as referring to that statute or statutory provision as it may from time to time be amended, modified, extended, re-enacted or replaced (whether before or after the date of this Agreement) and including all subordinate legislation from time to time made under it

15.10. Severance

In the event that any provision of this Agreement is declared by any judicial or other competent authority to be void, voidable, illegal or otherwise unenforceable or indications of this are received by either of the Parties from any relevant competent authority the Parties shall amend that provision in such reasonable manner as achieves the intention of the Parties without illegality or at the discretion of X it may be severed from this Agreement

15.11. No Assignment

This Agreement may not be assigned or otherwise transferred in whole or in part without the prior written consent of X but shall be binding upon and enure to the benefit of each of the Parties, their heirs, legal personal representatives and, where so permitted, assigns or other transferees

15.12. Survival of terms

The warranties and indemnities contained in this Agreement shall survive its termination

15.13.   Rights and Remedies Cumulative

All rights and remedies available to either of the Parties under the terms of this Agreement or under the general law or in equity shall be cumulative and no exercise by either of the Parties of any such right or remedy shall restrict or prejudice the exercise of any other right or remedy granted by this Agreement or otherwise available to it

15.14.   Further Assurance

At all times after the date hereof the parties shall at their own expense execute all such documents and do such acts and things as may reasonably be required for the purpose of giving full effect to this Agreement

AS WITNESS the hands of the parties the day and year first above written.

THE FIRST SCHEDULE

The Database

The database shall consist of information concerning the landscapes and figure subject painted in oil and water colour (and, if so determined by the parties, sketches and drawings in any other medium of artistic illustration) by Z and shall be organised in the following manner;-

[details to be supplied]

THE SECOND SCHEDULE

THE WORK

The work shall be derived from a Computer Generated database and shall document the landscapes and figure subjects painted by Z in oil and water colour (and, if so determined by the parties, sketches and drawings in any other medium or artistic illustration) containing the following chapters:-

Proposed chapter title   First draft to be written by

[details to be supplied]

SIGNED by X   )
in the presence of:)

SIGNED by Y   )
in the presence of:)

Appendix 14

INTELLECTUAL PROPERTY FORMS AND RELEASES

License to Use Museum Digital Image on Web Site

The Museum hereby grants to _____ a non-exclusive, worldwide license to display the images and text contained in Exhibit A hereto on its Web site according to the terms set forth herein. Subject to such license, the Museum retains all right and title to and interest in the license material. The following terms and conditions apply to such use:

1.   The digital files are for use on the Web site only and may not be used in any other way;

2.   The images and text may remain on the Web site until _____.

3.   After _____ (date), the digital files must be destroyed and written confirmation sent to the Museum of such destruction;

4.   The 'page' of the Web site which incorporate the images and/or text are subject to prior review and approval by the Museum before they appear on-line;

5.   For any 'page' which contains an image and/or text, the following language must appear at the bottom of the screen: 'Digital image and text © 199_ Museum'; and

6.   The Web site home page must include up front the following language 'Museum image files and associated text are to be used for non-commercial, personal and private use only. Any other use, including publication, copying or redistribution of Museum image files or text in any manner is prohibited without prior written permission from the Museum'.

AGREE:

_____

Name and Title

_____

Signature

_____

Date

License Agreement

I, _____, am the owner of certain materials described below, including copyright, that the Museum has requested to use and reproduce. (If not the copyright owner, please specify in the space below any additional permissions needed, if any, to grant these rights). I hereby grant to the Museum a royalty-free, irrevocable, and on-exclusive license to use the materials specified herein for standard non-profit museum uses, including educational, exhibition, archival, and research uses. I also grant permission to use my name, likeness and image in connection with advertising and promotion related to the use of my materials in standard museum projects. These materials may be used and reproduced for these purposes in any and all medium including, without limitation, the World Wide Web.

I understand that the Smithsonian often uses materials for other uses, including commercial products, and that all proceeds from the sales of products, both educational and commercial, are used to advance the research and educational missions of the Smithsonian. If permission is also granted to use these materials in commercial products such as posters, postcards, note cards, tote bags, t-shirts, and other products, please check here _____.

RESTRICTIONS ON USE OF MATERIALS, if any:

_____

TYPES OF MATERIALS (please check):
Photographs __   Illustrations __   Textual Materials __   Oral History/Interview __
Audiotape __   Videeotape __   Performance __   Other (describe)
_____.

DETAILED DESCRIPTION OF MATERIALS

_____.

(Please attach additional pages if necessary)
CREDIT LINE AND/OR CAPTION: _____

ADDITIONAL PERMISSIONS NEEDED, I ANY (for example, copyright owner, subjects in photographs, illustrations in text) _____
_____.

FEES (if any) _____

DISPOSITION OF MATERIALS AFTER USE (please check one):
__ Return to owner ___ May be retained

WARRANTY: I warrant and represent that I am the owner of the materials described, including copyright, and that I have the full authority to grant the requested license. If the materials include materials for which multiple permission are required (for example, subjects depicted in photographs), I warrant that I have obtained all necessary permissions, including without limitation, copyright and rights of privacy and publicity, from the rightsholders or have specified on the 'Additional Permissions' line above all additional permissions that the Museum must obtain in order to fully exercise the rights granted herein.

_____   _____

Name (please print)   Signature

Address _____

Telephone Number   FAX Number   E- mail Address

_____

Contracting Officer or authorized official

Participant Release

In connection with my appearance at the Museum in connection with
_____ ('the activity'), I hereby grant the Museum the following rights
and permissions on a perpetual, royalty-free, non-exclusive basis:

1.   To record, by any means including without limitation, audiotape,
videotape, and photograph, my voice and image while I perform, talk, play
music or attend any activities and events associated with the activity.

2.   To reproduce, display, transcribe, telecast, distribute and otherwise use
my voice and image as contained in the recordings authorized above for
standard Museum educational and promotional purposes in any media,
including print, video, still, moving photography, electronic media, the
internet, and others. Examples of possible uses include, but are not limited to,
production of educational video tapes, record albums, educational packets for
distribution to schools or public broadcast.

3.   To authorize other parties selected and approved by the Museum to
exercise the permission as granted above for non-profit museum, educational,
archival, or research uses.

In addition, I choose one of the following:

_____   Please give may name and address to other
organizations planning festivals or programs.

_____   Please do not give my name and address to other
organizations planning festivals or programs.

Any use of my name, address, recordings and image other than as authorized
above shall require my express written consent.

_____   _____
Participant signature   Participant name (print)

Date: _____

Web-Site Release Form

I grant permission to the Museum to use, reproduce and disseminate the following materials, and my name, voice, words, and image on and in connection with the Museum's World Wide Web site, on a royalty-free, irrevocable basis.

I also grant _____ do not grant _____ (check one) a license to the Museum to use the materials, and my name, voice, words, and image on and in connection with standard educational museum uses including, without limitation, exhibition materials, catalogues, brochures, exhibition promotion and advertising, archival and research uses.

I also grant _____ do not grant _____ (check one) a license to the Museum to use the materials, and my name, voice, words, and image on and in connection with the production of commercial products related to the Museum exhibition and/or other educational activities.

I warrant and represent that I am the owner of the materials, including all copyright and other intellectual property interests, and that I have the full authority to grant the rights granted herein.

MATERIALS: _____

_____

_____

Name (Printed)

_____

Signature

_____

Date

This sample document is intended to provide general direction and cannot cover every situation that may arise. It is not a substitute for a carefully document negotiated by the parties and tailored to their specific circumstances. An attorney should be consulted to address any specific cases, ambiguities or questions and to make sure that the use of any specific provision is advisable.

RELEASE AND ASSIGNMENT

I, _____, for good and valuable consideration received, hereby grant, convey, bargain, assign, transfer and deliver to the _____ Museum, and its successors and assigns, to have and hold forever, any and all rights, title and interest, including any and all copyrights and other proprietary rights or interests, in _____ ('Work'), and in all tangible and intangible property relating to the Work including without limitation _____, and similar information necessary for the practical utilization of the Work, that I may have or hold.

I, for myself and my executors, successors, and assigns, represent, warrant, agree and covenant that to the extent that I was commissioned for the Work, whether or not said commission constitutes a 'work made for hire' as define din the federal copyright law, that: the work was and is solely my own full power, right, and authority to convey, bargain, assign, transfer and deliver this assignment; and I will forever warrant and defend this assignment and indemnify and save Museum harmless against the claims of anyone whomsoever.

IN WITNESS WHEREOF, I have executed this assignment on the date written.

_____   _____
Signature   Date

_____
Street Address

_____
City, State, Zip Code

_____
Telephone Number

On this ___ day of _____ 199__, before me personally came _____, to me known, who being by me duly sworn, did depose and say that he acknowledged the foregoing instrument, by his subscribed, to be his free and voluntary act an deed as aforesaid.

_____
Signature of Notary Public   My commission expires:

This sample document is to provide general direction and cannot cover every situation that may arise. It is not a substitute for a carefully document negotiated by the parties and tailored to their specific circumstances. An attorney should be consulted to address any specific cases, ambiguities or questions and to make sure that the sue of any specific provision is advisable.

PHOTOGRAPHY RELEASE

I understand that the XXXXXXX Museum, through its XXXXXX Office, is creating a publication, tentatively entitled XXXXXXXXXXXXX.

I authorize and consent to being photographed, and to the display, reproduction, alternation or other use of any photographs of me, or in which I may be included with others, in connecting with the publication and any related promotional uses.

To the extent that I have any rights, title or interests in the photographs, I assign all such rights, title and interests to the Museum.

In giving this permission, without fee or limitation whatsoever, and in consideration of the opportunity to participate in the publication, I agree to release, discharge and hold harmless the Museum and its employees, from any and all claims, actions and demands of whatsoever nature, including but not limited to any claims of libel, or invasion of privacy, arising out of or in connection with the use of my photograph.

_____   _____
Name (Print)   Signature

_____   _____
Street Address   Date

_____
City, State, Zip Code

_____
Telephone Number

_____
Signature of Parent or Guardian (if minor)

_____

_____

Address (if different from Subject)

_____

Telephone Number (if different from Above)

This sample document is intended to provide general direction and cannot cover every situation that may arise. It is not a substitute for a carefully document negotiated by the parties and tailored to their specific circumstances. An attorney should be consulted to address any specific cases, ambiguities or questions and to make sure that the use of any specific provision is advisable.

INTERVIEW RELEASE AND ASSIGNMENT

I, _____, give to the XXXXXXXX Museum, the right and permission: to record any interview and performance; to copyright the recording of my interview and performance in its name; to use, re-use, publish and republish the recording in whole or in part in any medium and for any purpose whatsoever including, but not limited to, standard museum purposes (such as exhibitions, research, publications, educational materials and pubic relations), radio broadcast, sound recordings, other audio or video products, and books; and to use my name, image and likeness in connection with its use of the recording if it so wishes. Any proceeds from the Museum's use of my interview and performance will support the non-profit, educational activities of the Museum.

I also donate, convey and assign to the Museum, subject to any conditions written below, any rights and title to and interest in the recording of any interview and performance that may have, including any copyright interests.

This release and assignment is subject to the conditions written below, if any:
_____
_____
_____

Signed _____

Date_____

Interviewer_____ Date _____

FY199X–XXX

SMITHSONIAN INSTITUTION
Product Development and Licensing
Capital Gallery – Suite 260
600 Maryland Ave., SW
Washington, DC 20024
Phone: (202) 287-3620
Fax: (202) 287-3490

DATE

NAME
TITLE
COMPANY
ADDRESS
ADDRESS

Dear:

This letter will confirm the terms of the one-time license granted to **NAME COMPANY** to use an image of **NAME IMAGE** on its **NAME PRODUCT**. Permission to use the name and image is subject to the following terms and conditions:

1.   GRANT. Smithsonian grants to **NAME COMPANY** a one-time, nonexclusive, nontransferable license to use the image of **NAME IMAGE** (hereinafter called the image), in connection with its **NAME PRODUCT**. The image shall not be cropped or otherwise altered without obtaining the prior written permission of the Smithsonian Institution.

2.   PAYMENT. **NAME COMPANY** agrees to pay to the Smithsonian a one-time license fee of PRICE, payable to the Smithsonian Institution, cite fund No. 21830061, and mailed to:

DIRECTOR
PRODUCT DEVELOPMENT AND LICENSING
SMITHSONIAN INSTITUTION
600 MARYLAND AVE., SW SUITE 260
WASHINGTON, DC 20024

Payment shall be due immediately upon the signing of this agreement.

3.   QUANTITY. This license permits manufacture of no more than **STATE QUANTITY** of the **NAME PRODUCT** using the image. If **NAME COMPANY** wishes to produce additional quantities, it shall submit a written request to the Smithsonian. If Smithsonian grants permission to produce additional merchandise, it ma impose an additional licensing fee.

4.   DURATION. This agreement constitutes an exclusive one-time use only for the **NAME PRODUCT**, and **NAME COMPANY** shall not use, or authorize others to use, the image in any other manner without obtaining the prior written consent of the Smithsonian.

5.   MARKET. The **NAME PRODUCT** may be marketed and sold only in **STATE SALES TERRITORY**. Any and all marketing and/or selling by **NAME COMPANY** of **NAME PRODUCT** beyond the above-designated geographic area is hereby prohibited.

6.   QUALITY. **NAME COMPANY** understands and acknowledges that the Smithsonian has the right to inspect the quality of the products to ensure that they satisfy Smithsonian standards. To the end, **NAME COMPANY** shall submit tot he Smithsonian representative designated in paragraph 13 for prior written approval, applicable color proofs and mechanical of the **NAME PRODUCT** as well as any copy or textual material. **NAME COMPANY** shall make all requested corrections before manufacturing the **NAME PRODUCT**.

7.   CREDIT LINE. The credit line shall read as follows:

8.   COPYRIGHT DISCLAIMER.   Permission is granted only to the extent of the Smithsonian Institution's ownership of the rights relating to the request. Certain works may be protected by copyright, trademark, or related interests not owned by the Institution. The responsibility for ascertaining whether any such rights exist, and for obtaining all necessary permissions remains with the applicant.

9.   ADVERTISING.   Any advertising or promotion by **NAME COMPANY** for the **NAME PRODUCT** that uses the image mentioned herein must be approved in advance by the Smithsonian

10. USE OF NAME. Except as authorized herein, **NAME COMPANY** shall mean no reference to the Smithsonian Institution or to any of its bureaus in any manner, including without limitation, for publicity, advertising and promotion.

11. **NAME COMPANY** shall return any and all transparencies and slides provided by the Smithsonian to the Smithsonian within three (3) months of receiving the images and acknowledgment form. If the materials are returned after the three (3) month deadline, a $1,000.00 fine shall be imposed for each outstanding transparency or slide.

12. SAMPLES. **NAME COMPANY** shall provide to the Smithsonian three (3) samples of the **NAME PRODUCT** upon completion. These samples shall be sent to the address in paragraph 2.

13. SMITHSONIAN REPRESENTATION. For purposes of this agreement, the Smithsonian shall be represented by Alex Yi, Office of Product Development & Licensing, Smithsonian Institution, 600 Maryland Avenue, S.W., Suite 260, Washington, D.C. 20024.

Please sign in the space provided below and return agreement FY199X-XX with the licensing fee to the address in paragraph 2.

Sincerely,

Hannah Runge Mullin
Acting Director
Office of Product Development and Licensing

NAME COMPANY

_____
Approved by Name

_____
Title

_____
Date

Index

The International Bar Association Series

Other titles in this series:

Acquisition of Shares in a Foreign Country (Editors, M. Gruson, S. Hutter)
ISBN 1 85333 755 2

Agency and Distribution Agreements – An International Survey (Editor, A. Jausàs)
ISBN 1 85966 100 9

The Alleged Transnational Criminal (Editor, R.D. Atkins)
ISBN 0 7923 3409 4

Anti-Dumping under the WTO: A Comparative Review (Editor, K. Steele)
ISBN 90 411 915 3

Arab Comparative and Commercial Law – The International Approach,
Volumes 1 and 2
Volume 1 ISBN 0 86010 9771
Volume 2 ISBN 0 86010 987 X

Capital Markets Forum Yearbook vol 1/1993 (Editor, S.M. Revell)
ISBN 1 85966 066 5

Civil Appeal Procedures Worldwide (Editor, C. Platto)
ISBN 1 85333 725 0

Current Issues in Cross-Border Insolvency and Reorganisations (Editors,
F.B. Leonard, C.W. Besant)
ISBN 1 85333 958 X

The Developing Global Securities Market (Editor, F.W. Neate)
ISBN 0 86010 979 8

Due Diligence, Disclosures and Warranties in the Corporate Acquisitions Practice (2nd
ed.) (Editors, D. Baker, R. Jillson)
ISBN 1 85333 633 5

Economic Development, Foreign Investment and the Law (Editor, Robert Pritchard)
ISBN 90 411 0891 2

Energy Law '88 (Section on Energy & Natural Resources Law)
ISBN 1 85333 097 3

Energy Law '90 (Section on Energy & Natural Resources Law)
ISBN 1 85333 477 4

Energy Law '92 (Section on Energy & Natural Resources Law)
ISBN 1 85333 759 5

Enforcement of Foreign Judgments Worldwide (2nd ed.) (Editors, C. Platto, W.G. Horton)
ISBN 1 85333 757 9

Environmental Issues in Insolvency Proceedings (Editor, J. Barrett)
ISBN 90 411 0722 3

Environmental Liability (Editor, P. Thomas)
ISBN 1 85333 561 4

Global Offerings of Securities: Access to World Equity Capital Markets (Editors, M. Brown, A. Paley)
ISBN 1 85966 045 2

Insider Trading in Western Europe (Editors, G. Wegen, H-D. Assmann)
ISBN 1 85966 079 7

Joint Ventures in East Asia (Editor, J. Buhart)
ISBN 1 85333 739 0

Law Without Frontiers (Editor, E. Godfrey)
ISBN 90 411 0851 3

Legal Opinions in International Transactions (3rd ed.) (Editors, M. Gruson, S. Hutter, M. Kutschera)
ISBN 90 411 0944 7

Liability of Lawyers and Indemnity Insurance (Editors, A. Rogers, J. Trotter, W.G. van Hassel, J.R. Walsh, R.P. Kröner; Co-edited by K.C.J. Frikkee)
ISBN 90 411 0876 9

Life After Big Bang (Editor, S. MacLachlan)
ISBN 0 86010 982 8

Litigation and Arbitration in Central and Eastern Europe (Editors, D.W. Rivkin, C. Platto)
ISBN 90 411 0583 2

Managing and Disclosing Risks of Investing in Derivatives (Editor, M. Brown)
ISBN 90 411 0930 7

Mechanics of Global Equity Offerings (Editor, M. Brown)
ISBN 90 411 0855 6

Nuclear Energy Law After Chernobyl (Editors, P. Cameron, L. Hancher, W. Kühn)
ISBN 1 85333 110 4

Obtaining Evidence in Another Jurisdiction in Business Disputes (2nd ed.) (Editors, C. Platto, M. Lee)
ISBN 1 85333 082 5

Pre-Trial and Pre-Hearing Procedures Worldwide (Editor, C. Platto)
ISBN 1 85333 758 7

Privatisation – Current Issues (Editors, M.M. Brown, G. Ridley)
ISBN 1 85966 049 5

Research and Invention in Outer Space – Liability and Intellectual Property Rights (Editor, Sai'd Mosteshar)
ISBN 0 7923 2982 1

Transnational Environmental Liability and Insurance (Editor, R.P. Kröner)
ISBN 1 85333 778 1

The Impact of the Freeze of Kuwaiti and Iraqi Assets (Editors, B. Campbell, D. Newcomb)
ISBN 1 85333 558 4

Trial and Court Procedures Worldwide (Editor, C. Platto)
ISBN 1 85333 608 4

Using Set-Off as Security – A Comparative Survey for Practitioners (Editor, F.W. Neate)
ISBN 1 85333 363 8

Warranties in Cross-Border Acquisitions (Editor, M. Rubino-Sammartano)
ISBN 1 85333 946 6

Water Pollution – Law and Liability (Editor, P. Thomas)
ISBN 1 85333 874 5